The Chief Plays of Corneille

THE CHIEF PLAYS OF
Corneille

TRANSLATED INTO ENGLISH BLANK VERSE
WITH AN INTRODUCTORY STUDY OF CORNEILLE

BY

LACY LOCKERT

PRINCETON, NEW JERSEY
PRINCETON UNIVERSITY PRESS

1957

To

L O U I S E   A L L E N

to whom not this book only but
my whole life is dedicated.

CONTENTS

TRANSLATOR'S FOREWORD

I entitle this companion volume to *The Best Plays of Racine* not *"The Best"* but *"The Chief" Plays of Corneille.* For *Rodogune* is not, in my opinion, one of his best plays—or even a good play at all. Besides the five tragedies that are generally regarded as constituting his literary achievement of permanent value, I consider *Don Sanche d'Aragon, Attila, Pulchérie,* and *Suréna*—and even *Othon,* and perhaps even *Héraclius*—superior to it. But traditionally *Rodogune* has been looked upon as its author's sixth-best play and is certainly the sixth in fame; it was his own favorite above all (!) and it well exemplifies the faults which, accounted merits by him, led him after the *Cid* and *Polyeucte* not to still greater heights but downhill to a sad stultification of his genius. Therefore this tragedy, poor as it is, has a significance which makes it deserve inclusion in a book intended to give English-speaking readers a better knowledge of Corneille, in both his strength and his weakness. Some knowledge of both is necessary for an adequate comprehension of him, as of any author.

It is customary, I realize, to include only the best work of a dramatist in a volume of his selected plays. But the case of Corneille is peculiar. The really characteristic faults as well as the characteristic virtues of most playwrights can be discerned even in their finest productions. Any of the secular dramas of Racine, for instance, exhibits in some measure both his merits and his defects, omitting none of importance. It is not so with Corneille. A volume containing only the *Cid, Horace, Polyeucte,* and *Nicomède* would indeed display almost every phase of his genius and would leave readers with a more favorable impression of him. But this would not be a true impression of him. No one could guess from those four plays his frequent frigidity, which is revealed in *Cinna.* Nor would anyone guess, from them, his predilection for melodrama, his readiness on occasion to sacrifice character or credibility for sensational effects, his fondness for involved plots, the fascination that he found in stark criminal energy, or the extent to which he would submit to the influence of the Hôtel de Rambouillet and of the pseudo-historical romances then popular—all shown in *Rodogune.*

i x

Corneille's comedy *le Menteur* is often included in volumes of his selected works, and of recent years there has been some renewal of interest in his early comedies. But whatever the merits of any of these plays, it is as one of the two great French writers of tragedy that he is famous and is always thought of. True, there have been more performances of *le Menteur* than of any of his tragedies except the *Cid*; but similarly the performances of Racine's one comedy, *les Plaideurs,* have far outnumbered those of any of his tragedies, not excepting even *Phèdre,* and yet *les Plaideurs* is never considered one of his "chief" plays. To all the world Corneille is a tragic dramatist; and here are translations of his six most noted tragedies.

I have employed in this volume a different verse-form from that which I used in translating Racine. Just as the movement of the French alexandrine is intermediate between that of the English anapestic tetrameter,

> From the ends of the earth, from the ends of the earth,
> Where the night has its grave and the morning its birth,

(which appears superficially its analogue but gives much too jerky and jolty an effect to be suitable for translating it) and that of the English iambic pentameter (into which it is customarily and rightly rendered), so likewise neither our rhymed-couplet verse nor our blank verse is of the same degree of divergence from prose as the French alexandrine, which is between them in this respect. French has little accent—not enough, in fact, to establish a verse pattern by accent alone; it requires rhyme to distinguish it from prose. With its rhyme it is somewhat further removed from prose than is English blank verse, especially in view of the latter's great irregularities of rhythm. But even the freest, least end-stopped English rhymed couplet, since it has both a pattern of heavy accents and rhyme also, is further from prose than the French alexandrine, which practically has rhyme alone. The alexandrine is somewhere between these two English verse-forms in its departure from prose, and can be translated not inappropriately into either.

In any case, unless the translation were quite falsified with "embellishments," its appeal as dramatic verse must be quite other than that to which we are accustomed in English poetry.

x

The verse of seventeenth century French classicism, and of its English imitators such as Pope, has been said by some English critics not to be poetry at all. This, however, is a mere matter of definition; to assume that the English conception of poetry is right and the French conception wrong, is to beg the question. Let it be recognized only that these conceptions are largely different. Whereas we look in poetry for "fine surprises" of language, play of imagination, depth and subtlety of thought, and detailed treatment of nature, a French classicist looks for orderly arrangement of ideas and for precision, lucidity, and euphony of expression. Hence the true analogue of French classical poetry is not to be found in characteristic English poetry at all, but rather in the prose of Demosthenes and the other Attic orators, whose style, despite its apparent artlessness and simplicity, was far more carefully wrought than any English prose ever written. Of course the diction of the Greek orators was highly concrete and that of classical French tragedy somewhat abstract, but otherwise the parallel is interestingly close.

The smooth flow of Racine's polished verse seems to me best rendered by the English rhymed iambic pentameter couplet. But the closer adherence to the precise meaning of the original which blank verse permits makes this appear the more advisable medium for translating Corneille. In his fondness for intellection, which often becomes casuistry, he can be compared with only two other authors, of not dissimilar literary stature, Robert Browning and Friedrich Hebbel; when any one of these three men begins a chain of reasoning, there is no foreseeing with what conclusion it will end. To translate such a writer, a vehicle is needed in which the exact meaning of any passage can be reproduced if that is of paramount importance, and this cannot always be done in a rhymed version. But if blank verse is to be used, it should be a special kind of blank verse, one which allows any number of lines in succession to have some punctuation or voice-pause at the end of each, as the French alexandrines customarily have, without a disagreeable monotony of effect. Now unless the pauses usually come elsewhere than at the end of a line, there will be such monotony if the last syllable of nearly every line is accented, as it is in the blank verse of Milton, Tennyson, and most other

English poets. But there is one sort of blank verse in which the pauses can usually come at the ends of lines and yet no unpleasant sense of monotony will result: the sort of blank verse written by the later Elizabethan dramatists, including Shakespeare in his last phase, and especially by Fletcher, in which a large proportion of the lines end with an unaccented syllable, as in "To be, or not to be: that is the question," or "Farewell, a long farewell, to all my greatness." It is into this type of blank verse, in which the sense that each line is a unit, as in the French alexandrines, can be preserved wherever convenient and desirable, that I have translated these plays of Corneille. I have occasionally introduced rhymed verses, however, as Shakespeare and other Elizabethans did at times in the midst of their blank verse for various effects; I have done this most frequently in the *Cid*, where rhymes are particularly appropriate because of the almost lyric quality of its youthful passion.

Except Thomas Constable's *Polyeucte* (eloquent, but so free that it really is only a paraphrase) all English metrical translations of Corneille made within the last hundred years have been, to the best of my knowledge, in blank verse. Walter Federau Nokes has done a *Cid* (which I have never seen), an *Horace*, and a *Polyeucte*; Florence Kendrick Cooper a *Cid*; Paul Landis a *Cid* and a *Cinna*. I am indebted to the Nokes translation of *Horace* in not a few instances. Like Professor Landis I have made free use of Miss Cooper's spirited version of the *Cid*, familiar in anthologies, and he and I have often appropriated the same lines from her; from his own renderings, however, since they are much more recent, I have not considered it legitimate to borrow felicitous phrases except very rarely—perhaps once or twice in an act—though I may have echoed him unconsciously in other instances as a result of having read his translations several times in the past, and of course where two people translate the same original rather closely there will be many chance correspondences in their work. In the last line of the stanzas which conclude the first act of the *Cid*, and also in the last line of the first scene of its fifth act, I have followed Miss Cooper in departing from the letter of the French to reproduce more adequately in each instance the general sense and emotional effect of the passage as a whole. I have availed myself *ad libitum* of the excellent choice of diction in Roscoe Mongan's prose renderings of the *Cid* and *Cinna*.

In general, I have based my translations on the standard text of Corneille. I have restored, however, the first version of the opening of the *Cid*, which is commonly used by actors today, and also that of the last speech of Chimene. It was with this text that the play captivated all Paris and made history, and the subsequent alterations were not the result of the author's riper judgment but of fallacious criticism to which he bowed.

No English translator or critic of French classical tragedies has been consistent in altering or preserving the French names of the dramatis personae. All keep at least some of them, and all alter at least some to the forms familiar in English. I have, therefore, attempted no consistency in this respect—even within the limits of a single play. As a rule I have changed proper names to the form, classical or otherwise, that we customarily use in English. But "Chimene" is world-famous, whereas the Spanish legend of "Ximena" is known to few; and I should similarly have retained "Rodrigue" in preference to "Rodrigo" or "Roderick"—were it not for the fact that previous translators have set the fashion for calling him "Roderick," which is not unjustifiable in view of Southey's familiar Spanish hero, "Roderick, the last of the Goths." Also in deference to my predecessors I have used "Diegue" instead of "Diego." In *Polyeucte* and *Rodogune* I retain the French names of the characters which are the same as the names of the plays themselves (and, indeed, who knows what the real names of this native Armenian and this Parthian might be?) and I also retain "Pauline" since this is a familiar English name—just as nearly all translators of *The Divine Comedy* pronounce its heroine's name in the well-known English form (taken from the French) and not as the Italian quadrisyllable.

Among those who have helped me in the making of this book, I am especially indebted to Mrs. W. F. Peirce of Ithaca, N.Y., and to Dr. Charles Maxwell Lancaster of Vanderbilt University. They have patiently checked my translations for accuracy, and if in any instance I have departed unjustifiably from the meaning of the original, it has not been the fault of their supervision but of my judgment. As in my previous books of translations, Miss Louise Allen has been the chief constructive critic of my English verses. Dr. Philip W. Timberlake of Kenyon College also has helped me with his advice on various points, mainly in the Introduction.

The Chief Plays of Corneille

INTRODUCTION

The career of Pierre Corneille, called "the Great" by his admirers and thus conveniently distinguished from his younger brother Thomas, is perhaps without parallel in the history of literature. At the age of thirty he dazzled France with a masterpiece of tragic drama; he wrote three other very famous plays within the next half-decade; then in thirty years more he never again even approached the standard which he himself had set, and much of his work in that long period is simply execrable. Yet there was at no time any marked diminution in his poetic powers as with Wordsworth in later life, nor in his capacity for characterization, nor in his technical skill as a dramaturgist.

How, then, are we to account for the frustration of this author's undeniable genius? What was there in the man, in his life, in his environment, or in all three together, which can explain such a descent from the heights he had formerly reached? In seeking an answer, we may disregard his comedies and his productions for music and spectacle; only his serious dramas are of real significance.

I

Born at Rouen in Normandy in 1606, Corneille was educated for the profession of law. Between 1629 and 1636 he wrote eight plays—six of them called comedies and two called tragedies, though the earlier of this pair, *Clitandre*, is really an extravagant tragi-comedy and should not be (and never is) taken into account in any consideration of the tragedies of Corneille. The other, *Médée* (1635), his first genuine tragedy, is not altogether lacking in merit—though indeed, with Euripides and Seneca as guides, it would have been hard to spoil completely the subject of Medea's vengeance. There is nothing in the play as good as the later acts of Mairet's *Sophonisbe*, which had inaugurated French "classical" tragedy a few months before—nor anything to suggest that real genius was at work in that field and was on the point of bursting into full flower. Yet the very next year, Corneille wrote the *Cid*, his masterpiece.

INTRODUCTION

The literary Brahmins of the seventeenth century preferred *Cinna*, the literary Brahmins of today prefer *Polyeucte*, but the great mass of theater-goers and play-readers have never wavered in their allegiance to the *Cid*. It took Paris by storm and made its author the popular idol; "as beautiful as the *Cid*" became a proverbial phrase. It is the work which one instinctively associates in one's mind with Corneille, even more than one thinks first of *Phèdre* in connection with Racine or of *Hamlet* in connection with Shakespeare.

Nor is this to be wondered at. When the youthful playwright, by happy chance, went rummaging about in the vast store-house of material furnished by the national drama of Spain, then at its apogee, and lighted upon the *Mocedades del Cid* of Guillen de Castro, he found in that inchoate chronicle-play a subject which is perhaps more universal and irresistible in its appeal than any other in the dramatic literature of mankind. All the world loves a lover; and all the world can sympathize with a man's or a woman's devotion to the imperative claims of honor, whether or not the particular code that institutes those claims is still in vogue; and hence all the world must thrill to the story of Roderick, bound by honor to avenge the intolerable insult to his aged father by the father of the woman he loves, and of Chimene, obligated no less to seek his death in turn despite her love for him.[1] The nobility of the young lovers, their steadfast adherence to what they conceive to be their duty, and the greatness of their love for each other in spite of everything, have always captured and will always capture the hearts of people everywhere.

The *Cid* is an astonishing work. It is essentially the work of a young man; it has all the freshness and exuberance of youth. In this respect it is somewhat like Racine's *Andromaque* and still more like *Romeo and Juliet*. But there is also a note of Marlowe here: it makes the blood tingle, like a

[1] The compulsion under which Chimene acted may, indeed, have to be explained today to be rightly understood. In an age when it devolved on a slain man's family rather than on a public prosecutor to bring his slayer to justice, she was obligated to take every step against Roderick that her father would have wished to be taken. He being helpless in death, common loyalty made her his deputy, no matter if she herself thought his foe blameless. The situation is unfamiliar to us, but needs no further statement to be sufficiently comprehended.

flourish of trumpets in the morning. A minor French critic, in a literary manual intended for use in schools, has not only compared the *Cid* with *Romeo and Juliet* but has pronounced the two dramas approximately equal in greatness.[2] True, like a good patriot, he has been careful to point out to his adolescent readers only those details in which he thinks the play written by his fellow-countryman is superior to Shakespeare's, never those in which the case is the reverse; but his appraisal is correct: these two tragedies, so similar in nature and in their date in the careers of their respective authors, are indeed of a surprisingly exact parity of merit. The *Cid* does, however, in its best scenes rise to greater heights than its English rival ever attains.

Its chief defect is, obviously, the role of the Infanta. The struggle between her love for Roderick and her pride which forbids her to marry a man not of royal blood, a theme which often recurs in dramas of the period, does not vitally affect the action and is tiresome in itself, though the disingenuousness of her advice to Chimene at times and the uncertainty of how she may intervene in the course of events do increase in some small degree the tension of the tragic predicament. Almost every other alleged blemish proves, upon closer inspection, to be a positive excellence. Is Chimene's plea when she first comes before the King, demanding her lover's death, flamboyantly rhetorical? She speaks from a sense of duty, asking for what she does not really desire; the note of insincerity here, sounded by her exaggerated rhetoric, is precisely right. Are the arguments with which she and Roderick justify the positions they take oversubtle and wire-drawn, as Corneille himself felt to be the case? Yes, they are increasingly so as the play proceeds; and that is natural with certain people of an intellectual type who are enmeshed in an agonizing situation with which they try to deal rationally, reasoning their way through it, while the strain to which it subjects them increases steadily and makes their suppression of hysteria more and more difficult. Do they go to extremes in stickling for the "point of honor"? Jules Lemaître has cleverly ob-

---

[2] F. Hémon in *Cours de Littérature, le Cid*, Paris, 1930 ed., pp. 44-46.

served[3] that they often express not the sentiments which they have, but those which they think they ought to have; that they are conscious of the noble figure they cut, each in the other's eyes, and that they want to compel each other's admiration and prove themselves worthy of being loved; that constantly in all their anguish they thus are, after a fashion, making love to each other: it is a very delicate and beautiful touch. Is Roderick's boast of invincibility, when Chimene tells him to fight his best for her hand, outrageous rhodomontade? Nothing could be truer to life: he has been stumbling blindly through a dark maze from which he saw no prospect of escape; he has perceived at last a little glimmer of light and groped his way towards it; and then suddenly it is brighter than he could possibly have expected, and the path lies plain and straight before him with nothing required to gain his heart's desire but simple hard-hitting, in which he knows his adequacy. A man's instinctive reaction in such a case would be to throw up his head, square his shoulders, and shout aloud what he feels in his sheer relief: "I can thrash all creation!" And that, in the language of poetry, is just what Roderick says.

The twin peaks of the *Cid* are the two interviews between the lovers. Here are the essence and the greatness of the play. Each of these scenes is pivotal. The first of them clears up every possible misunderstanding that either Roderick or Chimene might have had of the other's attitude. "Roderick offers his life, and Chimene demands it; but in spite of the feud which a rigorous obligation imposes on them, they adore each other; they will adore each other even unto death, which (it is their sole hope) will reunite them soon."[4] The second interview breaks the deadlock established in the first; it shows to Roderick (and to us) that Chimene may yet be his, for a situation has developed in which she will accept this outcome rather than the only other alternative; it ends with her promise to wed him if he will save her from that, and he undoubtedly can. But far more wonderful than the dramatic effectiveness of these scenes, or even than their psychological insight,

---

[3] In L. Petit de Julleville's *Histoire de la Langue et de la Littérature française*, Paris, n. d., IV, pp. 278-279.

[4] Translated from L. Petit de Julleville: *Théâtre choisi de Corneille*, Paris, n. d., pp. 21-22.

is their emotional power—the beauty and vital force of the eloquent depiction here of the heart's true feelings bursting into irrepressible utterance despite every code and convention that would throttle them. This breath-taking triumph of sincerity is an almost incredible thing.

For, if we are to judge by its literature, there was never, perhaps, in all human annals an age more convention-ridden, a society more artificial, than that in which the *Cid* was written and first produced. The characters in the plays of that century were governed by catchwords rather than by realities; Racine's Andromache offers merely the most consistent and thorough-going example of the common vice. Legal relationships were of paramount importance; the Tomyris of Quinault, who is desperately in love with Cyrus and is forced into a detested marriage to save his life, thereupon finds her sense of duty to her "husband" so strong that she cannot kill, as she has planned to do as soon as she attains her object, the villain who has thus compelled her to wed him—and when Cyrus himself kills him, she feels that she is undeniably obligated to put her lover to death! Appearances were at any cost to be preserved. Everyone was forever posturing. "By this action I shall become an illustrious example"—of this or that—is the phrase which eternally recurs. Yet it was then, and at no other time, that a great dramatist represented a daughter letting herself be plighted to her father's slayer, within twenty-four hours of his deed—because he did only what he ought to have done, and he still really deserved her love, and she could not but love him still.

The audiences of the day were enraptured. Moralists were scandalized. Propriety joined hands with envy and enmity in an attack on the author. We need not review the famous "Quarrel of the *Cid*," which followed and which threw the subject finally into the hands of the French Academy. Suffice it to say that the judgment of that august tribunal, declaring the marriage of Chimene to Roderick so flagrant an affront to decency that it would have been better not to write a play at all than to set girls such an example, and condemning many other details of the plot as unethical, unseemly, or improbable, wrought a vital change in the nature of Corneille's work and affected all his subsequent career. We must not for a moment suppose that the verdict of the Academicians either crushed or curbed him; he could have defied it and triumphantly walked his own path, assured of the support of an idolatrous public. It did worse: it convinced him. Not immediately, for he resented it at first; but soon in large degree, and still more as time went on, though not so much in regard to its specific criticisms as in regard to the principles and viewpoint underlying it. In consequence, the great romantic dramatist that, as the *Cid* shows us, might have been (a figure such as Victor Hugo would have liked to be and doubtless did fondly imagine himself) never was. The extent of Corneille's metamorphosis may be measured by the fact that in his *Examen* of the *Cid* in the edition of 1660 he points out that his heroine never consents to wed Roderick; that she is silent when the King decrees that their marriage shall take place at the end of a year, and silence when royalty has spoken does not imply consent but the reverse; therefore we may well believe that she will persist in her refusal!

This argument is of course absurd—though it has been approved by certain modern critics who are the spiritual descendants of those who were shocked by the play when it first appeared.[5] In reality, Chimene's final speech and the King's speech that follows, taken together, permit no reasonable doubt that the lovers will "marry and live happily ever afterwards."[6] This, having been the outcome in the source of

[5] They surprisingly include Petit de Julleville (*op. cit.*, p. 222, note), whose discussion of the *Cid* is for the most part brilliant and penetrating.

[6] Chimene says that she has already revealed her love of Roderick, that she cannot deny it now, and that she is obligated to do whatever her sovereign bids her do—only she asks the King if he himself can sanction this marriage which he has commanded, and can justly use her to pay his own debt to Roderick in a manner that will dishonor her.

No, she does not ask even this; it is what the Corneille of 1660 substituted for the lines he had originally written and had let stand till then. The point about Roderick's value to the State had been raised by the Academy as the only possible justification for Chimene's union with him; that, beyond doubt, is what made Corneille introduce it at long last. Originally Chimene had said only that it would be a monstrous thing if *in one same day* she buried her father and wedded Roderick; this would be to compound her father's death, to be untrue to his memory, and to bring everlasting reproach upon herself.

It is this original speech, rather than its emended version, that the King's

Corneille's drama, is to be assumed, unless he specifically indicated the contrary. The audiences that first acclaimed the *Cid* understood it thus—or they perhaps would not have been so delighted. The people who censured it, including the Academy, understood it thus. The people who defended it understood it thus. If Corneille himself had meant it to be understood otherwise, he would most surely have said so dur-

---

reply directly answers: he says that it would be indeed unseemly for Chimene to wed Roderick on that very day, but that he has not prescribed the date; in a year it will be quite legitimate and she shall wed him then. Yet in either version the gist of the matter is the same: Chimene protests, but says she will obey the King's decision—"Vous êtes mon roi, je vous dois obéïr" ("You are my King; I ought to obey you") in 1637; "Quand un roi commande, on lui doit obéïr" ("When a king commands, he ought to be obeyed") in 1660—and the King answers her objection and decides that she still must marry Roderick.

The only evidence in support of the idea that Chimene will never relent is that cited by the aging Corneille from the scene earlier in Act V between her and Elvira. Here she declares that even if Roderick should prevail in his duel with Don Sancho, she will defy the royal mandate and refuse marriage with him. Corneille argues in 1660 that what she says in this scene has especial validity because she is speaking to her confidante, to whom she would not lie. But neither would she lie to the man whom she loves and honors—not at least in a matter of supreme importance when his action is based on his confidence in her good faith. The fact is that she no longer knows her own mind; she is the prey of veering impulses. A few moments after her statement adduced by Corneille, she tells Elvira that her love for Roderick is less potent than her aversion to Don Sancho in moulding her desires concerning the outcome of the duel. Let him believe it who can!

Dramatically, this declaration of Chimene's, that under no circumstances will she wed Roderick, is needed to maintain the suspense; for otherwise the denouement of the play would have been too obvious after their interview in V, i; that scene and her subsequent scene with Elvira, the mistake about the result of the duel, Chimene's public avowal of her love, Roderick's generous renunciation of his rights, her final forgiveness of him but objection to their nuptials, alternately presage and seem to thwart the ultimate solution that is reached only with the King's pronouncement at the very end of the drama. But Corneille, with the subtlety characteristic of his best work, has made a virtue of necessity. The uncompromising attitude taken by his heroine in talking with Elvira is psychologically explainable as her instinctive revulsion from having permitted herself, just previously, to assure Roderick that he can win her by winning the duel and that she wishes him to. When she thereupon goes to the opposite extreme and hysterically insists she will never wed him, she says also that she will raise up a thousand other champions to espouse her cause if Don

ing the controversy. The interpretation which he offered in the *Examen* of 1660 is hence merely a perverse and graceless attempt—like that of Tennyson in *Locksley Hall Sixty Years After*—to unsay in old age what he had said magnificently in youth. In the same *Examen*, Corneille admits that he would not write the two colloquies between the lovers, if it were to do over again!

II

What he did write, when three years after the *Cid* he first offered another play to the public, was a tragedy of early Rome, *Horace*, or, as it is often called, *les Horaces*. The latter would seem, to modern English ears, the more suitable title; for the theme here treated was the legendary combat of the Horatii and the Curiatii, and when the name "Horatius" is used, we think today rather of the Roman hero who held the bridge against the army of Lars Porsena as told by Macaulay —whereas "Horace" suggests the great poet of the Age of Augustus. But Corneille entitled his drama *Horace*, and that fact should refute those critics who have maintained that the play has two chief characters of equal importance, or that its hero is not the young warrior but his father. Corneille calls the father "le vieil Horace" ("Old Horatius"), the son "Horace" alone.

Yet this play is a study of the reactions not only of one man but of a number of people to a tragic situation in which conflicting claims are made on their loyalty. A similar situation had been the essence of the *Cid*; there the conflict between

---

Sancho fails; but in the end she accepts the outcome of a single duel as terminating her efforts to avenge her father, just as the arrangement had been that she would accept it; and similarly she may be expected to abide also by her promise to Roderick that she will marry him if he is victorious. Nor could she honorably do anything else, for it was on that condition alone that he would not let Don Sancho kill him. True, he releases her from her pledge—he knows best how to capture her heart utterly!—but he waives his claim to her hand only that he may first do whatever deeds are necessary to satisfy her. There has never been any suggestion that he would consent to live, if forgiven but deprived of her forever. They both know that. When Chimene surrenders her vengeance, she in effect surrenders herself also.

If she did not, the problem of the Infanta would be reopened and left unsolved; the play would not really end, but only terminate.

love and filial duty was long undecided, but love had the final word. In *Horace* the conflict is between love in its various phases on the one hand and patriotism on the other, and no two of the characters concerned react in the same way. To young Horatius, beside the claims of his country everything else is as nothing. In old Horatius the counterclaims of affection are no less inexorably rejected, but they make themselves felt more strongly—though the difference perhaps results only from the mellowing effect of age on a nature fundamentally much the same as his son's. The Alban champion, Curiatius, exemplifies normal humanity in contrast to these austere extremists. He feels the full force of both claims; like the brave man he is, he does his duty unhesitatingly, but with torn heart. Naturally it is he who falls in his combat with the single-minded zealot, Horatius.

The remaining major characters in the play are the two women, Sabina and Camilla. Alban by birth and Roman by marriage, at once the affectionate sister of the three Curiatii and the devoted wife of Horatius, Sabina finds no alternatives in prospect but the subjection of her adopted or of her native city, the death of her husband or of all her brothers; and her dominant wish, to which she recurs again and again in this intolerable position, is to escape from it by her own death. Horatius' sister, Camilla, is at the opposite extreme from him. With her, feeling is everything, principle nothing. When she sees Curiatius in Rome, she at first supposes him a deserter for her sake, and she is proud and happy to think that he loves her so much. Whichever side may win the triple duel, she will hate the victor who bereaves her of brother or lover; and when Horatius returns exultant with the blood of her betrothed on his hands, the only possible outcome of the meeting between this fanatical patriot and the frantic, resentful girl—who curses not only him but Rome also—is the swordstroke with which he punishes such blasphemy.[7]

---

[7] It should be noted, in illustration of Corneille's delicate sense of character, that he does not represent Camilla here as one whom grief and anger have made reckless of all consequences, even loss of life. His "Camille" is of too frail fiber for anything approaching heroism. Clearly she never conceives that her death may be the cost of her imprecations; she flees in panic when her brother attacks her.

11

This turn of the plot was believed by Corneille, no doubt rightly, to account for the original imperfect success of *Horace*; and it has been a target of adverse criticism ever since. It violates the only one of the famous three Unities that is of real importance, unity of action, by violating what has been called "the unity of peril": hitherto the subject of this drama had been the combat between the Horatii and the Curiatii, by which the life of the hero was endangered; but now, with that danger past, he is again in peril—in peril of being put to death for killing his sister—and the fifth act is concerned with the entirely new subject of his arraignment for this deed. Attempts to defend the play as written, or to suggest an improvement, have been unsatisfactory.

The murder of the Horatii's sister by her surviving brother and his escape from punishment for it when brought to trial are, however, a part of the legend itself which Corneille dramatized; and indeed something more than a duel successfully fought, even under the harrowing circumstances of such close ties between the combatants and when so much depends on its result, is necessary for an adequate tragic action. The native genius of the author, which was really remarkable, seems to have groped instinctively towards a right solution of his difficulty, and might have found it if he had not been governed at this time by unfortunate prepossessions.

That a character should undergo some change in the course of a play is universally regarded as one of the finest achievements of dramatic art. We are told it can rarely occur in classical drama, where the action takes place within the limits of a single day. Yet it occurs in *Horace*. When the young hero of this tragedy first appears—it is at the beginning of Act II— he knows that he and his brothers have been selected to represent Rome in the impending combat, but not that the Curiatii are to represent Alba. He is proud of the distinction accorded him, but modest withal. He feels that many others might better have been chosen than he—though he believes that the fervor and determination which he will bring to the task assigned can make him invincible. Then he discovers who will be his adversaries. He must kill the betrothed of his own sister, the brothers of his own wife, men whom he himself loves devotedly; or Rome will henceforth forever wear the yoke of Alba. The conflict which is waged in his soul is not portrayed in words, as that in Roderick's is portrayed in the *Cid* before he goes to meet the father of Chimene. Yet Horatius' inner struggle is no doubt truer to nature, if not so clear to an audience, in being wordless. Silent acting perhaps could partially reveal it. In the text it may only be inferred from his immediate change in tone and temper. When Curiatius is overwhelmed on learning that he and his brothers are to fight against the Horatii, Horatius tries to help him by arguing that the very poignancy of the situation, which is a challenge to their manhood, will augment their glory. Here something of strain and excess is already evident; and when Curiatius protests against the inhumanity of his attitude, he becomes arrogant and contemptuous. To attain to the unwavering, obsessive resolution which he considers needful in this crisis, he has had to do violence to his gentler feelings, and in the degree that this was difficult his self-esteem for having so done is magnified, and he cannot permit any question that he is right. It is true that he can still be moved by the distress of his wife and his sister—while the combat is still to be fought. But when it is over, and what he ruthlessly purposed he has actually performed no less ruthlessly, he comes home triumphant— great in his own eyes as he deems the importance great of Rome's victory, which was due to him alone—flaunting the spoils of his once-beloved antagonists, without comprehension or toleration of Camilla's anguish. And when finally he is tried for killing her, he is quite devoid of any sense of having disgraced himself by this brutal crime; standing on the scene of it, when his victim's body has scarce yet grown cold, he complacently asks for death because, he says, he has now reached the very pinnacle of heroic renown, and any further life that he might live must needs be less glorious!

It should be clear, then, what kind of ending this play ought to have. Hémon, to whom I am largely indebted for the substance of the preceding paragraph,[8] points out that even though our sympathies are with the temperate, warm-hearted Curiatius, we must realize that the man who can best serve his country in her hour of need is he who, when a great cause

---

[8] Cf. his *Cours de Littérature*, *Horace*, Paris, 1930 ed., p. 18ff.

is at stake, abandons himself to it utterly; and therefore the blind devotion of Horatius to the task entrusted to him was the right reaction at such a time, being the reaction most likely to bring success and hence most conducive to the public weal. But however right, it was ruinous to him as a man. It was right because in comparison with the fortunes of an entire people his individual fate was of slight importance, but its inevitable consequence was a perversion of his character. The violence done to his natural feelings, the identification of himself with his country's cause, could only result in callousness and egotism. Purely specious was his father's argument: that it was on impulse that Horatius slew his sister, and the impulse sprang from his patriotic ardor, a virtue in him, because of which he legitimately was enraged by Camilla's treasonous words. Even if he killed her in hot blood, he was cool and calm when later, at the bar of justice, he exhibited no vestige of remorse but only proud self-satisfaction. Regardless of the King's verdict, this drama is indeed the "tragedy" of Horatius; for to have become the man he is in the last two acts is assuredly tragic—and that he became such a man as a result of having answered his country's call in the best of all possible ways, may well excite in us both "pity and terror." And the fact, which we may also realize, that this perfect response of his, which enabled him to do his duty better than it could otherwise have been done, would have been impossible for anyone who did not have originally in his nature a certain imperfection—his "tragic flaw," which could develop as it did—is a part of the complexity and the wonder and the mystery and the truth of life.

But something more overtly and actively tragic than the mere demonstration of the impairment of Horatius' character is needed. Indubitable disaster should befall him, of a sort to make his error obvious—to the audience, at least, if not to him. One is perhaps safe in saying that it is of chief importance that his wife should kill herself. Many critics have found Sabina's role, with her often reiterated eagerness to die, monotonous and ineffectual. As the consummation of her recurrent desire and a pivotal feature of the denouement, her suicide would greatly lessen the force of that reproach. It would be a very hard blow to Horatius, who has shown a tendency to display human weakness only where she is concerned. And it would be a very natural step for her to take, and natural that she should take it directly in consequence of his murder of Camilla. Sabina might have reconciled herself to resume her wifely place at his side in spite of the death of her three brothers by his hand, for that was in fair fight and "in line of duty" by the necessity of war; and yet, even though she loved him still, she might have felt it impossible for her to live with a husband who had butchered his own sister merely because of the girl's frenzied grief and the vain words, however culpable, which it prompted—his sister, who was Sabina's sister-in-law and house-mate, of whom she had grown fond. These things she could have told Horatius with great dramatic effectiveness before taking her own life—and told him, too, that though Rome was so much in his debt that he could not be punished, everyone would recoil from association with him. After this it would make little difference what "curtain" might be devised for Horatius himself—whether suicide in his turn, or a stubborn refusal to believe that he was wrong, or a bewildered sense of isolation somewhat like Anthony's final "I no longer understand the world" in the *Maria Magdalena* of Hebbel.

But Corneille, who had been blamed for depicting in the *Cid* the triumph of love over duty as commonly conceived, was bent on showing in this next tragedy the triumph of the manly passion of patriotism, regarded as a supreme duty, over all gentler passions, with death the penalty incurred by one who put love highest and the infliction of that penalty excused if not vindicated. Hence he would not follow the logic of what his genius divined and perhaps despite him portrayed; he followed the old story, and even modified it in favor of Horatius, who in the legend was first sentenced to die but then was pardoned because of his great service to the State. The fifth act of the play, in large part devoted to formal speeches at the trial of the hero, is in consequence stiffly rhetorical; but indeed there is a certain rigidity about this drama as a whole, with its symmetrical differentiation of the several characters to illustrate the different possible attitudes towards the problem posed, and with its severe economy of dialogue. Another fault, which seems oddly to have escaped comment though

15

much of the general dissatisfaction with the latter part of *Horace* may be caused by it, is the failure to provide at the end of Act IV anything to make one look forward to what will follow. At this point one sees that Horatius' relations with his wife offer a problem, and of course one does feel that his killing of his sister must have serious consequences; but there is no definite indication that he will be prosecuted for murder, and there ought to be. Indeed, there is nothing said that would suggest any consequences whatever of his crime; as it stands, the drama might almost conclude with the end of the fourth act. Because of these defects, *Horace*, in spite of all its excellent features noted above and the martial vigor and magnificent swell and crash and resonance of its verse, is not to be reckoned like the *Cid* a truly great play, if one sets the standard of greatness as high as one should; but a very fine play it unquestionably is.

III

From rigidity, Corneille passes in *Cinna* to frigidity. This we encounter at its very outset, with a heroine who in monologue apostrophizes her "*impatients désirs d'une illustre vengeance*," weighs her love for Cinna against her hatred for Augustus, and, in connection with the latter passion, speaks also of her rage (*fureur, ardents transports, bouillant mouvement*) though hate cherished for many years because of an old wrong must surely be an emotion of cold malevolence rather than of flaming anger. A large part of the first act is consumed with an account, part summary and part verbatim quotation, of a previous impassioned harangue; and most of the second act is a formal debate in which one of the two participants does not argue sincerely. In Corneille's own day, however, *Cinna* was regarded as his masterpiece. Its somewhat too "stately" rhetoric was in keeping with the literary taste of the times; its discussion of whether a republic or a monarchy is the best form of government, whether justice or mercy is more to be commended in a ruler, and whether tyrannicide is justifiable were of absorbing interest in a period when these questions could not be argued save on the stage without risk of going to the Bastille; and in Emilia all recognized a portrait of one of the high-born ladies of that generation, such as

Madame de Chevreuse, Madame de Longueville, or the Princesse de Condé, who combined love and intrigue, who conspired ceaselessly against Richelieu and a few years later would create the Fronde. Yet modern critics tell us that in the age in which this play was most admired, it was not admired understandingly. Then, Cinna and "Emilie" were the center of sympathetic interest, Augustus was the adversary whose eventual change of heart fortunately spared them; and this view of the play, modern critics tell us, is wrong. Pointing to the complete title, *Cinna, or the Clemency of Augustus,* they explain how cleverly Corneille has wrought—how in the first act he lets Augustus be seen through the eyes of the conspirators as a ruthless tyrant and themselves as heroic champions of liberty, and how in the subsequent acts we bit by bit discover his noble qualities and the ingratitude, self-seeking, and perfidy of those who plot against him, until at last we behold him in all his greatness and them in all their baseness and pettiness. Such criticism forgets that to write a play thus is to ignore one of the cardinal facts of drama: that when the sympathies of an audience are once enlisted, they cannot afterwards be transferred effectively. In evidence of this fact is the stage-history of *Cinna*: whatever the pronouncements of literary authorities, theater-goers in general have always regarded Cinna himself and Emilia as the hero and heroine of the play.

I shall have the temerity to defend Corneille on this point, in part at least, against his scholarly admirers. He has not been as ill-advised as they represent him. If his intention had been to shift all sympathy from the conspirators to Augustus, he would never have made Cinna display such courage when confronted with the prospect of death—and still less, when Augustus reproaches Emilia for the way in which she has repaid his unnumbered acts of loving kindness, would she have been given the most impressive line in the entire play:

Ceux de mon père en vous firent mêmes effets.[9]

Professor Paul Landis comes much nearer the truth when he praises "the dexterity with which Corneille in *Cinna* first throws the sympathy to Cinna, then to Augustus, and finally

> Those of my father
> Produced the same results in thee.

extracts and unites the virtues of both."[10] While older than Roderick and Chimene, both Cinna and Emilia are still quite young; they are thrilled by the excitement of conspiring and by the picture they paint of themselves as the deliverers of Rome; they are easily thrown into a panic by the sobering threat of discovery. But there is true pathos in Emilia's cry, when faced with failure, that she has done all she could. Her incomprehension of Cinna's scruples and her readiness to assume the worst hypothesis to account for his hesitancy is a blemish only too characteristic of "lovers" in French classical tragedy, but she has the excuse that she has just been under great tension. As for Augustus, his eventual pardon of the conspirators is attributed by different critics to sagacity, humanity, or ambition to behave nobly. Professor Lancaster suggests that he may well have been actuated by all three at once.[11] But I think that his successive reactions to the successive disclosures warrant little doubt as to which was the dominant factor in determining his course. When he first learns of the conspiracy, his reflections leave him undecided, but at least he rejects the advice of Livia, which is to do precisely what he finally does. In the fifth act, at the end of his scene with Cinna, there is no hint of leniency: he says he will see whether Cinna's fortitude will persist unshaken to the end; and he tells the culprit to choose his own punishment according to what is just. Then the horrified Emperor discovers that Emilia, too, has conspired against his life, yet he still has no thought of mercy; she begs to be united with Cinna in a common doom, and he declares that he will indeed unite this treacherous and ungrateful pair and make the whole world blench at their punishment as at their crime. Then Maximus appears, his savior Maximus—and confesses to being the worst, the most perfidious, of all his foes. "Have I any subject still faithful!" cries Augustus, and forthwith pardons them all. Dramatically, the scene is defective, in that his change is too sudden to be easily understood; but that change, coming as it does, can only be a result of his realization that all his previous severity has left him no one whom he can trust, that

[10] *Six Plays by Corneille and Racine*, New York, 1931, p. xi.

[11] *A History of French Dramatic Literature in the Seventeenth Century*, Part II, Baltimore, 1932, p. 315.

this policy has ended in complete bankruptcy, and that there is nothing left for him to do but to try its opposite.

Even with such an interpretation of Augustus' conduct, and with the necessary modification of that extreme reversal of sympathies which modern criticism has seen in this play, we still must recognize that Corneille has overreached himself in his design. The difference between the Augustus described in the first act and the Augustus shown to us in the second act remains bewilderingly, unacceptably great. The temperate, kindly, conscientious ruler, whom we find anxiously debating the proper course to pursue, can never have been, by any stretch of the imagination, the blood-stained proscriber of whom we have heard; he seems to us more like George Washington deciding not to accept a third term as President and about to write his famous Farewell Address. And Emilia, too, is inconceivable, on any thoughtful envisagement of her conduct. Even waiving all questions of the ethical status of revenge in general (since it is true that no other theme has a more potent dramatic appeal at all times), many critics have declared that she could not be justified in taking vengeance, though for a father's death, upon one on whose bounty she had lived so long with pretended reciprocation of his love; but this is not really the main point of the difficulty about her. Life in a royal household would not involve nearly so close a relationship between its members as in a private family; yet with all necessary allowance made for that fact, the truth is that she could not have concealed so completely and so long the intense hatred which she felt for Augustus—not unless deceitfulness to a repulsive degree was a strong, fundamental trait in her nature, which Corneille certainly did not mean to be the case. Nor is it humanly possible that, having hated Augustus so bitterly for so many years, she could in a twinkling reverse her feelings towards him as one takes off or puts on a garment. She might indeed be convinced, when he pardoned all, that thanks and admiration and loyal service were now his due from her, instead of death. But she could have said only something like this: "Sire, I am overwhelmed by your magnanimity. I owe everything to you. After what you have just done, I could not conspire against you; I would henceforth give my life to serve you and defend you. But I cannot live in constant loving association with you, whose face, whose voice, whose person have been linked in my mind, since childhood, with all the hatred of which my soul was capable. Permit me, sire, to go to the farthest bounds of your empire, where I shall never see you again." The whole effect of the conclusion is that of the forced "happy ending" so frequently encountered in comedy and tragi-comedy. The facile supposition that people can let any and all bygones be bygones may be very convenient in bringing a drama to a pleasant close, but it is very untrue to life.

There is a similar want of imaginative grasp elsewhere in this play. Cinna claims that he could not avenge Emilia on Augustus if the Emperor were to abdicate; but though the conspiracy would of course collapse when it no longer had the object of regaining the liberties of Rome, as a private citizen Augustus could be killed all the more easily by one determined man.[12] It is unbelievable that any human being would have been fatuous enough to declare his love in the circumstances and in the manner in which Maximus declares his to Emilia; and, indeed, that he secretly loves her, and betrays the conspiracy in the hope of destroying his "rival" and winning her hand, is the most hackneyed of possible turns that the play could take. Augustus concludes his great soliloquy by expressing a sentiment, "Either let me die or let me reign," which it was conventional to ascribe to all sovereigns, but which is at complete variance with the feelings of this particular sovereign as previously and subsequently portrayed. *Cinna* contains much eloquence and some really striking thoughts and workmanship; but only the tenacious traditionalism which at all times has characterized the appraisals of French classical drama could have preserved for this tragedy a place beside or near its two immediate predecessors and *Polyeucte*, which followed it.

IV

In Corneille's own century *Polyeucte*, though a favorite of

[12] True, the plea of personal revenge for a past crime of Augustus might not, in that case, save the murderer if he were discovered—but this would be an inglorious consideration for the professed lover to be governed by! Neither Cinna nor Emilia ever envisages the situation.

the general public, was not held by "the judicious" to be one of his best plays. There were two reasons for its failure to win their plaudits. In the first place, they preferred the more elevated style of *Cinna*, whereas we consider the greater naturalness of expression in *Polyeucte* a point of excellence, and its verse is commonly thought today to be the finest its author ever wrote. In the second place, its religious subject was long deemed unsuitable for treatment on the stage.

This tragedy of an early Christian martyr seeks to depict the workings of Divine Grace in the human soul. With his fondness for symmetrical structure, Corneille offers three examples of this, in which the miraculous element is increasingly evident. The first instance, Polyeucte's resolve to interrupt a pagan sacrifice, break the images of the gods, and thus win martyrdom, does not seem miraculous at all, but merely the fervor of a newly baptized convert. The third and last instance, the sudden conversion of the ignoble, cowardly Felix, cannot possibly be anything but a miracle—and as such it is usually considered the chief defect of the play. The best that can be said for it is, that it is of a piece with the world of saints'-legends from which *Polyeucte* derives and something of whose atmosphere is preserved throughout this drama, nor could one easily imagine any other, more satisfactory ending that would conclude the action with sufficient finality to have been acceptable to its original public. Between these two manifestations of Grace there is yet another, the conversion of Pauline; this one is surprising in its suddenness and can be regarded as supernatural, but it also admits of rationalistic explanation as a consequence of the transfer of her love from Severus to Polyeucte. Her position between these two men— her lost lover and her husband—is the heart and core of the play.

Herein has lain always the principal interest in *Polyeucte*; and herein does modern criticism find grounds for maintaining that it is Corneille's masterpiece. In certain of its scenes—most of all in the great scene between Severus and Pauline in the second act—we encounter a strength, a subtlety, a maturity of genius which cannot be matched by anything in the *Cid* or elsewhere in his work. But by strange coincidence it was now, and only now, immediately on the heels of *Cinna*, that he repeated the fundamental mistake of that play and again asked of his audience an impossible shift of their sympathies. The shift would be less violent here; both Severus and Polyeucte were meant by him to be admired, but first the one and then the other in the higher degree. Yet even more surely here than in *Cinna*, what Corneille attempted was doomed to failure. There is nowhere—there never has been—an audience that would not give its heart, at once and beyond recall, to a worthy young man who is denied the hand of his sweetheart because of his poverty.

So it was from the first with this play. "Is there anyone," asked the Prince de Conti, the brother of the great Condé, "who would not be a thousand times more touched by the anguish of Severus when he finds Pauline married than by the martyrdom of Polyeucte?" In the next century Voltaire observed a secret joy in the audiences when they saw that Polyeucte was going to break the statues of the gods, because they anticipated that he would be put to death for it and Severus would then wed Pauline. One is safe in saying that this would still be, and will always be, the reaction of the average undirected spectator. But Corneille unquestionably intended to represent the change in his heroine's feelings as a growth from a youthful, romantic love for Severus—admirable enough in its way, but essentially earthly—to a nobler, higher, more spiritual love for her husband. Regardless of whether we like this change, we must recognize that he has motivated it with great subtlety and complexity. Many things have been pointed out as involved in causing it: her fear of her love for Severus, her wish to love Polyeucte, her instinctive cherishing of one for whom she has given up so much, the fact that it is now he (as it formerly was Severus) who is in a distressing situation and her heart goes out by nature and habit to the unfortunate, the necessity of declaring and emphasizing her love for him in order to put the strongest pressure that she can both on Felix to grant him mercy and on Polyeucte himself not to persist in his fatal resolution, her pique in being then rejected by him, and, most of all, the attraction of the mysterious and the unknown—the seemingly heroic and the professedly supernal—which she feels when he talks of religious values beyond her ken and renounces her and goes to his death for them, so that in comparison with him Severus, ready to accept her from his hand and uttering the conventional phrases of courtship, appears to her small and commonplace.[13] But all these factors combined could not have produced the result they did, if it had not been for one circumstance which Corneille supplied with the unerring instinct of genius working at its best: she had been married to Polyeucte only fourteen days. Her feelings towards him were still easily subject to change; he had won her esteem and affection by his kindly, considerate treatment of her as well as by displaying his own great love for her; she may even be said to have begun to love him at the opening of the play, though too little not to be torn by the more powerful tug of her old love when this was given fresh strength—but he must have been in large measure a stranger to her still. She could not yet have explored the major portion of his mind or soul. She had not yet had a long-continued daily life with him, which would have made him familiar to her beyond possibility of glamor. Hence, when she discovered him dedicated to an otherworldliness whose claims he asserted in lofty-sounding words, her imagination could invest him with the grandest qualities, and he speedily became almost a god to her, and the luckless Severus as nothing in comparison.

Now this representation of the change in Pauline is wonderfully well conceived in the only way in which it could have taken place. Most people in Corneille's lifetime, and long afterwards, doubtless were glad for the heroine to become a Christian in any way and so escape damnation. Modern scholarly critics, on their part, are so engrossed in admiring the masterly genius of the portraiture that they have not regarded with their natural human reactions the thing that is portrayed. But rightly considered, for people too far removed from the Middle Ages to believe in the excellence of martyrdom or in the supreme importance of correct theological dogma, the spectacle of a woman so dazzled by the aura of false saintliness which surrounds a religious enthusiast that she loses all love for her noble, greatly-tried lover, and will not

[13] This generally accepted interpretation of Pauline's character and conduct was first set forth by Sarcey. Cf. Lemaître in Petit de Julleville's *Histoire*, IV, 290, and Faguet in his *En lisant Corneille* (Paris, 1914).

marry him when fate at last removes every legitimate obstacle to their union, is decidedly unpleasant.

We must recognize today that Severus is altogether the more admirable man. Where religion is not concerned, Polyeucte exhibits many attractive qualities—a grave courtesy, an understanding and magnanimous nature, a zest for life, and a lack of jealousy which, one regrets to say, can hardly be paralleled elsewhere in French classical drama. He has served in war, we gather, with considerable distinction. But there is no reason to suppose that he could even have approached the achievements which made Severus the hero of the empire; and in the realm of the spirit, Polyeucte's inferiority is greater still. His chief concern in seeking martyrdom is to enjoy the delights of heaven sooner and to avoid the danger he would run of losing them by back-sliding if he continued to live. These are the considerations that he talks of most. Severus, on the other hand, is actuated wholly by principle—by a love of rectitude and nobility for their own sake—when he tries to save his rival and declares that he will intercede with the Emperor for the Christians though at the risk of his life. Both in abilities and in moral grandeur, the man who loses Pauline's heart is far above the man who wins it.[14]

The fact is that with enlightened people of today whose imagination is keen enough to make real to them what is depicted in literature, Polyeucte's behavior in the temple may well put him entirely beyond the pale of sympathy. Religious intolerance, carried to the point of using force, is particularly abhorrent to us. Granted that it appears in its least objectionable form in Polyeucte, who would have killed or harmed no one in the name of religion. He had a moral right to express his convictions publicly, denouncing the pagan faith and proclaiming the virtues and truth of his own. But his violation of the sanctities of others by doing this in the midst of their ceremonies of worship, which he broke up, and then

---

[14] Lemaître's idea, given unfortunate prominence by being stated in so notable a place as the pages of Petit de Julleville's great *Histoire*, that when Severus calls Pauline *"trop vertueux objet"* he reveals that he has hoped to seduce her, is exploded by reference to the text of the play. He calls her "too virtuous" when she reminds him that it was never in her power to marry him, for filial duty subjected her to her father's will.

destroying their sacred vessels and the statues of their gods, was an outrage for which he deserved to be very severely punished.

Pauline herself, even apart from her misguided change of affections, seems to me by no means so admirable as traditional criticism has pronounced her. No other heroine of Corneille, says Professor Lancaster, "unites such intensity of feeling with such understanding of others and such strength."[15] It is true that, like Severus, she acts from principle, according to what she conceives to be right, however intense her emotions; and she shrewdly realizes that no fear of punishment will make her husband abjure his faith, and is under no illusions about her father. But she continually, and always wrongly, expects the unworthiest conduct of Polyeucte and Severus in their relations with each other, though recognizing that her fears insult them both. A climax is reached in Act IV when she imagines that Severus' object in coming to see Polyeucte is to taunt him in his misfortunes![16] It may be the same persistent distrust of a man of admitted nobility which partly inspires her vehement assertion that nothing could make her wed one who was, however innocently, the cause of her husband's death; she probably believes that Severus will not do his best to save him if the least prospect remains of marrying her in case of Polyeucte's execution. At any rate, she here brings to mind by contrast Chimene, who can in the end marry one who deliberately, with his own hand, killed her father, since she knows that he was blameless in doing so; and we may be sure that the people who were horrified by Chimene applauded Pauline. But Chimene had never ceased to love Roderick, and Pauline by this time has almost completed the transference of her love to Polyeucte. Her last vestige of affection for Severus appears in her final words of this scene, when she tells him that if he is not generous enough to intercede for her husband's life, she

[15] *Op. cit.*, Part II, p. 325. Professor Lancaster's more sympathetic analysis of Pauline's character is the best succinct statement of the traditional view of her that I know of.

[16] This immediate, wholly gratuitous conjecture is, perhaps, in some degree a result of blind anger; her husband has just rejected her in favor of his religion, and it actually would seem from her words that she is on the point of leaving him to his fate; but Severus unluckily arrives at that very moment, and she vents her ill temper on him.

does not wish to know it. Thereafter, as Professor Lancaster observes,[17] he drops so utterly out of her thoughts and heart that when Polyeucte has suffered martyrdom and she has become a Christian, she exclaims on learning that her father, too, is converted,

> This glad change makes my happiness complete.

She says this in the presence of Severus himself, to whom, moreover, she speaks no word and pays no attention at any time in the entire scene. With her, out-of-love is indeed out-of-mind—and out of any sort of fondness whatever. Though she must believe that salvation depends on conversion, she feels not the slightest concern for the noble, heroic man whom she formerly has loved, who loves her still, and who has tried to save his rival for her sake.

I have stated the matter thus sharply because there is no other possible interpretation of her behavior in this concluding scene of the play, and it seems to me that here we have a sufficient answer, even without the other points discussed above, to those who see a spiritual development in her merely because her love for a gallant pagan soldier is supplanted by an infatuation for a Christian martyr. It is a blemish in any literary work if the characters whom the author meant to be esteemed cannot hold the sympathies of people in all subsequent times, as I believe Polyeucte and Pauline cannot. But this blemish, though serious, does not necessarily prevent a play which is marred by it from being a great play.[18] The very fact that different periods and different critics can interpret Polyeucte and Pauline differently and cannot agree in liking or disliking them, just as we differ about people in real life, is a proof of the complexity and lifelikeness of their portraiture. All, in fact, of the major characters in *Polyeucte* are masterfully drawn. No further comment on Severus is

---

[17] *Op. cit.*, Part II, p. 325.

[18] Molière's *Tartuffe* does not provide an exact parallel, for no one has ever sympathized with Orgon's conduct in casting his son out with almost murderous mood and trying to force his daughter to marry Tartuffe. But parental tyranny was formerly condoned enough, especially as a stage convention, for people to be satisfied with a denouement in which Orgon recognizes his error, whereas he now arouses emotions not so easily purged. Yet no one would deny the greatness of *Tartuffe*.

needed; and, except for his miraculous conversion, we have in Felix a wonderful study of base fatuity, where a large and delicious element of comedy, which is usually excluded from the French tragic stage, testifies to Corneille's powers in that vein. Though a religious drama, *Polyeucte* is its author's most broadly human play.

V

Since neither its subject matter nor its verse, however, had pleased those whose approval he most desired, he went back to Roman themes and resounding rhetoric in his next tragedy. *La Mort de Pompée*, which deals with matters leading up to and following the murder of Pompey (who is not himself a character in it), was considered in his own lifetime one of his supreme achievements, along with the *Cid, Horace,* and *Cinna;* and even yet in traditional repute it stands among his seven or eight best tragedies; but most modern critics would rank it among his worst. Imitating *Cinna,* it exaggerates the defects of the earlier play, with grandiose verse in long, formal speeches of debate or narrative. It does not really have a plot; "a mere sequence of events logically connected" does not constitute one. It has no conflict of opposites evenly enough matched, or maintained long enough, to create suspense. Many critics regard the brief role of Cornelia, Pompey's vengeful widow, as its sole excellence; but though the dramatist himself certainly intended her to be admired, she appears on adequate inspection a far from attractive figure. The "duty" to which Corneille's heroines consecrate themselves becomes more and more questionable; no credible logic could show it to be her duty to seek Caesar's death in retaliation for her husband's. The quarrel between these great men was political, not personal; Caesar in victory was eager to treat his vanquished foe with kindness and honor, was horrified by the murder of Pompey and pledged himself to avenge it. Cornelia's implacable hatred of him is in the blind and senseless spirit of a vendetta.

The chief offense to most people, however, in *Pompée* is its depiction of the love of Caesar for Cleopatra. According to this play, he fell in love with her when she came to Rome, while a young girl, with her father; he has written her almost daily letters throughout all his campaigns; he conquers the world only to lay it at her feet! A new influence has now become of major importance in the work of Corneille. Early in the seventeenth century the enormous vogue of D'Urfé's interminable pastoral romance, the *Astrée*, introduced into French drama its preoccupation with love, its strained conventions of gallantry and decorum, and its stereotyped love-jargon of "sighs" and "flames" and "conquests." This element, called "romanesque" because of its derivation from the *Astrée* and subsequent romances, was perpetuated and increased by the influence of the fashionable drawing-room society, which had its heyday from 1630 to 1650, upon French life and letters —particularly the influence of the coterie who frequented the famous *chambre bleue* of the Marquise de Rambouillet. These took as their models the heroes and heroines of D'Urfé.

Prominent authors had free access to the Hôtel de Rambouillet. It is said that Corneille read all his plays to the gatherings there, from the *Cid* to *Rodogune*—and that *Polyeucte* met with great disfavor. All these tragedies, like all others of their period, have romanesque touches, be it only some use of the conventional love-language; but in *Pompée* the romanesque element runs riot. There is but one thing that can account for its sudden extreme prominence in this drama: the advent just then of a new literary type, degenerative in its effect on the taste of cultured high society, at the very time when Corneille must have been anxious not to displease again. In place of the previous pastoral romances, the pseudo-historical or "heroic" romance was coming into vogue; and it is even possible that by 1642, the year in which *Pompée* was written, he had heard in the *chambre bleue* the opening chapters of Madeleine de Scudéry's *le Grand Cyrus*, with its wonderfully valiant and absurdly gallant heroes, in all whose doings of war or statecraft, as in those of Corneille's Julius Caesar, love such as the frequenters of the drawing-rooms would have love be was an important consideration. The first volume of this colossal work was not published until 1648; but its author's earlier romance, *Ibrahim* or *l'Illustre Bassa*, had appeared in 1641 and the first volume of La Calprenède's *Cassandre* in 1642. The latter, especially, anticipated the characteristics of *Cyrus*, and its setting in the Near East during the break-up of the empire of Alexander the Great pointed the way for dramatists to exploit the Hellenistic world, whose petty kingdoms, with obscure annals, allowed free scope to romanesque invention.

It was to this very world that Corneille, after writing two comedies, *le Menteur* and *la Suite du Menteur*, next turned. *Rodogune*, produced in 1644-1645, was his own favorite of all his plays, and therefore is significant as revealing what he came to value most in drama. An involved plot, largely of his own invention, with extraordinary situations which culminate in a sensational climax—it was on this that he especially prided himself; and here in a single drama, he asserted, are combined a beauty of subject-matter, power and fluency of verse, soundness of reasoning, violence of passions, and tenderness of love and affection, so that his other plays have few merits which *Rodogune* does not possess. But the fact is that its love is the gallant love of the romances, its passions are strained, its logic is often fantastic, its verse less grandiloquent than that of *Pompée* but still too rhetorical;[19] and its subject-matter and conduct are such that it is a melodrama rather than a tragedy.

Melodrama bears the same relation to tragedy that farce does to comedy; in both melodrama and farce the interest excited is found in the plot rather than in the characters. Hence in melodrama the characters are likely to be simplified —to be altogether good or altogether bad—and the plot is likely to be devised to secure the maximum possible tension and shock, frequently of a naive or crude sort, and sheer chance may be a factor in what occurs. And when, for the sake of the plot, something is made to happen as it would not happen in real life, or the consistency of a character is violated, the melodrama becomes bad melodrama. *Rodogune* is a bad melodrama.

The exposition of what has previously taken place and of the situation at the opening of this play is clumsier, perhaps, than any elsewhere in Corneille, and is so long that to make

[19] Its over-use of apostrophe in soliloquies is especially flagrant. Sometimes a speaker apostrophizes first one abstraction or inanimate object and then immediately afterwards another. E.g. the first speech in Act II and the first speech in Act V.

it endurable he had to interrupt it with scenes of a more dramatic nature and resume it after them. Demetrius Nicanor, king of Syria, was taken prisoner, it explains, by the Parthians and was reported dead. His wife, "Cleopatre,"—to use the French form of her name and avoid confusion with the famous Cleopatra of Egypt,—then married his brother, who at length died; and later she learned that Nicanor was still alive, an honored captive in his adversaries' hands. He would accept no excuses for her second marriage, and himself planned to wed Rodogune, the young sister of the Parthian king; but when he brought this princess home to marry her, the outraged Cleopatre killed him and subjected her to the cruelest imprisonment until her brother came with an avenging Parthian army and forced the Queen to agree to a treaty arranging for Rodogune to wed the elder of Cleopatre's twin sons, who would then mount the throne of Syria. At the opening of the play, these two young men have recently arrived from Egypt, where they were sent when little children for safe rearing in the troubled times through which their country has passed. Only the Queen knows which of them was born first— here at the outset we encounter one of the improbabilities frequent in melodrama—and she, unaware that both have fallen in love with Rodogune, tells them that she will name as the true heir to the crown the one that will kill the Princess for her. When they both refuse to do this, she tries to turn them against each other; but their mutual devotion is unshaken by her wiles, so she secretly stabs to death one of the twins, Seleucus, and feigning to be reconciled with his brother Antiochus and with Rodogune, intends to poison them at their wedding.

The supreme situation planned by Corneille for the climax of this drama was that now, in the fifth act, Antiochus should be faced with the certainty that either his mother or his bride seeks his life, but should not know which. For this, it was necessary that what he learns of Seleucus' death should clearly indicate that the murderer must be one of the two women and might be either of them. It was also necessary that there should have been something earlier in the play that would make Rodogune as natural an object of suspicion as the perfidious, sanguinary Queen herself. To supply this indispensable preparation for the culminating scene, Corneille gave the plot a startling turn indeed.

After Cleopatre has promised, in Act II, to yield the throne to whichever of the twins will kill Rodogune, they decide to ask the Princess herself to choose the one who shall wed her and reign. She has secretly been informed of the Queen's offer to them, and when they come to her to learn her preference, she tells them that she will wed whichever will avenge his father by killing his mother for her!

This instigation to matricide is introduced into the play purely by arbitrary will of the author, to enable him to have his climacteric scene and in violence to every other consideration. From Rodogune, who both earlier and later is a typical romanesque heroine, so atrocious a proposal is entirely out of character. Of course it produces a sensational surprise, but it lessens the effectiveness of her role by showing her to be no less savage and dangerous than her enemy, just when most sympathy for her should be evoked. In her predicament it was the worst possible maneuver. Corneille said that she made it only to avoid choosing either of the princes and to enlist them both in her defense by giving them equal hopes; but the result really to be anticipated from it was that she would alienate them both—perhaps make them think their mother was quite right in wanting to kill such a person.[20] She did alienate one of them.

Corneille also said that she did not expect or even wish her demands to be granted; but these explanations were made more than fifteen years after he wrote the play, and at the time when he misrepresented the conclusion of the *Cid*. Though Rodogune herself says much the same thing to Antiochus in the scene in Act IV in which she admits that she loves him, her statements then are sharply at variance with her soliloquy in Act III. There, after having been advised to find shelter from the Queen's hate in the love of the two princes, she deliberately works herself up, with frigid rhetoric and strained reasoning, to a determination to avenge her late betrothed. From this speech, one might well think that she loves

[20] Rodogune does not even excuse herself to them by explaining that she knows of the Queen's fell designs against her. To do so might risk the life of her informant.

31

Nicanor, who cannot have been dead very long, and his son also![21] She declares that it would be ignoble to ask the protection of men in love with her, that she becomes a free agent once more when Cleopatre breaks the treaty and when Antiochus and Seleucus let her choose between them, and that as a free agent it is her "duty" to seek vengeance for the man who was slain when about to wed her. But when the Queen pretends a reconcilement, Rodogune is all deference and amity again. It would seem that she is able not merely to hide her feelings; she can turn them on and off like water at a faucet.[22]

The circumstances of Seleucus' death which cast equal suspicion on both women are no less unnatural. Found dying, he gasps:

> A hand that was beloved by us
> Avenges a cruel deed's refusal thus.
> Reign; and, above all, brother dear,
> Of that same hand beware, beware.
> It is . . .

and then expires. No man at death's door with such information to impart would speak thus, withholding the all-important fact of his murderer's name so long—with the result that he dies before uttering it. This is but a familiar expedient of melodrama.

At least, the scene achieved at such cost is a tremendous one. *Rodogune* is mainly famous for it and for the stark figure of Cleopatre. She too, however, belongs essentially to melodrama; she is simply a human tigress, consumed by ambition and hatred, yet, with melodramatic naïveté, calling her own deeds "crimes" and making conventional references to the motherly instincts to which she did violence—as though she, portrayed as she is, would have any thoughts of such instincts! Her sons,

---

[21] Some recent critics have assumed that Rodogune must have been much older than the twins, merely because she had been engaged to their father! There is nothing improbable about a royal marriage being arranged for a monarch of forty or more with a princess of twenty or less.

[22] Corneille's characters, especially his women, again and again assert a complete mastery over their emotions. Pauline's claim of it is so extreme as to evoke a cry of anguished protest from Severus. Fortunately for truth-to-life, their strength of will generally proves to be much less potent than they suppose it to be. But in Rodogune it goes beyond the bounds of nature.

on the other hand, have generally been considered the play's worst blemish. Both of these youths appear at first as sighing lovers out of the *Astrée* or *le Grand Cyrus*, but Seleucus later exhibits shrewdness and a sense of values which make him the one really likable character in this drama. He wants no bride who bids him kill his mother, and he is aware of his mother's villainy and minces few words with her. Therefore it was inevitable that he should be less admired than his brother in an age when fashions in men were set by the Hôtel de Rambouillet, from whose ideas and gestures Antiochus never departs—and no less inevitable that it should be Antiochus who survives to wed and reign. The weight of tradition in the field of French "classical" tragedy is such that, amazingly, most critics ever since have also preferred this priggish young chevalier *à la mode*, who is always tenderly respectful to his mother and unshaken in his love for his heart's mistress, no matter what they do. When his brother cries out in horror at the Queen's malignant offer, this perfect son chides him:

Let us have more respect for natural ties.

When Rodogune makes an even worse demand and Seleucus exclaims that one so barbarous ought to be the daughter of Cleopatre, this perfect lover says:

Let us lament without blaspheming.

Unlike Seleucus, he does not cease to love either of them; and therefore critics speak approvingly of his "moderation" or "magnanimity"—even of his being the "maturer" of the twins. A lack of revulsion from people of abominable wickedness is not regarded elsewhere as moderation or magnanimity or maturity. Perhaps his magnanimity is to be seen in his professed willingness for Seleucus to have Rodogune, though he knows that it is himself whom she loves; without the slightest regard for *her* happiness, he must be the perfect brother also. In the final scene he wishes to die rather than find out which woman is the criminal, despite the fact that his death would leave the other one to her tender mercies; and, to crown all, when his mother, trapped at last, herself drinks the poisoned draft which she has prepared for him, and refuses all aid, he bleats:

Ah, live to change this hate to love!

Yet he has just learned that she had murdered his beloved twin-brother!

VI

Despite the criticisms which *Polyeucte* had incurred, Corneille, fortified by the success of *Pompée* and *Rodogune,* now undertook in *Théodore* another drama about an early Christian martyr. But his infatuation for extremes caused him to confront his heroine, as the greatest possible test of her constancy, with the choice of renouncing Christianity or being thrown into a house of ill fame—a situation that foredoomed the play to failure in an age which demanded strict decorum in its tragedies—and to represent her as vowed to perpetual virginity and so self-possessed in her cold otherworldliness that she is little shaken even by the prospect of her defilement, and to set her in isolation among baleful people, so that none of the dramatis personae elicits the slightest sympathy. The egregious badness of Act V suggests that when Corneille was writing it he may have known, at least subconsciously, that his labor was in vain.

He went back to melodrama—to melodrama so involved that *Rodogune* appears simple in comparison. For extreme complication his *Héraclius* (1646-1647) has become a legend; he himself said that no one could understand it completely on seeing it only once. The difficulty, which for the most part lies in the identity of the characters, is really by no means as great as that. Even in reading the play for the first time, one does not find it hard to keep track of them, and in actual performance, where they are before one's eyes, it would be much easier. As all too frequently in melodrama, the denouement is no logical consequence of the action which precedes it; but this action is, throughout, full of excitement, suspense, sudden turns, and striking situations; there is little "gallantry," and the characters nearly always behave as they naturally would under the circumstances—so that though *Héraclius* never equalled *Rodogune* in renown, and has no scene as theatrically effective as the last scene in *Rodogune* and no figure to match Cleopatre, a good argument might be made that it is the better play.

After *Andromède*, a production for music and spectacle, Corneille wrote *Don Sanche d'Aragon* (1649), which he called a *comédie héroïque*. It does not excite laughter, but with its acceptance of the old idea that people closely related by blood but unaware of their kinship are instinctively drawn to each other, an alleged attraction which here creates preposterous situations, it presents a slightly unreal, slightly conventionalized stage world. If not taken too seriously, it is one of the very best of Corneille's lesser plays, though the amazing verve and brilliancy of its first act, which is cloak-and-sword drama of the finest sort, is not sustained thereafter. The difference that its success might have made in his career is an interesting subject for speculation. In it he was again exploiting the chivalric world of the *Cid*, his natural field and one in which he seemed to recover immediately in some degree the qualities that characterized the masterpiece of his youth. But *Don Sanche* was a failure because it displeased a certain exalted personage, and just as its author turned from the Spain of the *Cid* to the Rome of *Horace*, so now he turned from the Spain of this "heroic comedy" to the Rome of *Nicomède*.

This time the Rome that he depicts is not the Rome of the kings, taking her first steps towards greatness, nor Rome at the height of her power, the assured mistress of the world, under her kingly emperors, but republican Rome (already the chief power throughout the Mediterranean area) in her dealings— now wily, now tyrannical—with the petty kings of Asia Minor; and he treats his subject from the viewpoint of those unfortunate monarchs. Among his contemporaries, Corneille enjoyed an especial reputation as a historical dramatist; but he allowed himself much license with prominent figures of history, altering at will their motives, their characters, and the events in their lives. What he was at pains to reproduce, as well as he could with the limited knowledge that people in his day had of the past, was the political background, the forces at work and in conflict, and the general nature of the periods in which he laid his tragedies. Nowhere else has he done this so notably as in *Nicomède*.

He chose for his hero, whose name the play bears, the son of King Prusias of Bithynia. According to history, Prusias tried to kill Nicomedes but was killed by him. Corneille rejected so terrible a denouement and made the really undistinguished prince an impressive figure by representing him as having learned the art of war from Hannibal during the great Carthaginian's last days in exile at the Bithynian court, as having already caused Rome anxiety by his conquests, and as embodying Asiatic nationalist resistance to Roman aggression, before which the cowardly Prusias cringes.

In Corneille's play, Nicomedes is the son of Prusias' first marriage; and the King's second wife, Arsinoë, hates her step-son and wants her own son to succeed to the throne in his stead. To her influence and her machinations, to the no less dangerous hostility of her ally, the Roman envoy Flaminius, and to the base jealousy and suspicions which Nicomedes' victories and the love felt for him by the populace excite in Prusias himself, he opposes a bold demeanor, a cool courage, and a barbed, eloquent tongue. Irony is the keynote of this drama, and admiration—not "pity or terror"—the feeling which it arouses. There results a somewhat too great monotony of effect: Nicomedes' successive clashes with his several adversaries, in which everybody is equally ironical, are too much alike; and his betrothed, Laodice, the Queen of Cappadocia, who also engages in duels of wits and words with them, is nearly—though not quite—his "double." These constantly repeated encounters are purely thrust and parry and counter-thrust; one may be hurt or angered or baffled in them, but no one (with a single exception) is influenced by what another says, as the characters in the *Cid* or *Polyeucte* are influenced, and hence the dialogue, though always spirited and often quite stirring, is not so dramatic as in those plays.

Lemaître sees in Nicomedes an earlier D'Artagnan, ever intrepid and ever capable—to the confusion of all miscreants. In reality, Corneille has not created so conventional a hero. This valiant, straight-forward soldier, marvelously competent in war, is without experience in Court intrigues and falls at once into the trap which Arsinoë sets for him; it is Laodice, not he, who divines that there must be something in the situation besides what meets the eye. But the trouble is that this play needs the conventional hero imagined by Lemaître. One who speaks always with the proud assurance characteristic of Corneille's Nicomedes must live up to his words, or he to some extent forfeits sympathy. This self-confident prince cuts an inglorious figure when, after all his "tall talk," the first and only real act against him finds him devoid of resources to thwart it, and he can do nothing but exclaim in helpless surprise, "Thou sendest me to Rome?" and owes his deliverance to no effort of his but to his despised brother, Attalus. Here we have one of the two or three serious defects in this excellent play.

Yet in some sense Nicomedes was, truly, himself the cause of his eventual triumph. It was his example—his bravery in the face of odds, his gallant bearing, his frank speech, his loftiness of soul—that first kindled the dormant spark of manhood in the breast of Attalus. The transformation of this youth, from the complacent protégé of Rome and spoiled darling of his mother to the noble lad who comes to his elder brother's rescue, is perhaps the finest single thing in *Nicomède*. Here we again have that great achievement of genius, so rare in plays of the "classical" type: a change or development of character, convincingly depicted, in the course of a drama.

The revelation that it was Attalus who saved Nicomedes is a very effective *coup de théâtre*. In other respects, the denouement of this tragedy is its weakest point. Even more than in *Cinna*, matters have gone too far, feelings have been too intense and purposes too grim, for any finale of forgiveness and reconciliation to be appropriate. Such an ending is palpably forced. It has been argued that Corneille made Prusias so ignoble a figure that, like Felix in *Polyeucte*, he arouses amusement rather than abhorrence; and beyond doubt the dramatist did intend to justify thus the way in which he concludes the play. There is, indeed, a large comic element in Prusias.[23] But though Felix was fatuous, craven, and selfish, he was not by nature unkindly, whereas Prusias was malignant as well as base. Nicomedes did not know of his father's intention to kill him and throw down his head to the rioters; but he might some day learn of it, perhaps from Attalus—and then what tolerable relations could exist between him and Prusias? The feelings which this vile king evokes in us, like those evoked

---

[23] This is particularly true in his scenes with Arsinoë, which may have suggested Molière's Argan and Béline in *le Malade imaginaire*.

by the Orgon of *Tartuffe*, cannot be placated by anything short of veritable disaster for him. And what faith can Nicomedes—or we—have in Arsinoë's professions of regret and amity?

Appreciation of *Nicomède* has grown steadily greater. Voltaire and La Harpe coupled it with *Sertorius* as merely one of the best tragedies of Corneille's long decline, inferior to his *Rodogune* and, of course, to his then-admired *Pompée*. In the nineteenth century it was generally thought to be next in merit to "the four masterpieces"—the *Cid, Horace, Cinna,* and *Polyeucte.* That is still the opinion of some critics—notably of Professor Lancaster, who is inclined to conservatism (quite properly in such work as his) in regard to the acceptance or rejection of traditional appraisals.[24] But, beginning with Lemaître, modern criticism has tended to rank this play above *Cinna* and consequently fourth among the dramas of its author, a place it surely deserves.

Unfortunately, Corneille again went from Roman tragedy to melodrama. *Pertharite roi des Lombards* (1651) has always been adjudged one of his very worst plays, and is of interest only because the situation in its first two acts is almost a duplicate, and evidently the model, of that with which Racine was to achieve the tremendous success of *Andromaque*. *Pertharite* failed so completely that Corneille resolved to write no more for the stage, and in this resolve he persisted for seven years.

VII

When at length, in 1659, he again addressed himself to

[24] Perhaps he would rate *Nicomède* higher, but for a strange error in his recollection of it. In his *History of French Dramatic Literature in the Seventeenth Century,* Part II, p. 692, he says: "Corneille apologizes for the fact that he makes Flaminius, the king, and the queen return at the end of the play after having set out to sail for Rome. . . . It is, indeed, difficult to believe that Prusias and Arsinoë would have returned merely to avoid an accusation of cowardice. . . . Apart from this slip the play is well constructed." Really, according neither to the play itself nor to Corneille's statement to which Professor Lancaster refers was Arsinoë one of the party who set out for Rome—nor was the king, strictly speaking—and Prusias declares that he and Flaminius returned to protect her from the mob or die in her defense.

dramatic composition, preciosity and gallantry reigned supreme. Madeleine de Scudéry's *Cyrus* had been followed by her still more extravagant *Clélie*, with its map of the Land of Tender Love; and, beginning with the *Timocrate* (1656) of Corneille's younger brother Thomas, romanesque plays dominated the stage, to which they brought all the absurdities, the complications, and the complete disregard of historical verisimilitude which were characteristic of the romances themselves. Amid such a world Pierre Corneille produced an *Œdipe*, in which he made of the grim story of King Oedipus of Thebes another involved melodrama and for "heart interest" created a daughter of Laius and Jocasta, Dirce by name, and made her the beloved of no less a personage than Theseus, who as here portrayed might have stepped from the pages of *Clélie* itself. During a large portion of the play their love is given greater prominence than the affairs of Oedipus. People who see in Corneille a resolute foe of the romanesque vogue do not take sufficient note of his *Œdipe*, in which he surrenders abjectly to prevailing tastes. Yet this sorry play was greeted with an enthusiasm which must have restored its author's faith in his power to please.

What his true preference was, however, when he felt he could safely follow it, can be learned from his next tragedies. The success of his brother's *Stilicon* and *Camma* in the interim had shown that the public would now again accept dramas of a less tinsel kind, grounded to some extent in actual history; and he accordingly produced *Sertorius* in 1662, *Sophonisbe* in 1663, and *Othon* in 1664. These are the most characteristic plays of the latter part of his career, and they embody the principles set forth in his critical writings, which appeared in 1660, and which were the ablest dramatic criticism in France up to that time. Love is a passion of too little impressiveness, he maintained, to serve as the chief subject of a tragedy, where it should not be absent but should be relegated to a secondary part. For this opinion, subsequent critics have never ceased to berate him; and they have pointed to his dramas of this period as lamentable proof of its erroneousness. Yet the trouble with these later tragedies of Corneille is not that love is stressed too little in them. The trouble is that it is stressed too much. Nearly every character is represented as in love with somebody.

In every decision on matters of great historical note, some love or other, generally invented outright by the author, is involved. The eternal recurrence of such factors, in the most important questions of war or policy, is annoying. It quite transforms history and the figures of history. Yet it does not make them more dramatic by introducing any violent passions, which result in stirring words or deeds. It merely keeps the characters in a state of indecision till the five acts required by invariable custom in French "classical" tragedy have run their course. Each of these plays consists of a dreary series of dialogues between two of the dramatis personae in continually new pairings, each new dialogue modifying an infirm purpose which has just been formed in a previous dialogue. The characters profess intense love; even when great things are at stake they frequently listen to love's promptings to an extent that would have horrified Chimene; but in the end they do not obey its promptings. Moreover, they talk about their love frigidly, and often in the conventional phrases of gallantry, so that though it intrudes into all their affairs, it seems almost an impersonal consideration.

Sertorius is the most typical example of tragedy according to this recipe. It has traditionally been regarded as the best of all the dramas written by Corneille after his seven years' retirement; for its poetry is superior to that of any of the others of this period, and style has always been accorded undue weight in the critical judgments of his countrymen. However, it has usually been placed on a par with *Pompée*; and that is indeed where, for better or worse, it should rightly stand. Significantly, Faguet and Lemaître, the most eminent French critics since Brunetière, have liked it least. *Sophonisbe*— Corneille's unsuccessful attempt to rival Mairet's *Sophonisbe* of some thirty years earlier, which was still played and admired —is universally considered one of his poorest tragedies. It contains, more than any of the others, nearly all the characteristic questionable features of its author's work subsequent to the *Cid*, and exhibits them in their worst form, much as a cartoon exaggerates the distinctive, salient details of someone's face. But at least its dramatis personae, in refreshing contrast to those of *Sertorius*, know their own minds and go straight towards the goal of their desires; and in this respect it is less typical than *Sertorius* of Corneille's later manner. In *Othon*, veering decisions again fill an entire play, but here he for once found a subject in which they are not inappropriate or objectionable: the struggle for power—even for survival— at the Court of the well-meaning but aged and pliable Roman emperor Galba. Some of Corneille's friends thought this tragedy equal or superior in merit to the finest achievements of his prime; and in recent years, also, it has had a few fervent admirers. The cold objectivity with which it depicts a corrupt Court no doubt endears it to modern lovers of disillusion, but a dramatist's coldness of detached observation should not be communicated to the characters and their passions—and here these, too, are mortally cold. Yet the motivation and conduct of the characters are in no instance unnatural, however frigid their speech; so that *Othon*, despite the fact that Otho himself takes no active part in its outcome, may be called a "good play."

Only his incredible mislabeling of *Agésilas* (1666) as a tragedy could have secured it a place among his serious dramas and brought down upon it the scorn of critics, from Boileau with his *"Helas"* to the present day, as the most insipid and worthless of them all. It is merely an inept experiment in a new kind of light comedy with a nominally classical setting; and when it was ill received, Corneille returned to weightier themes in *Attila* (1667).

Here, at last, genuine emotion reappears and with it a protagonist of tremendous impressiveness. Attila the Hun is the one gigantic figure that Corneille ever drew. He depicts him as a wily despot, a monstrous, gloating King Spider who winds his toils around all within the range of his power; and if we find it grotesque that this Attila feels too nearly the same sort of love that other characters of Corneille feel, and speaks of it in too nearly the same gallant language, we should realize that the model for his portrait is not the Mongolian barbarian of history but a very different kind of man not incapable of some refinements of speech and feeling: one of the ruffianly, scheming tyrants or condottieri of the Italian Renaissance, conscienceless and grandiosely ambitious, a Sforza or a Borgia, or even some wolfish, sardonic great French lord of the author's own lifetime—which, in view of the meager historical imagination then possessed by anyone, is probably as near as Corneille could come to divining what the real Attila was like. The fate which overtakes him, though in accord with history, is quite out of keeping with tragic dignity; the hero of a tragedy must not die of a "nose-bleed"; yet despite such a denouement, this play—instead of *Sertorius* as it was formerly held, or *Othon* or *Suréna* as some now hold—is the best of Corneille's later dramas, and ought to be more widely known.

It enjoyed a moderate success; but hardly more than eight months later, Paris was in ecstasies over Racine's *Andromaque*, and Corneille saw his laurels fade in the blaze of glory which attended the advent of a rival who could have challenged his supremacy in his palmiest days—a rival, moreover, whose themes and ideas were in extreme contrast to his own. Racine's depiction of men and women as the helpless prey of their passions must have seemed to him—who had always insisted on the sovereignty of the human will—profoundly immoral, insidious, even indecent. He was openly contemptuous of Racine's plays. Jealousy of each other's greatness increased the bad feeling between these two sensitive, acrimonious men, whose antipathetic conceptions would have bred hostility in any case. For three years Corneille wrote nothing; and all three of his subsequent plays seem to have been written in deliberate competition with Racine, in which he persisted in the tactical blunder of trying to surpass his rival in his rival's own special field, instead of attempting to show his superiority in tragedies in which he could follow his natural bent.

Tite et Bérénice (1670) is the first and poorest of the three. It was not written, we now believe, in competition with Racine's *Bérénice*; the truth seems to be that Racine discovered the subject of the new play on which Corneille was at work and hastened to write a play of his own on it, confident that his would be the better and that thus he would humiliate his enemy. Corneille probably undertook *Tite et Bérénice* in emulation, rather, of *Andromaque*; alone among his plays it has, exactly like *Andromaque*, a cast of characters consisting of four principals and their four confidants, and in it too the essential problem is: who will marry whom? It is another late-Corneillian drama of irresolution, in which Corneille's reaction against the frenetic emotionalism of *Andromaque* leads him to revert to something of the frigidity from which he had escaped in *Attila*; none of its characters excites sympathy, and one of them, Domitia, who has the longest role in the play, is extremely despicable, but the others continually refer to her fine qualities and excuse her worst behavior as "natural"! What are we to make of this? Did Corneille deliberately portray in her an odious woman, to match Racine's Hermione, and ironically pretend to justify her for those who had delighted in the characters of *Andromaque*? Or had he actually come to have no better discernment of what is good and what is bad—of what can be admired or at least sympathized with and what must be detested—than his presentation of Domitia would indicate? The whole matter of Racine's influence on the last plays of Corneille needs fuller study than it has yet received.

It is more probably *Pulchérie* (1672), his next drama, that was written in emulation of Racine's *Bérénice*. Its subject, also, is a royal marriage in which considerations of State oppose the dictates of the heart. Though it is another play that consists of a mere series of conversations without excitement or tension, it is surpassed among Corneille's later dramas only by *Attila*—and perhaps by *Suréna*, which followed it. Despite its quiet tone, one senses the presence of true emotion in its characters; with them, strong feeling seems restrained, not absent. They are all subtly and consistently portrayed; their conduct is natural; and the action progresses to the final outcome without being open to serious criticism at any point. But, doubtless because of its lack of violent passions and its unromantic conclusion, *Pulchérie* was little appreciated.

Suréna (1674), finally, is in emulation of Racine's *Bajazet* and possibly, to some extent, of *Mithridate* also. No other drama of Corneille has been so diversely appraised. When produced, it met with such scant favor that he once more abandoned play-writing, this time permanently. It was long looked upon as one of the feeblest of his tragedies; but Brasillach asserts that it is surpassed only by the *Cid* and *Polyeucte*, and Schlumberger thinks the role of its heroine comparable to none but that of Racine's Phaedra.[25] The truth lies, surely, between these extremes of praise and blame. *Suréna* is not a

[25] Brasillach, *Corneille*, Paris, 1938, p. 462. Schlumberger, *Plaisir à Corneille*, Paris, 1936, p. 258.

bad play, yet neither is it a very good play. It contains passages of no small eloquence, which reveal its author to be a great poet to the last. In its characters we again encounter, as in *Pulchérie*, intense but restrained emotions. With a cleverly devised plot, it depicts the stages by which two lovers, both of whom are required to wed someone else, gradually betray to others the secret of their love, which they try to conceal, and shows how in their misery they are unable to avert the doom which threatens the hero in consequence. He is that Parthian general who, history tells us, annihilated the Roman army of Crassus and then was put to death by his king for being too powerful a subject; in the play he could save his life by marrying the king's daughter, but to this the "heroine" (a figure probably suggested by Racine's Atalide in *Bajazet* and hardly less unattractive) cannot consent. Nobody in *Suréna* is really likable. The mature and war-hardened general declares in all seriousness that he will shortly die of grief at losing his beloved. She does die of grief when he is killed. With this climax of romanesque conventionalism, Corneille ends his career as a dramatist.

VIII

In our survey of his work we may observe four sharply differentiated periods. During the first of these, he wrote according to his own taste and judgment, following the impulses of his own native genius. Unhappily, after his apprenticeship, only the *Cid* was written under these conditions.

In the second period he wrote according to his taste and judgment as these had been modified by the storm of criticism which the *Cid* evoked. The fruit of the change thus wrought in him is to be found in *Horace, Cinna,* and *Polyeucte.*

In the third and by far the longest period, beginning with *Pompée* and extending (across his seven years' retirement in middle life) down to and including *Attila*, his work was further modified by the influence of the gallant pseudo-historical romances, which embodied and exaggerated the artificial ideals of the Hôtel de Rambouillet.

The fourth period, which produced *Tite et Bérénice, Pul-*

chérie, and *Suréna,* is that in which his work underwent a final
modification in consequence of his rivalry with Racine.

The sensitiveness—the responsiveness—to external influ-
ences which these successive radical changes in the matter and
manner of his plays reveal does not accord with the usual
conception of this "dramatist of the Will" as himself a heroic
figure. The truth is that there is no evidence to support such
a conception of him. The facts, as we have seen, all indicate
him to have been just the reverse of this; and, indeed, that
was the more natural presumption. It is the man who is himself weak, and who suffers from his weakness, that is most
likely to be fond of drawing inflexible supermen; thus vicari-
ously he enjoys the strength and heroism which he does not
possess. A dramatist who shared the resolute self-confidence
of Nicomedes would not have grown to regret his depiction of
Roderick and Chimene, or, having written the *Cid,* have gone
on to write *Cinna* and *Pompée* and *Rodogune* and *Sertorius*
and *Suréna.*

As though by a strange fatality, each time when it seemed
that he might adjust himself to the compromise which then
governed him and do better work than he had yet done under
its terms, some new thing persuaded him to write in a different and less effective vein. *Polyeucte* was his best play subsequent to the *Cid,* and after its ill success with the coterie of the
Hôtel de Rambouillet he surrendered to the conventions of the
romances which were their favorite reading. *Don Sanche
d'Aragon,* with its momentary promise, was a failure. In
Attila, Corneille at long last again depicted intense emotions
—and the vogue of Racine's emotional dramas of love drove
him to what was at once an imitation of them and a reaction
against them.

One cannot turn from one's natural bent, discard one's own
ideas of what is attractive and noble in deference to the ideas
of others, transform one's writing in compliance with prevailing literary fashion, save at a heavy cost. The verve and passion and warmth of human sympathies which characterized
the *Cid* were never quite captured by Corneille again; and,
anxious to please though he was, he was often unable to gauge
the effect of what he would offer to an audience when no
longer following his own instincts; hence the last act of

Horace, the change of sympathies that he vainly sought in *Cinna* and *Polyeucte*, the abject failure of *Théodore* and *Pertharite*, the lack of appeal in most of his later dramas. As the years passed, his plays grew colder and colder. And especially, and most naturally, did he who had distrusted and renounced his own sense of right-and-wrong become increasingly confused as to ethical values. In *Horace* he does with remarkable acuteness perceive them all in a highly complex situation and errs solely in his relative emphasis among them and in considering as palliable and pardonable an atrocity which is neither. But in both the hero and the heroine of *Polyeucte* he evidently approves of that which ought to be censured; and he proceeds in subsequent plays to expect sympathy and even admiration for characters whose conduct is vicious, absurd, or contemptible. Perhaps this descent to moral sanctions approximating those of the romances and of the minor romanesque dramatists is the most important single factor in Corneille's decline.

The pity of it all was that, though inferior to Racine as a poet, he seems to have been in some respects more richly endowed with the specific gifts of a dramatist. We have observed three instances—Horatius, Pauline, and Attalus—in which, despite the very limited time of the action in classical tragedies, he succeeded in depicting the change or development of a character in the course of a play; there is no example of this in any drama of Racine's.[26] Great characters, characters of an impressiveness such as Racine's Phaedra, Hermione, Athaliah, Roxana, Achmet, or Jehoiada, he has not drawn— except his Attila in a minor play. Yet these personages of Racine are delineated with the economy of means characteristic of classical art in general—with few, simple strokes that sketch a vividly conceived, obviously consistent and easily understood figure—in striking contrast to the detailed portrait-painting of Shakespeare, which has the complexities, the surprises, and the apparent irrelevances and contradictions of life itself. Aeschylus, Sophocles, and Euripides, though con-

---

[26] That alleged of Nero in Racine's *Britannicus* is not a change of character but merely a breaking away from restraint. It can be canceled, together with that alleged of Augustus in Corneille's *Cinna*, each being a spurious instance of this difficult achievement of dramatic genius.

strained to even greater brevity than the French classical dramatists, manage to achieve touches of subtlety and surprise and a complexity of characterization that can hardly be matched outside of Shakespeare. But Corneille, in depicting character and motivation, approaches the complexity of Shakespeare and of life more nearly than any other neoclassical dramatist, if not more nearly than any ancient one.[27]

Again and again both in Shakespeare and in Corneille we are surprised at some speech or act of someone. We ask ourselves: "Why did this character say—or do—that?" Has the author blundered, or are we lacking in perception? In the case of Shakespeare, except in his very early or very casual work, we can be certain that the fault is ours if the arresting detail seems—and even never ceases to seem—wrong.[28] But we can-

---

[27] We have remarked the covert love-making of Roderick and Chimene— in acting nobly before each other—throughout their ordeal, and the amazing multiplicity of factors involved in the transfer of Pauline's love from Severus to Polyeucte. For one further illustration of this lifelike complexity in Corneille's treatment of character, let us note the mingling of several motives which can be found in even so small a detail as Chimene's choice of Don Sancho to be her champion. Her main reason for it —probably her only conscious reason—is that, as he reminds her, she has promised him this honor. But the reason which Leonora and the Infanta impute to her, that she knows he will be no match for Roderick, may well have influenced her, too, though subconsciously. (She must have been conscious immediately, or the next instant, of the *fact* that he could not win the duel; but she would not have been false to her self-imposed task by deliberately choosing him *for that reason*.) Still another very possible unconscious reason may have been the resentment which she must have felt in her heart towards Don Sancho for telling her, when he escorted her home the night after her father's death, what she did not wish to hear, that she is indeed obligated to take vengeance, and for being eager to kill Roderick for her and thinking that he, forsooth, can do so. She will show him whether he can or not! And how much was it this resentment, and how much just a desire to be rid of his importunities as soon as possible so that she might surrender herself to her grief, and how much an instinctive grasp at the only help which had been offered her, that caused her to give him her promise in the first place?

[28] Nothing could be more unexpected, or more revelatory when its whole import is grasped, than his "Yet Edmund was beloved," perhaps the most wonderful brief utterance in all drama. Even in so poor a play as *All's Well that Ends Well*, Shakespeare's sense of character consistency does not fail him: it is not an accident that the scene of coarse badinage between Helena and Parolles, in the like of which none of his other heroines ever engages, was assigned to one whose later conduct, though tradi-

not have a similar assurance of inerrancy in Corneille, and the very challenge of the hazard thus involved in criticizing him is not without its fascination. With him, what seems botch-work may be precisely that instead of some unfathomed subtlety, yet it is really a subtlety so often that one does not feel altogether safe in pronouncing it botch-work in any instance. Perhaps his fitfulness of inspiration is, in some measure at least, another result of his conforming to literary fashion and ceasing to depict life in accordance with his own observation and instinctive sympathies. There is certainly no botch-work in the *Cid*, or even in *Horace*.

Why was Corneille, with all his genius, so much more than Racine a victim of his environment? Racine was no less sensitive to criticism than he—was, indeed, more deeply wounded by censure or by lack of appreciation, if the testimony of their contemporaries can be trusted—and began to write when the influence of romanesque conventions was far stronger than in Corneille's youth. The answer is to be found in part in the younger dramatist's unquestionably surer taste and greater capacity for self-criticism. We have seen that Corneille's creative instinct, with its keen sense of reality, was at times his master rather than his servant,[29] perhaps in unconscious rebellion against the constraint which his compromises placed upon it. We have observed in him, also, a perverse fondness for complication—he took pride in exhibiting his skill in it—and for melodrama, quite absent in Racine; this was doubtless partly innate. But still more important was a difference in their education. Racine's largely shaped his superior literary taste; and it furnished him with models of excellence in drama—such as Corneille did not have—to keep him from straying too badly from the path of true art.

Corneille's education did not give him Racine's knowledge of Greek. His chief acquaintance among the ancient classical dramatists was with the Latin Seneca, whose admiration for

---

tionally acceptable to a mainly male public (as Professor Lawrence has shown), would not have been that of any woman of any real refinement in any period of history.

[29] E.g. his portrayal of Nicomedes as the over-confident soldier unversed in intrigue, rather than as the hero equal to any situation—the sort of figure needed to secure the maximum sympathy of an audience.

gigantic energy even when directed to criminal ends he echoed, and whose rhetoric he imitated all the more readily because his own legal training (as well as his native mental endowment and temperament) made it—and hair-splitting distinctions, and reasoning carried to the point of casuistry—natural to him. Racine had from boyhood worshipped at the shrine of Sophocles and Euripides; their surviving masterpieces were for him the quintessence of greatness in tragedy, guiding stars towards which his ambition led him. It is, consequently, his peculiar distinction that, beginning his career in the trammels of a dramatic convention as frustrative of great achievement (because envisioning a very unreal, artificial world) as ever hampered a playwright, he nevertheless got free of them—and rose above them—to an extent to which no one else, so enmeshed at outset, ever did. Corneille, on the other hand, has the sad distinction of being the greatest dramatist both actually and potentially who could not escape from the toils of similar circumstances and was enwound and dragged down by them.

The Cid

CHARACTERS IN THE PLAY

THE KING, *Ferdinand the First, of Castile.*

THE INFANTA, *his daughter.*

THE COUNT DE GORMAS, *his most eminent warrior and captain.*

DON DIEGUE, *a Castilian nobleman, formerly of the same pre-eminence, now an old man.*

RODERICK, *son of Don Diegue.*

CHIMENE, *daughter of the Count de Gormas.*

DON ARIAS, *a Castilian nobleman.*

DON ALONSO, *another Castilian nobleman.*

DON SANCHO, *a young Castilian nobleman.*

LEONORA, *lady in attendance upon the Infanta.*

ELVIRA, *Chimene's duenna.*

A page.

Courtiers and guards.

The scene is laid in Seville, in medieval Spain.

"Diegue" rhymes with "re-beg" and "Chimene" with "re-pen" except that in both names the sound of "e" in the second syllable is prolonged a little.

The Cid

ACT I

Scene One

A room in the house of the COUNT DE GORMAS. *The* COUNT *and* ELVIRA *are discovered.*

ELVIRA.   Of all the lovers who with youthful ardor
  Worship thy daughter and seek aid from me,
  Don Roderick and Don Sancho seem the two
  In whom her beauty most hath kindled love.
  Not that Chimene doth hearken to their wooing
  Or by some look encourages their suit.
  Quite the reverse, as though towards all indifferent,
  She neither gives them hope nor robs them of it,
  And with no glance too cold nor yet too kind
  Awaits a husband from thy choice alone.

THE COUNT.   She acts discreetly. Both are worthy of her.
  Both are of noble blood, valiant and true,—
  Young, but revealing clearly in their mien
  The lofty virtues of their brave forefathers.
  Don Roderick especially displays
  Naught in his aspect which does not betoken
  A man of courage. From a family
  He comes which hath produced so many heroes
  That all its sons are born amid war's trophies.
  The prowess of his father, never equalled
  In his own day, was deemed miraculous
  So long as yet his strength endured. His exploits
  Are graven plainly on his furrowed brows,
  Which tell us still what formerly he was.
  Even such as I have seen the sire, the son,
  Methinks, will be; and, in a word, 'twill please me
  Well if my daughter loves him. Go and talk
  Of him with her; but in your conversation
  Conceal my feelings and discover hers.
  I wish to speak with thee concerning this
  On my return. The present hour calls me

Unto the council which is to be held.
The King must choose a tutor for his son,
Or, rather, must give me that honored office.
The deeds mine arm hath daily done for him
Forbid me to believe that anyone
Disputes my right to it. (*Exit* THE COUNT.)

ELVIRA (*to herself*). What blissful news
For these young lovers! And how everything
Shapes itself for their happiness!

Enter CHIMENE.

CHIMENE. How now,
Elvira, what must I expect? What fate
Is to be mine? What did my father say
To thee?

ELVIRA. Things which should very much delight thee.
He admires Roderick no less than thou
Dost love him.

CHIMENE. My good fortune is so great
That I distrust it. Can I really credit
Such words?

ELVIRA. He goes yet further; he approves
Of Roderick's wooing and will soon command thee
To plight thy troth with him. When they have left
The council, Roderick's father is to broach
The matter. Do thou judge, then, whether any
Better occasion could be found, and whether
All thy desires will soon be satisfied.

CHIMENE. It none the less seems that my troubled spirit
Cannot believe this joyous news, and finds
Itself o'erwhelmed by it. One moment oft
Gives a new aspect to one's fate. I fear
Some dire disaster from this great good fortune.

ELVIRA. Thou soon wilt see thy fear most happily
Proved needless.

CHIMENE. Let us go, and whatsoever
The outcome is to be, let us await it.

(*Exeunt.*)

Scene Two

A room in the apartments of the Infanta, *in the royal palace.*
The Infanta, Leonora, *and a page are discovered.*

The Infanta.   Page, go and tell Chimene for me that she
Hath waited somewhat overlong today
To come and see me, and that her tardiness
Grieves me, who am so fond of her.

(*Exit the page.*)

Leonora.   Each day,
Madam, the same wish moves thee, and I hear thee
In talking with her ask each day how fares
Her love.

The Infanta.   I do so not without good reason.
I almost have compelled her to receive
Its shafts, wherewith her heart is wounded now.
She loves Don Roderick; and it was my hand
That gave him to her,—with my aid that he
O'ercame the coldness of her maiden soul.
Having thus forged the chains which bind these lovers,
I needs must take an interest in their fortunes.

Leonora.   But, madam, when Fate seems to smile upon them,
Thou showest no joy thereat, but sore displeasure.
Does this their love, which fills them both with gladness,
Cause in thy noble breast so great a sadness?
And does this interest which thou takest in them
Make thee unhappy thus when they are happy?
But I am indiscreet, and go too far.

The Infanta.   My sorrow is increased by secrecy.
Hearken to what a struggle has been mine.
Learn to what trials I am still exposed.
Love is a tyrant that spares none of us.
This noble youth, this lover I have given
Unto Chimene—I myself love him.

Leonora.   *Thou*
Lovest him?

The Infanta.   Lay thy hand upon my heart
And feel how hard 'tis beating at his name,
Knowing its conqueror.

LEONORA.   Madam, pardon me
    If I presume to blame thee for this madness.
    Can a great princess so forget herself
    That she will love a simple cavalier?
    What would the King say? What would Castile say?
    Dost thou remember still whose child thou art?
THE INFANTA.   So well do I remember this that I
    Would kill myself ere I would stoop to be
    False to my station. I might well remind thee
    That in a lofty soul true worth alone
    Should light the fires of love; and if my feelings
    Sought an excuse, a thousand famed examples
    Could furnish them with one. But I would nowise
    Follow these precedents in any matter
    Where honor is concerned. Although my fancy
    Be captivated, my resolve stands firm,
    And ever do I tell myself that, being
    The daughter of a king, none but a king
    Is worthy of me. On finding that my heart
    Could not defend itself, I made a gift
    Of him I did not dare to take. I put
    Chimene in love's bonds in my stead, and lighted
    Love's mutual flames in them to quench mine own.
    Then be no more surprised if my wracked spirit
    Awaits their wedding so impatiently.
    Thou seest that now my peace depends upon it.
    Love lives by hope and dies when hope is dead.
    It is a fire that, lacking fuel, goes out;
    And, notwithstanding all that I have suffered,
    If once Chimene has Roderick for a husband,
    My hope must end, my wounded heart be healed.
      Till then, my anguish is beyond conception;
    For, till he weds, I cannot choose but love him.
    I do my best to lose him, and the loss
    Grieves me, and hence proceeds my secret woe.
    I see regretfully that love constrains me
    To utter sighs for one whose rank I scorn.
    I feel my soul divided: though my will
    Is strong, my breast is all aflame. This marriage
    Will mean my death! I fear it and desire it.

I dare hope from it only mingled joy
And pain. My honor and my love are both
So dear to me that I shall die if either
Of them surrenders or if either conquers.

LEONORA.   Madam, thy words leave naught for me to say.
I can but sigh with thee for thy ill fortune.
At first I blamed thee; now I pity thee.
But since in a mischance so dire yet sweet
Thou art too noble to accept its yoke
And yieldest not to its greatness nor its spell,
Thou wilt find peace again through fortitude.
Put trust therein, and in Time's kindly hand.
Put trust in heaven; 'tis too just to leave
Such virtue in such long-continued grief.

THE INFANTA.   My surest hope lies in the loss of hope.

(Enter the page.)

THE PAGE.   Chimene hath come to see thee, as thou badest.

THE INFANTA *(to* LEONORA*)*.   Go entertain her in yon gallery.

LEONORA.   Wouldst thou bide here in brooding reverie?

THE INFANTA.   Nay, I wish only for a little space
Of time in which I may compose my face,
Despite my misery. I shall follow thee.

(Exeunt LEONORA *and the page.)*

O righteous heaven, to which I look for comfort,
Set limits to the woe that doth possess
My soul. Grant peace to me. Grant honor to me.
Let me in others' happiness find my own.
This marriage equally concerns three hearts.
Oh, hasten it, or give me greater strength!
The nuptials that make these two lovers one
Will break my fetters and end all my torture.
But I am lingering. I will seek Chimene
And by our converse try to lull my pain.   *(Exit.)*

Scene Three

A hall in the royal palace. DON DIEGUE *and the* COUNT DE
GORMAS *are discovered.*

THE COUNT.   And so thou hast prevailed, and the King's favor
Confers on thee an office rightly mine.
Thou art to rear the young prince of Castile.

Don Diegue.   This proud distinction given my family
         Proves to all men how just our sovereign is
         And that he can reward past services.
The Count.   Kings, howso great they be, are like ourselves
         And, even as other men, can be mistaken.
         This choice will prove to every courtier
         That present services are ill rewarded.
Don Diegue.   Let us say nothing more about a preference
         So galling to thy soul. Kindness, perhaps,
         Hath swayed the balance quite as much as merit.
         But to a king whose power is supreme
         We owe too much respect to question aught
         That he hath willed. To the honor he has done me
         Add thou, I pray, another. Let us join
         By sacred ties thy house and mine. Thou hast
         An only daughter; I have an only son.
         Their marriage will forever make us more
         Than friends. Grant me this favor and accept him
         As son-in-law.
The Count.   Unto some loftier marriage
         This precious son of thine ought to aspire,
         And the bright splendor of thy new-won office
         Should make his heart swell with more vaunting hopes.
            Perform thy duties, sir; instruct the Prince.
         Teach him the way that one should rule a province,
         Should make his laws feared everywhere by all,
         Inspire the good with love, the bad with terror.
         Add to these lessons those a soldier needs;
         Show him how he must learn to laugh at hardships,
         To ply the trade of Mars without an equal,
         To pass whole days—yes, and whole nights—on horseback,
         Sleep fully armed, capture by storm a stronghold,
         And owe a victory to himself alone.
         Teach him by thy example; make him perfect,
         Setting before his eyes thy precepts' fruit.
Don Diegue.   To teach him by example, I but need—
         Despite thy jealousy—to let him read
         The history of my life. There in a long
         Succession of heroic deeds can he
         Discover how to subjugate a province,

Attack a fortress, marshal an armed host,
And by great exploits win himself renown.
THE COUNT. Living examples are the better guides.
A prince learns ill his duties from a book.
And, after all, what have thy many years
Wrought, that one day of mine cannot surpass?
Thou hast been valiant; I am valiant now.
On my strong arm this kingdom rests secure.
When my sword flashes, Aragon takes flight,
Granada trembles, and my name of might
Serves as a rampart unto all Castile.
Without me, ye would soon obey the mandates
Of aliens and have your foes for kings.
Each day, each moment, to increase my glory,
Adds victory unto victory, praise to praise.
The Prince, were he beside me, on the field
Would prove his mettle, guarded by my arm,
Would learn to conquer while he watched me conquer,
And, following soon his noble nature's bent,
Would find . . .
DON DIEGUE.   I know. Thou servest the King well.
I saw thee fight, and command, under me.
Now that old age hath clogged my veins with ice,
Thy signal valor sets thee in my place,
And, to avoid unnecessary words,
Thou art today what I was formerly.
Thou seest, however, that in our rivalry
A monarch finds some difference between us.
THE COUNT. Nay, thou hast stolen that which I deserved.
DON DIEGUE. He who prevailed o'er thee deserved it more.
THE COUNT. He who can use it to the best advantage
Is the most worthy of it.
DON DIEGUE.   To be refused it,
Is little sign of worth.
THE COUNT.   Thou wonnest it
By trickery, being an old, wily courtier.
DON DIEGUE. My deeds' high fame was my sole advocate.
THE COUNT. Say, rather, the King honors thy grey hairs.
DON DIEGUE. My age the King but measures by my deeds.
THE COUNT. For deeds, this honor was due me alone.

DON DIEGUE.   He who could win it not, deserved it not.

THE COUNT.   Deserved it not? I?

DON DIEGUE.   Thou.

THE COUNT.   Thine insolence,
    Thou rash old man, shall have fit recompense.

                (He strikes DON DIEGUE *across the face.)*

DON DIEGUE *(drawing his sword)*. Go on, and take my life, after this
       insult—
    The first that e'er made red with shame the brow
    Of any of my race.

THE COUNT.   And what dost *thou*
    Think thou canst do, weak as thou art?

                    (He disarms DON DIEGUE.)

DON DIEGUE.   O God!
    My worn-out powers fail me in my need.

THE COUNT.   Thy sword is mine, but thou wouldst be too vain
    Were I to carry off so poor a trophy.
      Adieu! Make the Prince read, in spite of sneers,
    For his instruction, thy life's history.
    This punishment of thy offensive words
    Will add to it no small embellishment. *(Exit* THE COUNT.)

DON DIEGUE.   O fury! O despair! Hateful old age!
    Have I, then, lived so long only for this
    Disgrace? In toil of war have I grown grey,
    To see my laurels wither in one day?
    And does the arm at which all Spain has marveled,
    My arm, which has so often saved this realm,
    So often given new strength to its king's throne,
    Betray my cause now and avail me none?
    O cruel remembrance of my vanished glory!
    A whole life's effort canceled in one moment!
      New office, fatal to my happiness,
    Thou eminence from which my honor falls,
    Must I behold De Gormas mar thy splendor?
    Must I die unavenged or live in shame?
    Be *thou*, Count, the instructor of my prince!
    That post belongs to none humiliated,
    And by this gross affront thy jealous pride,
    Despite the King's choice, doth unfit me for it.
      And thou, the glorious doer of my exploits,

But in mine age a useless ornament,
Sword, once so feared, which now in my dishonor
Servest for show and not for my defense,
Go, leave henceforth the most abject of men;
Pass, to avenge me, into worthier hands!

(*Enter* RODERICK.)

Roderick, art thou courageous?

RODERICK.   Any man
Except my father soon would find I am.

DON DIEGUE.   O welcome anger, balm unto my sorrow!
I recognize my own blood in that answer.
My youth again lives in thy wrath's quick flame.
Go, my son, my true son, blot out my shame.
Avenge me.

RODERICK.   Yes! For what?

DON DIEGUE.   So great an outrage
'Tis fatal to the honor of us both.
A blow in the face! I would have slain the man
Who struck me, had my nerveless arm not failed me;
And this sword, which my hand no more can wield,
I place in thine for chastisement and vengeance.
    Go prove thy courage 'gainst our haughty foe.
Nothing but blood atoneth for a blow.
Kill him or die. But I shall hide naught from thee.
I send thee to confront a paladin.
I have beheld him, covered with dust and gore,
Spread terror everywhere through a whole army
And shatter countless squadrons by his valor.
But there is something else to tell thee of him:
More than a mighty warrior, a great captain,
He is . . .

RODERICK.   Oh, speak!

DON DIEGUE.   The father of Chimene.

RODERICK.   The . . .

DON DIEGUE.   Answer not a word. I know thy love;
But he who can endure to live dishonored
Deserves not life. The dearer the offender,
The greater is the offense. Well, then! Thou knowest
My wrong; thou holdest vengeance in thy hand.
Enough! Avenge me, and avenge thyself.

Show that thou art thy father's worthy son.
Crushed by the woes that Fate hath laid upon me,
I go to mourn them. Fly thou and avenge them.

(*Exit* Don Diegue.)

RODERICK.

      Pierced to my bosom's core am I
By an unlooked-for dagger's mortal thrust;
Hapless avenger of a quarrel most just,
And wretched victim of Fate's cruelty,
I stand bewildered, and my soul, thus brought
      Low, can find help in naught.
So near at last to love's dear recompense,
      And learn—ah God, what pain!—
Of insult to my father; the offense
Was done him by the father of Chimene!

      Within my breast how wild a storm!
My honor is at stake, my love at stake.
If I avenge my sire, two hearts I break.
Honor incites me, love would stay mine arm.
Renounce my love or suffer all men's scorn—
      No choice have I, forlorn,
But these, yet from them must a choice be made.
      O God, what fearful pain!
Am I to leave an insult unrepaid?
Am I to slay the father of Chimene?

      Father or loved one; honor or love;
Self-conquest proud or bondage sweet—how choose?
My happiness or my fair fame I lose;
My life I blight or am unworthy of.
And thou, my sword, hope of my ardent heart
      Where love no less hath part,
Thou noble foe to all my dreams of bliss,
      Thou source of all my pain,
Hast thou been given me for this, e'en this:
To cut the ties that bind me to Chimene?

      Nay, better die at once! To her
I love, I owe no less than to my sire.
To avenge him will incur for me her ire;

To avenge him not will her contempt incur.
I must behave as though I do not love her
        Or be unworthy of her.
All search to cure my woes hath but increased
        Their number and their pain.
So, being bound to die, let me at least
Die without bringing sorrow to Chimene.

        What! die, and leave redress ungained?
Desire an ignominious death to die?
Endure that Spain should recollect that I
Have ill the honor of my house maintained?
Yield to a love which, I can plainly see,
        Holdeth no hope for me?
Let me henceforth shun thoughts so base and low,
        Thoughts which augment my pain!
Come, let me save my honor; for I know,
Whate'er I do, I needs must lose Chimene!

        Yes, I have erred. My father's claim
Stands first, not fealty to my heart's adored.
Whether I die of grief or by the sword,
I will not bring upon our ancient name
Disgrace. Already do I blush that I
        Did not to vengeance fly;
And, full of shame for hesitating so,
        Now I reck naught of pain.
Foul wrong was done my father, and I go
Forthwith to seek the father of Chimene.   (*Exit* Roderick.)

ACT II

Scene One

A hall in the palace. The Count de Gormas *and* Don Arias *are discovered.*

The Count. Between ourselves, I shall admit I *was*
        Somewhat too hot of blood, was too much moved
        By a few words, and went too far. But what
        Is done, is done; there is no remedy.
Don Arias. Let thy proud spirit yield to the King's wishes.
        He is most deeply stirred, and in his anger

Will use his whole authority against thee.
Moreover, there is naught which thou canst plead.
The grossness of the offense, and the high rank
Of him who suffered it, require of thee
Greater submissiveness and more amends
Than commonly suffice for satisfaction.

THE COUNT.   The King can take my life whene'er he pleases.

DON ARIAS.   Thou art too violent yet, after thy deed.
The King still loves thee. Mollify his wrath.
He says, "I wish this"; wilt thou disobey him?

THE COUNT.   Sir, to preserve all that I value most,
A little disobedience is no crime;
Yet were it e'er so heinous, my great service
Now to the realm would more than cancel it.

DON ARIAS.   However great and glorious are one's exploits,
A king is never in his subject's debt.
Thou flatterest thy pride, and thou shouldst know
That he who serves his sovereign well, does only
His duty. Sir, thou wilt destroy thyself
If in thy deeds thou puttest thy trust.

THE COUNT.   I shall not
Believe thee until thou hast been proved right.

DON ARIAS.   Thou shouldst dread more the power of a king.

THE COUNT.   I can outlive a single day's displeasure.
Let all the realm be armed for my destruction;
If I should perish, the whole State will perish.

DON ARIAS.   What! thou so little fearest thy sovereign's might . . .

THE COUNT.   Why should I fear a sceptered hand whose grasp
Is weaker than mine own? The King knows well
How much his fortunes are bound up with mine.
My head in falling would strike off his crown.

DON ARIAS.   Let reason, sir, resume its sway o'er thee.
Take counsel . . .

THE COUNT.   Counsel is already taken.

DON ARIAS.   What shall I tell the King? I have to make
Some report to him.

THE COUNT.   Say that I can never
Consent to my dishonor.

DON ARIAS.   But bethink thee
That kings would have their will supreme.

THE COUNT.   The die
    Is cast, sir; let us talk of this no further.
DON ARIAS.   Adieu, then, since I cannot change thy purpose.
    Beware the thunderbolt, despite thy laurels.
THE COUNT.   I shall await it unafraid.
DON ARIAS.   But not
    In vain.
THE COUNT.   Then Don Diegue will be content.

                                          (*Exit* DON ARIAS.)

    He who does not fear death, does not fear threats.
    My heart will rise above the worst misfortunes.
    I can be made to live without earth's blessings,
    But not induced to live bereft of honor.

                   Enter RODERICK.

RODERICK.   One word, Count.
THE COUNT.   Speak.
RODERICK.   First rid me of a doubt.
    Dost thou know Don Diegue well?
THE COUNT (*loudly*).   Yes!
RODERICK.   Nay, let us
    Talk quietly. Listen. Dost thou know that this
    Old man was in his day the epitome
    Of manhood, valor, honor?
THE COUNT.   That may be.
RODERICK.   The fire now kindled in mine eyes—dost thou
    Know it bespeaks his blood? Dost thou know that?
THE COUNT.   What matters it to me?
RODERICK.   At a few paces
    From here, Count, I will teach thee what it matters.
THE COUNT.   Presumptuous youth!
RODERICK.   Fly not into a passion.
    I am young, yes; but those of valiant lineage
    Do not await maturity for valor.
THE COUNT.   To measure swords with me! What can have made thee
    So vain—thee whom none ever saw bear arms!
RODERICK.   Men like me do not need a second chance
    To prove their quality. They are determined
    To make their maiden efforts master-strokes.
THE COUNT.   Dost thou indeed know who I am?

RODERICK.   I do.

    Anyone else, if he but heard thy name,
    Might tremble with affright. The palms wherewith
    Thy brows are crowned would seem to bear inscribed
    Upon their leaves the promise of my doom.
    Yet I dare face an arm always victorious.
    He who is brave enough, hath might enough.
    One can do marvels in a father's cause.
    Thou art unconquered, not invincible.

THE COUNT.   The lofty spirit which thy words reveal
    Has from thy face been long apparent to me.
    The future hero of Castile, naught less,
    I saw in thee, and joyfully my heart
    Destined for thee my daughter's hand. I know
    Thou lovest her, and now I am delighted
    To find that all thy dearest hopes give way
    To duty, that they have not sapped thy manhood,
    That thou art high of soul as I believed thee,
    And that in seeking for my son-in-law
    All that a knightly gentleman should be,
    I did not err when I made choice of thee.
    But thou awakenest my compassion. I
    Pity thy youth while I admire thy bravery.
    Let not thy first essay of arms be fatal.
    Release me from a combat so unequal.
    No honor could be mine in victory;
    To triumph without danger is inglorious.
    None would believe that thou wert hard to slay,
    And for thy death I could but feel regret.

RODERICK.   Thy arrogance turns to offensive qualms.
    Shall he who dares to rob me of my honor
    Fear to deprive me of my life?

THE COUNT.   Nay, go thou
    Hence.

RODERICK.   Go with me without more waste of breath.

THE COUNT.   Art thou so tired of life?

RODERICK.   Dost *thou* fear death?

THE COUNT.   Come, then! Thou doest thy duty. He is base
    Who will survive one hour his sire's disgrace.

                              (*Exeunt together.*)

Scene Two

A room in the apartments of the INFANTA. *The* INFANTA,
CHIMENE, *and* LEONORA *are discovered.*

THE INFANTA.   Nay, do not grieve so sorely, dear Chimene.
　　　　Display thy strength of soul to face misfortune.
　　　　A calm will follow soon this transient storm.
　　　　Only a small cloud shadoweth thy bliss,
　　　　And thou wilt lose naught though it be deferred.
CHIMENE.   My heart, o'erwhelmed with woe, dares hope for nothing.
　　　　The tempest which hath suddenly descended
　　　　Upon a smiling sea now threatens me
　　　　With certain shipwreck, and I cannot doubt
　　　　That I shall perish in the very harbor
　　　　Ere setting sail. I loved; I was beloved;
　　　　Our fathers both approved, and I was telling
　　　　The happy news of this to thee precisely
　　　　At the sad moment when their quarrel was born,
　　　　Whose fatal tidings were no sooner brought thee
　　　　Than all my sweet hopes were at once destroyed.
　　　　　　Cursèd ambition, odious mania
　　　　Whose tyranny the noblest spirits suffer!
　　　　Pride without pity for my dearest wishes,
　　　　How many sighs and tears thou art to cost me!
THE INFANTA.   This quarrel gives thee no just grounds for fear.
　　　　Born quickly, 'twill as quickly disappear.
　　　　'Tis too much talked of not to be composed.
　　　　The King already seeks to bring about
　　　　A reconciliation, and thou knowest
　　　　That I so sympathize with thy distress
　　　　That I would do the impossible to end it.
CHIMENE.   No reconciliation will avail.
　　　　Such insults are beyond all reparation.
　　　　In vain are prudence and authority;
　　　　And if the wound be healed, 'tis but in semblance.
　　　　The hate that is locked up within the heart
　　　　Burns secretly and with a fiercer flame.
THE INFANTA.   When marriage joins Don Roderick and Chimene,
　　　　Their fathers' enmity will fade, and we

Shall soon see love, stronger than any hate,
Efface all discord by your happiness.
CHIMENE. Thus I would have it, but my hope is scant.
    Don Diegue is too proud; and I know my father.
    I try to stanch my tears, yet still they flow.
    The past is anguish, and I fear the future.
THE INFANTA. What dost thou fear? an old man's feeble arm?
CHIMENE. Roderick is not a coward.
THE INFANTA.   He is too young.
CHIMENE. The brave are valiant the first time they fight.
THE INFANTA. But he should cause thee small anxiety.
    Too well he loves thee to bring pain to thee,
    And one word from thy lips would stay his anger.
CHIMENE. If he obeyed me not, what crowning pain!
    And if he did obey me, what would men
    Say of him! Being born his father's son,
    Is he, forsooth, to suffer such an outrage?
    Whether he yields or does not to the love
    Which binds him to me, I must either be
    Ashamed of his excessive pliancy
    Or crushed by his refusal, however just.
THE INFANTA. Chimene is high-souled, and with all at stake
    She cannot, still, have one unworthy thought.
    But if, until the day of reconcilement,
    I make her paragon my prisoner
    And thus deny all scope unto his courage,
    Would that offend her proud and loving heart?
CHIMENE. Ah, madam, then my cares would be no more!
        (*The* INFANTA *claps her hands. The page appears.*)
THE INFANTA. Page, seek out Roderick and bring him hither.
THE PAGE. He and the Count de Gormas . . .
CHIMENE.   O dear God!
THE INFANTA. Yes? Speak!
THE PAGE.   Together they have left the palace.
CHIMENE. Alone?
THE PAGE.   Alone, and seemingly at strife,
    Though talking in low tones.
CHIMENE.   Beyond all doubt
    They now are fighting!
               Naught remains to say.

Madam, forgive my haste. I cannot stay.
>   (*Exit* Chimene, *hurriedly. The page withdraws.*)

The Infanta. Alas, that such disquietude is mine!
  I weep her griefs, but Roderick thrills my heart.
  Calmness forsakes me; all my love revives.
  The fate that is to part him from Chimene
  Kindles at once my hope and woe again.
  Their separation fills me with regret
  But in my soul doth secret joy beget.

Leonora. What! does the lofty virtue of thy soul
  So soon give place to this unworthy passion?

The Infanta. Nay, call it not unworthy, when it now,
  Strong and triumphant, reigneth in my bosom.
  Respect it, since 'tis dear to me. My pride
  Indeed forbids it, but despite myself
  I hope, and, ill defended 'gainst such madness,
  My heart flies to a love Chimene hath lost.

Leonora. And thus thy noble resolution fails,
  And reason ruleth in thy mind no longer?

The Infanta. How little does one heed the voice of reason
  When such sweet poison worketh in one's breast!
  For when the sick man loves his malady,
  He takes the healing draft unwillingly.

Leonora. Thy hope beguiles thee; thou desirest no cure.
  But Roderick is in truth unworthy of thee.

The Infanta. Too well I know it; but if my pride forsakes me,
  Learn how love flatters those whom it enslaves.
    If Roderick is the victor in this combat,—
  If this great warrior falls before his valor,—
  I shall feel free to love him without shame.
  What can he not do, if he can o'ercome
  The Count! I dare to picture to myself
  That in the smallest of his mighty deeds
  Whole realms will pass beneath his sway. Already
  My fond heart is convinced I shall anon
  Behold him seated on Granada's throne,
  The vanquished Moors fearing yet loving him,
  Aragon welcoming her conqueror,
  Portugal, too, surrendering, and his exploits
  Bearing him proudly o'er the seas, to bathe

His laurels in the blood of Africa!
After this victory, I expect from Roderick
All that is told of the most famous captains,
Thinking to find my glory in his love.
LEONORA. But, madam, see how far thou carriest
His conquering arm beyond a duel which may not
Be fought!
THE INFANTA.   An insult calls for Roderick's vengeance.
The Count is author of the outrage. They
Went out together. Need we know aught more?
LEONORA. Well, grant they fight, since thou wilt have it so.
Will Roderick go as far as thy dreams go?
THE INFANTA. Bear with me. I am mad; my fancy roves.
Thou seest what evils love prepares for me.
Come to my chamber and console me there,
And leave me not, when I am so distraught.

                                                    (*Exeunt.*)

Scene Three

A hall in the palace. The KING, DON ARIAS, *and* DON SANCHO
are discovered.

THE KING. Pray, is this haughty Count bereft of sense?
Dares he expect free pardon for his offense?
DON ARIAS. I talked with him long in thy name. I did
All that I could, sire, and gained naught.
THE KING.   Just heaven!
Has any subject, then, such scant respect
For me? Does he so little care to please me?
He thus insults Don Diegue and flouts his sovereign?
In mine own Court he lays down laws for me!
Brave warrior, great commander though he be,
The power is mine to tame his haughty soul.
Valor itself were he—the god of battles—
He shall learn what it means to disobey.
Whatever punishment his deed deserved,
I wished at first to show him leniency;
But since he doth abuse it, go at once
And, whether he resists or not, arrest him.
DON SANCHO. A little time might make him less rebellious.

He was approached while seething from his quarrel.
Sire, in the heat of its first fierce emotions
So great a spirit yields not easily.
He knows that he is wrong, but lofty beings
Are not at once brought to confess a fault.

THE KING.   Don Sancho, hold thy peace, and understand
That he who takes his part, shares in his guilt.

DON SANCHO.   Sire, I obey, am silent . . . But permit me
One word in his defense.

THE KING.   What canst thou say?

DON SANCHO.   That he who is accustomed to brave deeds
Cannot abase himself to show contrition.
He can conceive of no apologies
Without dishonor, and 'tis the fear of that
Alone which makes the Count resist thy will.
He finds his duty as thy loyal subject
Somewhat too onerous. He would obey thee
Were he less great of heart. Command of him
That with an arm grown strong amid war's dangers
He shall at the sword's point give satisfaction
For his rash act, and he will do it promptly,
Sire; and whoe'er may wish to fight with him,
I, till he knows hereof, will answer for him.

THE KING.   Thou failest in respect, but I forgive thee,
For 'tis the ardor of a brave young heart.
    A king whom prudence teaches worthy aims
Is much more sparing of his subjects' blood.
I jealousy guard that of mine—conserve it
Even as the head guards well the limbs that serve it.
Thy reasoning is no logic, then, for me.
Thou as a soldier speakest; I must needs
Act as a king; and whatsoever any
May please to say or dare to think, the Count
Can lose no honor by obeying me.
Besides, his deed affects *me*; he insulted
The man whom I had chosen to teach my son.
To strike my choice is to beard me myself
And challenge my supreme authority.
No more hereof!
                    Ten vessels have been sighted

        Flying the flags of our old enemies.

        They boldly have approached the river's mouth.

DON ARIAS.   The Moors have learned to know thee all too well.

        So oft have they been vanquished that they fear

        To pit themselves against so great a monarch.

THE KING.   Ne'er will they see without a jealous pang

        My scepter ruling Andalusia.

        That lovely land, which they too long possessed,

        Is always looked upon by them with envy.

        That is the only reason why, ten years

        Ago, I made Seville my capital:

        To watch them better and by speedier action

        To foil at once whate'er they might attempt.

DON ARIAS.   They at the cost of their best chieftains' lives

        Found that thy presence makes secure thy conquests.

        Thou needest fear naught.

THE KING.   And naught must I neglect.

        Too utter confidence itself breeds danger,

        And thou must surely know how easily

        The rising tide could bring them even here.

        Yet 'twould be wrong of me to stir men's hearts

        To panic, when the news is so uncertain.

        The fright that could be caused by false alarms

        At night, which soon will fall, would agitate

        The city all too sorely. Let the guards

        Be doubled on the walls and at the harbor.

        That is enough, now.

                 (*Exit* DON ARIAS. *Enter* DON ALONSO.)

DON ALONSO.   Sire, the Count is dead.

        Don Diegue, through his son, has taken vengeance

        For the wrong done him.

THE KING.   I no sooner heard

        About that wrong than I foresaw revenge,

        And would have fain averted such misfortune.

DON ALONSO.   Chimene draws near, bringing her woe to thee.

        All bathed in tears she comes imploring justice.

THE KING.   Howe'er compassion for her moves my heart,

        What the Count did seems to have well deserved

        This punishment for his temerity.

        And yet, however just his fate, I cannot

Without regret lose such a mighty warrior.
After long service rendered to my realm,—
His blood poured out for me a thousand times,—
Although his arrogance aroused my wrath,
To lose him weakens me, and his death grieves me.

Enter CHIMENE, DON DIEGUE, *and* DON ARIAS.

CHIMENE. Sire, justice, justice!
DON DIEGUE.   Nay, sire, hear our pleas.
CHIMENE. I kneel before thy feet.
DON DIEGUE.   I clasp thy knees.
CHIMENE. I ask for justice.
DON DIEGUE.   Hearken to my defense.
CHIMENE. Punish the crime of an audacious youth.
      He has struck down the mainstay of thy throne.
      He has killed my father.
DON DIEGUE.   He avenged his own.
CHIMENE. A king owes justice to his subjects' blood.
DON DIEGUE. Just vengeance can deserve no penalty.
THE KING. Rise, both of you, and speak unhurriedly.
      Chimene, I share thy sorrow; with a grief
      No less than thine I feel my heart assailed.
      (*To* DON DIEGUE) Thou shalt speak later. Do not interrupt her.
CHIMENE. My father, sire, is dead. Mine eyes have seen
      His blood in great streams pouring from his side.
      That blood which hath so oft kept safe thy walls,
      That blood which hath so oft won battles for thee,
      That blood which, as it flowed, still smoked with anger
      At being shed for anyone but thee,—
      Which war, midst all its dangers, dared not drain,—
      Roderick hath in thy Court spilled on the earth.
      Thither I ran, pallid, with limbs unstrung;
      I found him lifeless. Sire, forgive my grief.
      My voice quite fails me at this fearful moment.
      My tears and sighs will tell thee the rest better.
THE KING. Take heart, my child, and know that from this day
      Thy king will be a father unto thee.
CHIMENE. Such honor, sire, doth not beseem my woe.
      I have already said, I found him lifeless.
      His wound gaped wide and, to incite me more,

His blood wrote in the dust my duty for me;
Or, rather, all his greatness, thus undone,
Spoke to me through his wound and urged me on,
And to be heard by the most just of monarchs
It borrows, using these poor lips, my voice.
    Sire, do not suffer it that beneath thy sway
License should reign before thy very eyes,
Exposing the most valiant warriors
To any hot-head's blows, nor that unpunished
An upstart youth should triumph over them,
Bathe in their blood, and flout their glorious fame!
If such a hero as thou hast been robbed of
Be not avenged, none will have zeal to serve thee.
My father is dead; I plead for vengeance for him—
More for thy sake than to appease my wrath.
The death of one like him is harm to all.
Avenge it by another's—blood for blood.
Exact a sacrifice—nay, not to me,
But to thy crown, thy kingdom, and thyself—
A sacrifice, sire, to the whole realm's good—
Of those who glory in this high-handed crime.

THE KING. Don Diegue, speak in answer.

DON DIEGUE.   How deserving

Of envy is the man who, when he loses
Life's vigor, loses life as well! and what
A miserable fate old age prepares
For noble-minded men before their end!
I, whose long labors won me so much honor,
I, followed once by victory everywhere,
See myself now, for having lived too long,
Insulted, vanquished, and yet still alive.
What neither fight nor siege nor ambuscade,
Nor all my foes, nor all my jealous rivals,
Could ever do, nor Aragon, nor Granada,
The Count de Gormas in thy Court hath done,
Almost in thine own presence—done because
Of envy at thy choice of me and pride
In the advantage which the helplessness
Of this my age now gave him over me.
    Sire, thus these hairs, grown grey beneath the helmet,

This blood, which was so often shed to serve thee,
This hand, which once the foemen's armies feared,
Would have gone down dishonored to the grave
Had I not had a son well worthy of me,
Worthy of his country, worthy of his king.
He loaned me his young arm; he slew the Count,
Restored my honor, washed away my shame.
If to show courage and a righteous anger,
If to avenge a blow, ought to be punished,
On me alone should fall the tempest's fury.
When the hand errs, the head must bear the blame.
In what we speak of, be it crime or not,
I am the head, sire; he is but the hand.
Chimene cries out that he has killed her father;
Could I have done it, he would not have done it.
Sacrifice, then, this head which years will soon
Bring low, but spare the hand that now can serve thee.
By taking *my* life, satisfy Chimene.
I shall oppose not, but accept, my doom;
And, far from murmuring at that decree,
Dying with honor, I shall die content.

THE KING.   This matter is a weighty one, and truly
Deserves to be debated in full council.
   Don Sancho, take Chimene back to her home.
Don Diegue will have my palace and his word
To hold him prisoner. Someone find his son.
   (*To* CHIMENE) I will accord thee justice.

CHIMENE.   It is just,
Great king, that he who kills a man should die.

THE KING.   Go, take some rest, my child. Restrain thy grief.

CHIMENE.   To rest brings greater anguish, not relief.

ACT III

Scene One

A room in the house of the deceased COUNT DE GORMAS. ELVIRA
is discovered. Enter RODERICK.

ELVIRA.   Roderick, what hast thou done? Why comest thou here,
Unhappy man?

RODERICK.   To follow the sad course
    Of my most woeful destiny.

ELVIRA.   Whence hast thou
    The brazenness and newly-found presumption
    To show thyself in places thou hast filled
    With mourning? What! wouldst thou come even here
    To challenge the Count's ghost? Hast thou not killed him?

RODERICK. That he should live was to my shame. My honor
    Required this deed of my reluctant hand.

ELVIRA. But thus to seek asylum in the house
    Of the dead man! Hath any slayer yet
    Ever made that his refuge?

RODERICK.   I have come here
    Only to give myself up to my judge.
    Look not with an astonished face at me;
    'Tis death I seek after inflicting it.
    My judge is my beloved—is my Chimene.
    I deserve death, having deserved her hate;
    And I have come here to receive the greatest
    Of blessings: my death-sentence from her lips,
    My death-blow from her hand.

ELVIRA.   Flee from her sight,
    Rather; flee from her feelings' violence.
    Shun the first transports of her grief; expose not
    Thyself to the first promptings of her anger.

RODERICK. No, no, this dearest object of my love,
    Whom I have so offended, cannot feel
    Too fierce an eagerness to punish me.
    I shall escape a hundred deaths if I
    Can fan her heart's wrath and the sooner die.

ELVIRA. Chimene is at the palace, crushed with woe,
    And she will not return home unaccompanied.
    Oh, Roderick, fly! Spare me such anxious fear.
    What would men say if they should find thee here!
    Wouldst have some slanderer, to complete her misery,
    Charge her with sheltering him who slew her father?
    She soon will come back.—She comes now! I see her.
    Hide, at least, Roderick, for her honor's sake.
    (RODERICK *goes into an adjoining room. Enter* CHIMENE
     and DON SANCHO.)

DON SANCHO. Yes, madam, thou must needs have blood for blood.
　　　Thy wrath is just, thy sore distress but natural.
　　　I would not try, by means of any words,
　　　To soothe thine anger or console thy heart.
　　　But if it is within my power to serve thee,
　　　Employ my sword for punishing the guilty;
　　　Employ my love to avenge thy father's death.
　　　In thy behalf, my arm will be resistless.
CHIMENE. Ah me!
DON SANCHO.　　　I beg of thee, accept my aid.
CHIMENE. I thus would wrong the King, who promised me
　　　Justice.
DON SANCHO. Thou knowest it proceeds so slowly
　　　That often crime escapes by its delays.
　　　Its tardy, doubtful course costs many tears.
　　　Suffer a cavalier to give thee justice
　　　By force of arms. That way is swifter, surer.
CHIMENE. It is the last resort. If I must finally
　　　Have recourse to it, and thou still pitiest
　　　My woes, thou shalt have leave then to avenge them.
DON SANCHO. To that one happiness my soul aspires,
　　　And with the hope of it I go, contented. (*Exit* DON SANCHO.)
CHIMENE. At last I am free, and can without restraint
　　　Show thee what great and bitter grief is mine.
　　　I can give vent to my sad sighs. To thee
　　　I can unpack my bosom's agony.
　　　　My father is dead, Elvira; and it was
　　　The first sword Roderick wielded that cut short
　　　His life. Weep, weep, mine eyes! dissolve in tears!
　　　One half my heart sends to the grave the other
　　　And by that fatal blow makes me avenge
　　　That which I lost on that which yet is left me!
ELVIRA. Be calmer and rest, madam.
CHIMENE.　　　　　　　Ah, how useless
　　　To talk of rest in misery like mine!
　　　How shall my sorrow ever be appeased
　　　If I can feel no hate for him that caused it!
　　　And what can I expect but endless torture
　　　If, punishing a deed, I love its doer!
ELVIRA. He killed thy father, and thou lovest him still?

CHIMENE. "Love" is too weak a word to use, Elvira.
    I worship him. My adoration of him
    Joins battle with a daughter's natural feelings.
    I find my lover in my enemy,
    And am aware that notwithstanding all
    Mine anger Roderick still within my breast
    Contends against my father. He attacks him,
    Drives him back, yields to him, defends himself,
    Now strong, now weak, and now victorious.
    But in this dreadful war of wrath and love,
    Although my heart is torn, my will is firm;
    And whatsoever hold my love hath on me,
    I shall not hesitate to do my duty.
    I walk unfalteringly the path of honor.
    Roderick is very dear to me. I grieve
    For him; my heart is with him; but despite
    Its struggles, I forget not that I am
    My father's daughter and that he is dead.

ELVIRA. Wouldst thou take Roderick's life?

CHIMENE.   Ah, cruel thought,
    And cruel path that I am forced to tread!
    I ask his head and fear to gain my prayer.
    My death will follow his, yet his I seek.

ELVIRA. Renounce, renounce, dear lady, such a purpose!
    Impose not on thyself so stern a task.

CHIMENE. What! when my father dies—in my arms, almost—
    Shall his blood cry for vengeance and I not
    Hearken to it? Shall my heart, shamefully
    Ensnared by other spells, believe it owes him
    Nothing but unavailing tears? And can I
    Let guileful love betray my filial duty
    And stifle to base silence honor's voice?

ELVIRA. Believe me, madam: all men would excuse thee
    From visiting such wrath on one thou lovest,
    One that so loves thee. Thou hast done enough.
    Thou wentest to the King. No further urge
    Thy suit. Persist not in thy fierce resolve.

CHIMENE. My honor is at stake. I must have vengeance.
    To noble souls every excuse seems vile,
    However strong their hearts' desires.

ELVIRA.   But loving
  Roderick, thou canst not wish him ill.
CHIMENE.   'Tis true.
ELVIRA. Feeling thus, what dost thou intend to do?
CHIMENE. To keep my fair fame safe and end my torment,
  Pursue him to his death, then die myself.
  (*Enter* RODERICK *behind her from the adjoining room.*
    He hears her last words.)
RODERICK. Without the trouble of pursuing me,
  Assure thy honor, taking now my life.
CHIMENE. Elvira, where are we? What do I see?
  Roderick in my house! before mine eyes!
RODERICK. Spare not my blood. Enjoy—for I resist not—
  The sweetness of my death and thy revenge.
CHIMENE. Alas!
RODERICK.   Nay, hear me.
CHIMENE.   I shall die.
RODERICK.   One moment.
CHIMENE. Go; let me die.
RODERICK.   Grant me a few words only;
  Then answer me with nothing but this sword.
  (*He draws his sword and holds it out to her by the blade.*
    She recoils.)
CHIMENE. What, dripping e'en yet with my father's blood!
RODERICK. Dearest Chimene . . .
CHIMENE.   Take that accursed thing
  Away. The sight of it recalls thy deed
  And thus reproaches me that still thou livest.
RODERICK. Look on it, rather, to excite thy hatred,
  To increase thy anger, and to speed my doom.
CHIMENE. 'Tis stained with my own blood.
RODERICK.   Plunge it in mine
  And make it thus lose every trace of thine.
CHIMENE. What cruelty in one day to kill the father
  By the sword's thrust, the daughter by its sight!
  Take it away; I cannot bear to see it.
  Thou wishest me to hear thee, and thou slayest me!
RODERICK (*sheathing the sword*). I do thy will, but I preserve the hope
  Of ending at thy hands my wretched life.
  Yet still do not expect, although I love thee,

7 9

A base repentance for a righteous deed.
The irreparable act of hot, swift anger
Humiliated my father and shamed me.
Thou knowest what a blow means to a man
With any pride. Part of the insult fell
On me. I sought its author out. I found him,
And so avenged my honor and my father;
And I would do it again, were it still to do.

    Not that my love did not indeed long struggle
For thee against my father and myself.
Judge of its strength when, after such an outrage,
I could debate whether to seek for vengeance.
Forced to displease thee or to live disgraced,
I still accused myself of too great haste.
I feared that I was too impetuous!
And thy fair face might well have turned the scale
Had I not set this thought against thy spell:
That without honor I would not deserve thee;
That, though I had a place within thy breast,
Thou, who hadst loved me when a gallant man,
Wouldst hate me when I had become ignoble;
And that to hear my love and heed its voice
Would bar me from thee and condemn thy choice.

    I tell thee this, and, though it wrings my heart,
I will repeat it with my dying breath:
I wronged thee sorely, but I was forced to do it
To blot my shame out and be worthy of thee.
Now, with the claims of honor and my father
All met, I come to give thee satisfaction.
Thou seest me here to offer thee my lifeblood.
I did my duty; I still do my duty.
I know thy father's death must arm thy heart
'Gainst me, nor would I rob thee of thy victim.
Sacrifice boldly to the blood outpoured
The man who takes a pride in having spilled it.

CHIMENE.   Ah, Roderick, the truth is that, though thy foe,
I cannot blame thee for refusing shame;
And howsoe'er my grief bursts forth, I do not
Accuse thee, I lament my evil fortune.
I know how ardently a noble nature

Is moved by honor after such an insult.
Thou hast but done thy duty, as a brave man;
But thou, in doing it, hast shown me mine.
Thy fatal valor in thy victory
Over thyself instructs me. It avenged
Thy father and preserved thy fair fame. *I*
Must be as scrupulous. I have—alas!—
My father to avenge, my name to soil not.

    But oh! thy part herein drives me to madness!
If something else had robbed me of my father,
My soul would in the joy of seeing thee
Have found the only solace possible,
And midst my grief I would have felt it sweet
For thy dear hand to wipe away my tears.
But I must lose thee after losing him!
Honor requires that I suppress my love,
And this dread duty, whose demands will kill me,
Bids me myself to seek for thy destruction.

    For still do not expect, although I love thee,
Any base hesitance to punish thee.
Howe'er in thy behalf our love pleads with me,
My strength of soul must be no less than thine.
In wronging me thou provedst thyself worthy
Of me. By *thy* death I must prove myself
Worthy of thee.

RODERICK.   Defer no longer, then,
What honor claimeth. Honor demands my head;
I give it to thee freely. Make of it
A sacrifice unto this noble duty.
The death-stroke will be welcome, like the sentence.
To wait, after my crime, for tardy justice,
Delays thy glory, as it does my death.
I shall die happy, dying by thy hand.

CHIMENE.   Go; I am not thine executioner
But thine accuser. If thou offerest me
Thy head, have I the right to take it? I
Must lay claim to it, but thou must defend it.
Another, not thyself, must give it to me,
And I must prosecute, not slaughter, thee.

RODERICK.   Howe'er in my behalf our love pleads with thee,

Thy strength of soul must be no less than mine.
To borrow other arms to avenge a father,
Believe me, dear Chimene, is not like me.
My hand alone avenged my father's shame;
Thy hand alone ought to avenge thy father.

CHIMENE.   Cruel man! why stand so stubbornly on this point?
Without aid thou avengedst thyself, and thou
Wishest to give me *thy* aid. I shall follow
Thine own example; I have too proud a heart
To let thee share the praise that will be mine.
My father and my honor shall owe nothing
To promptings of thy love or thy despair.

RODERICK.   'Tis thou that standest on a point of honor.
Whate'er I do, can I not win this mercy?
In thy dead father's name, for our love's sake,
In vengeance, or at least in pity, slay me!
Thy wretched lover would far happier die
By thy dear hand than live when hated by thee.

CHIMENE.   Nay, go. I do not hate thee.

RODERICK.   But thou shouldst.

CHIMENE.   I cannot.

RODERICK.   Holdest thou so lightly blame
And false report? When all men know my deed
And know thou lovest me still, what will the tongues
Of censure and of malice not proclaim?
Compel their silence, and without more words
Save thy good fame by slaying me.

CHIMENE.   My fame
Will shine the brighter if I slay thee not,
And I shall hear the voice of blackest slander
Lift to the skies mine honor and mourn my woe,
Knowing that I love thee and yet seek thy life.
Go; show no more to me in my great sorrow
What I must lose although my love continues.
Hide thy departure in the shades of night.
If thou wert seen, my honor might be sullied.
The sole occasion for a slanderous word
Is, that I have allowed thy presence here.
Give no one grounds to assail my character.

RODERICK.   Oh, let me die!

CHIMENE.   Leave me.
RODERICK.   What wilt thou do?
CHIMENE.   Although my fervent love precludes all hate,
    I mean to try my best to avenge my father;
    But notwithstanding duty's stern requirements,
    My dearest wish is to accomplish nothing.
RODERICK.   O miracle of love!
CHIMENE.   O weight of woe!
RODERICK.   What tears and misery our fathers cost us!
CHIMENE.   Roderick, who would have thought . . .
RODERICK.   Could have foretold . . .
CHIMENE.   That bliss so near us would so soon be lost!
RODERICK.   Or that so near the port a sudden storm
    So unforeseen would shatter all our hopes!
CHIMENE.   Oh, mortal griefs!
RODERICK.   Regrets without avail!
CHIMENE.   Leave me, I say. I will not hear thee more.
RODERICK.   Farewell! I go to live a death-in-life
    Till thy pursuit of me shall take it from me.
CHIMENE.   If I obtain that end, I pledge my word
    I shall not live one instant after thee.
    Farewell! Go, and above all, be not seen.

                       (*Exit* RODERICK.)

ELVIRA.   Madam, whatever evils heaven sends us . . .
CHIMENE.   Vex me no further. Leave me to myself.
    I need but silence and the night, to weep.

      (*Exit* ELVIRA. CHIMENE *is alone as the curtain falls.*)

Scene Two

A street in Seville, at night. Enter DON DIEGUE.

DON DIEGUE.   We never taste a perfect happiness.
    All our success hath sadness mingled with it.
    Ever do cares attend the consummation
    Of what we most desire, and mar its rapture.
    In my good fortune now I feel their pang;
    Amidst my joy I tremble with sharp fear.
    I have seen lying dead the foe who shamed me,
    But nowhere can I find my dear avenger.
    In vain I seek him and with fruitless toil,

Though an old, broken man, scour the whole city.
The remnant of my strength that age hath left me
Is futilely expended in my search.
Each moment, everywhere, in this black night
I think to see and clasp him—and I clasp
Only a shadow; and my love, misled
By such false semblance, conceives dread suspicions
Which double my anxiety. I cannot
Discover any sign that he hath fled.
I fear the dead Count's friends and followers.
Their number drives me frantic with dismay.
Roderick no longer lives, or is held prisoner! . . .
    Just heaven! do appearances still mock me?
Do I at last behold my life's one hope?
'Tis he—ah, no more doubt!—my prayers are answered,
My fears dispelled, my troubles at an end!

                          (*Enter* Roderick, *distractedly*.)

    Oh, Roderick, God hath finally let me see thee!
Roderick.   Alas!
Don Diegue.   Nay, mingle with my joy no sighs.
    Ah, let me catch my breath that I may praise thee!
My valor hath no reason to disavow
Thine own. Thou well hast imitated it,
And thy brave daring maketh live again
In thee the heroes of my race. From them
Thou art descended, and thou art my son.
Thy sword's first blow hath equalled all I smote,
And, with a glorious ardor fired, thy youth
Attains a like renown by this great proof!
    Support of mine old age, my crowning blessing,
Touch these white hairs, restored by thee to honor.
Come, kiss this cheek, remembering 'twas the place
Where fell the blow whose stain thou didst efface!
Roderick.   Honor was due thee; I could do no less,
Sprung from thy loins and nurtured 'neath thy care.
'Twas my good fortune, and I am glad to learn
That my first blow pleased him who gave me life.
But midst thy joy, begrudge it not if I,
Having done *thy* will, now should do mine own.
Let my despair find voice without restraint.

Enough and all too long thy words have stayed it.
Nowise do I repent my having served thee;
But—give me back the things my deed hath cost me!
I armed my hand against my love, for thee,
And with one blow I cleft my heart in twain.
Say nothing more to me. I have lost all
For thee. Whate'er I owed thee, I have paid it.

DON DIEGUE.   Prize, prize more highly thy great deed's results.
I gave thee life; thou givest me back my honor;
And as I value honor more than life,
So much the more I owe thee, in my turn.
But cast this weakness from a noble heart.
We have one honor; ladies fair are many.
Love is but pleasure. Honor is a duty.

RODERICK.   Ah, what is this thou sayest?

DON DIEGUE.   What thou shouldst know.

RODERICK.   *My* outraged honor claims its penalty,
And thou darest urge me to inconstancy!
The craven warrior and the faithless lover
Are infamous alike in equal measure.
Do not insult my heart's fidelity.
Let me be brave—but also be unperjured.
Bonds such as mine cannot be broken thus;
My vows still bind me though I hope no longer;
And as I cannot leave, nor win, Chimene
The death I seek will soonest end my pain.

DON DIEGUE.   This is not yet the time to seek for death.
Thy sovereign and thy country need thine arm.
The fleet we feared hath entered this great river
To take the city unawares and sack it.
The Moors are coming, and the tide and night
Will bring them in an hour to our walls.
The Court is in confusion, and the people
Are terrified. On all sides are cries and tears.
'Twas my good fortune, in this hour of need,
To find five hundred of my friends, who, hearing
Of the affront I suffered, came to me
With one accord, to offer to avenge me.
Thou hast already done so, but their hands
Will be more nobly dyed in Moorish blood.

Go at their head, where honor bids thee go.
'Tis thou this gallant band would have to lead them.
Go, face the onset of our ancient foes.
There, if thou wishest to die, find a brave death.
Seize the occasion for it that is offered.
Make the King owe his safety to thy loss—
Or, better still, come back with wreath-crowned brows.
Be not content with vengeance for an insult;
Go on to greater glory; by thy valor
Compel thy sovereign to grant pardon to thee,
Chimene to say no more. If thou dost love her,
Know this: that to return a conqueror
Is the sole way to win again her heart.

But time is now too precious to be wasted
In words. I stay thee, talking, and I fain
Would have thee fly! Come, follow me. Go fight,
And show thy king that whatsoever he
Lost in the Count, he hath regained in thee.

(*Exeunt.*)

ACT IV

Scene One

A room in the house of the deceased COUNT DE GORMAS. CHI-
MENE *and* ELVIRA *are discovered.*

CHIMENE. 'Tis not a false report? Thou art sure, Elvira?
ELVIRA. Thou never wouldst conceive how all admire him
And make the heavens echo, with one voice,
With this young warrior's glorious achievements.
The Moors who met him have gained naught but shame.
Swift was their coming, swifter still their flight.
Three hours of battle left to our defenders
A complete victory and two captive kings.
Nothing withstood the prowess of our leader.
CHIMENE. And Roderick hath wrought all these miracles?
ELVIRA. The two kings are the prize won by his valor.
His hand o'ercame them; *his* hand captured them.
CHIMENE. By whom hast thou been told this wondrous news?
ELVIRA. The populace sing everywhere his praises,

Call him the author of their joy, their hero,
Their guardian angel, their deliverer.
CHIMENE. And the King—how does he regard such exploits?
ELVIRA. Roderick still dares not appear before him,
But Don Diegue presents to him in chains
These two crowned prisoners in the victor's name,
With glad pride, and requests our noble sovereign
To look today on him who saved the realm.
CHIMENE. Is Roderick wounded?
ELVIRA.   As to that, I know not . . .
Thou turnest pale. Take heart again.
CHIMENE.   Nay, let me
Take, rather, my heart's fading wrath again!
Must I, in thinking but of him, forget
My proper feelings? All men boast his deeds,
They praise him, and I hear them with delight,
My honor mute, my sense of duty weak.
Be silent, love! balk not my grim intent.
Though he o'ercame two kings, he slew my father.
This mourning garb, which tells of my misfortune,
Is the first consequence of his great might;
And whatsoe'er is elsewhere said of him,
Here all reminds me of the wrong he did me.
    Ye who can fill me best with bitterness—
Veils, crape, funereal robes, the somber pomp
His earliest victory hath made me wear—
Uphold my honor in my heart's despite,
And when my love becomes too strong in me
Speak to my soul of my sad obligation
To seek, unfalteringly, this conqueror's death.
ELVIRA. Restrain thyself. See: here is the Infanta.

Enter the INFANTA *and* LEONORA.

THE INFANTA (*to* CHIMENE). I come not hither to console thy grief;
Rather I come to add my tears to thine.
CHIMENE. 'Twere better if thou sharedst the common joy,
Tasting the happiness which heaven sends thee,
Madam; I, only, have a right to weep.
The fact that Roderick rescued us from danger
And with his arm assured the public safety

Still permits tears today to no one else.
He saved the city, he served well his king;
To me alone his valorous arm brings woe.

THE INFANTA. 'Tis true, Chimene, he has accomplished marvels.

CHIMENE. The unwelcome news thereof hath reached mine ear
Already, and I hear him everywhere
Proclaimed aloud as no less brave in war
Than he hath been unfortunate in love.

THE INFANTA. But why should such news be unwelcome to thee?
This youthful Mars won formerly thy favor.
Thy soul was his. He lived but to be thine.
To extol his prowess honoreth thy choice.

CHIMENE. Everyone else can rightfully extol it,
But unto me its praise brings added pain.
To set his worth so high, augments my grief.
I see how much I lost in losing him.
Ah, cruel torture to a heart that loves!
Its flame burns more, the more I hear his greatness;
Yet ever is my sense of duty stronger,
And though I love him I will seek his death.

THE INFANTA. That sense of duty won thee yesterday
The highest admiration. Then, the struggle
Thou madest for its sake seemed so heroic,
So noble, that the whole Court was filled with wonder
At thy brave spirit and pity for thy love.
But wouldst thou heed a faithful friend's advice?

CHIMENE. To heed thee not, would be most wicked of me.

THE INFANTA. What was then just, is just no more today.
Now, Roderick is our country's sole support,
The hope and idol of an adoring people,
Castile's defense, the terror of the Moor.
In him alone—the King himself is well
Aware of this—thy father lives again;
And, if thou wishest me to say all in brief,
Thou seekest in his death the nation's ruin.
What! to avenge a father is it ever
Right to consign one's country to her foes?
Is thy revenge lawful as touching *us*?
We shared not in the crime. Must *we* be punished?

'Tis not as though 'twere planned thou still shouldst wed
Him by whose sword thou knowest thy father dead.
I would myself not wish thee to do *that*.
Deprive him of thy love; leave us his life.

CHIMENE.   Ah, it is not for me to show him mercy!
My obligation hath no metes nor bounds.
Though my love pleads with me in his behalf,—
Though the land worships him, and a king honors him,—
Though all the bravest warriors gather round him,—
My cypress boughs shall seek to blight his laurels.

THE INFANTA.   'Tis truly noble when to avenge a father
We try to take the life of one so dear,
But 'tis more noble still for us to place
Our country's interests above ties of blood.
Nay, trust me, 'tis enough to quench thy love.
The loss of that will punish him enough.
Let the realm's welfare guide thee. . . . And what is it,
Indeed, that thou dost think the King will do?

CHIMENE.   He may refuse me, but I must not fail
To try my utmost.

THE INFANTA.   Chimene, consider well
What course thou wishest to take. Adieu. Thou canst,
Without haste, choose it when thou art alone.

CHIMENE (*as the* INFANTA, LEONORA, *and* ELVIRA *withdraw*).
My father dead, no choice is left me—none.

Scene Two

A hall in the palace. The KING, DON DIEGUE, RODERICK, DON
ARIAS, DON SANCHO, *courtiers, and guards are discovered.*

THE KING (*addressing* RODERICK).   Brave son of an illustrious house,
which always
Was the defense and glory of Castile,
Whose many ancestors' exceptional valor
The first display of thine already equals,
My power to reward thee is too small,
For it is less than are thy just deserts.
    The land's deliverance from a savage foe,
Thy strengthening of my grasp upon the scepter,
The Moors' defeat ere, amid night's alarms,

I could take measures to repulse their army
Are exploits that now do not leave thy sovereign
The means or hope of recompensing thee.
But the two kings, thy prisoners, will reward thee:
They both alike have in my presence called thee
Their CID, and in their language "Cid" means "lord,"
Nor should I grudge thee such a glorious title.
    Be henceforth named "THE CID": to that proud name
Let everything succumb; let it dismay
Granada and Toledo. Let it show
To all of those who live beneath my sway
How great thou art, how much to thee I owe.

RODERICK.   Sire, will thy Majesty spare my confusion?
Thou valuest too highly such small service
And makest me blush before my gracious king
For having merited so very little
The honors now accorded me. I know
That to the welfare of thy realm I owe
The blood within me and the breath of life,
And had I lost them in that sacred cause,
I would have only done a subject's duty.

THE KING.   Not all men whom this duty binds to serve me
Discharge it with a courage such as thine;
And valor, unless carried to extremes,
Never accomplishes such mighty deeds.
Let thyself, then, be praised, and at more length
Tell me the story of thy victory.

RODERICK.   Thou knowest, sire, that in this hour of danger
Which threw the city into so great panic
Some friends who at my father's house had gathered
Besought me, still distracted as I was . . .
But pardon, sire, my boldness! if I dared
Lead them without authority from thee,
The peril now was nigh, their band was ready,
To appear before thee was to risk my head,
And if I had to die I would much rather
Have taken leave of life while fighting for thee.

THE KING.   I pardon thine avenging of a wrong.
This land thou savedst pleads thy cause. Chimene

Henceforth, be very sure, will speak in vain,
And I shall hear her but to comfort her.
Say on.

RODERICK.   Then under me this band proceeded,
With brave determination in each face.
Five hundred when we set forth, by the time
We reached the port we were three thousand strong,
So soon, on seeing us march so resolutely,
Did those most terrified regain their courage.
Two-thirds of us I hurriedly concealed
In the holds of vessels which were lying there;
The rest, whose numbers grew with every hour,
Impatient for the fray, remained with me.
They lay flat on the ground and noiselessly
Waited through no small portion of the night.
By my command, the harbor guards did likewise,
Keeping themselves well hidden, to aid my ruse;
For I pretended boldly that I had
From thee the orders which they saw me now
Carrying out, and which I gave to all.

The dim light of the stars revealed at last
Thirty sail coming in upon the tide.
Its heaving swell upbore them, and the Moors
Entered the harbor with the sea at flood.
None stayed them; all seemed tranquil; soldiers nowhere
Along the quays nor on the city walls.
Deceived by such deep silence, they now could not
Doubt that they had surprised us. Fearlessly
They neared, cast anchor, disembarked, and rushed
Forward—to fall into our waiting hands.

We sprang up then and lifted, as one man,
A shout to heaven from a thousand throats.
Those in our ships answered that battle cry;
They stood forth armed; the Moors were sore dismayed.
Terror possessed them when but half had landed,
And ere the fight began, they deemed it lost.
They came to pillage; they encountered war.
We pressed them hard, alike on sea and shore.
We made their blood, in rivers, flow before

Any resisted or could form in ranks.

   At length, despite us, their chiefs rallied them.
Their courage was reborn, their fear forgotten.
The shame of being slain without a struggle
Restored their discipline and renewed their valor;
They faced us stoutly with their scimitars,
And our blood mingled in dread streams with theirs,
While earth and wave, the harbor and their fleet
Were fields of carnage over which death reigned.

   How many brave, how many brilliant deeds
Went without notice in the darkness, where
Each man saw only his own mighty blows
And could not tell to which side Fate inclined!
I, who went everywhere, encouraging
Our soldiers, bidding some advance and giving
Others aid, marshaling those who came up later
And sending them in turn into the fray,
Knew not how went the battle, until day.
But finally the dawn disclosed our victory
Unto us, their defeat unto the Moors.
They suddenly lost heart, and when they spied
Fresh reinforcements which arrived to help us,
The fear of death replaced their zeal to conquer;
They gained their ships, they cut the cables, making
The welkin ring with their affrighted cries,
And in confusion fled, without once asking
Themselves if their two kings escaped with them.
Their panic was too great for loyalty.

   The tide's flood brought them; its ebb took them hence,
While their kings, fighting in our midst, together
With a few followers badly wounded by us,
Strove like brave men to sell their lives right dearly.
I myself called out to them to surrender;
They stood at bay and would not hearken to me;
But when they saw at last that all their warriors
Lay at their feet and that they must unaided
Defend themselves to no avail, they asked
Who was our leader, I said that I was he,
And they surrendered. I sent them both to thee

At the same time, and thus the combat ended,
There being none to fight.

                    'Twas in this manner
That, in thy service . . .

          Enter DON ALONSO.

DON ALONSO.   Sire, Chimene approaches
  To plead with thee for justice.
THE KING.   Sorry news
  Is this, with an unwelcome task for me.
    (*To* RODERICK) Go; I would not compel her to behold thee.
  For thy sole thanks, I needs must drive thee hence!
  But ere thou goest, come, let thy king embrace thee.
             (*He embraces him.* RODERICK *withdraws.*)
DON DIEGUE. Chimene pursues him with her vengeance, wishing
  The while to save him.
THE KING.   I have heard she loves him,
  And I shall test her. Look more sorrowful.
               (*Enter* CHIMENE *and* ELVIRA.)
  Be satisfied at last, Chimene; thou hast
  Thy will. Though Roderick overcame our foes,
  He just now died before us, from their blows.
  Give thanks to heaven, which hath avenged thee on him.
    (*To* DON DIEGUE) See how already she is drained of color!
DON DIEGUE. But look: she swoons, and in that swoon supplies
  The proof, sire, of a love that hath no bounds!
  Her grief betrayed the secrets of her soul.
  Thou canst no longer doubt her real feelings.
CHIMENE (*reviving*). What! Roderick, then, is dead?
THE KING.   No, no! he lives
  And with unchanging fervor loves thee still.
  Cast off this grief that seized thee for his sake.
CHIMENE. Sire, one can faint for joy as well as sorrow.
  We all grow weak from too great happiness,
  And when 'tis sudden, it o'erwhelms our senses.
THE KING. Thou wishest us to believe the impossible
  For thee? Chimene, thy grief was too apparent.
CHIMENE. Well then, sire, add this climax to my misery
  And call my swoon the consequence of grief.
  A natural bitter disappointment caused it.

His death would save his head from me, who seek it.
Died he of wounds got in his country's service,
My vengeance would be lost, my aims defeated.
An end so fair would satisfy me little.
I ask his death, but not a glorious death,
Not one so splendid that it would exalt him,
Not one in battle, nay, but on a scaffold,
One for my father, not one for his country,
One that will stain his name and blight his memory.
Death for one's native land is no sad fate;
To die thus, is to win immortal fame.
    I can rejoice in Roderick's victory, then,
Rightfully, and I do. It saves the State
And leaves me still my victim, nobler now,
Illustrious now above all other warriors,
A captain not with flowers crowned but laurels,
And one who is, to speak in brief my thought,
A worthy offering to my father's shade.
    Alas, in what vain hopes do I indulge!
Roderick has nothing more to dread from me.
What can unheeded tears avail against him?
The whole realm is for him a place of safety.
Where'er thou rulest, he can do no wrong.
O'er me, as o'er his enemies, he prevails.
Justice, whose voice he stifled in their blood,
Makes a new trophy for this conqueror's crimes.
Like the two kings his prisoners, we follow
His chariot, while he tramples on the law.

THE KING. Thy words, my daughter, are too violent.
When one dispenses justice, one weighs all.
Thy father, whom he slew, brought on the quarrel.
Justice itself bids me be merciful.
Before thou blamest me for my clemency,
Consult thine own heart; Roderick reigns within it,
And secretly thou needs must thank thy king,
Whose favor preserves for thee such a lover.

CHIMENE. For me? My foe? The object of my wrath,
The author of my woes, my father's murderer?
My righteous plea is looked upon so lightly
That 'tis a favor to me not to hear me!

    Since to my tears thou dost refuse all justice,
    Allow me, sire, to have recourse to arms.
    It was by arms alone he injured me,
    And thus in turn I should avenge myself.
    Of all thy cavaliers I ask his head—
    Yes, and whoever brings it to me, I
    Shall be his prize. Let them, sire, fight with him.
    If Roderick be slain, I wed his conqueror.
    Confirmed by thy decree, let this be published.
THE KING. That custom anciently established here
    Under the pretext of redressing wrongs
    Weakens a State with loss of its best warriors.
    Oft the sad outcome of this evil practice
    Destroys the good and lets the wicked live.
    I exempt Roderick from it. He is too precious
    To me to be exposed to Fate's caprice.
    If one so noble could commit a crime,
    The Moors in flight bore it away with them.
DON DIEGUE. What, sire! for him alone annul the laws
    Which all thy Court so oft have seen observed?
    What will thy people think or envy say
    If he takes shelter under this exemption
    And makes of it a pretext not to go
    Where men of honor seek a gallant death?
    His glory would be tarnished by such favors.
    Give not his victory a reward that shames him.
    The Count insulted me; he punished him.
    He was a brave man then, and still must be one.
THE KING. Since thou desirest it, I will let him fight.
    But in each vanquished warrior's place a thousand
    Others will stand; the prize Chimene hath promised
    His conqueror, will make every knight his foe.
    For him to face them all, would be unjust.
    Once only shall he enter, then, the lists.
       Choose whom thou wilt, Chimene, but choose with care;
    For I will grant to thee no further prayer.
DON DIEGUE. Not thus afford excuse to those who fear him.
    Leave the field open; none will enter it.
    After the prowess Roderick hath displayed,
    Who has the courage to dare fight with him?
    Who against such a foe would risk his life?

Who is so valiant?—nay, who is so rash?

DON SANCHO.   Open the lists. Thou seest his adversary.
I am that rash man—nay, that valiant man.
        (*To* CHIMENE) Vouchsafe this favor to my heart's devotion,
Madam. Thou knowest what thou didst promise me.

THE KING.   Chimene, dost thou consign thy cause to him?

CHIMENE.   He hath my promise, sire.

THE KING.   Tomorrow, then.

DON DIEGUE.   No, sire; there is no reason for delay.
One who is brave is always ready.

THE KING.   What!
Fight at once, having just come from a battle?

DON DIEGUE.   Roderick has rested while he told thee of it.

THE KING.   My will it is that he shall have at least
An hour or two in which to get his breath.
But lest this duel should appear to set
A precedent, and that I may show plainly
With what reluctance I permit a thing
So sanguinary, which I never liked,
I shall not witness it, nor shall my Court.
        (*To* DON ARIAS) Thou shalt preside, alone, over this combat.
See that both combatants fight honorably,
And when 'tis over, bring to me the victor.
Whiche'er he be, the prize will be the same.
I wish, myself, to give him to Chimene,
And his reward shall be her plighted troth.

CHIMENE.   What, sire! impose on me this cruel sentence?

THE KING.   Thou murmurest at it, but if Roderick triumphs,
Thy heart without a murmur will accept him.
Cease to protest against my kind decree;
To him who conquers I will marry thee.

ACT V

Scene One

A room in the house of the deceased COUNT DE GORMAS. CHI-
MENE *is discovered. Enter* RODERICK.

CHIMENE.   What, Roderick! In broad daylight? Whence this boldness?
'Twill rob me of my honor. Go. Please, go!

RODERICK.   I go to die, madam, and I have come,
        Before my death-blow falls, to say farewell.
        The faithful love which bows me to thy will
        Bids me, ere taking leave of life, to see thee.
CHIMENE.   Thou goest to die?
RODERICK.   I rush to that glad moment
        When my shed blood will satisfy thy vengeance.
CHIMENE.   Thou goest to die? Don Sancho is so mighty
        That he brings terror to thy dauntless heart?
        What makes thee now so weak, or him so strong?
        Roderick goes forth to fight, and talks of dying!
        One who feared not my father nor the Moors
        Goes forth to fight Don Sancho, and despairs
        Already! Thus, then, does thy courage fail thee?
RODERICK.   I do not go to fight, but to be punished;
        For when thou seekest my death, my soul's devotion
        Takes from me all wish to defend myself.
        My courage is the same, but not my arm
        When I protect a wretch who hath displeased thee.
        Ere this I would have died in last night's fray,
        If I had then fought in my own defense;
        But when it was my king that I defended,
        His people, and my country, to defend
        Myself but ill, would have been false to them.
        Life is not yet so hateful unto me
        That I desire to die dishonorably.
        Now that I, only, am concerned, when thou
        Wouldst have my heart's blood, to thy will I bow.
        For thy revenge, thou choosest another's hand.
        (It would have been too sweet to die by thine.)
        I shall make no resistance. I owe more
        Respect to anyone who fights for thee;
        And, full of joy to think the mortal blows
        Are really dealt by thee because it is
        Thy quarrel that thy champion's sword sustains,
        I shall present to them a naked breast,
        Adoring, in his hand that slays me, thine.
CHIMENE.   Though duty forces me, against my will,
        To hound relentlessly unto his death
        A man such as thou art, if hence thy love

Prescribes for thee in turn so strict a course
As to require thee to make no resistance
To anyone who fights for me, forget not,
In this blind fervor, that thy fame is now
At stake as surely as thy life. However
Great the renown of Roderick while he lives,
When it is known that he has met his death,
'Twill be believed by all that he was vanquished.

  I am less dear to thee than is thine honor,
For in my father's blood it dyed thy hands
And led thee to renounce, although thou lovest me,
Thy fondest hope, that I was to be thine.
Yet now I see thee care so little for it
That thou wouldst be laid low without a struggle.
How changeful is thy valor! Why dost thou
Have it no more, or why didst thou once have it?
What! art thou brave only to injure me?
When I cannot be wronged, hast thou no courage?
And wilt thou cheapen thus my father's memory:
First conquer him, then let thyself be conquered?
Go; do not seek thy death. That task is mine.
If naught thou valuest life, defend thy fame.

RODERICK.   After the Count's fate and the Moors' defeat
Does my renown demand yet other deeds?
I can disdain, now, to defend myself.
Men know that there is nothing that I shrink
From undertaking, nothing that my valor
Cannot accomplish, nothing under heaven
That is more precious to me than my honor.
Nay, in this combat—think whate'er thou wilt—
Roderick can fall with no risk to his fame,
With none to venture to impugn his prowess
Or deem he was o'ercome or met his match.
Men will say only: "He adored Chimene.
He would not live when he had caused her pain.
Unto the will of hostile Fate he bowed,
Which forced his heart's beloved to seek his blood.
She asked it; and, high-souled, he deemed withal
That to refuse it, would be criminal.
To avenge his honor, he put love aside;

And to avenge her whom he loved, he died,
Cherishing, though she might have been his wife,
Honor more than Chimene, her more than life."
 Thou seest, then, that 'twill not bedim my glory
To end thus, but will only make it brighter.
My voluntary death has this distinction:
That it alone could give thee due redress.

CHIMENE. Since life and honor have too scant appeal
To hold thee back from hastening to thy death,
Dear Roderick, if thou hast ever loved me,
Defend thyself to save me from Don Sancho!
Fight to release me from a cruel compact
Which gives me otherwise to one I loathe.
Oh, must I say yet more to thee! Go, fight
To o'ercome my scruples; force them to be silent,
Remembering, if thy heart still loves Chimene,
As victor thou wilt love her not in vain.
Adieu! these words have set my cheeks ablaze.
      (*Exit* CHIMENE, *hastily.*)

RODERICK. Where is the foe I cannot conquer now!
Come on, Navarre, Morocco, and Castile!
Come, every valiant hero, if ye will,
And to oppose me in one host unite.
My single arm shall match your gathered might.
Against a hope so fair, the whole of Spain
Would be too weak. I fight for my Chimene! (*Exit* RODERICK.)

Scene Two

A room in the apartments of the INFANTA. *The* INFANTA *is discovered, alone.*

THE INFANTA.
 O pride of birth, shall I still hark to thee,
  That feelest for my love disdain?
 Or, love, that biddest me 'gainst pride's tyranny
 Revolt, shall I instead hear thy sweet strain?
   To which, poor princess, of these twain
   Oughtest thou to give thy loyalty?
 Roderick, thy valor merits anyone;
 But, howso brave, thou art no monarch's son.

Pitiless fate, which sets a cruel abyss
     Between my rank and my heart's cry!
If I should choose a hero such as this,
Must I find great unhappiness thereby?
     Ah heaven, for how many a sigh
     Must I prepare myself, I wis,
If I can ne'er, tortured by love and shame,
Accept my lover or put out love's flame!

But I too long have wavered, and to mine own
     Mind do my qualms now bring dismay.
Though one like me should wed with kings alone,
Roderick, I well could live beneath thy sway.
     Since two kings thou tookest today,
     Couldst thou fail to win a throne?
And that great name of CID now thine—how plain
Its presage of o'er whom thou art to reign!

Yes, he is worthy of me, but he unto
     Chimene belongs. So little hate
A father's death can breed between these two,
Her filial duty hounds him with regret.
     Thus from his deed no gain I get,
     From all my pain doth naught accrue,
Since destiny, to punish me, decrees
That they shall still love, although enemies.

                              (*Enter* LEONORA.)

     Why comest thou, Leonora?

LEONORA.   'Tis to praise thee,
     Madam, for having finally recovered
     Thy soul's peace.

THE INFANTA.   How should I find peace again
     When most my soul is torn?

LEONORA.   Hast thou not said,
     "Love lives by hope and dies when hope is dead."
     Roderick indeed can charm thy thoughts no longer.
     Thou knowest the duel in which Chimene involves him.
     Since he will perish then or be her husband,
     Thy hope must end, thy wounded heart be healed.

THE INFANTA. How far from that!

LEONORA.   What is it thou canst expect?

THE INFANTA.   Rather, what hope is now forbidden me?
          Though Roderick does fight under these conditions,
          I can invent a thousand ways to evade them.
          Love, the sweet source of all my bitter pain,
          Teaches too many wiles to lovers' wits.
LEONORA.   Canst *thou* do aught, after a father's death
          Could not enkindle discord in their bosoms?
          For by her conduct Chimene clearly shows
          That hate does not inspire her efforts 'gainst him.
          She wins the King's consent unto a combat,
          And for her champion she at once accepts
          The first who volunteers. She does not have
          Recourse to one of those heroic arms
          Far-famed for their unnumbered glorious deeds.
          Don Sancho satisfies her and deserves
          Her choice because he now for the first time
          Confronts a foe. She prizes in her champion
          His inexperience, and as he is
          Without renown, she is without misgivings.
          The readiness of her acceptance of him
          Ought to convince thee that she seeks this combat
          Because her sense of duty bids her do so,
          But that she wishes it to be a duel
          Which will give Roderick an easy victory
          And yet will seem to satisfy her honor.
THE INFANTA.   Only too clear it is; yet I adore,
          In rivalry with her, this conqueror.
          What shall I do! O miserable me!
LEONORA.   Remember better what thy lineage is.
          Thou needs must wed a king; thou lovest a subject!
THE INFANTA.   He whom I love is not the same. I love
          Roderick, a simple cavalier, no longer.
          Not thus do I now think of him. The man
          I love is he that did such mighty deeds,
          The valiant CID, the master of two kings.
          Yet I shall conquer, none the less, my heart—
          Not from a fear of censure, but because
          I do not wish to wrong a love like theirs.
          Even if, for *my* sake, he received a crown,
          I would not take again that which I gave.

Since he is sure to triumph in this encounter,
Let us once more bestow him on Chimene;
And thou, who knowest my inner strife and pain,
Come, see me finish that which I began.

(Exeunt.)

Scene Three

A room in the house of the deceased COUNT DE GORMAS. CHI-
MENE *and* ELVIRA *are discovered.*

CHIMENE.   How terrible my sufferings are, Elvira!
How very greatly I am to be pitied!
I can but hope, and I have all to dread.
No prayer escapes me that I would acknowledge;
A swift repentance follows every wish.
Two rivals have I made cross swords for me;
The happiest result will cost me tears;
And be Fate e'er so kind to me, my father
Must have no vengeance or my lover die.

ELVIRA.   In either case I see no lack of solace.
Thou wilt have Roderick or wilt be avenged.
Whate'er it be that Fortune may decree,
Thy fair fame will be safe, and thou shalt wed.

CHIMENE.   Him I detest or him whose death I sought!
The slayer of my father or of Roderick!
In either case I shall be given a husband
Stained with the blood of him that I held dearest.
My soul shrinks from the thought of either of them,
And more than death I fear what will ensue.
Vengeance and love, which fill my heart with turmoil,
Away with you! ye have no charms for me
At such a price as this. And thou, almighty
Dispenser of my grievous destiny,
Conclude this duel with no decisive outcome
And neither of the twain victor or vanquished!

ELVIRA.   That would be too unkind to thee. This combat
Would only bring new torture to thy spirit
If it should leave thee still compelled to plead
For justice, still compelled to show resentment
And seek continually thy lover's death.

Madam, much better were it that his prowess
Should crown his brow and force thee to be silent,—
That the conditions of the duel should stifle
Thy sighs, and that the King should make thee follow
Thy true desires.

CHIMENE.   If Roderick prevailed
Dost thou suppose that I would ever yield?
My duty is too clear, my loss too great;
And neither the conditions of the duel
Nor the King's will can govern me herein.
Roderick can easily o'ercome Don Sancho
But not the sense of duty of Chimene.
No matter what the King hath promised him,
I shall raise up a thousand foes against him.

ELVIRA.   Beware lest heaven should finally grant thee vengeance
To punish thee for such perversity.
Wilt thou reject the happiness of being
Able at last to accept a reconcilement
Honorably? What, then, is this sense of duty?
What does it hope for? Will thy lover's death
Restore to thee thy father? Does one stroke
Of great misfortune not suffice for thee?
Must thou add loss to loss and grief to grief?
Stubborn and wilful as thou art, thou dost not
Deserve the lover who is destined for thee,
And we shall see the righteous wrath of heaven
Give thee instead, by Roderick's death, Don Sancho
For husband.

CHIMENE.   I have woe enough, Elvira;
Double it not by this dire prophecy.
I wish to escape them both, if I can do so.
If I cannot, Roderick has all my prayers.
Not that insensate love inclines me thus—
Nay, but because if he were conquered I
Would be Don Sancho's. From the fear of that
Springs my desire . . . What do I see, unhappy
Girl that I am! Undone! I am undone!

    (*Enter* DON SANCHO. *He carries a sword, which he offers,*
      holding it by the blade, to CHIMENE.)

DON SANCHO.   'Tis mine to bring this sword unto thy feet . . .

CHIMENE.   What! reeking with the blood of Roderick still?
          Perfidious wretch, dost thou dare show thyself
          Before my face, when thou hast taken from me
          That being who was dearest to me? Speak out,
          My love! thou hast no more to fear. My father
          Has been avenged. Cease to restrain thyself.
          By one blow has my good fame been assured,
          My soul plunged in despair, my heart set free.
DON SANCHO.   With calmer spirit . . .
CHIMENE.   Art thou still talking to me,
          Vile murderer of the hero I adore?
          Begone! Thou slewest him treacherously. A man
          So valiant never would have fallen before
          An adversary such as thou. Hope naught
          From me! No service hast thou done me. Thinking
          To avenge me, thou hast robbed me of my all.
DON SANCHO.   With this strange error, far from hearing me . . .
CHIMENE.   Wouldst have me hear thee boast of killing him,—
          Hear thee with patience while thou arrogantly
          Tellest of his death, my crime, and thy great prowess?
             (*Enter the* KING, DON DIEGUE, DON ARIAS, *and* DON ALONSO.)
            Sire, I need try no longer to conceal
          What all my efforts could not hide from thee.
          I loved, thou knowest; and to avenge my father
          I sought to have the head of him I loved.
          Thy Majesty himself, sire, could observe
          How I have made my love give way to duty.
          Roderick is dead at last, and by his death
          Has changed his unrelenting enemy
          To a grief-stricken maid whose heart is his.
          I owed revenge to him who gave me life,
          And now I owe these tears to my dear lover.
          Don Sancho hath in my defense undone me,
          And I am the reward of his fell arm!
            If pity, sire, hath power to move a king,
          Revoke, I beg thee, a decree so dreadful
          To me. To recompense his victory,
          Which takes from me the one thing that I love,
          All that I have is his; let him consent
          Only to leave me to myself, that I

May in a cloister weep incessantly,
Till my last sigh, my father and my lover.
DON DIEGUE. So now she speaks the truth, sire; she no longer
Deems it a crime to avow the love she feels.
THE KING. Chimene, be undeceived: thy Roderick lives.
Don Sancho, who was vanquished, misinformed thee.
DON SANCHO. Sire, it was her impetuousness, despite me,
Which thus deceived her. I came straight from the combat
To tell her its result. That noble warrior
Who hath her heart said, when he had disarmed me:
"Fear nothing; I would leave my victory doubtful
Sooner than take a life risked for Chimene.
But since my duty calls me to the King,
Go thou and tell her of our duel, for me;
And bring to her thy sword, my gift to her."
I came here, sire; and seeing me return
Bearing my sword, she thought I was the victor,
And instantly her anger and her love
Betrayed her into such a violent outburst
That I could not obtain a moment's hearing.
For my part, although conquered, I account
Myself most fortunate, and despite the interests
Of my own heart and all my infinite loss
Am happy still in my defeat, which brings
To fair fulfilment such a perfect love.
THE KING. My daughter, there is naught to make thee blush
For what thou feelest or seek to disavow it.
No shame can rightfully be thine. Thy honor
Is without stain; thy duty has been discharged;
Thy father's claims are satisfied. Enough
His death has been requited when so often
The death of Roderick has been sought by thee.
Thou seest that heaven is disposed to save him.
Hence, having for thy father done so much,
Take thy reward, and do not be rebellious
'Gainst my authority, which gives to thee
A husband whom thou lovest with all thy heart.

Enter the INFANTA, LEONORA, *and* RODERICK.

THE INFANTA. No longer weep, Chimene. Receive with joy

This hero from the hand of me, thy princess.

RODERICK (*to the* KING, *going to* CHIMENE *and kneeling before her*).
Be not offended, sire, if in thy presence
My reverent love now casts me at her feet.
   (*To* CHIMENE) I come not here to claim my victory's guerdon;
I come again to offer thee my head,
Madam. My love will not avail itself
Of either the duel's terms or the King's will.
If all that hath been done is still too little,
Tell me what else thou dost require of me.
Must I needs fight with countless other rivals,
Extend my triumphs to earth's utmost bounds,
Unaided storm a camp or rout an army,
Surpass the deeds of heroes of romance?
If thus my crime against thee finally
Can be atoned, I dare to undertake
All of these things, and I can do them all.
But if thy fierce, inexorable sense
Of duty cannot be appeased without
The death of him who wronged thee, send no more
The might of mortals 'gainst me. See, my head
Is bowed before thee; do thou avenge thyself.
Unto thy hand alone the power is given
To slay the invincible. Take, then, a vengeance
That no one could take for thee. But at least
Let death, I pray, suffice to punish me!
Banish me not from thy dear memory;
And since by dying I make thee honored more,
Keep in return my image in thy heart
And sometimes say, with sorrow for my fate,
"Had he not loved me, he would not be dead."

CHIMENE. Nay, Roderick; rise.
                        I must confess it, sire—
I have said too much to thee e'er to unsay it—
Since he is what he is, I cannot hate him.
And thou—thou art my king; I must obey thee.
But though thou hast decreed my fate already,
How, sire, would it appear, with this sad marriage,
For one same day both to begin and end

My mourning, and place me in Roderick's arms
And in the tomb my father? This too much
Savors of a connivance at his death,
Makes me unfaithful to his sacred ashes,
And soils my honor with the eternal shame
That with a father's blood my hands are stained.

THE KING. Time often renders lawful that which seems
At first to be inseparable from guilt.
Roderick has won thee, and thou must be his;
But though thou art today his valor's prize,
I needs would be thy fair fame's enemy
Should I so soon reward his victory.
To put these nuptials off breaks not my promise,
Which gives thee to him but saith not at what time.
Take, if thou wilt, a year to dry thy tears.
    Roderick, thou meanwhile must resume thine arms.
Already hast thou here at home defeated
The Moors, foiled their intent, and hurled them back.
Carry the war now into their own country.
Command my armies and lay waste their land.
The mere name of THE CID will make them tremble.
They have already given thee this title
Of "lord"; they soon will wish thee for their king.
    But midst thine exploits remain ever true
To her thou lovest; return still worthier
Of her, if that be possible; and force her
By thy great deeds to have in thee such pride
That she will then rejoice to be thy bride.

RODERICK. To win Chimene and serve my sovereign, too,
What is there, sire, I cannot, will not, do!
Though for a time I shall not see her face,
That I can hope, is enough happiness.

THE KING. Trust in thy courage; trust in my pledged word.
Over her heart thou art already lord.
The point of honor that resists thee now
To time, thy valor, and thy king will bow.

Horace

(THE HORATII)

CHARACTERS IN THE PLAY

TULLUS, *King of Rome.*
OLD HORATIUS, *a Roman nobleman.*
HORATIUS, *his son, the eldest of three brothers.*
CURIATIUS, *the eldest of three brothers, a young Alban nobleman, betrothed to Camilla.*
VALERIUS, *a young Roman nobleman, in love with Camilla.*
SABINA, *wife of Horatius and sister of Curiatius.*
CAMILLA, *the betrothed of Curiatius and sister of Horatius.*
JULIA, *a Roman lady, intimate friend of Sabina and Camilla.*
FLAVIAN, *an Alban soldier.*
PROCULUS, *a Roman soldier.*
Guards.

The scene represents a hall in the home of the Horatii, in Rome.

The Horatii

ACT I

SABINA and JULIA are discovered.

SABINA.   Bear with my weakness. Do not blame my grief.
 'Tis too well justified in such misfortune.
 Terror is seemly in the noblest hearts
 When such dire storms will burst so soon upon them;
 And the least apprehensive, bravest nature
 Could not maintain unwaveringly its courage.
 However dazed I am by these dread happenings,
 The sorrow in my bosom brings no tears;
 And though to heaven ascend my woeful sighs,
 My self-control at least still rules mine eyes.
 To manifest no further one's distress,
 If short of man's full strength, is more than woman's.
 All that can be expected of our sex
 Is not to weep at such a time as this.

JULIA.   That is enough, perhaps, for common souls,
 Which at the slightest danger feel despair.
 But so great frailty shames a noble breast.
 Where there is doubt, it dares to hope the best.
 The opposing camps are pitched beneath our ramparts,
 But Rome still knows not how to lose a battle.
 Far from dismay, thou shouldst feel joy for her.
 She goeth forth to fight, and hence to conquer.
 Have done, have done with fears so vain, and learn
 Better what thoughts are worthy of a Roman.

SABINA.   I am a Roman, for Horatius is.
 I became one when I became his wife.
 Yet marriage bonds would be but chains of slavery
 If they forbade me to recall my birthplace.
 Alba, where first I breathed the breath of life,
 Mine own dear city and my earliest love,
 Alas, in war 'twixt us and thee, I dread
 Our victory no less than our defeat.
   Rome, if thou deemest me a traitor to thee

111

In feeling thus, make choice of enemies
Whom I can hate. When from thy walls I see
Thine army and their foes', in one my husband
And in the other my three brothers, how
Without impiety can I find words
For prayers and ask of heaven thy success?
I know thy realm, still in its infancy,
Cannot assert its power without wars.
I know that thou must grow, and that thy great
Destiny makes thee no mere Latin state,—
That heaven hath promised that thou shalt rule the world,
And that thou canst not do this, save by war.
Far from opposing thy sublime ambition
Which followeth heaven's will in seeking greatness,
I fain would see thy legions, crowned with laurels,
Cross with victorious tread the Pyrenees,
Carry their cohorts into Eastern lands,
Go plant their standards all along the Rhine,
And shake with pulse of marching feet the Pillars
Of Hercules. But still respect the town
Which gave thee Romulus. Ungrateful city,
Remember that unto its royal seed
Thou owest thy name, thy walls, and thy first laws.
Alba is thy one source. Stop and bethink thee
That with the sword thou stabbest thy mother's breast.
Turn elsewhere thy triumphant arms. What joy
She then will manifest at thy good fortune!
And with maternal love allowed full sway,
If thou no more assailest her, she will pray
Only for thy success.

JULIA.   Thy words surprise me,
Seeing that ever since the time our warriors
Took arms against her people, I have noted
That thou hast shown as scant concern for her
As if thou hadst been born of Roman parents;
And I admired the strength of mind which made thee
Able to suppress thy natural loyalties
In favor of thy husband's, and I consoled thee
When thou didst fear, 'twould seem, for Rome alone.

SABINA.   So long as there were only skirmishes

Which could result in neither city's ruin,
And hopes of peace could soothe my heart's distress,
Yes, I took pride in being wholly Roman;
And if I with the least regret beheld
Rome's fortunes prosper, straightway I condemned
That secret sorrow; and when Fate frowned on her
And for my brothers' sake I felt some joy,
I promptly stifled it within my breast
And wept when glory made itself their guest.
    But now when Alba needs must fall or Rome,
One or the other cannot but succumb,
And when after their battle there can be
Nothing to stay the conqueror and no hope
For the defeated, I would have to hate
My city savagely if I could still
Be wholly Roman and if I could ask
The gods to give to you a victory
That would cost so much blood so dear to me.
I cannot think entirely of one man.
I cannot pray for Alba or for Rome.
I fear for both alike in this last fray
And unto them shall cleave who lose the day.
Neutral until the victory has been won,
I then will share the lot of those undone.
I keep, amid such pain and anguish sore,
Tears for the conquered, hate for the conqueror.

JULIA. How oft in the same trials are displayed
By different hearts quite different emotions!
How unlike thee Camilla does! Thy husband
Is one of her three brothers; her betrothed
Is one of thy three. Yet she seems to view
With very different eyes than thine her flesh
And blood in one host and her heart's beloved
In the other. When thy soul was still all Roman,
Her own, irresolute and sure of naught,
Dreaded the hazards of the smallest encounter,
Cursed an advantage gained by either side,
Gave her tears always to the piteous fate
Of those who fell, and thus within her bosom
Cherished continual grief. But yesterday,
When she had learned the time had finally

Been fixed on for a battle to be fought,
Then suddenly, joy lighting up her face . . .

SABINA.   Oh, Julia, how I fear a change so swift!
She yesterday greeted with smiles Valerius.
My brother hath been discarded for this rival,
'Tis plain. Her heart, beset by suitors near her,
Can find no love, after two years have passed,
For one still absent. . . . But forgive my outburst
Of sisterly affection. My concern
For him hath made me fear the worst in her.
I form suspicions on too trivial grounds.
In such dread times as these, love does not change
Nor is one pierced with shafts of a new love.
Amid such dire events, one's thoughts are different,
But one does not then in sweet converse deal
Nor feel such happiness as she seems to feel.

JULIA.   Its cause from me is hidden, as from thee,
And no conjecture satisfies my mind.
'Tis enough fortitude, in such great danger,
To see it and await its coming calmly;
But to be joyful is to go too far.

(Enter CAMILLA.)

SABINA.   Lo, some good spirit fitly sends her hither!
Attempt to make her speak about these matters.
Too much she loves thee to hide aught from thee.
I leave you.
    (*To* CAMILLA) Sister, talk with Julia.
I feel ashamed to manifest such grief,
And, crushed beneath unnumbered cares, my heart
Seeks solitude where it may hide its sighs.   (*Exit* SABINA.)

CAMILLA.   How wrongly she wants me to talk with thee!
Does she believe my grief is less than hers,—
Think that, more callous to so great misfortunes,
I mingle with my sad words fewer tears?
My soul is terrified by equal fears.
Like her, I lose by either army's loss.
I shall behold my lover, my sole joy,
Die for his country or mine own destroy.
Yes, he I love will midst my anguish be
One to be mourned or hated. Alas me!

JULIA. Yet she is to be pitied more than thou art.
One can change lovers; one cannot change husbands.
Forget Curiatius and accept Valerius,
And thou needst tremble for both sides no longer.
Thou wilt be wholly ours; thy heart, untorn,
Will then have naught to lose in our foes' camp.

CAMILLA. Give me advice more honorable to follow.
Sympathize with me without bidding me
Be wicked. Though I scarce can bear my woes,
I sooner would endure them than deserve them.

JULIA. What! dost thou call a change so wise, then, wicked?

CAMILLA. Does broken faith seem pardonable to thee?

JULIA. What bond can bind us to an enemy?

CAMILLA. What can release us from a solemn vow?

JULIA. Thou vainly wouldst conceal a thing too plain.
I saw thee talking with Valerius
Yesterday, and thy gracious manner with him
Gives him a right to indulge in sanguine hopes.

CAMILLA. If yesterday I talked with him and smiled,
Imagine naught from that to his advantage.
It was not he that caused my heart's contentment.
But hear the whole truth and be undeceived.
I have too great a love for Curiatius
To let thee any longer think me faithless.
    Thou wilt recall that hardly had his sister
Been wedded happily unto my brother
When, to complete my joy, he won my father's
Consent that his true love should be rewarded
By giving me to him. That day was both
Kind and disastrous to us. It united
Our families and set our kings at strife.
The selfsame instant sealed our marriage contract
And brought us war; it gave our fond hopes birth
And straightway dashed them ruthlessly to earth,
Robbed us forthwith of all it promised us,
And made us lovers but to make us foes.
What a cruel disappointment then was ours!
What curses then he hurled against the gods,
And in what streams the tears ran down my cheeks!
I say no more of this; thou sawest our partings.

Thou hast seen, since, the turmoil of my soul.
Thou knowest how love has made me pray for peace,—
How I have wept at every turn of fortune,
Now for my country, now for my betrothed.
   In my despair, with hope so long deferred,
I sought at last the voice of oracles.
Listen, and judge if the response vouchsafed me
Yesterday ought to calm my anxious heart.
That far-famed Greek who hath for many years
Foretold our fates beneath Mount Aventine—
He whom Apollo ne'er hath let speak falsely—
Thus promised me the end of all my grief:
   "Alba and Rome shall peace tomorrow see.
      Thy prayer is heard; their conflict will be o'er;
      And thou shalt with thy Curiatius be
         United. Ye thenceforth will part no more."
   This oracle completely reassured me,
And, as it promised more than I had hoped,
I let my soul be filled with ecstasy
Beyond the transports of the happiest lovers.
Judge thou of its excess. I met Valerius
And, unlike other times, he could not vex me.
He spoke to me of love without my feeling
Angry. I scarce knew that I talked with him.
I could not treat him with disdain or coldness.
Each face I saw seemed that of Curiatius;
Each word said to me told me of his love;
And every word I spoke told him of mine.
The armies will today be locked in battle;
I heard that yesterday, yet recked not of it.
Lulled with sweet hopes of marriage and of concord,
My heart refused to think of such grim matters.
Last night hath stripped me of these fond illusions.
Countless dire dreams, countless cruel images—
Nay, countless heaps of carnage and of horror—
Have banished joy and given me back my fears.
I have seen blood and corpses—naught connected;
A vision scarce had risen ere it was gone.
One blotted out another, and each picture
Redoubled my affright by this confusion.

JULIA. Dreams mean the opposite of what they show us.
CAMILLA. I ought to think so, for I so would have it,
      Yet now I find myself, despite my wishes,
      Faced with a day of conflict, not of peace.
JULIA. Thereby the war will end, and peace will follow.
CAMILLA. If thus alone our ills are to be cured,
      May they ne'er end. Whether it shall be Rome
      That falls or Alba that wears chains, dear lover,
      Expect no more to be someday my husband.
      No man shall ever, ever, have that name
      Who is my city's conqueror or slave.

                              (*Enter* CURIATIUS.)
      But what new sight appears before me here?
      Is't thou, Curiatius? Can I trust mine eyes?
CURIATIUS. Yes, doubt them not, Camilla; and thou beholdest
      Neither the slave nor conqueror of thy city.
      Have no more fear of seeing my hands red
      With shame of fetters or with Roman blood.
      I knew thy heart's pride and thy love for Rome
      Would make thee scorn my chains and loathe my triumph,
      And since in this dilemma I had fear
      No less of victory than of servitude ...
CAMILLA. Enough, Curiatius; I divine the rest.
      Thou fleest a strife so fatal to thy hopes;
      And, wholly mine, thy heart, to lose me not,
      Deprives thy people of thy valiant arm.
      Let others judge the rightness of thy conduct
      And blame thee, if they will, for having loved me
      Too much. 'Tis not Camilla's place to esteem thee
      Any the less for this. The more thy love
      Is shown for her, the more she ought to love thee;
      And if thy debt is great unto the city
      That gave thee birth, the more thou dost forsake
      For me, the more thy love is manifested.
      But hast thou seen my father, and will he
      Permit thee to come boldly to his home?
      Cares he not for the interests of the State
      More than for those of his own family?
      Cares he not more for Rome than for his daughter?
      Now is our happiness indeed assured?

Did he receive thee as a son-in-law
Or enemy?

CURIATIUS.　　　　A son-in-law, and so
Affectionate was his greeting that it showed
Beyond all question his wholehearted joy.
But he did not behold in me a traitor
Unworthy to set foot within his house.
Nowise do I forsake my city's cause.
I love Camilla, but I still love honor.
So long as the war lasted, I was found
As true a patriot as I am a lover.
I gave my love and Alba, both, their due;
I yearned for thee even while I fought for her;
And if we were again to come to blows,
I would fight for her while I yearned for thee.
Yes, despite all the longings of my heart,
Were there still war, I would be with our army.
'Tis peace which lets me enter thy home freely—
Peace, unto which our love owes this good fortune.

CAMILLA.　Peace? How can I believe this miracle!

JULIA.　Have faith, Camilla, in thy oracle,
And let us learn by what blest means it was
That on the verge of battle peace was made.

CURIATIUS.　'Twas past belief! Already the two armies,
Each fired with equal ardor for the fray,
With threatening glances and defiant mien,
Awaited only the command to charge,
When our dictator stood forth from our ranks,
Asked your monarch for a moment's silence,
And, having gained it, said:
　　　　　　　　　　　"What are we doing,
Romans? What demon makes us fight each other?
Let reason now shed light upon our souls!
Neighbors are we; our daughters are your wives,
And marriage links us with so many ties
That few among our sons are not your grandsons.
We are one blood, one people, in two cities.
Why should we rend ourselves in civil wars,
Where every death amidst the vanquished weakens
The conquerors and the most glorious victory

Is stained with tears? Our common enemies
Await with joy the time when the defeat
Of one of us shall make the other one
An easy prey, exhausted, half undone,—
Triumphant, but in consequence thereof
Stripped of the aid it hath itself destroyed.
They have too long rejoiced at our dissension.
Let us henceforth combine our strength against them
And in oblivion drown these petty quarrels
Which make of such good soldiers such bad kinsmen.
For if the ambition to have sway o'er others
Puts in the field today your troops and ours,
Far from dividing us, it will unite us
If we can be content to shed less blood.
Let us choose men to fight in place of all;
Let each side trust its fortunes to its champions;
And even as Fate decrees concerning them,
Let Rome or Alba, one, obey the other,
The subject people subjects but not slaves,
With no dishonor for such valiant warriors,
No shame, no tribute, no constraint but this,
To follow everywhere the victor's banners.
Thus our two cities shall become one realm."

    It seemed that at these words our strife was ended,
And everyone, scanning the hostile ranks,
Espied a brother-in-law, cousin, or friend.
They were amazed that they had heedlessly
Come thus with would-be fratricidal hands,
And every face displayed forthwith a horror
Of any battle now, and all were eager
To choose their champions. Thus was the proposal
Accepted, and the peace that all desired
Was sworn at once, on the proposed conditions.
Three on each side will fight, but both commanders
Wish for a little time, to choose the best.
Yours now is with the Senate, ours in his tent.

CAMILLA. O Gods! what balm these tidings bring my soul!
CURIATIUS. Within two hours at most, it was agreed,
    Our champions' combat will decide our fate.
    In the meantime, we are free till they are named.

Rome now flocks to our camp, our camp to Rome.
On either side, entrance is granted all.
Everyone hastens to renew old friendships.
Love made me follow, for my part, thy brothers,
And such success hath crowned my heart's desires
That he who gave thee birth has promised me
The bliss tomorrow of thy hand in marriage.
Thou wouldst not be rebellious to his will?

CAMILLA.   It is a daughter's duty to obey.

CURIATIUS.   Come, then, and from his lips hear words so sweet,
Which are to make my happiness complete.

CAMILLA.   I follow thee, but to see again my brothers
And learn from them, too, that our woes are over.

JULIA.   Go, and meanwhile before our altars I
Will thank for both of you the gods on high.

(Exeunt.)

ACT II

HORATIUS *and* CURIATIUS *are discovered.*

CURIATIUS.   So Rome hath let no others share her preference.
She deemed that to choose elsewhere would be wrong!
In thee and thy two brothers this proud city
Finds her three warriors of the greatest prowess,
And with her noble ardor, matched by none,
Defies us all with your one house alone.
Seeing her fortunes wholly in your hands,
We should imagine that there were no Romans
Except Horatius' sons. Her choice could crown
Three families with glory and forever
Hallow them in the memories of men.
The honor which this choice confers on you
Could well have left the names of three immortal;
And, since 'tis here that kind fate and my love
Made me bestow my sister and choose a wife,
The ties I have, and am to have, with you
Cause me to claim what share of it I can.
But there are thoughts that chill, perforce, my joy
And mingle with it great anxiety.
The war hath so much signalized your valor

That I must fear for Alba and foresee
Her downfall. Since 'tis ye who are to fight,
Her ruin is assured. By having you
Named as Rome's champions, destiny decrees it.
Thereby do I perceive her fell intent
Only too plainly, and I count myself
E'en now one of your subjects.

HORATIUS.   Far from trembling
For Alba, thou shouldst pity Rome, beholding
Those she hath quite forgotten and the three
She hath selected. 'Tis a fatal blindness,
With such a wealth of choice, to choose so ill.
A thousand of her sons much worthier of her
Could better far than we uphold her cause.
But though this combat means my death, the glory
Of being chosen swells my heart with pride.
My soul conceives a manly confidence.
I dare to hope great things from my scant might,
And, whatsoe'er ungenerous Fate intendeth,
I nowise count myself one of your subjects.
Rome thinks too well of me; but, honored thus,
I shall not fail her, short of being slain.
He who would die or conquer rarely dies.
One reckless of his life is hard to vanquish.
Rome shall at least know naught of vassalage
Till my last gasp confirmeth my defeat.

CURIATIUS.   Ah me! 'tis hence that I complain of Fate.
That which my country seeks, my friendship dreads.
Oh, cruel alternatives: Alba subdued,
Or victor at the cost of thy dear blood;
And the one blessing that she strives to gain
Can be bought only with thy dying breath!
What can I wish? what happiness expect?
In any case I shall have tears to shed.
In any case my fond hopes are betrayed.

HORATIUS.   What! thou couldst weep for me if I should die
Serving my country? For a noble heart,
That is the fairest of all deaths. The glory
Which follows it, permits no tears; and I
Would welcome it, blessing my happy fate,
Should this in some wise benefit the State.

CURIATIUS.   Allow thy friends to fear it, still, for thee.
    In such a death they, only, are to be
    Pitied. Thine is the glory, theirs the loss.
    Thine is immortal fame; sorrow is theirs.
    One loses all, losing a friend so dear.

                                    (*Enter* FLAVIAN.)

    But Flavian brings some message to me here.
    (*To* FLAVIAN) Has Alba chosen her three combatants?
FLAVIAN.   I came to bear the news of this to thee.
CURIATIUS.   Well, then, what three are they to be?
FLAVIAN.   Thy two
    Brothers and thou.
CURIATIUS (*aghast*).   Who!
FLAVIAN.   Thou and thy two brothers.
    But why this face of gloom, this stony stare?
    Art thou displeased?
CURIATIUS.   No, but I am astonished.
    I deemed myself unworthy of an honor
    So great.
FLAVIAN.   Shall I report to the Dictator,
    Who sent me with this news here, that thou heardst it
    With such scant joy? This cold, dejected welcome
    Thou givest it, astounds me in my turn.
CURIATIUS.   Tell him that friendship, family ties, and love
    Cannot deter the three Curiatii
    From serving Alba 'gainst the three Horatii.
FLAVIAN.   Against *them*? Ah! these few words make all plain.
CURIATIUS.   Take him my answer. Leave us to ourselves.

                                    (*Exit* FLAVIAN.)

    Henceforth let heaven and hell and the whole world
    Unite their fury to make war upon us.
    Let all mankind, the gods, the fiends, and Fate
    Contrive against us a combined assault.
    To put us in worse plight than now we are,
    I challenge Fate, the fiends, the gods, and men.
    All that is cruel, ghastly, and terrible
    That they can do is truly far less dreadful
    Than is the honor given to us both.
HORATIUS.   Fate, opening the lists of glory to us,
    Offers a noble trial to our manhood.

It does its utmost to devise ill fortune
Which best will take the measure of our worth,
And, thinking us no ordinary folk,
It sets for us no ordinary test.

    To meet in mortal combat for one's country
An enemy and face some stranger's blows,
Is but an act of any man of courage.
Thousands have done it, thousands more could do it.
Death for one's country is a death so glorious,
So beautiful, that untold numbers seek it.
But to attempt to kill, for public weal,
A màn one loves, to fight one's other self,
To assail the cause of those that, to defend it,
Have chosen a warrior who is the brother
Of one's own wife and also is the lover
Of one's own sister—to break all these ties
And in one's country's service draw one's sword
To take a life that one would give his own
To save—such strength of will is ours alone.
Few will be jealous of this great distinction,
For in few hearts is honor prized enough
For them to dare aspire to such renown.

CURIATIUS. 'Tis true our names henceforth can never die.
A glorious chance is offered us; we must
Embrace it. We indeed shall be examples
Of a rare strength of will. But there is something
Barbarous in thy inflexible resolve.
Few of the noblest hearts would find a pride
In thus achieving immortality.
However much one values aught so vain,
Oblivion is better than such fame.

    For my part, I can say—and this thou knowest—
That I have ne'er thought twice in doing my duty.
Neither long friendship, love, nor family ties
Could make me vacillate a single instant;
And, since the choice of Alba shows that she
Values me quite as much as Rome does thee,
I shall serve her as well as thou shalt Rome.
Yet, though as high-souled, I am but a man.
I see that duty bids thee spill my lifeblood

And gives me one sole aim, to pierce thy breast,—
That, when about to wed thy sister, I
Must slay her brother, and that my destiny
Is thus cruel for my country's sake. Yet though
Unflinchingly at duty's call I go,
My heart recoils; I shudder with revulsion,
Deem my lot hard, and look with envious eye
On those who in our war ere this could die.
But none the less I would not shun my task.
This great and grievous honor paid to me
Moves me but does not shake my resolution.
I prize it, and I mourn for what it costs me.
If Rome requires a more exalted manhood,
I thank the gods that I am not a Roman
So as to keep some human feelings still!

HORATIUS.   If thou art not a Roman, be at least
Worthy to be one; and if thou art equal
To me, give better evidence that thou art.

  The stalwart manhood of which I have boasted
Permits no weakness in its sturdy fiber;
And ill the augury when one looks back
While taking the first step on honor's pathway.
Great our misfortune is—yea, past all measure.
I see the whole of it, yet I do not quail.
No matter against whom my country sends me,
With joy do I accept this honor blindly.
The glory of receiving such assignments
Should stifle in our breasts all other feelings.
He who when called to serve his native land
Thinks of aught else prepares himself but badly
To do his duty; and that sacred trust
Nullifies every claim except its own.
Rome hath made choice of me; I ask no questions.
With eagerness no less than that I felt
To wed thy sister, I shall face her brother.
And let me now cut short this useless talk:
Alba names thee, and I no longer know thee.

CURIATIUS.   I know thee still; that is what breaks my heart;
But such stern manhood is unknown to me.
Like our misfortunes, it is past all measure.

Let me admire it, but not imitate it.

HORATIUS.   Nay, nay, do not be noble 'gainst thy will;
And since thou findest more charms in lamentations,
Without restraint enjoy so sweet a pleasure.
Here comes my sister to make moan with thee.
I go to thine, that I may give her strength
To forget never that she is my wife,
To love thee still if by thy hand I fall,
And, come what may, to feel as Romans feel.

(Enter CAMILLA.*)*

Knowest thou what honor is done Curiatius,
Camilla?

CAMILLA.   Woe is me! my hope is gone.

HORATIUS.   Find fortitude and show thyself my sister;
And if I die and he returns triumphant,
Receive him not as one that slew thy brother
But as a man who bravely did his duty,
Who served his country well and proved to all
By his great deeds that he is worthy of thee.
As though I still were living, marry him.
But if, instead, my sword cuts short his life,
Accept my victory in the selfsame spirit;
Do not reproach me with thy lover's death.
    Thy tears, I see, must flow; thy heart is heavy.
Unpack it of all weakness, now, with him.
Blame heaven and earth, curse Fate, but when the combat
Is over, think no more about the dead.
    (To CURIATIUS*)* Only a moment I shall leave thee with her;
Then I shall go with thee where honor calls us.

(Exit HORATIUS.*)*

CAMILLA.   Wilt thou indeed go, Curiatius;
And does this fatal "honor" charm thy soul
At the expense of all our happiness?

CURIATIUS.   Alas, whate'er I do, I needs must die
Either of grief or by Horatius' hand.
I go to this proud task as though to misery.
I curse a thousand times the honor done me.
I hate the prowess for which Alba chose me.
In my despair, love makes me impious:
I call the gods to account; I dare to blame them.

I pity thee and me—yet go I must.

CAMILLA.   I know thee better. Thou wouldst have me plead
With thee, so that my power over thee
Should serve to excuse thee in thy country's sight.
Thou hast enough fame from thy former deeds.
All that thou owest to Alba they have paid her.
None in this war hath borne himself more nobly
Than thou; none with more dead hath strewn our land.
Thy name cannot grow greater; it lacks naught.
Let someone exalt his in turn.

CURIATIUS.   What! suffer
Before mine eyes the immortal laurels now
Awaiting me to deck another brow,
Or all my country to reproach me, saying
That, had I fought, it would have won the day,
And that my valor's drowsing, lapped in love,
Hath crowned my exploits with such infamy?
Nay, Alba, since thou so hast honored me,
It is through me thou shalt succumb or conquer.
Thou hast committed unto me thy fate,
And I will answer for it to thee and live
Without reproach or perish without shame.

CAMILLA.   Canst thou not see that thus thou wilt be false
To me?

CURIATIUS.   My duty first is to my country.

CAMILLA.   But, for its sake, to slay thy brother-in-law,
Thy sister's husband!

CURIATIUS.   Such is our dire plight:
The choice which Rome and Alba made destroys
All sweetness in ties formerly so sweet.

CAMILLA.   Then thou couldst bring to me his head, cruel man,
And as thy victory's guerdon claim my hand?

CURIATIUS.   These things must not be thought on any more.
To love thee without hope is all I now
Can do. Thou weepest, Camilla?

CAMILLA.   I must needs
Weep. My unfeeling lover bids me die,
And when the marriage torch is lighted for us,
He quenches it and sends me to my grave.
His ruthless soul is bent upon my death.

While saying that he loves me still, he kills me!
CURIATIUS.　How eloquent are a loving woman's tears,
　　And with their help what power is in her glance!
　　How my heart melts at this sad sight! Against her
　　It strives unwillingly to preserve its firmness.
　　　Try not my honor further with such grief,
　　And let me save my manhood from thy sobs.
　　I feel it waver and ill defend itself.
　　The more I am thy lover, I the less
　　Am Curiatius. When I am already
　　Weak from resisting friendship, how can I
　　Conquer at the same time both love and pity?
　　Go, go! love me no more and weep no more,
　　Or I shall strike back to defend myself
　　Against such potent weapons. I could better
　　Endure thine anger, and, to merit this,
　　I tell thee now that I no longer love thee.
　　Avenge thyself. Punish my faithlessness. . . .
　　Thou art not hurt on being outraged thus?
　　I love thee not, and thou still lovest me!
　　Is it not enough? . . . I break off our betrothal.
　　　Can I, the victim of a cruel duty,
　　Nowise resist without the aid of crime?
CAMILLA.　Commit none other, and I swear to heaven
　　I shall not hate thee but will love thee more—
　　Yes, cherish thee whate'er thy faithlessness,
　　If thou wilt cease to aspire to fratricide.
　　Why am I Roman? or why art thou not Roman?
　　Then with mine own hand I would wreathe thy laurels;
　　I would encourage thee, and not dissuade thee
　　But treat thee as I oft have done my brother.
　　Alas! my prayers today were made in blindness:
　　They were against thee when they were for him!
　　　He comes back. Ah, what woe if his wife's love
　　Hath no more power o'er him than mine o'er thee!
　　　　　　　　　(*Enter* HORATIUS *and* SABINA.)
CURIATIUS.　Sabina comes with him. To shake my heart,
　　Gods, doth Camilla not suffice?
　　　　　　　(*To* HORATIUS) To her
　　Must thou needs add my sister? Didst thou grant

The conquest of thy great soul to her tears
And bring her here to triumph o'er me also?

SABINA.   Nay, nay, my brother, nay! I come here now
Only to clasp thee and to say farewell.
Too noble is thy blood. Fear nothing base
From it in me—nothing to shame the firmness
Of lofty natures. If this unmatched mischance
Shook either of you, I would disavow him,
Whether it were my brother or my husband.
Might I, however, make one prayer, most meet,
To such a husband and to such a brother?
I wish to rid your honorable strife
Of impiousness, to render the distinction
Attending it devoid of sin or stain,
To leave its glory unbedimmed by horror—
I wish, in short, to make you lawful foes.

I am the bond between you—I alone.
When I shall be no more, ye will have none.
End your connection; break the link that forms it;
And since your duty requires deeds of hatred,
Buy with my blood the right to hate each other.
'Tis Alba's will, and Rome's; ye must obey them.
One of you kill me; one of you avenge me.
Then there will be naught strange about your combat,
And one, at least, will justly press the fight
In vengeance for his sister or his wife.

But no! ye would impair your glorious fame
If any cause like this inspired you partly.
Your patriotism forbids all other motives.
'Twould be less noble if your ties were less.
It claims the slaying of a brother-in-law
Done without wrath. Defer no longer, then,
What ye should do.

     (*To* CURIATIUS) Begin by shedding first
A sister's blood.

     (*To* HORATIUS) Begin by stabbing first
A wife's breast.

      (*To both*) Both of you begin forthwith,
By sacrificing me, to make a worthy
Sacrifice of your lives for your dear cities.
In this great combat we all three are foes—

Thou of Rome, thou of Alba, I of both.
Shall I be left to see a victory
In whose proud pageantry I must behold
The laurels of a brother or a husband
Reeking with blood I have so dearly cherished?
Could I between you thus divide my heart,
Discharge the duties of both wife and sister,
Embrace the slayer while I mourn the slain?
No; ere that time I shall have ceased to live.
I shall be dead, no matter by whose hand.
Refuse me yours, ye force me to use mine.
Come! what restrains you? Come, cruel men; I have
Too many means by which to make you kill me.
Upon the field of combat ye shall find
This body, interposed, will stay your swords;
And though ye will not pierce me with them now,
Ye then must pierce my breast to pierce each other.

HORATIUS.   O my wife!

CURIATIUS.   O my sister!

CAMILLA.   Courage, Sabina!
Their hearts are touched.

SABINA.   Ye sigh. Your cheeks turn pale.
What fear hath seized you? Are these those lofty beings,
Those heroes Rome and Alba chose for champions?

HORATIUS.   What have I done to thee, Sabina—how
Have I offended—that thou must seek such vengeance?
When I but do as duty bids, do I
Wrong thee? And by what right dost thou come here
To try with all thy power to daunt my manhood?
Be satisfied with having shaken it,
And let me now finish this great day's work.
Thou hast unnerved me strangely. Love thy husband
Enough, dear wife, to push thy triumph no further.
Go; do not make my victory uncertain.
This controversy hath already shamed me.
Let me, I pray, with honor end my days.

SABINA.   Fear me no more. Succor for you has come.

Enter OLD HORATIUS.

OLD HORATIUS.   What are ye doing here, my children—hearkening

To love and wasting time with women still?
Soon to shed blood, do ye now heed their tears?
Fly hence, and leave them to bewail their woe.
Their plaints are too affectionate and artful;
They presently would make you share their frailty.
Only by flight can one avoid such influence.

SABINA.   Fear naught for them; they are well worthy of thee.
Thou shouldst expect them, despite all our efforts,
To be the son and son-in-law thou'dst have them;
And if our weakness hath impaired their honor,
We leave thee here to give their hearts new strength.
  Come, come, my sister; shed no more vain tears.
They are poor weapons against men so valiant.
In nothing but despair can we find aid.
Go, tigers, fight! And we—let us go die.

(Exeunt SABINA *and* CAMILLA.)

HORATIUS.   Father, restrain these women; they are frantic;
And above all, I beg thee, do not let them
Go forth. Their love would bring them, with great noise
Of cries and tears, to hinder our encounter;
And what they are to us would make it natural
That folk should think their coming thus a vile
Artifice we contrived. The honor done us
When we were chosen would be too dearly bought,
Were we suspected of a thing so base.

OLD HORATIUS.   I will see to it. Go. Thy brothers wait.
Think only of thy duty to thy country.

CURIATIUS (*to* OLD HORATIUS).   What can I say to thee in parting?
    How
Express . . .

OLD HORATIUS.   Ah, do not stir my feelings now!
To hearten thee, my tongue can find no words.
I do not have clear thoughts. In this farewell
Mine eyes are full of tears too ill suppressed.
Go. Do thy duty. Leave to heaven the rest.

(Exeunt HORATIUS *and* CURIATIUS.)

ACT III

Sabina is discovered, alone.

SABINA. Take sides, my soul, in this dire pass, and be
Horatius' wife or Curiatius' sister.
Cease to divide thy futile apprehensions.
Have some real wish, and not so many fears.
But oh, which side to choose in such a strife!
Which deem my foe, a husband or a brother?
Love pleads for one, blood ties plead for the other,
And obligations bind me to them both.
Then let us, rather, do like them our duty;
Be one's wife and the other's sister, too;
Regard their honor as our chief concern;
Copy their firmness and henceforth fear nothing.
The death which threatens them is a death so noble
That without dread we should await its tidings.
Let us not, then, call Fate a barbarous tyrant.
Think in what cause, not by whose hands, they die;
Behold the victors without being mindful
Of aught except the glory which their victory
Bestows upon their house, and, not considering
At the expense of whose dear blood their valor
Exalts them, make the interests of their family
Our interests. In one home I am a wife,
A daughter in the other, and I am linked
By such strong bonds to both that neither of them
Can triumph now save by the might of those
Whom I can claim as mine. Whatever sorrows,
Fortune, thy cruelty can bring to me,
I can find joys in them, and hence can view
Today the combat without fear, the dead
Without despair, the slayers without horror.

   Flattering delusion, error sweet and gross,
Vain effort of my soul, hope's feeble ray
Whose false gleam fain would dazzle me, how briefly
Thou canst endure, how soon thou vanishest!
E'en like a flash of lightning—which can bring
Day to the blackest shadows, and then is gone,

Leaving the night more somber than before—
Thou smotest upon mine eyes for but an instant,
Only to plunge me into deeper darkness.
Too much didst thou allay mine agony,
And heaven, offended thus, already makes
That moment's respite cost me heavily.
I feel my sad heart pierced by all the blows
Which rob me of a brother or a husband,
And thinking of their death, which I envision,
I think not in what cause but by whose hand
They die, and when I shall behold the victors
Exalted presently, I shall consider
Only at the expense of whose dear blood.
The family alone of those who fall
Can move me. In one home I am a wife,
A daughter in the other, and I am linked
By such strong bonds to both of them that neither
Can triumph now save by the death of those
Whom I must claim as mine. So this is, then,
That tranquil heart which I so much desired!
Too gracious gods, how have ye hearkened to me!
What thunderbolts would ye in anger hurl,
If even your favors show such cruelty;
And in what way would ye requite wrongdoing,
If thus ye treat the prayers of innocence?

(*Enter* JULIA.)

  Is it over, Julia? What news dost thou bring me?
News of my brothers' or my husband's death?
Has the grim outcome of their impious fray
Made victims of all six of those that fought;
And, grudging me my loathing of the conquerors,
Hath heaven required my tears for all alike?

JULIA. What! thou still knowest not that which hath occurred?
SABINA. Art thou indeed surprised that I know nothing?
Art thou then ignorant, Julia, that this house
Was made a prison for me and for Camilla?
We are confined here, for our tears are dreaded,
Or else we would have rushed between their weapons
And, with the desperation of true love,
Have roused at least some pity in both armies.

JULIA. There was no need for that pathetic sight.
 The sight of them was obstacle enough.
   As soon as they stood forth, ready to fight,
 A murmur, plainly heard, ran through both hosts.
 On seeing such friends, men with such close ties, come
 To meet in mortal fury, each for his country,
 Some pitied them, and some were seized with horror,
 Some wondered at so fierce a patriotism,
 Some praised their matchless ardor to the skies,
 Some dared to call it brutal and unhallowed;
 But with these different feelings all united
 To blame their leaders and denounce such choices.
 They will not let these champions meet in combat.
 They cry out, they push forward and separate them.

SABINA. Great gods, who heard my prayers, what thanks I owe you!

JULIA. It is not yet, Sabina, as thou thinkest.
 Hope thou canst cherish; thou hast less to fear;
 But there is still enough cause for thy woe.
   These cruel heroes let none take their places.
 'Tis vainly sought to save them from their doom.
 The glory of being chosen is so precious
 To them and charms so much their lofty souls
 That when their fate is mourned, they deem themselves
 Blest and the pity felt for them an insult.
 The soldiers' protest blocks their path to fame.
 They would fight Rome's and Alba's hosts combined
 And perish by the hands that would restrain them
 Before they would renounce the honor paid them.

SABINA. What! did these hearts of steel remain unsoftened?

JULIA. Yes, but both armies rose in mutiny
 And, loudly clamoring, with one common voice
 Demanded battle now, or other champions.
 Not much respect was shown for the commanders;
 Their power was doubtful, their voice little heeded.
 The King himself stood dazed. He finally said:
 "Since our dissension hath too much enflamed us,
 Let us consult the high gods' sacred will
 And learn if this change doth accord therewith.
 What impious man would dare oppose their wishes
 When in a sacrifice they have revealed them?"

He ceased; and these few words seemed magical.
Even the six combatants laid down their arms,
And notwithstanding their blind eagerness
For glory, which had made them shut their eyes
To all things else, they reverenced the gods.
Their ardor yielded to the advice of Tullus;
And whether from regard for him or sudden
Scruples, both armies let it be their law
As though they both acknowledged him their king.
The victims' bodies will disclose the rest.

SABINA. The gods will never sanction such a wicked
Combat. My hopes are great, when 'tis deferred;
And I begin to see my prayers answered.

(*Enter* CAMILLA.)

(*To* CAMILLA) Oh, sister, let me tell thee some good news!

CAMILLA. I think I know it, if so it must be called.
'Twas told my father, and I then was with him;
But I see nothing in it to assuage
My woe. Postponement of misfortunes makes them
The harder to be borne and merely lengthens
The time anxiety can torture us.
The only good that we may look for from it
Is to mourn later those whom we must mourn.

SABINA. Not vainly have the gods inspired this outbreak.

CAMILLA. Say rather, sister, that one consults them vainly.
These same gods inspired Tullus in his choice.
The people's voice is not always their voice;
They prompt those of such low estate less often
Than they do kings, their earthly images,
Whose absolute and divine authority
Is guided by an inner light from heaven.

JULIA. To seek their voice beyond their oracles
Is to wish stubbornly to find something adverse;
And to believe thou shalt lose all, thou must
Declare untrue the words thou lately heardest.

CAMILLA. An oracle always conceals its meaning,
Which is least clear whenever it seems clearest;
And far from being assured by what it says,
He who finds naught obscure therein should deem
That it is wholly dark.

SABINA.   Let us accept
    More trustingly the boon accorded us
    And dare to cherish reasonable hopes.
    When heaven half-extends a kindly hand,
    One who expects no favor, deserves none.
    He often will prevent its being bestowed
    On him; or if it is, by his rejection
    Of it he causes it to be withdrawn.

CAMILLA. Heaven in such matters acts regardless of us
    And is not influenced by our thoughts or feelings.

JULIA. It roused thy fears but to be gracious to thee.
    Farewell. I go to learn what now is happening.
    Be less afraid. I hope that I can talk
    Wholly of love with thee, on my return,
    And that we shall employ this day's last hours
    In preparations for thy happy marriage.

SABINA. I still dare hope it.

CAMILLA.   *I* have no hope of aught.

JULIA. The end will prove to thee that we were right.   (*Exit* JULIA.)

SABINA (*to* CAMILLA). Even amid our sorrows let me chide thee.
    I must blame such confoundment of thy soul.
    What wouldst thou do, dear sister, in my place,
    Hadst thou as much to fear as I must fear
    And couldst expect from those death-dealing swords
    Such woes and losses as I must expect?

CAMILLA. Speak with more insight of thy woes and mine!
    Each sees her own not as she sees the other's.
    Yet weigh them both aright, and thine will seem,
    Compared with mine, the figment of a dream.
      Thou hast Horatius' death alone to dread.
    Beside a husband, brothers are as nothing.
    Marriage, when it creates the tie that binds us
    To another family, dissolves the tie
    That bound us to the family of our childhood.
    One values differently such different bonds.
    She leaves her first home for her husband's sake.
      But if, before they wed, he whom she loves,
    And whom her father gave her in betrothal,
    Is less dear to her than a husband would be
    But not less dear to her than brothers are,

Her feelings must be fluctuant between them,
Her prayers confused, her choice impossible.

Thus in thy woe thou hast at least, my sister,
Something to pray for, something not to fear;
But I, if heaven will not abate its ire,
Have everything to fear, naught to desire.

SABINA.　When one of two we love must kill the other,
This reasoning of thine is bad indeed.

Although the ties, sister, are very different,
Those of the home we left are not forgotten.
Marriage cannot efface our first dear memories.
To love one's husband breeds no hate of brothers.
Their bond with us keeps always the same strength.
One wishes nothing that must cost their lives.
They, like our husbands, are our other selves,
And all griefs are alike when very great.
But the mere lover who hath charmed thy heart,
And whom thou yearnest for, is unto thee,
After all, only what thou makest him.
Ill humor or a little jealousy
Oft drives a lover's image from one's fancy.
Let reason do that which caprice can do,
And with thy flesh and blood compare none else.
'Tis wrong to hold of equal sacredness
Ties voluntarily assumed and those
Which birth itself perforce hath fashioned for us.
I, then, if heaven will not abate its ire,
Have everything to fear, naught to desire;
But as for thee, amidst thy lamentations
Thy duty points out unto thee a goal
For thy desires—which gained, thy fears must end.

CAMILLA.　It is plain, sister, thou hast never loved.
Thou knowest naught of love nor of its ways.
We can resist it when it first is born,
But cannot banish it when grown our master
And when a father's sanction seals our troth
And ratifies its empire in our heart.
It comes in gentleness but reigns in might,
And souls that once have tasted of its sweetness
Have not the power to wish to love no more,

For they can then wish only what love wishes;
Its chains are no less strong than they are dear.

Enter OLD HORATIUS.

OLD HORATIUS.   I come to bring you grievous news, my daughters;
But I would not attempt to hide from you
What could not long be hidden. Even now
Your brothers fight; the gods have willed it so.

SABINA.   I must avow, this news amazeth me,
For I imagined in divinity
Much less injustice and much greater kindness.
Attempt not to console us. In misfortune
Like this, the voice of pity speaks in vain
And that of reason is importunate.
It lies in our own hands to end our sorrows.
Those who can dare to die can scorn all woe.
While in thy presence, we could easily
Make our despair seem to be self-control;
But when we can be weak without disgrace,
To feign a strength we do not have is base.
We leave to men such usage, nor in aught
Would we appear to be what we are not.
   We nowise ask that thou, who art so great
Of heart, should stoop like us to rail at Fate.
Without a quaver, see our mortal fears;
Behold our tears and shed, thyself, no tears.
We ask but this amid our miseries:
Maintain thy firmness, but permit our sighs.

OLD HORATIUS.   So far am I from censuring your tears
That all my firmness scarce can hold back mine;
And I might yield to such cruel blows of Fate,
Had I as much at stake as ye have now.
Not that the choice of Alba makes me hate
Thy brothers. They are all still dear to me.
But friendship is quite different, in its nature
And its intensity, from love and blood-ties.
I do not feel the anguish that assails
Sabina as their sister or Camilla
For one of them, whom she so dearly loves.
I can regard them as our foes, and give

137

My undivided hopes to mine own sons.
   Thank the gods, they are worthy of our country!
No fear hath sullied their bright fame, and I
Have seen their glory become twice as great
When they refused the pity of both armies.
Had they been weak enough to sue for it,—
Had they not valiantly rejected it,—
I resolutely would have taken vengeance
Upon them for the shame incurred by me
Through their faintheartedness. But when, in spite
Of them, others were sought to take their places—
I shall not hide it—I joined my prayers to yours.
Had heaven been merciful and heard my voice,
Alba would needs have made a second choice;
We could ere long have seen the Horatii triumph
With hands unstained by Curiatian blood,
And on the outcome of a more humane
Combat the honor of the name of Rome
Would have depended now. The gods on high
Have in their wisdom decreed otherwise.
My soul doth bow to their eternal will.
It fortifies itself with generous thoughts
And finds its happiness in the public weal.
   Seek ye like solace for your woe, and do not
Fail to remember ye are Roman women.
Thou *(to* SABINA*)* hast become one; and thou *(to* CAMILLA*)*
    still art one.
That proud distinction is a precious treasure.
The day will come, will come, when everywhere
Rome will be feared no less than heaven's bolt;
And, when the whole earth trembles 'neath her sway,
Kings will aspire to the great name of "Roman."
To our Aeneas the gods promised this.

                   (Enter JULIA.*)*

   Bringest thou, Julia, news of victory?
JULIA.   Not so, but of the combat's dire result.
   Rome is 'neath Alba's yoke. Thy sons are vanquished.
   Two have been slain. Only her husband lives.
OLD HORATIUS.   O truly dire result of a dire combat!
   Rome is 'neath Alba's yoke, and to preserve her

From it he did not fight to his last gasp?
No, no, that cannot be. Thou errest, Julia.
Rome is beneath no yoke, or he is dead.
I know my son, he knows his duty, better.

JULIA. Thousands, like me, beheld it from our ramparts.
He won the applause of all until his brothers
Had fallen; but when he saw he was alone
Against three adversaries and about
To be surrounded, his flight saved his life.

OLD HORATIUS. And did our men, whose trust he thus betrayed,
Not kill him? Did they open then, instead,
Their ranks and give asylum to the dastard?

JULIA. I had no wish to see aught, after this.

CAMILLA. Ah me! my brothers!

OLD HORATIUS. Nay, weep not for them all.
Two met a fate their father envies them.
Let fairest flowers be strewn upon their grave.
The glory of their death consoles me for them.
This blessing their unconquered hearts have won:
That while they lived they ever saw Rome free,—
Saw her obey no man except her king
Nor be the province of a neighboring State.
Weep for that third one; weep for the disgrace
His cowardice hath brought on all our race,—
Branding our brows,—which nothing can efface,
The eternal shame of the Horatii.

JULIA. What wouldst thou have him do 'gainst three men?

OLD HORATIUS. Die;
Or in the courage of despair find aid.
Had his defeat one moment been delayed,
Rome that much later would have been enslaved,
He would have left my grey hairs crowned with honor,
And life was not too much for him to pay
For this! He owed his country all his blood.
Each drop that he withheld stains his fair fame.
Each moment of his life, after such baseness,
Displays so much the more my shame and his.
I will cut short that life and in just wrath,
Using a father's rights against the miscreant,

Will by his punishment proclaim to all
My disavowal of his infamy.

SABINA.　Hearken less to thy noble indignation
And do not make our misery complete.

OLD HORATIUS.　Easily is thy heart consoled, Sabina.
　Thus far, our evil fate hath touched thee lightly.
　Thou hast not yet a share in our misfortunes.
　Heaven hath spared thy husband and thy brothers.
　If we are vassals, it is to thy Alba.
　We are betrayed; the Curiatii conquer;
　And seeing the heights their glory hath attained,
　Thou reckest not of our humiliation.
　But since thou lovest so dearly thy vile husband,
　Thou soon shalt have, like us, good cause to mourn.
　Naught will thy tears avail in his defense.
　I swear before the almighty gods that, ere
　This day is over, my hands—yes, my own hands—
　Shall wash out, with his blood, the shame of Rome.

(Exit OLD HORATIUS.*)*

SABINA.　Quick! let us follow him; he is mad with rage.
　Gods! shall we know naught but calamities?
　Must we needs always dread the worst, and fear
　Always those nearest to us and most dear?

(Exeunt SABINA, CAMILLA, *and* JULIA.*)*

ACT　IV

OLD HORATIUS *and* CAMILLA *are discovered*

OLD HORATIUS.　Plead not with me for such a caitiff! Let him
　Flee from me as he fled from his wife's brothers.
　Unless he shuns the sight of me, he yet
　Shall fail to save the blood he deemed so precious.
　Let his Sabina look to it, or else,
　By the almighty gods again I swear . . .

CAMILLA.　Ah, father, be more lenient! Thou wilt see
　Rome herself treat him very differently.
　And, howsoe'er brought low by heaven's will,
　Excuse his brave heart's being dismayed by numbers.

OLD HORATIUS.　Little I care whether Rome pardons him,
　Camilla, or condemns him. As a father,

I have my own prerogatives. I know
Too well how one with genuine courage acts.
Numbers o'erwhelm him but dismay him not.
His manly powers succumb to greater might;
But, always brave, he ne'er gives up the fight.
    Be silent. Let us learn Valerius' mission.

Enter VALERIUS.

VALERIUS.   Sent by the King to offer to a father
    Condolence and express to him . . .
OLD HORATIUS.   Nay, spare
    Thy pains. I do not need such consolation.
    Those whom a foe's hand hath just taken from me
    Are better dead than covered with disgrace.
    Both for their country fell like men of honor.
    I am content.
VALERIUS.   The third, though, is thy joy.
    He now should fill the place of all, for thee.
OLD HORATIUS.   Would the Horatian name had perished with him!
VALERIUS.   Thou alone censurest him for what he did.
OLD HORATIUS.   'Tis mine alone to punish his base deed.
VALERIUS.   What baseness seest thou in his heroism?
OLD HORATIUS.   What heroism seest thou in his flight?
VALERIUS.   Flight was glorious on this occasion.
OLD HORATIUS.   Thou doublest my confusion and my shame.
    Truly, 'tis strange and worth remembering
    For one to find in flight a path to glory!
VALERIUS.   What shame or what confusion can be thine
    In having bred a son who saved us all,—
    Who made Rome triumph and gained an empire for her?
    What greater honors can a father crave?
OLD HORATIUS.   What honors, triumph, empire can Rome have
    When Alba hath imposed her sway on us?
VALERIUS.   Of Alba and her sway why talkest thou thus?
    Dost thou still know but half of what befell?
OLD HORATIUS.   I know he by his flight betrayed Rome's cause.
VALERIUS.   He would have, if when fleeing he had brought
    The combat to an end; but he soon showed
    That he had fled only because he saw
    This was the way to win the day for Rome.

OLD HORATIUS. What! Rome, then, is victorious?

VALERIUS.   Learn, oh, learn

> The great worth of that son thou wrongly blamest.
> When he was left, alone against three foes,
> All of them wounded and himself alone
> Without a wound, not strong enough to o'ercome
> All three, too strong for any one of them,
> He saw how he might extricate himself
> From this predicament. He fled to fight
> Better, and by that ruse he cleverly
> Deceived and separated those three brothers.
> With equal eagerness they all pursued him
> At the best speed they now could run, which differed
> As the severity of the wounds of each
> Was different; and this fact strung out the chase.
>   Horatius, when he saw them far apart,
> Turned and already reckoned them half-vanquished.
> He waited for the first one—thy intended
> Son-in-law—and this adversary, outraged
> That he dared do so, manfully closed with him
> But vainly, being weak from loss of blood.
> The Albans in their turn began to fear
> Defeat. They shouted to their second champion
> To come and help the first. He tried to run
> Faster, tired himself out to no avail,
> And reached them but to find his brother dead.

CAMILLA. Woe's me!

VALERIUS.   Gasping for breath, he took his place

> And gave Horatius soon another victory.
> His courage without strength could aid him not,
> And by the side of him he would avenge
> He himself fell. The air resounded now
> With cries which both the armies raised to heaven—
> Alba's of agony and Rome's of joy.
>   When our brave hero saw his triumph near,
> Success was not enough; he boasted loudly:
> "Two have I slain as offerings to my brothers;
> To Rome I give this last antagonist.
> It is to her that I shall sacrifice him."
>   He spoke, and rushed upon him instantly.

The issue of their combat was not doubtful.
The Alban, pierced with wounds, scarce dragged himself
Onward, and like a victim at the altar
Seemed to present his throat to the mortal blow,
And thus, almost without defense, received it.
His death established Rome's supremacy.

OLD HORATIUS.   O my son! my life's joy! pride of our days!
Unhoped-for savior of a tottering realm!
True seed of Rome! true offspring of our house!
Our country's bulwark and the Horatii's glory!
When can I smother in my arms' embrace
The wrong I did thee through my grievous error?
And when can I bathe thy victorious brow
With tears of happiness and tenderest love?

VALERIUS.   Thou soon canst give free scope to thy affection.
The King will very shortly send him to thee.
We till the morrow leave the solemn rites
Of offerings to the gods for our good fortune.
Today we shall discharge our debt to heaven
By songs of victory and by vows alone.
In these the King employs him now, and meanwhile
Sends me to express to thee his grief and joy.
Yet words of mine seem insufficient to him;
He will himself come here, perhaps today.
He deems such valor too little signalized
Unless his own lips speak of it to thee
In thine own house, and of how much Rome owes thee.

OLD HORATIUS.   Thanks from his lips would honor me too greatly.
I hold myself amply repaid by thine
For one son's service and the two others' deaths.

VALERIUS.   He knows not how to honor one by halves.
The rescue of his scepter from the foe
Makes the distinction which he would accord thee
Less than the father's or the son's deserts.
I go to tell him what nobility
Thy lofty soul displays in all thy feelings
And how great ardor in his cause thou showest.

OLD HORATIUS.   I am much indebted to thee for thy kindness.

(*Exit* VALERIUS.)

My daughter, this is now no time for tears.

'Tis ill to shed them when we have such honor.
One should not weep for personal misfortunes
When victory for the State is their result.
Rome triumphs over Alba. That should be
Enough for us; and we should gladly purchase
With all of our bereavements such an outcome.
Thou losest but one man by thy lover's death,
Whose loss can easily be repaired in Rome.
After this victory there is no Roman—
None—who would not be proud to wed with thee.
    But I must tell the news, now, to Sabina.
'Twill be indeed a cruel blow to her.
Three brothers dead, slain by her husband's sword,
Will give her better cause for tears than *thou* hast;
But I believe that it will not be hard
To dry them, and that with a little counsel
I soon can make the loyal love she owes
Her husband reign in her devoted bosom.
Do thou, meanwhile, suppress thy shameful grief,
And when he comes, receive him worthily.
Show him thou art his sister, formed by heaven
In the same womb and of the selfsame blood.

                               (*Exit* OLD HORATIUS.)

CAMILLA (*alone*). Yes, I will show him unmistakably
That a true love defies the Fates' decrees
And will not be submissive to those tyrants
Whom inauspicious stars give us for parents!
    Thou blamest my grief; thou darest to call it shameful.
I nurse it all the more as it offends thee,
Merciless father, and I justly wish it
To be as great as my misfortunes are.
    When was there ever any mortal's lot
Which took so many turns so suddenly,—
Which was so often sweet, so often bitter,
And bore such buffets ere the final death-blow?
Was ever heart in one day so assailed
By joy and sorrow, hope and fear, the slave
Of more occurrences, the wretched plaything
Of more vicissitudes? An oracle
First reassures me; then a dream affrights me.

Peace calms the terror which the battle caused me;
My marriage is prepared for; and the next
Moment the man I love is chosen to fight
Against my brothers. This selection fills me
With black despair; then all refuse to accept it.
The project is abandoned, but the gods
Revive it. Rome seems vanquished, and alone
Of the three Albans Curiatius
Hath still not dyed his hands in blood of mine.
Ah heaven! did I feel too little sorrow
For Rome's defeat and for two brothers' deaths?
Was I o'er-sanguine when I dreamed I yet
Might love him without sin, might cherish some hope?
I am but too well punished by his fate
And by the cruel way in which the tidings
Of it were borne to my distracted heart.
His rival told me of it and recounted
Its piteous details before my face.
He openly displays his exultation
Less at the State's good fortune than my woe,
And builds air-castles on another's death.
He no less than my brother triumphs o'er him.
    But all these things are nothing to compare
With that which follows, now. I am commanded
To take delight in this accursed day,—
To applaud the exploits of the conqueror
And kiss the hand that stabs me to the heart!
With such a great and proper cause for tears,
To mourn is shameful and to sigh is wicked!
Their barbarous virtue would have everyone
Consider oneself happy; and if one
Is not devoid of feeling, one is base!
    Well, let me, then, be the degenerate daughter
Of such a high-souled father. Let me be
The ignoble sister of my noble brother.
'Tis glorious to be deemed contemptible
When inhumanity is accounted virtue.
Burst forth, my grief! why shouldst thou be restrained?
When all is lost, what more is there to fear?
Let us have no respect for this cruel hero.

Let us not shun him; let us cross his path,
Denounce his victory, excite his wrath,
And seek some pleasure in offending him.
He comes now. Let us try to make him know
At every moment how a woman should
Behave towards him that slew the man she loved.
(*Enter* HORATIUS *and* PROCULUS. PROCULUS *carries the
swords of the three Curiatii.*)

HORATIUS.   Sister, behold the arm that hath avenged
Our brothers' deaths, the arm that hath reversed
The course of hostile fate, that hath subjected
Alba to us; behold, in short, the arm
Which hath alone decided on this day
The fortunes of two cities. Look on these spoils,
These tokens of my glorious deeds; accord
The honor which thou owest my victory.

CAMILLA.   Take, then, my tears. They are its due from me.

HORATIUS.   After such exploits, Rome would fain not see them;
And our two brothers, fallen by the chances
Of war, too well are paid for now with blood
To require tears. When vengeance hath been taken
For any loss, it is a loss no longer.

CAMILLA.   Since the blood spilled hath made atonement for them,
I shall henceforth display for them no grief,
And shall forget their death, which thou avengedst.
But who is to avenge me for the death
Of him I love, or make me in one instant
Forget his loss?

HORATIUS.   What sayest thou, wretched girl?

CAMILLA.   O Curiatius, my beloved!

HORATIUS.   O monstrous
Effrontery of a most unworthy sister!
I come home, victor o'er my country's foe,
And find his name upon thy lips, his love
Within thy breast—a love that craves revenge!
Thy tongue demands it and thy soul longs for it.
Hearken to thy passion less, rule thy heart better,
And make me blush no more to hear thy sighs.
Henceforward extirpate this wicked passion;
Banish it from thy bosom, and instead

Think only of the honors I have won.
Do thou hereafter speak of them alone.

CAMILLA.   Then give me, barbarous man, a heart like thine.
Or wilt thou have me reveal mine to thee?
Give back my Curiatius unto me
Or leave me free to show how I adored him.
My joy or grief depended on his fortunes.
I loved him living, and I mourn him dead.
    Think not to find the sister whom thou knewest.
I am a woman robbed of her heart's love,
Who like a fury now will hound thy steps
And ceaselessly reproach thee for his death.
    Bloodthirsty tiger, who forbiddest my tears,
Who wishest me to take pleasure in his fate,
To extol thy deeds to heaven's utmost height,
And myself slay him thus a second time!
May such great miseries attend thy life
That thou wilt finally come to envy me,
And mayest thou sully by some infamy
That glory which thy savage heart holds dear!

HORATIUS.   O gods! Hath anyone e'er seen such frenzy?
Thinkest thou that I reck naught of grossest insults,—
That I will tolerate such foul dishonor
In those of mine own blood? Rejoice, rejoice
In this death, necessary for our welfare;
And to the memory of one man prefer
The good of Rome. Thy duty is to her.

CAMILLA.   Rome, which I hate, the source of all my pain!
Rome, for whose sake thou hast my lover slain!
Rome, which thou worshippest, which gave thee birth!
Rome, which I loathe for holding great thy worth!
May all her neighbor States, to undermine
Her power ere stronger, in one league combine;
And if all Italy is not enough,
Let East and West take arms against her, both—
A hundred peoples, from earth's farthest plains,
Cross, to destroy her, seas and mountain chains!
May civil strife devour her, overthrow
Her walls, and lay her open to the foe!
May heaven's wrath, kindled by my prayers, send down
A rain of fire on that accursed town!

May I with mine own eyes see the storm fall,
Her homes aflame, thy laurels dust, withal—
See the last Roman heave his final sigh!
Let *me* cause this, and I with joy shall die.

HORATIUS (*drawing his sword and rushing out in pursuit of her as she
         flees from him*).
    I have heard too much. My patience rightly ends.
    Go, and in Hades mourn thy Curiatius.

CAMILLA (*within*). Ah, dastard!

HORATIUS (*re-entering*).   Thus whoever dares lament
    An enemy of Rome should find swift payment.

PROCULUS. What hast thou done?

HORATIUS.   Only an act of justice
    Such guilt deserves no other penalty.

PROCULUS. Thou shouldst have treated her more mercifully.

HORATIUS. Tell me not that she was of mine own blood,—
    Was mine own sister. Thinkest thou that my father
    Could call her now his daughter? She who curses
    Her native land forfeits all family ties;
    Such loving names no longer can be hers.
    Those nearest akin to her become her foes.
    Their common lineage makes them hate her vileness
    The more. The speediest vengeance is the best;
    For such impiety, while powerless,
    Should like some monster be destroyed at birth.

                                            (*Enter* SABINA.)

SABINA. Why does thy noble rage stop here? Come, see
    Thy sister dying in her father's arms.
    Yes, feast thine eyes upon so sweet a sight,
    Or, if thy hand hath not grown weary yet
    With these heroic deeds, now offer up
    To the dear country of the brave Horatii
    This last unhappy remnant of the blood
    Of the Curiatii. So prodigal
    Of thine, do not spare ours. Add to Camilla
    Sabina; to thy sister add thy wife.
    Our guilt was equal, even as our woe.
    I grieve like her, and sorrow for my brothers,
    Offending more 'gainst thy stern code than she,
    Because she mourned but one, while I mourned three,

And mourn them still after her punishment.

HORATIUS. Sabina, dry thy tears, or hide them from me.
Be worthy of the name of my true wife.
Seek not to rouse in me unworthy pity
Wrongly. If our pure love's resistless power
Must make us be as one in thought and soul,
It is for thee to lift thyself to *my* plane,
And not for me to sink instead to thine.
I love thee, and I know the grief that racks thee.
Draw on my strength to overcome thy weakness.
Share in my glory; do not stain it. Try
To make it thine, rather than strip me of it.
Art thou so fierce a foe to my fair fame
That thou preferrest to see me sunk in shame?
Be less a sister than a wife, and model
Thy conduct upon mine, taking me always
For thy example.

SABINA.   Find more perfect people
To imitate thee. Not at all do I
Blame thee for the bereavements I have suffered.
I feel about them as I ought to feel,
And blame Fate for them, rather than thy duty.
But I will have none of your Roman virtue
If to possess it I must be inhuman,
Nor in myself can see the victor's wife
Only, and not the sister of the vanquished.
   Let us participate in the public triumph
In public. In our own home let us mourn
Our private woes and think not of the blessings
Common to all, but heed alone the heartache
Belonging to ourselves. Why wishest thou,
Cruel man, to act not in this manner? Leave,
On entering here, thy laurels at the door.
Mingle thy tears with mine. What! such base words
Arm not thy manhood 'gainst my wretched life?
My aggravated crime stirs not thy wrath?
Happy Camilla! she could anger thee.
She hath received from thee what she desired
And found among the shades him whom she lost.
   Dear husband, dear cause of mine agony,

Hearken to pity if thy rage hath cooled.
Show toward me, in my pain, one or the other.
Chastise my frailty or end my sorrows.
I beg for death, in punishment or kindness,
Dealt me from love or from a sense of justice,
No matter which; its sufferings all will seem
Sweet to me, coming from a husband's hand.

HORATIUS.   Oh, how unjustly heaven suffers women
To wield such power o'er the noblest hearts,
And finds delight in seeing even these
So 'neath the conquering sway of such weak beings!
To what a state my manhood is reduced!
Now naught can save it except flight. Farewell.
Follow me not, or else restrain thy grief.

(*Exeunt* HORATIUS *and* PROCULUS.)

SABINA (*alone*).   O rage, O pity, deaf to all my prayers,
My crime ye heed not; my sighs weary you.
Both chastisement and mercy are refused me.
Let us try tears once more, and then rely
Upon no other hand than ours to die.

A C T   V

HORATIUS *and* OLD HORATIUS *are discovered.*

OLD HORATIUS.   Let us now turn our thoughts from this grim subject
And wonder at the providence of the gods.
When glory makes our bosoms swell with pride
Which soars too high, they easily confound it.
They ever mingle with our dearest joys
Some sadness, with defects they mar our virtues,
And rarely do they grant to our ambitions
The honor of entirely noble conduct.
I pity not Camilla; she was wicked.
I pity, more than her, myself and thee—
Myself for having given birth to a daughter
With heart so little Roman, thee for having
Stained with her blood thy hand. I do not think
Thy deed unjust or hasty; but thou, my son,
Couldst well have spared thyself the stigma of it.
Her crime, though heinous and most worthy of death,

Had better gone unpunished than been punished
By thee.
HORATIUS.   Do with me as thou wilt. The laws
    Give power to thee o'er my life. I deemed
    I owed it to the city of my birth.
    If what I did was evil in thy sight,—
    If it must ever bring reproach on me
    And brand me with eternal infamy,—
    Thou canst with one word end my mortal lot,
    Taking the blood back which thou gavest, of which
    My baseness hath befouled the purity.
    I could not tolerate crime in any child
    Of thine. Do thou refuse to tolerate
    A soilure on the name of the Horatii.
    In matters in which honor is involved
    A father such as thou must show least mercy.
    Love should be silent where excuse is none;
    He himself shares the fault if he denies it;
    And he too little guards his own fair fame
    If he doth not chastise what he doth blame.
OLD HORATIUS.   He is not always without leniency.
    He often spares his sons to spare himself.
    He fain would lean on them in his old age,
    And for his own sake does not punish them.
    I see thee with quite different eyes than thine.
    I know . . . But the King comes. These are his guards.
    (*Enter guards of* TULLUS, *followed by* TULLUS *himself*
       and VALERIUS.)
      Ah, sire, this is to show me too great honor.
    It is not here that I should see my king.
    Let me on bended knee . . .
TULLUS.   Nay, rise, my father.
    I do but that which a good ruler should.
    A service so exceptional and so great
    Deserves the greatest, most exceptional honors.
    Valerius hath already pledged them to thee,
    And I did not wish to defer them longer.
      I learned from him—and had not doubted it—
    That thou hast borne the loss of two sons bravely.
    I knew that for a heart so resolute

My words of consolation would be needless.
But I have just been told what dire occurrence
Followed the victory of thy valiant third son,
And how in his too ardent patriotism
He hath bereft thee of thy only daughter.
That is a blow to shake the stoutest soul,
And I felt doubtful how thou bearest her death.

OLD HORATIUS.   Sire, with much sorrow, but with resignation.

TULLUS.   Such fortitude beseemeth well thy years.
Many have learned, like thee, from a long life
That evil cometh hard on the heels of good;
Yet few can take to heart like thee this lesson.
When 'tis themselves that are concerned, their courage
Fails them. If thou canst for thy sore distress
Find any solace in my sympathy,
Know that 'tis no less great than thy misfortune
And that I pity thee no less than I love thee.

VALERIUS.   Sire, in as much as heaven consigns its justice
And its authority to the hands of kings,
And as the realm expects of a good monarch
Rewards for virtues, penalties for crimes,
Permit a loyal subject to remind thee
That punishment, not pity, here is due.
Permit . . .

OLD HORATIUS.   What! punish one who conquered for us?

TULLUS.   Let him speak on, and I will dispense justice.
I love to accord it, always, everywhere;
A king in doing so is most like a god;
And the chief reason for which I pity thee
Is that now, after all his services,
Justice can be invoked against thy son.

VALERIUS.   Permit, then, O great king, most just of kings,
That all good citizens may speak through me.
'Tis not that we are jealous of his honors.
If he hath many, his great deeds deserve them.
Give him yet more of them, rather than fewer.
All of us would be glad still to contribute
To them; but now when he has demonstrated
That he is capable of such a crime,
Why, let him triumph as a conqueror,
But as a criminal be put to death.

Stay his mad rage and from his sword protect,
If thou wouldst reign, thy people that are left.
The issue is their safety or destruction.

   So bloody and so grim hath been this war,
And marriage-ties in earlier, happier times
So oft united those who were near neighbors,
That scarcely any of us were not affected
By someone's death in the opposing ranks
(A son-in-law's or else a brother-in-law's)
And were not forced to weep for their own private
Sorrows amid the general thanksgiving.
If this wrongs Rome, and if his arms' success
Gives him the right to punish such a crime,
Whose blood will this inhuman victor spare,
Who could not pardon his own sister's tears
Nor could excuse the clamorous grief with which
Her lover's fate afflicts a woman's heart
When, just before the nuptial torch was lighted,
She saw her dearest hopes with him lie dead?
This author of Rome's triumph, as her master,
Assumes o'er us the power of life and death,
So that our sinful days can last no longer
Than he is pleased, in mercy, now, to let them.

   Enough as to Rome's welfare! I could add:
Such a deed is unworthy of a man.
I could ask that before thine eyes the victim
Of this great exploit of his conquering arm
Should now be brought. Thou wouldst behold her blood
Flow in the presence of so cruel a brother,
Accusing him; thou wouldst, by seeing her,
Be filled with unimaginable horror,
So greatly would her youth and beauty move thee.
But I detest such tricks of artful pleaders.

   Tomorrow we shall offer sacrifices.
Thinkest thou that the gods, who are avengers
Of innocence, will find joy in rites performed
By one whose hands are stained with monstrous crime?
Such sacrilege will draw their wrath on thee.
Regard him only as a man they hate,
And think like us that in his triple combat
Rome's destiny, more than his arm, prevailed,

Since these same gods who granted him the victory
Allowed him straightway to becloud its glory,
So that this mighty hero, who had done
A deed most memorable, could deserve
Death in the very hour of his triumph.

  Sire, 'tis hereof thy judgment must decide.
Rome in this house saw her first fratricide.
Its consequences and the wrath of heaven
Alike are to be feared. Preserve us from him
And hold the gods in awe.

TULLUS.   Defend thyself,
  Horatius.

HORATIUS.   Why should I defend myself?
Thou knowest my deed; thou wert just told of it.
That which thou deemest it, decrees my fate.

  Sire, 'tis not easy to defend oneself
In opposition to a king's opinion,
And the most innocent man becomes a criminal
When to his sovereign he appeareth guilty.
'Tis wrong to make excuses to one's king.
Our lives are his; he can dispose of them;
And we should realize, when he takes them from us,
That he would not do this without just cause.
Then give thy verdict, sire; I bow to it.
Others love life, but I should not love mine.
I care not with what fervency Valerius,
Who hoped to wed my sister, now assails me.
Today my wishes are at one with his.
He seeks my death, and I, like him, desire it.
There is one point alone on which we differ,
That thus I fain would make my glory certain;
And both of us aim at the selfsame goal,
I to assure my honor, he to blight it.

  Sire, 'tis but rarely that a chance is offered
For a great soul to display all its greatness.
It usually reveals only as much
Of this as fits the occasion, and hence may seem
Mighty or commonplace to the beholder.
The populace, who judge by outward show,
Gauge one entirely by the things he does,

And they would have his deeds all of like stature.
If he hath once achieved a miracle,
Never must he do less. After an exploit
Perfect, stupendous, dazzling, anything
Not so resplendent ill doth satisfy
Their expectation. They would have one's actions
Ever the same at all times, in all places,
Nor think of whether one could then do more,
Or whether, if they do not always see
Marvels, the opportunity is less
And not the heroism. Thus their injustice
Belittles and dishonors noble names.
The greatness of the first feat dwarfs the second;
And when one's fame hath become eminent,
One must do nothing more, or it declineth.

    I shall not boast the valor of my arm.
Thy Majesty hath seen my threefold combat.
'Tis most improbable there should be again
One like it, or a similar situation,
Or that with all my courage my achievements,
After such great deeds, should not be inferior.
Hence, to preserve my glory and to leave
Behind me an illustrious memory,
My death today is necessary. Rather
It should have followed close upon my victory,
For I have even now outlived my honor.
A man like me deems his fair fame is sullied
When he incurs the slightest risk of shame.
My hand already would have saved me from it
But dared not end my life without thy sanction.
That life belongs to thee; thou must consent
For me to take it—otherwise, I rob thee.
Rome does not lack for gallant warriors.
Enough without me will maintain her glory.
With me, thy Majesty, henceforth dispense;
And if my deeds deserve some recompense,
Let me, O great king, with this conquering sword
Slay myself for my own sake, not my sister's.

Enter SABINA.

SABINA.   Sire, hearken to Sabina. See in her
   The sorrows of a sister and a wife,
   Who, brokenhearted, at thy revered feet
   Weeps for her brothers, trembles for her husband.
   'Tis not my aim by any artifice
   To snatch a criminal from the hands of justice.
   Despite his services, treat him as one;
   Punish in me this noble malefactor.
   Let my poor life atone for all his guilt.
   Thou wilt not substitute a different victim
   Or show him undeservèd mercy thus,
   But rather take from him his dearer half.
   The bonds of marriage and his fervent love
   Make him live more in me than in himself,
   And if thou wilt but let me die today,
   He will die more by *my* death than by his.
   The fate which I implore, and needs must have,
   Will bring him greater suffering and end mine.
    Consider, sire, how my cup overflows
   And in what fearful plight I find myself.
   How horrible to clasp a man whose sword
   Has cut the thread of my three brothers' lives!
   And what an impious sin to hate a husband
   For serving well his family, Rome, and thee!
   Love a hand red with my three brothers' blood?
   Not love a husband who preserved our freedom?
   Sire, save me by a kind death from the crime
   Of loving him or of not loving him,
   And I shall count my death-sentence a boon.
   My hand can give me what I beg of thee,
   But such a fate will be far sweeter to me
   If I can from all shame absolve my husband,—
   If with my blood I can appease the wrath
   Of heaven, which he aroused by his fierce virtue,
   Can satisfy Camilla's piteous ghost,
   And can preserve for Rome her valiant champion.

OLD HORATIUS.   Sire, it is I, then, who must speak to answer

Valerius, for my children conspire with him
Against their father. All three would fain undo me.
They most unreasonably take up arms
Against the remnant left me of my family.

   (*To* SABINA) Thou, who from grief that clashes with thy duty
Wouldst quit thy husband to rejoin thy brothers,
Go, rather, and consult their noble shades.
They died, but 'twas for Alba; blest are they.
Since heaven willed that she should be Rome's subject,
If any feelings can outlive man's life,
They deem this outcome a less cruel blow,
Seeing what honor falls thereby on us.
They all would chide the sorrow that o'erwhelms thee,
The tears thou weepest, the sighs thou utterest,
The horror which thou showest of a brave husband.
Sabina, be their sister; do thy duty
As they did theirs.

   (*To the King*) Valerius rages vainly
Against her noble lord. A sudden impulse
Hath never yet been reckoned a great crime;
And praise instead of punishment is due
When manly patriotism caused this impulse.
To love one's country's foes beyond all measure,
In anger o'er their death to curse one's country,
To pray that infinite woes may fall upon it—
These things are reckoned crimes, and these he punished.
His love for Rome alone impelled his hand;
He would be innocent, had he loved her less.
What do I say? he is, sire; and my arm
Already would have slain him, were he not.
I well know how to use the authority
Which fatherhood allows me over him.
Too much do I love honor, nor am I one
To brook disgrace or crime in mine own family.
Hereof I need no witness but Valerius.
He saw what sort of welcome for Horatius
My wrath prepared when, knowing but half the fight,
I thought he had betrayed us by his flight.

   Who gave Valerius, sire, charge o'er my household?

Why does he wish, despite me, to avenge
My daughter? Why does he feel more concern
About her just death than her father does?
He fears my son may, after her, kill others!
Sire, we have part but in the shame of those
Of our own blood; and what another doeth,
Not touching us, gives us no cause to blush.

    Thou canst weep, then, Valerius, even before
Horatius' eyes. He takes not to himself
The crimes of any who are not his kindred.
One of a different family cannot shame
The deathless laurels that begird his brows.
Ye laurels, sacred wreaths which some would blight,
Ye which could shelter him 'gainst heaven's bolts,
Will ye abandon him to the vile axe
With which the executioner beheads criminals?
Romans, will ye permit one to be slain
But for whom Rome today would not be Rome?
Will ye permit a Roman to attempt
To rob a warrior of his fair fame
To whom all owe so glorious a name?
Tell us, Valerius, tell us: if thou wishest
That he should die, where dost thou think to find
A fit place for his death? Is it to be
Within these walls which many a thousand voices
Still make resound with talk of his great exploits?
Is it to be outside, upon the plain
Still reeking with the Curiatii's gore,
Midst their three graves, or on that field of honor
Which saw his valor and our happy fortune?
Thou couldst not slay him in a place which does not
Recall his victory. Inside the walls,
Outside the walls, all brings to mind his glory;
All balks the unrighteous task thy love hath set thee,
To stain with such brave blood so bright a day.
Alba herself could not endure to see
This done, and Rome would with her tears oppose it.

    Thou canst forestall them, sire. By a just verdict
Thou wilt contrive to safeguard her best interests.

What he did for her, he can do again.
He still can be her shield 'gainst hostile Fate.
Grant nothing, sire, to my declining years.
Today Rome saw me father of four children.
Three have ere sunset perished in her cause.
One of them still is left. Save him for her.
Deprive her not of such a mighty arm.
 And let me, now, say some few words to him.
 (*He turns to* HORATIUS.) Horatius, deem not the dull popu-
  lace
Absolute arbiter of a man's renown.
Their clamorous voice is often loudly heard;
But, raised one moment, it is stilled the next,
And all that it contributes to our glory
Is ever in a twinkling gone like smoke.
'Tis kings, 'tis folk of noble birth and feelings,
That see one's nature in one's smallest actions;
'Tis they alone from whom true fame is had;
They alone make a hero's memory live.
Ne'er cease to be Horatius; and through them
Famous, illustrious, great will be thy name
Always, though Fate permit but lesser deeds
And the ignorant multitude be disappointed.
Then wish no more to die. Live for my sake
And to serve still thy country and thy king.
 Sire, I have said too much, but this affair
Concerns thee, and through me all Rome hath spoken.

VALERIUS. Sire, let me . . .
TULLUS.   Nay, Valerius, 'tis enough.
Their words have not effaced my memory
Of thine. I well recall thy forceful plea,
Thy arguments, and everything thou saidst.
 This monstrous deed, done almost in our presence,
Outrages nature and offends the gods.
That it resulted from a sudden impulse
Is no excuse for such a crime as his.
On this point even the mildest laws agree,
And if we follow them he ought to die.
On the other hand, while we must hold him guilty,

His crime, though great, monstrous, beyond excuse,
Was perpetrated by the same arm and sword
Which have just made me master of two States.
That now I have two scepters and that Alba
Obeyeth Rome speak loudly in his favor.
But for him, I would serve instead of reigning,
Would be a vassal instead of doubly king.

   In every country many worthy subjects
Show by good will alone their loyalty.
All men can love their sovereign, but not all
Can by heroic deeds preserve his realm.
The skill and might to make secure a throne
Are gifts which heaven bestows on very few;
'Tis in such subjects that a king's strength lies;
And such as they are hence above all laws.
Let law be silent, then; let Rome not heed
In thee what she ignored in Romulus.
She well can overlook in her deliverer
That which she overlooked in her first founder.

   Live, then, Horatius; live, too high-souled warrior.
Thy great worth sets thy glory above a crime
Which was the consequence of thy noble fervor.
What springs from such a cause must needs be borne with.
Live to serve Rome. Live, but with kindliest feelings
Of friendship for Valerius. Let there be
No hate or anger between him and thee.
Whether he spoke from love or sense of duty,
Resolve to look on him without resentment.

   Sabina, hearken less to thy sore grief.
Rid thy brave heart of weakness. 'Tis by drying
Thy tears that thou wilt show thyself indeed
The sister of those three for whom thou weepest.

   But we tomorrow owe the gods an offering,
And heaven will not listen to our prayers
Unless the priests, before they sacrifice,
Find means to purify this man. His father
Will see to that. He can at the same time
Also appease Camilla's outraged ghost.
I pity her and, because her fate was cruel,

Will do what most her loving heart would wish.
Since in the same day the same patriot zeal
Cut short her lover's life and hers as well,
Lo, now: let this same day which saw them die
See them in one same grave together lie.

Cinna

CHARACTERS IN THE PLAY

Octavius-Caesar-Augustus, *Emperor of Rome.*
Livia, *the Empress.*
Cinna, *grandson of Pompey; leader of the conspiracy against Augustus.*
Maximus, *another leader of the conspiracy.*
Emilia, *daughter of the tutor of Augustus, whom Augustus had proscribed during the Triumvirate.*
Fulvia, *female attendant of Emilia.*
Polyclitus, *freedman of Augustus.*
Evander, *freedman of Cinna.*
Euphorbus, *freedman of Maximus.*
Courtiers and guards.

The scene is laid in Rome, in the palace of Augustus.

Cinna

ACT I

The scene represents a room in EMILIA'S *apartments in the palace of* AUGUSTUS, *in Rome.* EMILIA *is discovered, alone.*

EMILIA. Ye restless longings for a noble vengeance
Which were begotten by my father's death,
Impetuous offspring of my hate, whereto
My grief infatuate blindly clings, your empire
Over my soul hath grown too absolute.
Allow me some few moments to draw breath
And to reflect, in this my present plight,
Upon both what I risk and what I seek.
When I behold Augustus in his glory
And ye recall to my sad memory how,
Murdered in cold blood by his hand, my father
Served as the first step to the throne on which
I see him sitting,—when ye raise before me
The bloody picture of his fury's victim,
The cause of all my hatred,—I surrender
Myself to your fierce frenzies, and I deem
For that death he deserves a thousand deaths.
Yet in the midst of all my righteous rage,
More than I hate Augustus I love Cinna,
And I can feel my burning ardor cool
Because, if I indulge it, I must hazard
My lover's life. Yes, Cinna, I become
Furious with myself when I consider
The dangers into which I hurry thee.
Though in my service thou hast fear of nothing,
To ask thee for his blood endangers thee.
No one can smite such an exalted head
And not call down a tempest on his own.
The outcome is uncertain, the peril sure.
One treacherous comrade can betray thy purpose;
Misplanning, or a failure to seize rightly
An opportunity, can bury thee

Beneath the wreckage of thine enterprise,
Can turn 'gainst thee the blows thou fain wouldst deal,
Or bring thee to destruction with thy victim.
Yes, whatsoe'er thou doest because thou lovest me,
He well may crush thee, in his fall, beneath him.
Ah, rush not, then, into this mortal danger!
To die avenging me is no real vengeance.
A heart is all too cruel that findeth charms
In joys marred by the bitterness of tears,
And we should reckon among the worst misfortunes
A foe's death which we buy with so much sorrow.
  But can one weep when one hath taken vengeance
For one's own father? Is there any loss
Which doth not seem little to pay for that?
And when his murderer falls beneath our blows,
Ought we to think of what this death may cost?
Cease, fruitless fears—cease, cowardly affections—
To breed unworthy weakness in my heart;
And thou, that by thy vain anxiety
Begettest them, O love, aid me to do
My duty, and oppose it now no longer.
Thy glory lies in thy submission to it,
Thy shame in thy frustration of it. Show
That thou art noble; let it be thy master.
The more thou givest, the more thou shalt be given,
And duty's triumph shall with honor crown thee.

(Enter Fulvia.)

  I have sworn, Fulvia, and again I swear it,
Though I love Cinna, though my soul adores him,
If he would win me, he must slay Augustus.
He cannot gain my hand save at the price
Of *his* head. I prescribe to him the terms
Which obligation hath imposed on me.
Fulvia. They too legitimately may be censured.
So great a purpose ought to make thee deemed
A worthy child of him thou wouldst avenge;
Yet still permit me, for this once, to tell thee
That thou shouldst somewhat cool thy natural fervor.
Augustus seems by daily acts of kindness
To have atoned sufficiently for the wrongs

He did thee; and so manifest appeareth
His graciousness towards thee that thou art she
Who in his household stands pre-eminent,
And often his most favored courtiers
On bended knee beg thee to speak for them.

EMILIA. All his boons do not give me back my father,
And howsoever I may be regarded,
Lapped in wealth or powerful in my influence,
I remain ever a proscribed man's daughter.
Favors do not do always what thou thinkest;
They are offensive from a hand abhorred.
The more we lavish them on those that hate us,
The more we arm those that would fain betray us.
Augustus day by day confers them on me,
Yet still he changes not my resolution.
I am the same I was, and have more power;
And with the very gifts that he doth shower
Upon me, I turn Roman hearts against him.
I would accept from him the place of Livia
As offering surer means to seek his death.
For one who taketh vengeance for a father,
There are no crimes, and to be overcome
By kindness is to sell one's flesh and blood.

FULVIA. But what need is there to seem so ungrateful?
Canst thou not hate without displaying hate?
Others besides thyself have not forgotten
The cruelties on which his throne was founded.
So many brave, so many noble Romans,
Wickedly sacrificed to his ambition,
Have left such heritage of deathless grief
Unto their children that in taking vengeance
For their own wrongs they will avenge thine, too.
Many have set about it now; a thousand
Others will follow them; and he who liveth
Hated of all, cannot have long to live.
Resign unto their arms your common interests,
And aid their plans only with secret prayers.

EMILIA. What! hate him without trying to injure him?
Shall I, then, wait till chance destroyeth him,
And shall I satisfy my obligations

By covert hate and ineffectual prayers?
His death, for which I long, would leave me bitter
If anyone should slay him in revenge
For any other person than my father,
And thou wouldst see my tears flow for his death
If he should die and I not take my vengeance.
'Tis cowardice to leave to others' hands
Public interests bound up with our own.
Let us unite the pleasure of a parent's
Avengement with the glory that one gains
By punishing a tyrant. Let us cause it
To be proclaimed throughout all Italy:
"Emilia hath achieved Rome's liberty.
Her soul was wrung, her heart was won; but only
At such a price would she bestow her love."

FULVIA. At this price it is but a fatal gift
Which bringeth certain doom unto thy lover.
Think well, Emilia, to what peril thou
Exposest him, and how many have already
Made shipwreck on this reef. Blind not thyself
When clearly can his coming death be seen.

EMILIA. Ah, thou canst strike me at my tenderest point!
When I conceive the risks I make him run,
With fear for him I almost die e'en now.
My troubled spirit battles with itself.
I would, then would not; am all flame, then dare not;
And my whole sense of duty, dulled, bewildered,
Dismayed, doth yield to my rebellious feelings.
    Nay, soft, my passion; be not quite so violent.
Thou seest many dangers; they are great,
But 'tis no matter. Cinna is not lost
By merely being risked. Whatever legions
May guard Augustus, and whatever cares
He takes, whatever course he may pursue,
One who disdaineth life is *his* life's master.
The more the peril, the sweeter is the fruit.
Honor impels us; glory will result.
Whoe'er shall die—Augustus be it or Cinna—
I owe this victim to my father's spirit.
Cinna promised it me when we were plighted,

And only this deed makes him worthy of me.
'Tis, after all, too late to change my mind.
Today the band meet, and the plot takes shape;
The hour, the place, the arm are chosen today;
And I, if need be, can die after him.

(Enter CINNA.)

But he is here! Cinna, are not thy comrades
Disturbed at all by fear of danger? Canst thou
See from their faces whether they are ready
To hold to that which they have promised thee?

CINNA.　Ne'er hath an enterprise against a tyrant
Permitted hopes of such a happy outcome.
Ne'er with such ardor hath one's death been sworn.
Ne'er were conspirers better in accord.
All show themselves transported with such joy
That each appears, like me, to serve a mistress;
And all exhibit such a violent hatred
That each doth seem, like thee, to avenge a father.

EMILIA.　I well foresaw that for this undertaking
Cinna could choose brave men, and that he would not
Place in bad hands the interests of Emilia
And of the Roman people.

CINNA.　　　　　　　　Would to heaven
Thou couldst thyself have seen how zealously
This band embarked on such a noble task!
At the mere words "Caesar," "Augustus," "emperor,"
Thou wouldst have seen their eyes ablaze with fury,
And, in the selfsame instant, with effects
The opposite of each other, seen their faces
Grow pale with horror and grow red with rage.
"My friends," I told them, "this is the glad day
Which is to consummate our lofty aims.
The gods place in our hands the fate of Rome,
And her redemption hangs on one man's death,
If he deserves the name of 'man' who hath
No human qualities—this tiger, avid
For every drop of Roman blood. How often
Hath he intrigued to shed that blood! how often
Hath he changed parties and alliances!
Now Antony's friend, and now his enemy,

169

And never arrogant and cruel by halves!"
    Then, with a long recital of the woes
Undergone in our childhood by our fathers,
Reviving both their memories and their hatred,
I doubled in their hearts their thirst for vengeance.
I drew for them pictures of those sad battles
When Rome with her own hands tore out her vitals,—
When eagle smote down eagle, and our legions
On both sides strove against their liberty,—
When our best soldiers and our bravest leaders
Found all their glory in becoming slaves,—
When, to be surer of the shame of chains,
All sought to fasten the whole world to their fetters;
The honor vile of giving it a master
Made them all love the odious name of "traitor";
And Romans fought 'gainst Romans, kinsmen fought
'Gainst kinsmen only to make choice of tyrants.
    I added to these pictures the dread picture
Of that alliance, impious, terrible,
And pitiless, fatal to honest men,
To men of property, and to the Senate—
I mean, in one word, their Triumvirate.
But I could find no colors dark enough
To represent its tragic history.
I painted these men to them, emulating
Each other in their boasted massacres,
The whole of Rome bathed in her children's blood,
Some of the victims slain in public places,
Others cut down amid their household gods,
The wicked led to crime by its rewards,
The husband in his bed killed by his wife,
The son all reeking with his father's gore
And carrying in his hand his father's head,
Asking for payment; but I could not succeed,
With all these horrible details, in giving
A true conception of their blood-bought peace.
    Shall I name o'er to thee those noble figures,
Whose deaths I told them of to rouse their hearts—
Those famous men proscribed, those demi-gods,
Who were not spared even at the very altars?

But could I tell thee to how great impatience,
To what revulsion and what violent feelings,
All the conspirators were stirred on hearing
Of these foul deaths, however ill portrayed?
I seized the occasion, noting how their anger
Made them afraid of naught and ripe for all things,
And said these few words more:
                            "Such cruelties,
The rape of worldly goods and liberties,
The laying waste of fields, the sack of cities,
And the proscriptions and the civil wars—
These are the sanguinary steps by which
Augustus hath contrived to mount the throne
And to give laws to us. But we can change
Our baleful fate, since of three tyrants he
Only is left to us and, doing good
For once, he hath deprived himself of all
Support, destroying, so that he might reign
Alone, two villains like himself. Him dead,
We have no vengeful enemy nor master.
With freedom, Rome herself shall be reborn,
And we shall well deserve the name of Romans
If with our hands we break her yoke of slavery.
Let us embrace our opportunity
When 'tis propitious. He intends to offer
A sacrifice tomorrow at the Capitol.
There let him be the victim; let us do
Justice to the whole world before the eyes
Of the immortal gods. For retinue
He will have hardly anyone but our band.
He takes the cup and incense from my hand;
And for our signal this same hand shall give him
Not incense, but a dagger in his breast.
Thus, smitten with a deadly blow, will he
Show whether I am of great Pompey's blood.
Do ye show whether ye, like me, remember
The glorious ancestors from whom ye spring."
    Scarce had I ended, when they all renewed
With noble oaths their vow of faithfulness.
They liked the plan, but each desired to have

The honor of striking the first blow, which I
Had taken for myself. Reason at last
Controlled the enthusiasm which possessed them.
Half of them, led by Maximus, will secure
The doors; the other half will follow me,
And will surround Augustus and stand waiting
For the least sign that I may give to them.
   That, fair Emilia, is how far we went.
Tomorrow I shall win men's hate or favor,
The name of monster or deliverer,
Caesar the name of great prince or usurper.
On what success we have 'gainst tyranny
Depends our glory or our infamy.
The populace, fickle regarding tyrants,
Detests them dead but worships them in life.
For me, let heaven be harsh or favorable,
Lift me to glory or to death consign me,
Let Rome itself be for us or against us,
To die to serve thee will seem sweet to me.
EMILIA.   Fear not that aught will soil thy memory.
Either success or failure brings thee glory;
And in a task like thine, to lack good fortune
Endangereth thy life but not thy honor.
Look on the fate of Brutus and of Cassius.
Hath that bedimmed the splendor of their names?
Did they die utterly with their lofty aims?
Are they no longer reckoned the last Romans?
Their memory is precious still in Rome,
Even as Caesar's life is odious.
There, if their conqueror reigns, they are regretted,
And in the hearts of all, their like are longed for.
   Go; follow in their steps where duty beckons,
But cease not to be careful of thy safety.
Remember that love's flame burns in us both,
And that Emilia as well as glory
Is thy reward, and that thou owest me
Thy heart, and that my favors wait for thee,
And that my life hangs on thy life so dear
To me. . . .

(Enter EVANDER.*)*

But what now brings Evander here?

EVANDER *(to* CINNA*).* Sir, Caesar calls for thee, and Maximus with thee.

CINNA. And Maximus with me! Art thou sure, Evander?

EVANDER. Polyclitus still awaits thee at thy house.
He would have come, himself, with me to seek thee
Had I not had the ingenuity
To keep him from it. He is very urgent.
I tell thee this to save thee from surprise. *(*EVANDER *withdraws.)*

EMILIA. Calls for the leaders of the enterprise!
Both! At the same time! Your plot is known.

CINNA. Nay, let us hope not.

EMILIA.   Cinna, I have lost thee!
The gods, determined we shall have a master,
Have put among thy loyal friends some traitor.
'Tis beyond doubt: Augustus hath learned all.
What! both! and just when ye had made your plans!

CINNA. I cannot hide it from thee, his command
Dismays me. But he often summons me.
Maximus is, like me, his confidant,
And we perhaps are needlessly alarmed.

EMILIA. Be not so good at self-deception, Cinna.
Drive me not to the limit of my endurance;
And, since hereafter thou canst not avenge me,
At least remove thyself from mortal danger.
Flee the relentless anger of Augustus.
I have enough wept for my father's death;
Do not augment my grief with a new anguish.
Ah, do not force me to bewail my lover.

CINNA. Shall I, reduced to panic by false fears,
Betray thy interest and the public cause,
And by this cowardice denounce myself
And give up all for which I should dare all?
What will our friends do if thou art mistaken?

EMILIA. What will become of thee if the plot is known?

CINNA. If there are souls so vile as to betray me,
At least my courage will forsake me not.
Thou shalt behold it, shining on the brink
Of doom, crown me with glory in defying
Tortures, make Caesar envious of the blood

He spills, force him to tremble while he slays me.
But I shall rouse suspicion if I longer
Delay. Farewell. Strengthen thy gallant heart.
If I must bear the blows of hostile Fate,
I shall die happy and unhappy also—
Happy to lose life in thy service thus,
Unhappy to die thus ere I could serve thee.

EMILIA.   Yes, go; and hear no more my voice that stays thee.
My mind's confusion clears; my reason returns.
Forgive this weakness of my loving heart.
Thou wouldst flee vainly, Cinna, I confess.
Were all revealed, Augustus would be able
To take from thee the power to escape.
Bear, bear into his presence manly boldness,
Worthy both of our love and of thy birth.
Die, if thou needs must die, as doth become
A Roman citizen, and with a glorious
Death crown a glorious purpose. Do not fear
That when thou diest aught can keep me here.
Thy death will draw my soul unto thine own,
And my heart straightway pierced with the same blows . . .

CINNA.   Ah, grant that though I die I still may live
In thee, and let me at least hope in dying
That thou canst take due vengeance for thy lover
As well as for thy father. There is nothing
For thee to dread. None of our friends hath knowledge
Of thy desires or what was promised me;
And when I spoke just now of Rome's misfortunes
To them, I said no word about the death
From which our hate was born—because I feared
My ardor, where thy interests were concerned,
Might well betray the secret of our love.
'Tis known but to Evander and thy Fulvia.

EMILIA.   I go, then, less afraid to Livia
Since in thy peril I have still the means
To use her influence and mine to aid thee.
But if my friendship there is unavailing,
Hope not that in the end I will survive thee.
I make thy fate decide mine own, and I
Will save thee or will follow thee in death.

CINNA

CINNA. For my sake, be less cruel to thyself.
EMILIA. Go, and remember only that I love thee.

(*Exit* CINNA.)

ACT II

The scene represents the cabinet of AUGUSTUS. AUGUSTUS,
CINNA, MAXIMUS, *and a number of courtiers are discovered.*

AUGUSTUS. Let all withdraw and no one enter here.
Thou, Cinna, stay; and thou, too, Maximus.
(*Exeunt all the others. There is a pause. Then* AUGUSTUS
    addresses CINNA *and* MAXIMUS.)
This absolute empire over land and sea,
This sovereign power of mine o'er all the world,
This greatness without limit, this lofty station
Which of old cost me so much blood and suffering—
In short, all that the wearisome flatteries
Of courtiers praise in my exalted fortunes—
Hath no attraction save a brilliancy
Which dazzles but which one no longer loves
When he hath once attained that eminence.
Ambition palls when it is satisfied,
Its cravings are succeeded by their opposite,
And as our spirits, even to our last breath,
Are always filled with yearnings towards some goal,
They on themselves recoil when all is gained,
And having reached the heights, long to descend.
I wished for empire, and I have achieved it;
But wishing for it, I knew not what it was.
In its possession I have found no charms,
But fearful cares, endless anxieties,
A thousand secret foes, death everywhere,
No pleasures unalloyed, and never peace.
Sulla before me had this power supreme;
My father, too, great Caesar, hath enjoyed it.
But they so differently regarded it
That one resigned it and the other kept it.
The first, though cruel and fierce, died well beloved
Like a good citizen, at home, serenely.
The other, ever kindly, saw his life

175

Cut short by murderers in the Senate-house.
From these examples I could learn enough,
Should we be guided wholly by examples.
The one bids me to follow it, the other
Frightens me; but example oft is only
A mirror that deceives, and the decree
Of destiny, which circumscribes our thoughts,
Is not always revealed by past events.
Sometimes one man is broken where another
Is saved, and what destroys one man preserves
Another.
         That, my dear friends, is the thing
Which troubles me. Ye who have taken the place
Agrippa and Maecenas held with me,
Assume, to settle this (debated also
With them), the power which they had o'er my mind.
Pay no attention to this regal grandeur
Loathed by the Romans and a burden to me.
Treat me not as a monarch, but as a friend.
Augustus, Rome, the realm, are in your hands.
Ye shall put Europe, Africa, and Asia
Under a sovereign's rule or a republic's.
Your counsel shall be law for me, and by it
I shall be emperor or a simple citizen.

CINNA.   Despite surprise and my inadequacy
I shall obey thee, sire, with honest frankness.
I put aside the deference which might keep me
From combating a view thou seemest to favor.
Allow this to one jealous for thine honor,
Which thou wilt sully with too dark a stain
If thou dost welcome such ideas so far,
Even, as to condemn all thou hast done.
    One does not renounce greatness attained rightly.
One keeps without remorse what one hath gained
Without crime; and the nobler, grander, lovelier
The thing is which one puts aside, the more
Doth he who dareth to surrender it
Declare it ill acquired. Do not imprint
This mark of shame on those great virtues, sire,
Which made thee emperor. Thou legitimately

Art that, and 'tis without the least wrongdoing
That thou hast changed our form of government.
Rome is beneath thy sway by right of conquest,
The right by which Rome governs all the world.
Thy arms have conquered her, and not all conquerors
Are tyrants merely by usurping power.
When they reduce a country to obedience
And govern justly, they are hence true princes.
That is what Caesar did, and thou today
Must needs impeach his memory or do like him.
If thou condemnest power unlimited,
Then Caesar was a tyrant; his death was just;
And to the gods thou owest a reckoning
For all the blood with which thou hast avenged him
In mounting to his station.
                  Fear not, sire,
His hapless destiny. A guardian spirit
More powerful than his protects thy life.
Ten times it hath been sought, without success,
And he who fain would take it, hath assured it.
Many conspire, but nothing is accomplished;
There are assassins, but there is no Brutus;
Yet even if Caesar's fate should be expected,
To die as master of the world is glorious.
That is, in brief, what I shall dare to say;
And I believe that Maximus thinks the same.

MAXIMUS.   Yes, I agree, Augustus has a right
To keep the empire that his merit alone
Brought him, and at the cost of his own blood
And at the peril of his head he made
A righteous conquest of the Roman State.
But that he cannot, without blackening
His name, lay down the burden of which he tires;
That he thereby would charge with tyranny
Caesar, or of his death approve—these things
Do I deny.
               Rome is thine, sire; the empire
Is thy possession. Everyone can freely
Dispose of his own property. As he chooses,
He can retain it or be rid of it.

Couldst thou alone not do as others can,
And so become, for having conquered all,
A slave unto the greatness which thou wonnest?
Sire, be its master; let it not be thine.
Be not its prisoner; make it yield to thee;
And in brief, proudly demonstrate to all
That all which it embodieth is beneath thee.
Thy Rome erewhile gave birth to thee; thou wishest
To give to it thy power supreme; and Cinna
Imputeth to thee as a capital crime
Thy generosity towards thy native land!
He calls "remorse" the love one bears one's country!
Exalted virtue, then, doth blight fair fame
And is a thing worthy of our disdain
If infamy rewards its best endeavors.
I shall indeed own that an act so noble
Gives Rome much more than thou derivest from her;
But is it an unpardonable crime
When gratitude goes far beyond the gift?
Hark, hark to heaven, which inspires thee, sire!
Thy glory doubles with thy scorn of empire;
And thou shalt be renowned hereafter, less
For having achieved it than for having left it.
Good fortune may lead men to sovereignty,
But to renounce it, character is needed,
And few are so high-souled as to despise,
When they have gained a throne, the joys thereof.
    Consider also that thou reignest in Rome,
Where, by whatever name thy Court may call thee,
A monarchy is hateful and the title
Of emperor, though cloaking that of king,
Is heard with no less horror. He is deemed
A tyrant there who makes himself men's master,
And he who serveth him a slave, and he
Who loveth him a traitor; any man
Who will endure him is considered base,
Spineless, and spiritless; and every effort
To free oneself from him is reckoned virtuous.
Sire, thou hast all too certain proof of this.
Ten vain attempts against thee have been made.

Perhaps the eleventh is about to follow.
Perhaps this impulse which assails thy heart
Is but a secret warning sent to thee
By heaven, that hath no other way to save thee.
Invite no more some sudden, tragic fate.
To die as master of the world is glorious,
But the most glorious death will mar one's memory
When one could live and make his glory greater.

CINNA. If love of country here should take precedence,
Rome's good alone should be considered by thee.
This freedom which appears so precious to her
Is for Rome, sire, only a fancied blessing
Less useful than injurious, far inferior
To that which a good ruler brings his realm.
With ordered wisdom he distributes honors;
With judgment he rewards and punishes.
He deals with all things as their rightful owner,
Unhurried by a fear of his successor.
But when the people rule, all is confusion.
The voice of reason is never heard in counsel;
Honors are purchased by the most ambitious;
Authority is left to the most factious.
Our petty kings, elected for one year,
Seeing their power confined to such brief time,
Make even the best conceived design miscarry
In their anxiety lest the fruit of it
Be left to those that follow them. As they
Own little of that which they administer,
They reap rich harvests in the public field,
Assured that everyone will readily
Pardon them in the hope of faring likewise.
Government by the people is the worst
Of governments.

AUGUSTUS.   And nevertheless it is
The only sort acceptable to Rome.
This hate of kings which for five hundred years
Her children have imbibed with their first milk
Is too deep-rooted to be torn from out them.

MAXIMUS. Yes, sire, Rome is too stubborn in her sickness.
Her people love it and would flee its cure.

Tradition ruleth them, instead of reason.
This ancient error, which Cinna would o'erthrow,
Hath made them prosper, and they worship it;
For the whole world, subjected to their sway,
Hath seen them tread upon the necks of sovereigns
And fill their coffers with the loot of kingdoms.
What more could any prince have done for them?

   I dare assert, sire, that in every clime
Most forms of government are little liked.
Each nation hath its own, best suited to it,
Which none could alter without injuring it.
Such is the law of heaven, whose just wisdom
Filleth the world with this diversity.
The Macedonians love monarchy,
And all the other Greeks free institutions.
The Parthians and the Persians would have kings.
The consulate alone befitteth Romans.

CINNA. 'Tis true that heaven in its infinite wisdom
To every nation gives a different genius,
But not less true that heaven's dispensation
Changes with time just as it does with place.
From kings Rome had her walls and her beginnings;
From consuls she derived her power and glory;
And thanks to thy rare virtues she now reaches
The highest peak of her prosperity.
'Neath thee she is no more the spoil of armies;
The gates of Janus have been closed by thee,
Which only once occurred under her consuls
And once ere that, under her second king.

MAXIMUS. Changes of government caused by heaven's ordinance
Cost no blood and contain naught perilous.

CINNA. 'Tis heaven's ordinance, without exception,
That we must buy at a price somewhat dear
The greatest blessings that are offered us.
The Tarquins' exile drenched our land with blood,
And our first consuls cost us bitter wars.

MAXIMUS. Then Pompey, thy grandfather, was opposing
Heaven in fighting to defend our freedom?

CINNA. If heaven had not wished that we should lose it,
By Pompey's hands it would have been preserved.

Heaven chose his death to signalize forever
With due impressiveness so great a change,
Owing the shade of such a man this honor,
That with him ended Roman liberty.

   Liberty—long now its name hath served
Only to dazzle Rome, and her own greatness
Prevents her from enjoying it. Since she
Hath seen herself the mistress of the world,
Since wealth abounds within her walls, and since,
Fruitful of glorious deeds, she hath produced
Citizens who are mightier than kings,
The great have bought up votes to grow in power,
And arrogantly enslaved the sovereign people,
Who let themselves be bound with golden chains,
Obeying laws instead of giving them.

   These great men, envious of one another,
Used intrigue always, and in their ambition
Contracted thence bloody alliances.
Thus Sulla grew jealous of Marius,
Caesar of my grandfather, and Mark Antony
Of thee; thus freedom hath no other function
But to breed civil war, in all its fury,
When, seized with madness ruinous to the world,
One will accept no master, one no equal.

   Sire, to save Rome, she needs must be united
Under a noble chief, obeyed by all.
If still thou wouldst be gracious to her, take
From her the means henceforth of all division.
When Sulla finally resigned the office
He had usurped, he opened wide the field
To Caesar and to Pompey, a misfortune
That we would not have seen at length if he
Had kept the power in his family.
What did the cruel murder of great Caesar
Accomplish, save to raise up against thee
Antony then and Lepidus, who would never
Have sought to destroy Rome by means of Romans
If he had left the empire in thy hands?
If thou resignest that empire, thou wilt plunge it
Again into those evils whence it scarcely

Yet hath recovered, and another war
Will drain it, sire, of the little blood still left it.
  Let love of country, let compassion move thee.
Rome at thy feet speaks to thee through my mouth.
Think of what price it was that thou hast cost her—
Not that she deems she purchased thee too dearly;
For woes she suffered she was well repaid;
But one real fear still keeps her heart afraid.
If, jealous of her lot and tired of ruling,
Thou givest her a gift she cannot guard,
If thou preferrest not *her* good to thine own,
If she must buy another at thy price,
And if this dread gift drives her to despair,
I dare not tell thee here what I foresee.
Preserve thyself, and let her have a master
Under whom her true happiness begins
To be reborn, and better to assure
The welfare of us all, name a successor
Who may be worthy of thee.

AUGUSTUS.   Let us not
  Deliberate further. Pity hath prevailed.
My peace is very dear to me, but Rome
Hath a yet stronger claim; and howsoever
Great the disaster which can overtake me,
I will embrace destruction to save Rome.
My heart sighs for tranquillity in vain.
Cinna, as thou advisest, I shall retain
The empire, but I shall retain it only
To share it with you both. I clearly see
That frank and guileless are your hearts towards me,
And that each one of you, in his advice
To me, thought only of the State and me.
Your love hath caused this conflict of opinion,
And both of you shall be rewarded for it.
  Maximus, I make thee governor
Of Sicily. Go and dispense my laws
Unto that fertile land. Remember always
That in my stead thou governest, and I
Will be responsible for what thou doest.
  Cinna, I give thee, for a wife, Emilia.

Thou knowest that she hath taken Julia's place,
And that if our misfortunes and necessity
Have made me deal severely with her father,
My bounty since, as lavish in her favor,
Should have assuaged her bitterness for that loss.
As sent by me, see her and try to win her.
Thou art a man whom she cannot disdain;
Thy wooing of her will enrapture her.
Farewell. I wish to bear the news to Livia.

(Exit AUGUSTUS. CINNA *and* MAXIMUS *remain.)*

MAXIMUS. What is thy purpose, after these fine words?
CINNA. The same that I have had, and shall have always.
MAXIMUS. A leader of conspirators can flatter
    A tyrant!
CINNA.   And a leader of conspirators
    Can wish to see a tyrant go unpunished!
MAXIMUS. I wish to see Rome free.
CINNA.   And thou must know
    That *I* wish both to free and to avenge her.
     What! is Octavius to sate his fury,
    Plunder our very altars, take our lives,
    Fill all the land with horror, pile Rome with dead,
    And be forgiven afterwards because
    Of what he does in his remorse? When heaven
    Hath by our hands prepared his punishment,
    Shall cowardly repentance shield his head?
    Impunity for him would make his course
    Seem too alluring, and would invite another
    To imitate him. Nay, let us avenge
    Our fellow citizens. Let his punishment
    Dismay whoe'er aspires after his death
    To wear the crown. Let us expose the people
    No more to tyrants. Had they punished Sulla,
    Caesar would have dared less.
MAXIMUS.   Yet the death
    Of Caesar, which thou deemest so meet and right,
    Served as a pretext for Augustus' cruelties.
    In his desire to win our freedom, Brutus
    Acted amiss. Had he not punished Caesar,
    Augustus would have dared less.

CINNA.   The mistake
    Of Cassius and his panic-breeding fears
    Brought Rome again beneath the sway of tyrants;
    But we shall see no similar mishap
    When Rome is following less imprudent leaders.
MAXIMUS. We still are far from giving any proof
    We shall conduct ourselves more prudently.
    It showeth little prudence not to accept
    The blessing which we risk our lives to win.
CINNA. It showeth still less when one expects to cure
    So great an ill, yet strikes not at its root.
    To use mild remedies in such a cure
    Is to put poison in the wound thou closest.
MAXIMUS. Thou wishest the cure to be a bloody one,
    And makest it doubtful.
CINNA.   And thou wishest it
    To be a painless one, and makest it shameful.
MAXIMUS. One never blushes to escape from chains.
CINNA. Escape from them is base, except through valor.
MAXIMUS. Liberty never ceases to be dear,
    And 'tis for Rome ever a priceless boon.
CINNA. Perhaps 'tis not a boon which she esteems
    Given by a hand tired of oppressing her.
    She hath a heart too brave to see herself
    Gladly the cast-off leavings of a tyrant
    Whose prey she was, and all true followers
    Of honor hate him far too much to love
    His gifts.
MAXIMUS.   Emilia, then, is hated by thee?
CINNA. To have her from his hand would mortify me.
    But when I have revenged what Rome hath suffered,
    I can defy him where he lies in hell.
    Yes, when I have deserved her by his death,
    I wish to take her hand in mine, blood-stained,
    To wed her o'er his ashes, and to make
    A tyrant's gifts, after our task is done,
    Reward my slaying of him.
MAXIMUS.   But is it likely,
    My friend, that thou, stained with the blood of him
    She loves as her own father, canst delight

Her heart? Thou art not one who would compel her.

CINNA.　Friend, in this palace somebody may hear us,
And we perhaps talk too imprudently
In so ill-chosen a place for confidences.
Let us go hence, to where we safely can
Discuss the best way to do what we plan.

(*Exeunt.*)

ACT III

The scene represents a room in the apartments of EMILIA, *as in Act I.* MAXIMUS *and* EUPHORBUS *are discovered.*

MAXIMUS.　He himself told me all. Their love is mutual.
He loves Emilia; he is loved by her.
But she will not be his till he avenges
Her father, and it really is to win
Her hand that he hath led us to conspire.

EUPHORBUS.　I am surprised no longer that he urged
Augustus with such vehemence to retain
His power. Should he resign, our plots would end.
Every conspirator would be his friend.

MAXIMUS.　We vied in furthering unwittingly
The passion of one man, who feigns to serve
Rome's interests, but who really serves his own;
And I, by a misfortune never equalled,
Thought I served Rome and really served my rival.

EUPHORBUS.　Art thou his rival?

MAXIMUS.　　　　　　　　　　Yes; I love Emilia.
I always have concealed it cleverly.
I wished, ere I disclosed my secret feelings,
By some great exploit to be worthy of her;
But I behold him, helped by mine own hands,
Rob me of her. His plan means my undoing,
And it is I who am achieving it!
I speed results where death must be my prospect,
And lend him mine own arm to murder me.
Into how dire a plight hath friendship plunged me!

EUPHORBUS.　Escape from it is easy. Act for thyself.
Avert the fatal blow that would destroy thee.
Denounce thy rival, and thus win her thou lovest.

Augustus, when thou wilt have saved his life,
Cannot refuse Emilia to thee.

MAXIMUS.   Betray my friend?

EUPHORBUS.   Love renders all things lawful.
One really in love recks not of friends,
And 'tis but justice to betray a traitor
Who, for his love's sake, dares betray his sovereign.
Forget his friendship. He forgetteth thine.

MAXIMUS.   The example of misdeeds should not be followed.

EUPHORBUS.   All is legitimate against schemes so black.
He does no wrong who punishes a crime.

MAXIMUS.   A crime by which Rome gains her liberty!

EUPHORBUS.   Beware at every turn a soul so base.
The common weal is nowise what concerns him.
Self-interest, not honor, fires his heart.
He would love Caesar, if he were not in love—
In short, is only an ungrateful man
Instead of being noble.
                    Dost thou think
That thou hast read his inmost soul? Beneath
The public cause he hid from thee his love,
And may still hide from thee, beneath that passion,
The abominable flame of his ambition.
Perchance he hopes, after Augustus' death,
Instead of freeing Rome, to be her master,
And reckoneth thee, e'en now, one of his subjects
Or foundeth his whole plan on thy destruction.

MAXIMUS.   But how accuse him and not name the others?
My story would bring doom on all our comrades,
And we would thus see shamefully betrayed
Those whom their country's good alone involves
With us. I cannot do so vile a thing.
'Twould slay too many innocent men to punish
One guilty man. I dare do all 'gainst *him*,
But shrink from every risk to them.

EUPHORBUS.   Augustus
Is weary now of being so severe.
On such occasions, tired of death and tortures,
He punishes the leaders and grants pardon
To their accomplices. Yet if for them

Thou fearest his anger, when thou speakest to him
Speak in the name of all.

MAXIMUS.   In vain we argue,
And it is only folly to expect
To win Emilia by Cinna's death.
To take life's light from him she loveth best
Is not the way to soften her fair eyes.
For my part, I care little for Augustus
To give her to me; for I wish to gain
Her heart more than her person, and I set
Not the least value on possession of her
If I can have no share in her affection.
Can I deserve her by threefold offenses?
If I betray her lover, foil her vengeance,
And save the life that she would fain have taken,
Can I have any hope that she might love me?

EUPHORBUS.   To tell the truth, that is a difficulty;
Yet may some artifice be useful here.
One must be found forthwith that will deceive her,
And for the rest, time can do everything.

MAXIMUS.   But if in his defense he should name her
As his accomplice, and Augustus should
Decide to punish her along with him,
Can I claim from the Emperor, to reward me
For my disclosure, her who made us plot
His death?

EUPHORBUS.   Thou couldst oppose to me so many
And so great obstacles that to surmount them
Miracles would be needed, yet I hope
By dint of pondering . . .

MAXIMUS.   Go, now. I soon
Will talk with thee again. Cinna approaches,
And I desire to draw him out, the better
Then to decide what I intend to do.

                    (*Exit* EUPHORBUS. *Enter* CINNA.)
        (*To* CINNA) Thou seemest thoughtful.

CINNA.   Not without good reason.

MAXIMUS.   May I know what it is that troubles thee?

CINNA.   Emilia and Caesar; both distress me.
One seems to me too kind, too cruel the other.

CINNA

Would to the gods that Caesar to more purpose
Had taken pains to make her love him better,
Or that he had loved me a little less!
Would that his boons could soften her who charms me,
And move her heart as much as they disarm me!
Within my breast I feel a thousand pangs
Of keen remorse, which bring back all his favors
Afresh before mine eyes. His acts of kindness,
So many and so ill appreciated,
Are killing me with constant sharp reproaches.
Especially I always seem to see him
Putting his sovereign power into our hands,
Listening to our advice, approving mine,
And saying, "Cinna, as thou counselest,
I shall retain the empire, but I shall
Retain it only to share it with you both."
And I can plunge a knife into his breast?
Ah! sooner . . . but alas, I love Emilia!
An oath accurst binds me to serve her hate.
Her detestation of him renders him
Odious to me. I must, whate'er I do,
Offend alike mine honor and the gods,
Must be forsworn or be a murderer,
Must needs be false to one or to the other.

MAXIMUS.   Thou didst not feel just now this agitation.
Thou seemedst then more resolute of purpose.
Thy heart knew no remorse and no reproaches.

CINNA.   One knows them only when the deed draws near.
One hath no comprehension of such crimes
Before the hand prepares to execute them.
Till then the soul, possessed by its intentions,
Clings blindly to its first idea. But later
What spirit would not grow perturbed? Or rather,
What spirit would not be confounded then?
I think that even Brutus, however highly
Men may esteem him, wanted more than once
To abandon his whole enterprise, and felt
Within his breast, before he struck the blow,
More than a single seizure of remorse,
And more than once repented.

188

MAXIMUS. He had a soul
Too noble to be so disturbed. He deemed not
That he was guilty of ingratitude,
But felt himself aroused against a tyrant
So much the more because he had received
Favors from him and was beloved by him.
As thou dost imitate him, do às he did
And be remorseful for a better reason:
For thy bad counsels, which alone prevented
The glad rebirth of Roman freedom. Thou
Alone this day hast robbed us of it. Brutus
Would have accepted it from Caesar's hands
Nor e'er would have allowed a trivial matter
Of vengeance or of love to leave it doubtful.
No longer hear the voice, now, of a tyrant
Who loves thee and would have thee share his power,
But hear Rome crying to thee on every side:
"Cinna, give back, give back to me what thou
Withheldest from me! And if thou didst put
Just now thy love before me, do not put
The tyrant who oppresses me before me!"

CINNA. My friend, cease to upbraid a wretched man
Who basely doth pursue a noble plan.
I know my crime against our countrymen
And soon will give them back those things whereof
I have deprived them. Pardon the last throes
Of old affection, which cannot expire
Without my feeling pity, and permit me,
I pray, while waiting for Emilia,
To give free rein to my unhappiness.
My sorrow vexes thee, and my wracked spirit
Wishes to be alone to curb such grief.

MAXIMUS. Thou wishest to tell her from whom thou hast
Love's wound about the goodness of Octavius
And thine own weakness. Lovers' colloquies
Need secrecy. Farewell. I shall withdraw
Like a discreet friend. (*Exit* MAXIMUS.)

CINNA (*alone*). Give a worthier name
Than "weakness" to the power of noble feelings
Which virtue rouses in me and which honor

189

Opposes to the overhasty blow
Of my ingratitude and infamy.
Nay, better shouldst thou call it "weakness" still,
Since 'tis so weak when she I love is near,
Since it respects a love that it should conquer,
Or, if it strives against this, lacks the courage
To triumph over it. In this great crisis
What should be my decision? To which side
Should I incline? To whom should I be loyal?

   What anguish doth an honorable soul
Feel when it falls! Whatever fruits I hope
To pluck thereby—the joys of love and vengeance,
The glory of setting free my native land—
Are insufficient to beguile my reason
If I must gain them only by foul treason,—
If I must pierce the breast of a great ruler
Who holds my little worth in such esteem,
Crowns me with honors, weighs me down with kindness,
And as to reigning, heeds no voice but mine!
O treacherous blow, unworthy of a man!
Let Rome remain enslaved, enslaved forever;
Let my love perish, let my hopes all perish,
Or e'er my hand shall do a deed so black!
Does he not offer me all that I desire,
All that my love buys at his life's expense?
To enjoy his gifts, must I needs murder him,
And must I snatch by force what he would give me?

   But I am bound by three things: my rash oath,
Emilia's hate, the memory of her father.
My faith, my heart, my arm are pledged to them,
And I can do naught more without their warrant.
It is for them to say what I must do.
It is for thee, Emilia, to forgive him.
Thy will, alone, ruleth his destiny
And by my hands decreeth his life or death.
O gods, who made her be adorable
Like your own selves, make her be like yourselves
Not deaf unto my prayers! Since I cannot
Free myself from her sway, let me be able

To bend her to my will.
But she is here
Again, this cruel and enchanting woman.

Enter EMILIA.

EMILIA. Thank all the gods, my fears were needless, Cinna.
None of thy friends hath failed in faith to thee,
And I had no occasion to employ
Myself in thy behalf. Octavius
Told Livia, in my presence, everything
And by his news restored my life to me.

CINNA. Wilt thou disown it; and wouldst thou delay
The happy consummation of his gift
To me?

EMILIA.   That lies in thy hands.

CINNA.   Nay. In thine.

EMILIA. I am the same still. My heart does not change.
To give thee me is not to give thee aught.
It makes a present to thee of what is thine.

CINNA. And yet thou canst . . . O heaven, dare I say it?

EMILIA. What can I? and what fearest thou?

CINNA.   I tremble,
I groan, and I can see that if our hearts
Had like desires, I would not find it needful
To explain my groans. Thus I am all too sure
I shall displease thee; but I dare not speak
And I cannot be silent.

EMILIA.   Nay, too much
Thou torturest me! Speak out.

CINNA.   I must obey thee.
I shall displease thee, then, and thou wilt hate me.
    Emilia, I love thee, and may heaven
Blast me if in thy love I do not find
My entire joy, and if I do not love thee
With all the ardor that a noble heart
Can feel for someone worthy of its love.
But see the price I pay for thy heart's gift.
Thou makest me infamous in making me
Happy. Augustus' goodness . . .

EMILIA.   That suffices.

I understand. I see that thou regrettest
Thy vows and art inconstant. So prevail
A tyrant's favors o'er thy promises.
Thy love, thine oaths yield to his blandishments.
Thy credulous mind imagines that Augustus,
Being supreme, can bend me to his wish.
Thou'dst have me as *his* gift, instead of mine;
Yet think not that I thus shall e'er be thine.
He can make all the earth shake 'neath his tread,
Depose a king and give his realm away,
Redden with his proscriptions land and sea,
And change at will the governance of the world;
But o'er Emilia's heart he hath no power.

CINNA.   Hence unto thee alone I fain would owe it.
I always am the same, true to thee always.
My sense of pity does not make me recreant.
Without reserve I shall obey thy wishes
And, more than I have sworn, champion thine interests.
     Without committing perjury or crime,
I could, thou knowest, have let thy noble victim
Escape thee; for if Caesar had relinquished
His sovereign power, he would have taken from us
Every pretext for slaying him, the whole
Conspiracy would then have been dissolved,
Thy purpose foiled, thy vengeance cheated. I,
I alone, reassured his wavering spirit
And so re-crowned him but to sacrifice him
To thee.

EMILIA.   To sacrifice him to me, traitor?
Thou wishest that I myself should stay thy hand!
Thou wishest that he should live and I should love him
And be the prize of him who dares to spare him
And whose advice prevailed on him to reign!

CINNA.   Condemn me not, when I have served thy will.
Had it not been for me, thou wouldst have had
No longer any power to assail him;
And yet, despite his kindnesses to me,
I give up all for love, when I resolve
That he shall perish or owe his life to thee.
Beside the first vows of my homage to thee

Let this weak effort of my gratitude
Find place; let me attempt to overcome
A hate unworthy of thee, and to inspire thee
With the same love for him he feels for thee.
A generous soul, a soul that virtue guides,
Flies from the shame of such words as "ungrateful"
And "treacherous"; it loathes the infamy
Of them, even in connection with success,
And accepts nothing at the cost of honor.

EMILIA. For mine own part, I glory in that shame.
'Tis noble to be treacherous to a tyrant,
And when one puts an end to wretched bondage,
The most ungrateful hearts are the most generous.

CINNA. Thou makest virtues of thy hate's desires.

EMILIA. They are virtues worthy of a Roman woman.

CINNA. A truly Roman heart . . .

EMILIA.   Dares all, to take
The hateful life of one who makes it serve him.
As worse than death it dreads the shame of slavery.

CINNA. One serves with honor when one serves Octavius,
And often have we seen kings kneel before us
Asking our aid, slaves though we be. Augustus
Abases at our feet the pride of crowns.
He makes us masters o'er their sovereign greatness;
He takes from them tribute for our enrichment
And sets on them a yoke we do not wear.

EMILIA. Oh, how unworthy is thy heart's ambition!
Thou takest pride in being more than kings!
Is there, between the two ends of the earth,
A king so vain that he believes himself
The equal of a Roman citizen?
Antony drew our wrath down on his head
By stooping to a queen's love. Attalus,
That mighty king, when long grown grey with reigning,
Said that he was the Roman people's freedman;
And though all Asia then obeyed his will,
He prized his throne less than he prized that title.
Think of thy race; maintain its dignity;
Be noble as all Romans should be, knowing
There is not one whom heaven did not create

193

         To impose his will on kings and have no master.

CINNA. Heaven hath shown too clearly in such crimes
         That it hates murderers and will punish ingrates,
         And that, whatever one attempts or does,
         When it sets up a throne, it will avenge
         That throne's fall. Heaven takes the side of those
         Whom it makes reign. The blow with which one slays them
         Draws blood that cries out long; and when the will
         Of heaven decrees their punishment, 'tis only
         By heaven's bolt that they should be chastised.

EMILIA. Say rather that *thou* takest their side, in leaving
         To heaven's bolt the punishment of tyrants.
           I will no longer talk of this with thee.
         Go. Be a slave of despotism. Abandon
         Thy soul to its base nature; and to restore
         Peace to thy strife-torn heart, forget alike
         Thy birth and the reward awaiting thee.
         Though thou lend not thy hand to serve my wrath,
         I can avenge my country and my father.
         I would myself already have the honor
         Of the great deed, if love had hitherto
         Not stayed mine arm. 'Twas love that, holding me
         Subservient to thy wishes, made me careful,
         For thy sake, of my life. Acting alone
         Against a tyrant, I would have to die
         By his guards' hands in slaying him. My death
         Would take from thee e'en her whom thou hast won;
         And since for naught but thee love bade me live,
         I vainly tried to cherish life for thee
         And let thee prove that thou wast worthy of me.
           Forgive me, ye great gods, if I deceived
         Myself when I supposed I loved a grandson
         Of Pompey, and, misled by false resemblance,
         Have loved a slave that occupied his place.
         Yet still I love thee, whosoe'er thou art;
         And if thou must betray thy lord to win me,
         A thousand other men would do the same
         If they could win me at the selfsame cost.
         But fear not that another shall possess me.
         Live for thy precious tyrant, while I die

Still thine. My days, with his, speed to their end—
Because, thou coward, thou darest not deserve me!
Come, see me, bathed in his blood and in mine,
Perish accompanied by my courage only,
And dying, say to thee, with heart content:
"Blame not my fate; thou alone broughtest it on me.
I find a grave to which thou hast condemned me,
Where glory follows me that was meant for thee.
I die destroying a despotic power,
But I would live for thee, hadst thou so willed it."

CINNA.   Well, then, I must do all as thou desirest.
Rome must be freed, thy father be avenged,
Against a tyrant righteous blows be launched.
But know that less than thou art is Augustus
A tyrant. If he robs us at his pleasure
Of our possessions, wives, and lives, he hath not
Up to this time constrained our consciences;
But the inhuman power thy beauty wields
Does violence even to our thoughts and wills.
Thou biddest me prize that which dishonors me;
Thou biddest me hate him whom my heart reveres;
Thou biddest me shed one's blood for whose protection
I ought to risk all mine a thousand times.
Thou wishest it; I fly to do it; my word
Is pledged; but next, my hand, turned 'gainst my breast,
Will sacrifice to the shade of such a monarch
Thy lover, and unite my punishment
To the crime forced upon me; and this deed,
Commingled with the other, will restore
Mine honor unto me as soon as lost.
Farewell!   (*Exit* CINNA.)

FULVIA.   Thou hast reduced him to despair.
EMILIA.   Let him discharge his vow, or cease to love me.
FULVIA.   He will obey thee at his life's expense.
Thou weepest!
EMILIA.   Alas! Run, Fulvia, after him.
If thy affection makes thee fain to help me,
Pluck from his bosom his resolve to die.
Tell him . . .

FULVIA.   That thou wilt let Augustus live
    For *his* sake?
EMILIA.   Ah, that would be too unjust
    Unto my hate!
FULVIA.   Then what?
EMILIA.   That he must needs
    Acquit him of his promise, and that he
    Can afterwards choose either death or me.

                        (*Exit* FULVIA.)

ACT IV

Scene One

The scene is again the cabinet of AUGUSTUS. AUGUSTUS, EUPHORBUS, POLYCLITUS, *and guards are discovered.*

AUGUSTUS. All that thou tellest me is incredible,
    Euphorbus.
EUPHORBUS.   Sire, the very words are fearsome.
    One scarcely can conceive of such mad frenzy.
    One quakes with horror even to think of it.
AUGUSTUS. My dearest friends! What! Cinna? Maximus?
    The two I honored with such high esteem,
    To whom I bared my heart, and whom I chose
    For the most important, noblest offices!
    After I placed my empire in their hands,
    They both conspire to rob me of my life!
    Maximus saw his fault and sent me warning.
    Plainly his soul is touched by true repentance.
    But Cinna!
EUPHORBUS.   He alone clings to his rage,
    The more intransigent as thou art kind.
    He alone still opposes the right course
    To which remorse impels his fellow plotters.
    Despite their terror and regrets, he tries
    To impart new firmness to their shaken spirits.
AUGUSTUS. Alone incites them and alone corrupts them!
    O thou most faithless of the sons of earth!
    O treason hatched in some fell Fury's breast!
    O wound too cruel from so beloved a hand!

Cinna a traitor!
                    Listen, Polyclitus.
                                        (*He whispers in his ear.*)
POLYCLITUS.   All thy commands, sire, shall be carried out.
AUGUSTUS.   At the same time let Erastus go and tell
        Maximus to come hither and receive
        Our pardon for his crime.
EUPHORBUS.   He hath adjudged it
        Too heinous not to punish himself for it.
        Hardly had he returned home from the palace
        When with wild eyes and a distracted look,
        With sighing bosom and with sobbing mouth,
        He cursed himself and the conspiracy,
        Informed me in detail of its whole plan,
        And having ordered me to warn thee, added:
        "Tell him that I have justly estimated
        My crime, and that I am not ignorant
        Of what I now deserve." Then suddenly
        He flung himself headlong into the Tiber;
        And the swift, turbulent water and black night
        Veiled his sad history's ending from my sight.
AUGUSTUS.   Too quickly he succumbed to his remorse
        And put himself beyond the reach of kindness.
        There is no crime against me which repentance
        Will not efface; but (*turning to* POLYCLITUS) since he hath
            preferred
        Not to accept my mercy, go and look
        After the rest, and see that care be taken
        To keep in a safe place this faithful witness.
                    (*Exeunt* POLYCLITUS, EUPHORBUS, *and guards.*)
            (*Alone*) To whom, O heaven, wouldst thou have me hence-
                forth
        Entrust the secrets of my inmost heart
        And the protection of my life? Take back
        The power thou hast committed to my hands
        If sovereigns lose their friends when given vassals,
        If 'tis the destiny of regal grandeur
        That their best favors win them naught but hate,
        And if inexorably thou doomest them
        To cherish those whom thou inspirest to slay them.

Monarchs have no security. He who can
Do everything must needs fear every man.
  Master thyself, Octavius, and no longer
Complain. Wouldst thou be spared, who sparedst none?
Think of the blood wherein thine arms were bathed—
How much made red the fields of Macedon,
How much was shed in Antony's defeat,
How much in that of Sextus, and once more
Behold Perugia weltering in gore
With all of her inhabitants. Behold
Again with thy mind's eye, after such carnage,
The sanguinary scenes of thy proscriptions,
When thou thyself becamest thine own friends' murderer
And sankest a dagger in thy tutor's breast—
Then dare to accuse Fate of injustice to thee
Because thou seest thine own friends take arms
To punish thee, and, led by thine example,
In seeking thy destruction, violate
Those sacred claims which thou hast not respected!
Their treason is just and authorized by heaven.
Lose thine exalted state as thou didst gain it.
Grudge not to faithless men thy faithless blood,
And bear with ingrates, having been ungrateful.
  But how my reason takes flight in this my need!
What madness, Cinna, to accuse myself
And pardon thee—yes, thee who treacherously
Hast made me keep this sovereign power for which
Thou wishest to punish me,—who accountest me
A criminal, yet hast thyself alone,
By re-establishing a lawless throne
Merely to cast it down, caused all my crime,
And cloaking brazenly with zeal for me
Thy purpose, didst oppose, to murder me,
The welfare of the State! Could I compel
Myself to forget this? And thou wouldst live,
Live quietly, after having made me tremble?
No, no, I am a traitor to myself
In thinking of it. He who readily
Pardons, invites offenses. Let us punish
The assassin and proscribe his fellow plotters.

CINNA

What? always blood and always punishing!
I weary of cruelty, yet I cannot stop.
I wish to make men fear me, and I only
Embitter them. Rome is, for me, a hydra.
One head cut off produces countless others
To take its place; and if I shed the blood
Of thousands of conspirators, I render
Myself more execrated, but no safer.
Octavius, do not wait for some new Brutus.
Die; rob him of the glory of thy fall.
Die; thou wouldst basely, vainly seek to live
If such a multitude of brave men vow
Thy death and all the noble youth of Rome
Undertake, each in turn, to kill thee. Die,
Since beyond cure is this ill case. Die lastly
Because thou must slay everyone or perish.
Life is a small thing, and the remnant left thee
Is not worth buying at so grim a price.

   Die, but at least take leave of life not tamely.
Put out its torch in this vile ingrate's blood.
In dying, slay him for his treachery to thee.
Fulfil his aims, but punish his foul crime.
Let thine own death be naught save torment for him.
Yes, make him witness it, yet not enjoy it.
Thyself enjoy his punishment instead,
And if Rome hates thee, triumph o'er its hatred.

   O Romans! O revenge! O sovereign power!
O bitter struggle in my wavering heart,
Which flies from every alternative
At once that it proposes to itself!
Prescribe some policy for a hapless ruler.
Which course ought I to shun, and which to follow?
Oh, either let me die or let me reign!

(Enter LIVIA.*)*

   Treason assails me, madam; and the hand
Which smites me leaves my spirit crushed with grief.
Cinna, the traitor Cinna . . .

LIVIA.   Euphorbus told me
All, sire, and as I listened to his account,
My face grew pale repeatedly. But wouldst thou

CINNA

What? always blood and always punishing!
I weary of cruelty, yet I cannot stop.
I wish to make men fear me, and I only
Embitter them. Rome is, for me, a hydra.
One head cut off produces countless others
To take its place; and if I shed the blood
Of thousands of conspirators, I render
Myself more execrated, but no safer.
Octavius, do not wait for some new Brutus.
Die; rob him of the glory of thy fall.
Die; thou wouldst basely, vainly seek to live
If such a multitude of brave men vow
Thy death and all the noble youth of Rome
Undertake, each in turn, to kill thee. Die,
Since beyond cure is this ill case. Die lastly
Because thou must slay everyone or perish.
Life is a small thing, and the remnant left thee
Is not worth buying at so grim a price.

Die, but at least take leave of life not tamely.
Put out its torch in this vile ingrate's blood.
In dying, slay him for his treachery to thee.
Fulfil his aims, but punish his foul crime.
Let thine own death be naught save torment for him.
Yes, make him witness it, yet not enjoy it.
Thyself enjoy his punishment instead,
And if Rome hates thee, triumph o'er its hatred.

O Romans! O revenge! O sovereign power!
O bitter struggle in my wavering heart,
Which flies from every alternative
At once that it proposes to itself!
Prescribe some policy for a hapless ruler.
Which course ought I to shun, and which to follow?
Oh, either let me die or let me reign!

(Enter LIVIA.*)*

Treason assails me, madam; and the hand
Which smites me leaves my spirit crushed with grief.
Cinna, the traitor Cinna . . .

LIVIA.   Euphorbus told me
All, sire, and as I listened to his account,
My face grew pale repeatedly. But wouldst thou

Hearken unto the counsel of a woman?
AUGUSTUS. Alas, what counsel can my soul adopt?
LIVIA. Sire, thy severity, without producing
          The slightest fruit, hath been till now notorious.
          No one is frightened by another's doom.
          Dead Salvidienus evoked Lepidus.
          Then came Murena; Caepio followed him.
          The tortures that robbed both these twain of life
          Chilled with no fear the fury of Egnatius,
          Whose place now Cinna fills unflinchingly;
          And midst the lowliest ranks the basest born
          Have sought to win renown by such great aims.
          Vainly has their audacity been punished;
          Try upon Cinna clemency instead
          And see what it can do. Punish him only
          By shaming him. On this occasion use
          The most effective means. His execution
          Might well exasperate a seething city.
          To pardon him may serve to enhance thy fame,
          And those whom harsher measures made defiant
          Will be, perhaps, touched by thy gracious mildness.
AUGUSTUS. Let us completely win them by resigning
          This empire, which doth make us hated by them
          And against which their plots are aimed. Too much
          By thine advice have I debated whether
          To do so. Never counsel such debate
          Again. I shall no longer hesitate.
              Cease, Rome, to sigh for liberty. If I
          With chains have bound thee, I myself will break them
          And give thee back thy realm, my prize of war,
          Greater, more tranquil than it was before.
          If thou wouldst hate me, hate me openly.
          If thou wouldst love me, love—and fear not—me.
          Weary as Sulla of the power and honors
          That he had, I would fain like him be happy.
LIVIA. Too long hath his example charmed thy thoughts.
          Thy lot may be the opposite of his.
          The unparalleled good fortune that preserved him
          Would not be called "good fortune," were it usual.
AUGUSTUS. Well, if it be too much to hope for this,

CINNA

I leave my lifeblood to whoever craves it.
After long tempests one desires a haven,
And I must choose for mine my peace or death.

LIVIA. Wouldst thou give up the fruit of so much toil?

AUGUSTUS. Wouldst thou still keep what breedeth so much hatred?

LIVIA. Sire, to proceed to such extremes is only
Despair, instead of loftiness of spirit.

AUGUSTUS. To reign and yet caress a hand so treacherous
Is to display weakness instead of courage.

LIVIA. 'Tis to reign o'er thyself and, choosing nobly,
To exercise the virtue worthiest
Of monarchs.

AUGUSTUS. Thou indeed didst promise me
A woman's counsel. Thou hast kept thy word
To me; for, madam, that is what thine is.
After I had laid low my many foes
Stretched at my feet, I reigned for twenty years.
I know the virtues that beseem a king.
I know their different sorts, and of what nature
A ruler's duties are on such occasions
As this. To try to kill him is to strike
A blow at all his subjects; and to think,
Even, of doing so is an offense
Against the State, a crime against the whole
Country, which he must punish, or else cease
To be a ruler.

LIVIA. Trust thy passion less.

AUGUSTUS. Be thou less weak or less ambitious.

LIVIA. Nay,
Do not treat good advice so ill.

AUGUSTUS. The gods
Will teach me what I ought to do. Farewell.
We but waste time.

LIVIA. I will not leave thee, sire,
Until my love hath had its prayer accorded.

AUGUSTUS. It is the love of greatness that doth make thee
Importunate.

LIVIA. I love thyself, and not
Thy greatness . . . (*Exit* AUGUSTUS.)
He hath fled me. Let us follow

201

And make him see that he can really strengthen
His power by showing mercy, and that, indeed,
Clemency is the noblest attribute
By which the world can recognize true monarchs.   (*Exit.*)

Scene Two

The scene is again a room in the apartments of Emilia, *as in
Acts I and III.* Emilia *and* Fulvia *are discovered.*

Emilia. Whence comes my joy, and how unseasonably
My soul, despite me, is entirely tranquil!
Caesar hath summoned Cinna, yet no fears
Are mine. I heave no sighs, I shed no tears.
'Tis even as though I knew by secret promptings
That all must end as I would have it end.
Did I hear rightly? Didst thou say so, Fulvia?
Fulvia. I had persuaded him to seek to live;
And I was bringing him again to thee
In a more tractable and gentle mood
To try again to appease thy wrath, and I
Was feeling proud of this, when suddenly
Came Polyclitus, by whom usually
Augustus makes his wishes known, to find him
And in the Emperor's name led him at once
Quietly, without armed escort, to the palace.
Augustus seems much troubled; none knows why.
Everyone's guess is different, but all think
That he has some great reason for anxiety
And sent for Cinna to take counsel with him.
But what disturbs me—what I have just learned—
Is that two unknown men have seized Evander,
That for some cause Euphorbus is arrested,
And that uncertain rumors are abroad
Even about his master; people say
Despair hath overwhelmed him; there is talk
Of Tiber's wave, but silence veils the rest.
Emilia. What grounds for terror—none for hope! and yet
My sad heart doth not deign to murmur. Heaven
In every instance fills it with emotions
The opposite of those it ought to feel.

Just recently a needless fear possessed it,
And when I ought to tremble, 'tis unmoved.

    I understand, ye mighty gods: your goodness,
Which I adore, cannot consent that I
Should stoop to any sob or tear or sigh,
And hence ye give me strength to meet misfortune.
Ye fain would have me die with the same courage
That made me undertake a work so glorious,
And I will gladly perish as ye decree
And in the temper ye inspire in me.

    O liberty of Rome! shade of my father!
I have done all that I had power to do.
Against your tyrant I have leagued his friends
And dared for your sake more than was vouchsafed me.
If I have failed, my glory is not less.
Since I could not avenge you, I shall die,
But burning still with such a noble wrath
And by a death so brave, so worthy of you,
That ye at once will surely recognize
The blood of those great men from whom I sprang.

                        (Enter MAXIMUS.)
Thou, Maximus, and 'twas said that thou wert dead!

MAXIMUS.   Euphorbus with that false report deceived
    Augustus. When he found himself arrested
    And the conspiracy discovered, he
    Pretended I was dead, to save my life.

EMILIA.   What is the news of Cinna?

MAXIMUS.   That his greatest
    Regret is to have learned that Caesar knows
    Thy entire secret. He in vain denies it
    And any knowledge of it; for Evander
    Told all, thus hoping to excuse his master,
    And by Augustus' order someone now
    Is coming to arrest thee.

EMILIA.   He to whom
    That order was entrusted is too slow
    In executing it; for I am ready
    To follow him and tired of waiting for him.

MAXIMUS.   He waits for thee at *my* house.

EMILIA.   At *thy* house!

MAXIMUS. That news surprises thee, but learn the care
　　　　　Which heaven hath taken of thee. He is one
　　　　　Of the conspirators, and will flee with us!
　　　　　Let us embrace the opportunity
　　　　　Before we are pursued. We have a ship
　　　　　Beside the river bank, for our escape.

EMILIA. Dost thou not know me better, Maximus?

MAXIMUS. I have done all that I can do for Cinna,
　　　　　And seek to rescue from our dire disaster
　　　　　The dearest part of him that still remains.
　　　　　　Let us preserve our lives, Emilia,
　　　　　Saving ourselves to come back and avenge him.

EMILIA. Cinna it is, in his misfortune, whom
　　　　　We ought to follow and ought not to avenge
　　　　　For fear we might survive him. Anyone
　　　　　Who seeks, after his loss, to save himself
　　　　　Does not deserve the life he tries to keep.

MAXIMUS. What blind despair doth drive thee to such madness?
　　　　　O gods, the frailty of one so brave!
　　　　　This gallant heart offers such slight resistance
　　　　　And falls before the first harsh blow of fate.
　　　　　Resume, resume thy splendid courage. Open
　　　　　Thine eyes at last. Know Maximus aright.
　　　　　In me dost thou behold another Cinna.
　　　　　In me, heaven gives thy lover back to thee;
　　　　　And since our friendship made our two souls one,
　　　　　Love in his friend the lover thou hast lost,
　　　　　And I can love thee with the selfsame ardor
　　　　　Which . . .

EMILIA.　　　　　Thou darest love me and thou darest not die!
　　　　　Thy hopes are aimed, indeed, somewhat too high;
　　　　　But show thyself at least, whate'er their aim,
　　　　　Worthy of that to which thou layest claim.
　　　　　Cease to fly basely from a glorious death,
　　　　　Or cease to offer me a dastard's faith.
　　　　　Force me to envy thy heroic courage,
　　　　　So that I may regret thee though I cannot
　　　　　Love thee. Show a true Roman's utmost manhood,
　　　　　And since thou canst not have my heart, deserve
　　　　　My tears. If as a friend thou carest for Cinna,

Thinkest thou 'tis friendship to woo her he loves?
Learn, learn from me what duty is. Show me
The practice of it, or let me show thee.

MAXIMUS. Thy natural grief is too impetuous.

EMILIA. Thine too ingeniously serves thine ends.
Thou speakest to me already of triumphant
Return, and midst thy sorrow love is born!

MAXIMUS. Yet in its very birth this love is great.
It is my friend I love in thee—thy lover—
And with the same keen ardor that consumed him . . .

EMILIA. Maximus, thou goest beyond all prudence.
Sudden disaster still leaves clear my mind.
In my despair I am in no wise blind.
I rule my soul; 'tis constant; and I see,
Despite myself, more than I wish to see.

MAXIMUS. What! thou suspectest me of some infamy?

EMILIA. Yes, I do, since thou wishest me to say it.
The arrangements for our flight are too well planned
To leave thee unsuspected of dishonor.
The gods would be in our behalf too lavish
Of miracles if they without thine aid
Removed all obstacles to our escape.
Flee without me. I do not want thy love.

MAXIMUS. Ah, thou hast said too much!

EMILIA.   I think still more.
Fear not that I shall burst into revilings,
But do not hope to dazzle me with false vows.
If I now wrong thee in distrusting thee,
Come, die with me to prove thine innocence.

MAXIMUS. Live, fair Emilia, and let thy slave . . .

EMILIA. I will not hear thee save in Caesar's presence.
Come, Fulvia, come.

                          (*Exeunt* EMILIA *and* FULVIA.)

MAXIMUS.   Bewildered, without hope,
And worthy, if possible, of a rejection
Yet crueler, Maximus, what wilt thou do?
What sort of punishment will thy better nature
Prepare for thy vain trickery? No illusions
Henceforth should flatter thee. Emilia
Will make known everything before she dies,

And on one scaffold will her death display
At once her glory and thy ignominy.
Her end will leave to future generations
The odious memory of thy faithlessness.
A single day hath seen thee, with false cunning,
Betray thy sovereign lord, thy friend, thy love.
Yet with so many obligations all
In one day violated and two lovers
Sacrificed to a tyrant, there remains
To thee no fruit except the shame and fury
Which vain remorse enkindles in thy breast.
    Euphorbus, this is the result of thy
Base counsels; but indeed what else can be
Expected from one such as thou? A freedman
Is never anything but a vile slave.
Though his condition changes, in his soul
He changes not. Thine, servile still, with freedom
Hath found no spark of true nobility.
Thou madest me uphold unlawful power;
Thou madest me belie mine honored birth;
My heart withstood thee, and thou hast assailed it
Until thy knavery defiled its virtue.
That costs my life, costs my fair fame, and I
Deserve it all for trusting to thy guidance.
Yet heaven will let me make a sacrifice
Of thee in wrath before these lovers' eyes;
And I dare hope, despite my great offense,
My blood will be sufficient recompense
For them if with *thy* blood my vengeful arm
Can cleanse me of the crime of hearkening to thee.

A C T   V

The scene is again the cabinet of AUGUSTUS. AUGUSTUS *is discovered.* CINNA *enters.*

AUGUSTUS.   Cinna, sit down. Sit down, and be most careful
    To do exactly as I order thee.
    Hear, without interrupting, what I say.
    Break in upon it with no word nor outcry.
    Lock fast thy lips, and if this utter silence

Should do some violence to thy feelings, later
Thou canst at any length answer me fully.
Upon this one point satisfy my wishes.
CINNA. I shall obey thee, sire.
AUGUSTUS.   Remember, now,
To keep thy promise. I, too, will keep mine.
    Thou livest, Cinna, but those who gave thee life
Were enemies to my father and to me.
'Twas in their camp that thou wert born, and when
After their death thou fellest into my power,
Their hatred, deeply rooted in thy bosom,
Had armed thy hand against me. Even before
Thy birth thou wert mine enemy, and when
Thou knewest me, thou wert still mine enemy,
Nor hath thy inclination e'er belied
Thy blood, which placed thee on my foemen's side.
    In so far as thou couldst, thou didst oppose me;
My only vengeance was to let thee live.
I made thee prisoner to heap favors on thee.
Thy prison was my Court; gifts were thy bonds.
First I restored to thee thy patrimony;
Next I enriched thee with the spoils we took
From Antony; and well thou knowest, since then,
I have, whene'er the chance was offered me,
O'erwhelmed thee with my liberality.
Every distinction for which thou didst ask me
I granted thee at once and willingly.
I gave thee preference even o'er those whose kindred
Held formerly in my camp the highest rank—
O'er those who bought my power with their blood
And who preserved in me the breath of life.
I have, in brief, so treated thee that the victors
Are jealous of the fortune of the vanquished.
When heaven willed, in calling hence Maecenas,
To show me after so much kindliness
A little wrath, I gave his place to thee
In that sad hour and thenceforward made thee,
As he had been, my dearest confidant.
This very day, when my uncertain heart
Urged me to lay aside my sovereign power,

I sought advice from thee and Maximus
Alone, and it was thine, in spite of him,
That I have followed. Yet more, on this same day,
I gave Emilia to thee, a prize
Worthy of any man in Italy,
One whom my love and care have set so high
That, had I crowned thee king, the gift were less.
Thou must remember, Cinna; so much honor
And so much happiness cannot so soon
Have faded from thy memory. But a thing
Which none could e'er imagine, Cinna, is
That thou rememberest and yet wouldst kill me.

CINNA (*starting up*). I, sire? I? Have I a soul so treacherous?
So base a purpose . . .

AUGUSTUS.   Ill thou keepest thy word.
Sit down. I have not yet said all I have
To say. Clear thyself later—if thou canst.
In the meantime, listen; and keep thy promise better.
    Thou'dst kill me in the Capitol, tomorrow
During the sacrifice, and for a signal
Thy hand would give to me, instead of incense,
The fatal blow. Half of thy fellow plotters
Were to secure the doors; the other half
To follow thee and lend thee aid. Am I
Well informed, or suspicious wrongly? Shall I
Tell thee the names of all these murderers?
Proculus, Glabrio, Virginianus,
Rutilus, Marcellus, Plautus, Lenas,
Pomponius, Icilius, Albinus,
And Maximus, whom next to thee I loved.
The rest are quite unworthy to be named—
A pack of men ruined by debts and crimes,
Hard beset by the workings of my laws,
And without hope of shunning them hereafter,
Who cannot live if all is not o'erthrown.
    Now thou hast naught to say, and keepest silent
More from confusion than obedience.
What was thine aim? What didst thou mean to do
When I lay dead before thee in the temple?
Set free thy country from monarchial rule?

If I just heard aright thy theories,
Her welfare is dependent on a sovereign
Who, to save all, hath in his hands all power;
And if thou strovest for her liberty,
Thou'dst not have kept me from restoring it;
Thou'dst have accepted it in the whole land's name
And not have wished to win it by a murder.
What soughtest thou, then? To reign here in my place?
Destiny threatens Rome with strange misfortune
If, when thou fain wouldst mount the throne and rule her,
Thou findest in her no obstacle but me
And if she is in such an abject state
That thou art, after me, her foremost man
And the great burden of the Roman Empire
Can fall into no better hands than thine.
  Nay, learn to know thyself; see what thou art.
Men honor thee in Rome; they court thee, love thee,
Tremble before thee, address petitions to thee.
Thy eminence is great, and thou canst do
Whate'er thou wilt, but even those to whom
This gives offense would pity thee if I
Were to abandon thee to thy deserts.
Dare to gainsay me; tell me of thy worth;
Name o'er to me thy virtues, thine achievements,
The rare abilities that pleased me—all
That raises thee above the common herd.
My favor made thee great; thence comes thy power.
It alone lifts thee high, alone sustains thee.
'Tis this that men adore, and not thyself.
Thou hast no influence nor rank at all
Except as this hath given them to thee;
And I e'en now, to make thee fall, need only
Withdraw the hand that is thy sole support.
Yet I would rather let thee have thy will;
Reign if thou canst, though at my life's expense.
But darest thou think that the Servilii,
The Cossi, the Metelli, Pauli, Fabii,
And all the rest indeed whose valorous hearts
Are those of their heroic ancestors,
Could so forget their pride of noble blood

That they would suffer thee to reign o'er them?
Speak, speak! 'tis time thou didst.

CINNA.   I stand confounded.
Not that thy anger or my imminent death
Daunts me; I see that I have been betrayed,
And thou beholdest me wondering who betrayed me.
I search my mind to know this, all in vain.
    But not hereon alone ought I to think.
I am a Roman, sire—of Pompey's blood.
A father and his two sons, foully slain,
Were not avenged enough by Caesar's death.
That is the honorable and only cause
Of our great purpose; and now that treachery
Exposes me to thy relentless wrath,
Look not for base repentance, vain regrets,
Or shameful sighs from me. Fate is to thee
As kind as it is cruel to me. I know
What I have done; I know what thou must do.
Thou needs must make of me a dread example.
My death is necessary to thy safety.

AUGUSTUS. Thou bravest me, Cinna, with a lofty air,
And far from seeking to deny thy guilt
Thou gloriest in it. Let us try and learn
Whether thy constancy will abide with thee
To the very end. Thou knowest what is thy due.
Thou seest that I have found out everything.
Sentence thyself. Choose thine own punishment.

Enter LIVIA, EMILIA, *and* FULVIA.

LIVIA (*to* AUGUSTUS). Thou knowest not yet all his accomplices.
Thine own Emilia is one of them,
Sire. Here she is.

CINNA.   'Tis she herself, O gods!

AUGUSTUS. Thou, too, my daughter!

EMILIA.   Yes, all that he did
He did to please me, sir. I made him do it
And promised him my hand for his reward.

AUGUSTUS. What! hath the love whose seed I sowed today
Within thy heart already grown so great
That thou wouldst die for him? Thy soul abandons

Itself too easily to love. Too soon
Thou dotest on this lover whom I gave thee.

EMILIA. The love for which I shall incur thine anger
Was not born suddenly at thy command.
Its secret flames were kindled in our bosoms
More than four years ago, without thy bidding.
But though I loved him and he pined for me,
Hate, stronger even than love, ruled both of us.
I would not give him any hope till he
Assured me that he would avenge my father.
I made him swear it. He sought aid of friends,
But heaven forbade me the success I vowed.
I now have come to offer to thee, sir,
A victim—not to save *him* by accusing
Myself of guilt. His death is naturally
The consequence of his attempt, and every
Excuse in crimes of State is unavailing.
To die with him and join again my father
Is all that brings me here; 'tis my one hope.

AUGUSTUS. How much and why, O heaven, wilt thou make use
Of shafts against me out of mine own house?
I banished Julia thence for wantonness;
I chose Emilia to take her place;
And now I find Emilia no less
Unworthy than herself of such distinction.
One robbed me of mine honor, and the other
Is thirsty for my blood. With both of them
Taking alike their passions for their guide,
One is unchaste and one a parricide.
O daughter mine, is this, then, the reward
Of all my kindliness?

EMILIA.   That of my father
Produced the same results in thee.

AUGUSTUS.   Ah, think
How lovingly I reared thee in thy childhood!

EMILIA. He reared thee in thy childhood no less fondly.
He was thy tutor, and thou wert his murderer.
Thou hast marked out for me the road to crime.
Mine in this point alone differs from thine,
That thy ambition made thee slay my father,

Whereas the righteous wrath with which I burn
Would slay thee to avenge his innocent blood.

LIVIA. Thou goest too far, Emilia. Stay; bethink thee
That he hath unto thee more than repaid
Thy father's kindness, and that thy father's death,
The memory of which stirs thy fury, was
Octavius' crime and not the Emperor's.
   All crimes of State, committed for a crown,
Are pardoned us by heaven when heaven accords it
To us, and in the sacred station where
The grace of heaven sets a king, the past
Is justified, the future should be safe.
He who attains that station is not guilty;
Whatever he hath done or he may do,
He is inviolable. We owe to him
All that we have, our lives are in his hand,
And none hath claims above a monarch's claims.

EMILIA. Hence, in the words which thou hast heard, I spoke
To anger him, not to defend myself.
   (*To* AUGUSTUS) Then punish, sir, those wicked charms that make
Thy favorites show such great ingratitude.
Cut short my sad life to assure thine own.
If I corrupted Cinna, I may well
Corrupt yet others, and I am the more
One to be feared and thou art more in danger
If I have both a father and a lover
To avenge.

CINNA.   Thou, sayest thou, hast corrupted me!
And must I needs endure to be still more
Dishonored even by her whom I adore?
   The truth must now be told, sire. I had formed
This purpose ere I loved her. Finding her
Deaf to my holiest wishes, I believed
She might be moved by other means. I spoke
Then of her father and thy ruthlessness,
And with my heart I offered her my sword.
How sweet is vengeance to a woman's soul!
Thus I beset her; thus I won her love.
She was indifferent to my little worth

But could not be indifferent to the arm
Which would avenge her. She was in the plot
Only through my devices. I alone
Contrived it; she is merely an accomplice.
EMIILIA.   Cinna, what darest thou say? Is this to love me,
Depriving me of honor when I must die?
CINNA.   Die, but in dying do not filch my glory.
EMILIA.   If Caesar will believe thee, mine is less.
CINNA.   And mine quite lost if thou thyself dost claim
All credit owed to such a noble aim.
EMILIA.   Well, take thy share of it and leave me mine.
To weaken that, would be to weaken thine.
Glory and happiness, and shame and pain—
All should be had in common by true lovers.
(*To* AUGUSTUS) Sir, our two spirits are two Roman spirits.
We love as one, and also hate as one.
Our bitter memories of our dear ones' deaths
Taught us our duty in the selfsame instant.
Our hearts were joined in this brave enterprise;
Together we conceived it, and together
We seek the honor of an illustrious fate.
Thy wish was to unite us; do not part us.
AUGUSTUS.   I will unite you, treacherous and ungrateful
Pair that ye are, and more mine enemies
Than Antony or Lepidus! Oh, yes,
I will unite you, since ye so desire.
We must appease the fires with which ye burn,
And make the whole world, seeing my heart's wrath,
Blench at the punishment as at the crime.
(*Enter* MAXIMUS.)
But heaven smiles on me at last: it saves
Maximus from the fury of the waves.
Come, thou sole friend who I have found was faithful!
MAXIMUS.   Sire, do not honor thus a guilty wretch.
AUGUSTUS.   Speak not of guilt now, after thy repentance—
After thou hast preserved me from such danger.
It is to thee I owe my life, my throne.
MAXIMUS.   Know better who is worst of all thy foes.
If thou still reignest, sire—if thou still livest—
Thou owest that only to my jealous frenzy.

Honest remorse did not assail my breast;
'Twas to destroy my rival that I revealed
His plot. Euphorbus feigned that I was drowned,
For we both feared that thou wouldst send for me.
I sought to have the chance then to deceive
Emilia, to strike terror to her soul,
And to persuade her to leave Italy—
As I believed I could by holding out
To her the hope of coming back someday
To avenge her lover. But she did not swallow
Such simple bait. Her courage was redoubled
When she was thus beset. She read my heart.
Thou knowest the rest, and hence there is no need
For me to tell thee aught of it. Thou seest
The outcome of my shameful trickery.
Yet if some favor is my due because
Of my disclosures, let Euphorbus die
Amid the cruelest torments, and let me
Perish before the eyes of these two lovers.
I have betrayed my friend and my beloved,
My master, mine own honor, and my country—
All by this villain's counsel; yet would I
Think my good fortune boundless if I first
Could punish him and afterwards myself.

AUGUSTUS.   Is it not enough, O heaven? Hath Fate, to harm me,
One of my people still left to seduce? . . .
Though to its efforts it join aid of hell,
I am earth's master and mine own as well.
I am. I will be so. O centuries
To come, O minds of men, preserve forever
The memory of my final victory!
I triumph over the most righteous wrath
That even posterity shall e'er recall.

Cinna, let us be friends. 'Tis I who ask it.
Life did I give thee when thou wert my foe,
And now, despite the rage of hate displayed
In thy base purpose, life do I again
Give thee when thou wouldst be my murderer.
Let us begin a contest that will show
By how it endeth which of us shall have

The better of it, he who gives or he
Who doth receive. My favors did not make thee
Loyal; I will redouble them. I have heaped them
Upon thee; they shall overwhelm thee now.
With this fair lady whom I bestowed on thee,
Receive the consulate for the coming year.
> (*Turning to* EMILIA). Daughter, love Cinna with this noble
> office.

Prefer its purple to my purple blood.
From my example learn to quell thine anger.
In giving back to thee alive a husband,
I give back more to thee than any father.

EMILIA. And I am conquered, sire, by such great kindness.
It lends me light for clearer vision now.
I see my crime, which I had thought was justice,
And—what no fear of death could make me do—
I feel a great repentance born within me,
And secretly my heart consents thereto.
> Heaven hath resolved that thou shalt be supreme.

To prove it, sire, I am myself sufficient.
I proudly dare lay claim to such distinction;
Since heaven doth change my heart, it surely wishes
To change Rome, too. My hate, which I believed
Immortal, soon will die . . . 'tis dead already,
And I am now thy loyal subject. Looking
Henceforth with horror on that hate, I shall
Replace it with an eagerness to serve thee.

CINNA. Ah, sire, what shall I say when our offense
Meets with rewards instead of punishments?
O matchlesss goodness, clemency which makes
Thy power the more just, my crime the greater!

AUGUSTUS. Stay me no longer from forgetting it,
And join me, both of you, in pardoning
Maximus. He betrayed us all, but thus
Kept you from crime and gives me back my friends.
> (*To* MAXIMUS) Resume thy wonted place with me again
And have once more thy influence and fair fame.
All three forgive Euphorbus in his turn,
And (*indicating* CINNA *and* EMILIA) let the morrow crown
> their love with marriage—

Thy punishment, if still thou lovest her.

MAXIMUS. I murmur not at this; it is too just;
And I am more confused, sire, by thy mercy
Than jealous of the bliss of which thou robb'st me.

CINNA. Sire, let the virtue in my heart reborn
Pledge thee a faith which I have once forsworn
But which is now so constant, so unwavering,
That were the heavens to fall, 'twould not be shaken.
May the great fashioner of fair destinies
Cut short our years but to prolong thy days,
And grant me, as a boon that all shall envy,
The loss a hundred times o'er, for thy sake,
Of all I hold from thee.

LIVIA.   Sire, hearken still.
A heavenly flame illuminates my heart
With a prophetic ray. Hear what the gods
Would have thee know through me. Thus they decree
Unalterably thy happy destiny:
After this, thou hast nothing more to fear.
Without complaining, men will wear thy yoke,
And the most stubborn will renounce all plots
And think it glorious to die thy subjects.
No shameful purpose, no ungrateful envy,
Will e'er assail so fair a life. Henceforward
There shall be no assassins nor conspirers,
For thou hast learned the way to rule men's hearts.
Rome with a joy both keen and deep consigns
Unto thy hands the empire of the world.
Thy kingly virtues make it very plain
That happiness for her requires thy reign.
Her mind from ancient error wholly free,
She now desireth naught but monarchy.
She rears to thee already shrines and altars;
Heaven finds a place for thee among the immortals;
And everywhere posterity will make thee
Serve as a pattern for the noblest rulers.

AUGUSTUS. I hail thy prophecy, and I dare to hope
'Tis true. Thus always may the gods vouchsafe
To inspire thee. Let our grateful sacrifices,
Offered to them 'neath better auspices,

Tomorrow be of twice their usual size;
And let the rest of the conspirators
Hear this official proclamation made:
"Augustus hath discovered all their plot,
And yet hath willed that all shall be forgot."

Polyeucte

CHARACTERS IN THE PLAY

FELIX, *Roman Governor of Armenia.*
POLYEUCTE, *an Armenian nobleman, son-in-law of Felix.*
SEVERUS, *a Roman gentleman, favorite of the Emperor Decius.*
NEARCHUS, *an Armenian nobleman, friend of Polyeucte.*
PAULINE, *daughter of Felix and wife of Polyeucte.*
STRATONICE, *friend of Pauline.*
ALBINUS, *friend of Felix.*
FABIAN, *servant of Severus.*
CLEON, *servant of Felix.*
Guards.

*The scene represents a room in the Governor's palace at Meli-
    tene, Capital of Armenia.*

In this translation the names "Polyeucte" and "Pauline"
are retained with the final "e" unpronounced as in the French.
The names "Severus," "Nearchus," "Stratonice" (four syllables), and "Albinus" are each accented on the next to the last
syllable, as is the name of the city, "Melitene" (four syllables).

Polyeucte

A C T   I

POLYEUCTE *and* NEARCHUS *are discovered.*

NEARCHUS.   What! do thy wife's dreams stay thee? Such slight things
    Trouble thy lofty spirit? Is thy heart,
    So often tried in war, alarmed at dangers
    A woman saw in visions of the night?
POLYEUCTE.   I know what a dream is, and how small credence
    A man should give to its extravagances,
    Which a confused conglomerate of night's vapors
    Forms of vain things that vanish when we waken.
    Thou knowest not what it means to have a wife.
    Thou knowest not her hold upon one's heart
    When, after she hath long enchanted us,
    The marriage torches have at last been lit.
    Pauline, unreasonably filled with woe,
    Dreads and expects e'en now to see my death,
    Of which she dreamed. Sore weeping, she opposes
    The purpose that I formed, and tries to keep me
    From issuing from the palace. I disdain
    Her terrors; I have yielded to her tears.
    She rouses pity in me, but no fears;
    And, touched though unafraid, my heart can nowise
    Make her to whom it doth belong unhappy.
    Is there, Nearchus, so great need for haste
    That I must pay a loved one's sighs no heed?
    Let us console her by a slight delay,
    Then freely do what she prevents today.
NEARCHUS.   But canst thou know with certainty that thou
    Wilt live till then or feel the same as now?
    Hath God, who holdeth in his hand thy soul,
    Thy life-days, promised thee as high a mood
    Tomorrow? He is ever just and good,
    But not always with the same efficacy
    His grace descends on us. When we have waited
    Too long with our delays, its beams no more

Transfix the soul; he ceases to dispense them,
Or else our hearts are hardened 'gainst his grace
And keep it out. His hand, which gave it freely,
Grows parsimonious, and that blessed zeal
Whence good proceeds is felt by us but seldom
Or not at all. The fervor which hath urged thee
To hasten to baptism wanes already
And is no more the same; and for the sake
Of a few sighs which thou hast heard, its flame
That fired thee flickereth and will soon be dead.
POLYEUCTE.   Thou knowest me ill. I burn with no less ardor.
My longing is the more as its fulfilment
Is further off. Those tears, which I behold
With a fond husband's eye, leave me at heart
As much a Christian as thyself thou art.
But although I prefer above the splendors
Of empire, as the one supreme good thing
To which my soul aspires, the consecration
By that life-giving water which doth cleanse us
Of sin, makes pure our hearts, unseals our eyes,
And gives us back man's lost inheritance,
I think that I can wait one little day
To soothe a loving wife's anxieties.
NEARCHUS.   Thus doth the foe of all mankind beguile thee.
When force avails him not, he useth craft.
Jealous of righteous aims, which he would foil,
If he cannot suppress them he diverts them.
Thine he will thwart with hindrance after hindrance,
Today with tears, each day with something new;
And this dream, filled with black imaginings,
Is but his first device wherewith to stay thee.
He uses prayers and threats and all things else;
Ever he strikes and never doth he tire;
He deems that he can do at last whatever
He cannot do yet, and that anyone
Who will delay is half o'ercome already.
  Frustrate his first attack. Let Pauline weep.
God wants no heart which worldly things possess
Or which looks back or, doubtful of its choice,
When *his* voice calls it, hears some other voice.

POLYEUCTE. Must he who gives himself to God love no one?
NEARCHUS. We may love all. He so permits, commands.
    But to be frank with thee, this Lord of lords
    Doth wish to stand first in our love and honor.
    As naught can equal him in majesty,
    We must love naught but after him and in him,
    Must in his service leave wife, wealth, and rank,
    And for his glory pour forth all our blood.
    But think how far thou art from that devotion,
    Required of thee, which I would have thee feel!
    I cannot speak except with tearful eyes.
    Polyeucte, we are hated everywhere,
    And men believe they do the realm a service
    In persecuting us, and any Christian
    Is subject to the cruelest tortures. How,
    Then, canst thou rise superior to such trials
    If thou canst not resist a woman's tears?
POLYEUCTE. Thou dauntest me not. The pity that I feel
    Beseems the stoutest heart; 'tis not a weakness.
    Beauty moves greatly men like me, Nearchus.
    We fear to cause it pain, though death we fear not;
    And if I needs must face the cruelest tortures
    And find my happiness and pleasure in them,
    Thy God, whom still I do not dare call mine,
    Will give me strength in making me a Christian.
NEARCHUS. Hasten to be one, then.
POLYEUCTE.   I will, Nearchus.
    I long to bear the glorious mark of one.
    But Pauline grieves and cannot suffer me
    To leave the house, so much this dream dismays her.
NEARCHUS. All the more, then, will thy return delight her.
    One hour hence, at latest, thou wilt dry
    Her tears, and then the joy of seeing thee
    Again will seem the sweeter unto her
    The more she will have wept so dear a husband.
    We are awaited. Come.
POLYEUCTE.   Then calm her fears.
    Assuage the woe with which her soul is pierced.
    She is here!
                        (*Enter* PAULINE *and* STRATONICE.)

NEARCHUS.   Fly.

POLYEUCTE.   I cannot.

NEARCHUS.   But thou must.

    Fly from an enemy who knows thy weakness,
    Who strikes thee through it with ease, the very sight
    Of whom o'ercomes thee, and who still doth charm
    Thy heart when doing thee the deadliest harm.

POLYEUCTE.   Let us fly, since we must.

                      Goodbye, Pauline,
    Goodbye. In one short hour I shall come back.

PAULINE.   What is so urgent that it calls thee forth?
    Is, then, thine honor, or thy life, at stake?

POLYEUCTE.   More is at stake.

PAULINE.   What can this secret be?

POLYEUCTE.   Thou shalt know some day. With regret I leave thee,
    But I must leave thee.

PAULINE.   Dost thou love me?

POLYEUCTE.   Yes,
    Far more, heaven be my witness, than myself.
    But . . .

PAULINE.   But my unhappiness cannot move thee.
    Thou hast thy secrets which I may not share.
    Oh, what a proof of love! In wedlock's name,
    Grant to my prayers, I beg thee, this one day.

POLYEUCTE.   Thou fearest a dream.

PAULINE.   Its presage hath no weight.
    I know that. But I love thee, and I therefore
    Am none the less afraid.

POLYEUCTE.   Fear no ill thing
    In one brief hour of absence. Fare thee well.
    Thy tears have too much influence on me.
    I feel my heart already prone to yield,
    And only by my flight can I resist thee.

               (*Exeunt* POLYEUCTE *and* NEARCHUS.)

PAULINE.   Go. Pay my tears no heed. Fly to encounter
    Thy death, whereof the gods foretold me. Follow
    That fatal agent of thine evil fortune,
    Who may deliver thee into murderers' hands.
      See, Stratonice, in what times we live!
    See how great power we have over men's hearts.

    See what remains to us, how much we keep,
    Of all the love and promises men proffer.
    While they are only suitors, we are sovereigns;
    And we like queens are treated till they win us,
    But after marriage they in turn are kings.
STRATONICE.   Polyeucte hath had no lack of love for thee.
    If he doth not take thee entirely now
    Into his confidence,—if he goes forth
    Despite thy tears,—this is but prudence in him.
    Grieve not thy heart thereat; believe with me
    That there are reasons he should not tell thee why.
    Be sure that what he doeth is for the best.
    'Tis well that husbands should hide something from us,
    Preserve some freedom, and not abjectly render
    Account to us of everywhere they go.
    Husband and wife should have a single heart,
    Sharing the same misfortunes; but this heart
    Hath diverse qualities, and the bond of marriage,
    Which makes the twain be one, doth not require
    That he should always tremble when thou tremblest.
    What rouseth fear in thee may not alarm him;
    He is Armenian, and thou art Roman;
    And thou canst understand that our two peoples
    Have not the same beliefs regarding dreams.
    A dream, to our mind, is a thing for jest.
    It leaves us neither hope nor fear nor doubt.
    But dreams are heeded in Rome reverently
    As true foreshadowings of destiny.
PAULINE.   However little they are credited
    Here, I believe thy fright would equal mine
    If the same ghastly vision had been thine
    Or if I even had described it to thee.
STRATONICE.   To tell one's troubles, often lightens them.
PAULINE.   Then listen. But for better understanding
    Of my sad story it is necessary
    That I should tell thee more and thou shouldst know
    Of my heart's frailty and its other love.
    An honorable woman can avow
    Without confusion those spontaneous feelings
    Which reason quells; 'tis by such tests that virtue

Reveals itself; and none is sure of any
Heart which hath never been assailed.

                         In Rome,
Where I was born, this luckless face had won
The love of a young Roman gentleman.
Severus was his name. Forgive the sigh
Which that dear name still forces me to utter.

STRATONICE. Was it he who lately at his life's expense
Saved from the foe your emperor, Decius,—
He who in death snatched victory from their hands
And turned the scale from Persia to Rome,—
He who among the bodies of the slain
Was never found—at least not recognized—
And to whom Decius, for his heroism,
Erected finally such great monuments?

PAULINE. Alas! 'twas he, and ne'er hath Rome produced
A nobler heart or seen a worthier man.
Thou knowest of him; hence I need say no more.
I loved him, Stratonice; he deserved it.
But what does merit avail when one is poor?
His soul was great, his worldy goods were scant:
A mighty obstacle, which the best of lovers
Can rarely in a father's eyes surmount!

STRATONICE. How excellent a chance for constancy!

PAULINE. Say, rather, for mad, wicked obstinacy.
Whate'er a daughter gains by such a course,
She alone deems it good who fain would err.
The whole time when I so much loved Severus
I was expecting that my father's will
Would give to me a husband, and I always
Was ready to accept one, and my mind
Never approved my heart's insurgency.
Severus had my love, my thoughts, my longings;
I did not hide from him how much I loved him;
We wept together, mourning our ill fortune;
But I could give him only tears, not hope,
And though his vows were sweet and dear to me,
My sense of filial duty was unshaken.
    At last I left Rome and my heart's ideal,
Coming here with my father to his province,

And my despairing lover joined the army
To win undying fame by a brave death.
The rest thou knowest. When I reached this land
I met Polyeucte and in his sight was pleasing,
And as he is the foremost of your nobles
My father was delighted when he wooed me,
And thought by this alliance to make himself
More powerful and respected here. He sanctioned
Polyeucte's love and plighted me to him;
And I—when I thus found myself betrothed,
I gave, as duty bade me, unto him
Who was to be my husband that affection
Which my heart's wish had given to the other.
If this thou doubtest, judge of it by the fear
Wherewith today thou seest me overcome.

STRATONICE.   It showeth, of a truth, how well thou lovest him.
But what dream was it that so frightens thee?

PAULINE.   I saw, last night, that same ill-starred Severus,
His hand with vengeance armed, his eyes ablaze
With rage. He was not clad in those sad vestments
Which a disconsolate ghost brings from the grave.
He was not mangled with those glorious wounds
Which took his life and gave him deathless fame.
He seemed triumphant, like our Caesar entering
Rome in his chariot, crowned with victory.
I was a little frightened at the sight
Of him, and then he said to me: "Transfer
To whom thou wilt the love that is my due,
Thou faithless woman; and when this day is over,
Thou wilt have ample time to mourn the husband
Whom thou hast chosen to wed instead of me."

I shuddered at his words; my soul was shaken;
And thereupon an impious band of Christians,
To hasten the fulfilment of that utterance,
Hurled Polyeucte prostrate at his rival's feet.
I begged my father to come quick and aid him.
Alas! what followed is what so confounds me.
My father's self I saw, dagger in hand,
Enter with arm upraised to pierce his breast!
Then my great anguish made the dream confused.

> Polyeucte's blood was shed to glut their fury.
> I know not either how or when they killed him,
> But in his death I know they all had part.
> That was my dream.

STRATONICE.   'Tis true, it was a bad one;
> Yet must thy spirit needs resist its terrors.
> That which thou sawest was horrible in itself
> But gives thee no just grounds to be afraid.
> Canst fear a dead man? or canst fear thy father,
> Who loves thy husband and is revered by him,
> And whose own choice hath given thee to that husband
> To gain in him a firm and sure support?

PAULINE.   So hath he told me, laughing at my panic,
> Yet still I dread the Christians' plots and spells.
> I fear they will take vengeance on my husband
> For all their brethren's blood shed by my father.

STRATONICE.   Their sect is mad, impious, and sacrilegious,
> And in its worship uses sorcery;
> Yet in their rage they only break our altars;
> They vent it on the gods, and not on mortals.
> However harshly they are dealt with, they
> Suffer without a murmur and die gladly,
> Nor, in the time in which they have been treated
> As guilty of high crimes against the State,
> Could they be charged with even a single murder.

PAULINE.   Be quiet! My father comes.

Enter FELIX *and* ALBINUS.

FELIX.   With what strange fright,
> My daughter, thy dream moves me, even as thee!
> I dread so greatly the fulfilment of it
> Which seems to be at hand!

PAULINE.   What sudden fear
> Hath seized thee thus?

FELIX.   Severus is not dead,
> After all.

PAULINE.   How can that fact injure us?

FELIX.   He is the favorite of the Emperor Decius.

PAULINE.   Having preserved him from the enemy's hands,
> He had a right to expect such eminence.

Fate, which to noble hearts so oft is adverse,
Sometimes decides it will be just to them.
FELIX. He himself comes here.
PAULINE.   Comes here!
FELIX.   Thou wilt see him.
PAULINE. Nay, 'tis too much! . . . But how dost thou know this?
FELIX. Albinus met him not far from the city.
    A throng of courtiers accompanied him,
    Showing well what his rank and influence are.
        Albinus, tell her what these people told thee.
ALBINUS (*to* PAULINE). Thou knowest the story of that mighty battle
    Which by his loss ended so happily
    For us—in which the Emperor, taken prisoner,
    Was rescued by his hand, and thereupon
    Rallied our already wavering army,
    While he himself, despite his valor, fell
    O'erwhelmed by numbers; and thou knowest also
    What honors to his memory were paid
    When he could not be found among the dead.
        The King of Persia, too, had ordered search
    Made for him, and had had him borne away.
    A witness of his bravery and exploits,
    This monarch wished to look upon his face.
    He placed him in the royal tent, where, even
    Pierced as he was with wounds and dead to all
    Appearance, thousands envied him. No sooner
    Did he exhibit any signs of life
    Than this magnanimous ruler was o'erjoyed
    And in his joy, despite his late defeat,
    Honored the valor of the arm that caused it.
    He had Severus cared for, secretly,
    And when, after a month, his body's soundness
    Was thoroughly restored, offered him wealth,
    High rank, and even alliance with himself
    By marriage, in a vain attempt to win him—
    Then, having praised him greatly for refusing,
    Sent Decius a proposal for his exchange,
    And the delighted Emperor at once
    Gave the King's brother and a hundred chosen
    Captains for him. Thus to the camp returned

Severus, the great hero—to receive
The guerdon of his bravery; for this
The Emperor's favor was his fit reward.
  The war went on. Our army was surprised,
Yet this disaster served to increase his glory.
He alone then re-formed the broken ranks
And won the victory—a victory
So great and so complete and signalized
By deeds so wondrous that the enemy
Offered us tribute, and we made peace with them.
The Emperor, whose love for him seems boundless,
After this triumph hath sent him to Armenia.
He comes to bring here the glad news and render,
With sacrifice, thanks to the gods therefor.

FELIX. Ah heaven! to what straits am I reduced!

ALBINUS. One of his retinue told me all this,
  And I have sped to inform thee of it, sir.

FELIX. Oh, daughter, beyond doubt he comes to wed thee.
  The sacrifice is unimportant to him;
  'Tis a false pretext given to serve his love.

PAULINE. That could well be the case. He loved me dearly.

FELIX. What scope will he not give to his resentment!
  And how far will a righteous wrath combined
  With so great power not carry his revenge!
  He will destroy us, child.

PAULINE.   He is too generous.

FELIX. Thou reassurest in vain thy wretched father.
  He will destroy us, child. It drives me mad
  That I did not love naked worth. Alas,
  Pauline, thou hast obeyed me all too well!
  Thy heart was wise; thy sense of duty wronged it.
  How fortunate for me would thy rebellion
  Have been! How 'twould have saved me from this plight!
  If there is any hope for me, it lies
  In the absolute power alone which he once gave thee
  Over his soul. Use in my aid the love
  For thee that fills him, and from the same source
  From which my ills proceed, effect their cure.

PAULINE. I? I? Again behold him, now a hero,
  And meet those eyes that pierce my bosom's core?

Father, I am a woman, and I know
How weak I am. I feel my heart already
Moved by him, and despite my marriage vows
I shall be sure to heave some sigh unworthy
Of me and thee. I will not see him!

FELIX.   Be not
So much afraid.

PAULINE.   He still is lovable,
And I am still a woman. With the power
He had o'er me of old, I dare not trust
My virtue fearlessly. I will not see him.

FELIX. Thou needs must see him, daughter, or thou wilt be
False to thy father and all thy family.

PAULINE. I must obey, since thou commandest this.
But oh, the perils to which thou dost expose me!

FELIX. I know thy purity.

PAULINE.   It will prevail,
Indeed. 'Tis not the outcome that I dread.
I shrink from the hard struggle and the turmoil
Of soul which my insurgent feelings make
In me already. But, since I must battle
Now with an enemy whom I love, allow me
A little time, that I may arm my heart
Against itself, and so prepare to see him.

FELIX. I have to go outside the walls to greet him.
Rally thou, meanwhile, thy stunned faculties,
Remembering that our fate lies in thy hands.

(Exeunt all but PAULINE.)

PAULINE. Yes, I shall quell whate'er is in my breast,
Once more a victim as thou orderest.

A C T   I I

SEVERUS and FABIAN are discovered.

SEVERUS. While Felix gives the orders which are needful
In preparation for the sacrifice,
Could I not seize a time so favorable
To my heart's prayers? Could I not see Pauline
And pay to her fair face the selfsame homage
That soon is to be paid unto the gods?

I have not hidden from thee that this it is
Which brings me here; all else is but a pretext
To lull my pain. I come to sacrifice,
But 'tis unto her beauty that I come
To make an offering of my heart and soul.

FABIAN. Thou'lt see her, sir.

SEVERUS.   Ah, what supreme delight!
This dear and lovely being will receive me!
But have I still some hold upon her heart?
Doth she still show some trace of love for me?
What pleasure or confusion doth my coming
Beget in her? Can every hope be mine
From this glad meeting? For I would rather die
Than wrongly use the Emperor's favoring letters
To win her hand. They are for Felix only,
Not to prevail o'er her. My heart was never
Rebellious to her wishes, and if hers
Hath changed in consequence of my ill fate,
I shall o'ercome my feelings and seek naught.

FABIAN. Thou'lt see her. That is all that I can tell thee.

SEVERUS. Nay, wherefore art thou trembling? Why that sigh?
Doth she no longer love me? Tell me that.

FABIAN. Sir, wilt thou hearken to me? Do not see her.
Confer on someone of a higher rank
The honor of thy love. In Rome thou canst
Find many hearts to accept it; for thy power
And fame are such that even the greatest ladies
There would account it a rare prize.

SEVERUS.   Thou thinkest,
Then, that my soul could stoop to thoughts so base
That I could deem Pauline unworthy of me!
She hath the nobler nature; I must try
To be like her. I value my success
But to deserve her better. Let us see her
Now, Fabian. Thy words vex me. Let us go
And lay my lofty fortunes at her feet.
By chance I won them on the field of battle
While seeking a death worthy of her lover.
Thus do my rank, the favor I enjoy,

POLYEUCTE

Derive from her; and I have verily
Nothing save what I have because of her.

FABIAN. Nay—but once more I beg thee, do not see her.

SEVERUS. Ah! 'tis too much. Now tell me plainly this:
Did she seem cold when thou besoughtest her for me?

FABIAN. I fear to say it. She is . . .

SEVERUS.   Go on.

FABIAN.   Wedded.

SEVERUS. Upbear me, Fabian! This thunderbolt
Strikes me the harder, being so unexpected.

FABIAN. What has become, sir, of thy gallant courage?

SEVERUS. Here fortitude is hard to put in practice.
Such sorrows crush the most heroic soul;
The manliest nature is bereft of strength;
And when a heart kindles to love so sweet,
Death makes it tremble less than such a shock.
I am no longer master of myself
On hearing these dire words: Pauline is wedded.

FABIAN. She has been wedded fourteen days. Polyeucte,
One of the foremost nobles of Armenia,
Enjoys the blessing of her hand in marriage.

SEVERUS. At least I cannot blame her choice. Polyeucte's
Name is well known. He is of royal blood.
Weak solace for a woe that hath no cure!
Pauline, I shall behold thee now another's.
O heaven, which brought me back to life despite me!
O Fate, which bade my love to hope again!
Take back your favor shown me, and allow me
To have that death which ye have robbed me of!
But I will see her, and in this sad spot
Take leave of life in bidding her farewell,
That, carrying her image in my heart
Among the dead, I may with my last sigh
Pay homage to her.

FABIAN.   Think, sir . . .

SEVERUS.   All is thought of.
What can one fear who is devoid of hope?
She does consent to see me, does she not?

FABIAN. Yes, my lord, but . . .

SEVERUS.   Enough!

FABIAN.   Thine anguish thus
    Will only be made greater.

SEVERUS.   This is not
    An ill I fain would cure. I wish for nothing
    Except to see her, breathe one sigh, and die.

FABIAN.   Thou wilt lose all thy self-control before her.
    A thwarted lover is devoid of deference.
    In such a meeting he lets passion guide him
    And utters only insults and fierce curses.

SEVERUS.   Deem otherwise of me. My reverence for her
    Yet lives unchanged. In my intense despair
    I still adore her. And what reproach have I
    A right to utter, and of what can I
    Accuse her, who ne'er gave me any promise?
    She is not perjured; she is not inconstant.
    Her duty, my ill fortune, and her father
    It was that have undone me; but her duty
    Was genuine, and her father was quite right.
    To my ill fortune I ascribe all blame.
    A little less success, earlier attained,
    Would have prevailed o'er him, and thus have won her
    And kept her mine; too well, but all too late,
    Have I attained it, and have lost her now.
    Let me, then, see her, breathe one sigh, and die.

FABIAN.   I will assure her that in thy great woe
    Thou wilt be strong enough to rule thy soul.
    She feared, like me, those first spontaneous feelings
    Which a disaster unforeseen provokes
    In lovers, and the violence of which
    Creates sufficient frenzy in their minds
    Without the presence of her whom they have lost
    To rouse them further and redouble it.

SEVERUS.   Fabian, I see her.

FABIAN.   Sir, recall . . .

                       (*Enter* PAULINE *and* STRATONICE.)

SEVERUS.   Alas!
    She loves another! is another's wife!

PAULINE.   Yes, I do love him, sir, nor do I seek
    To excuse myself for this. Let all but me
    Mislead and flatter thee. Pauline is high-souled

And speaks straight from her heart. 'Tis not at all
The story of thy death that has undone thee.
If heaven had left my marriage to my choice,
I would have given myself to none but thee,
And all the bleakness of thy former fortunes
Would vainly have been urged against thy merit.
I saw in thee such noble traits that I
Preferred thee even to the most blest of monarchs;
But since my duty decreed otherwise,
Whatever man my father chose for me,—
E'en hadst thou joined the splendors of a crown
To the attractions which thine own worth gave thee,
Hadst thou been here, and had I hated him,—
I would have sighed, but I would have obeyed,
And reason, sovereign in me o'er my feelings,
Would have condemned my sighs and quenched my hate.

SEVERUS. How fortunate thou art, when a few sighs
Can promptly heal all thy unhappiness!
Thus always mistress of thy heart's desires,
Thou art undaunted by life's greatest changes.
At will thou turnest the most ardent feelings
To cold indifference—nay, perhaps to scorn—
And with thy firmness easily canst make
Favor succeed disdain, love succeed hate.

How some share of thy nature or thy virtues
Would soothe the misery of this broken heart!
A sigh, a tear regretfully let fall,
Would have consoled me for thy loss already.
My reason, too, would be all-powerful
Over my feeble love, and from indifference
I would proceed even to forgetfulness,
And my love thus conforming to thine own,
I could find happiness in another's arms.

O too much loved, who charmedst my soul too well!
Is it thus, then, that one loves? Or didst thou love me?

PAULINE. Too well I have shown thee that I did, Severus;
And if my heart could quench that love's last fires,
Gods! what cruel anguish I would then escape!
My reason, it is true, controls my feelings,
But whatsoe'er its mastery over them,

It rules them by compulsion, like a tyrant,
And though I give no outward sign thereof,
Within me all is turmoil and rebellion.
Some spell thou hast which draws me to thee still.
Though reason rules me, I can see thy worth.
I see it yet, as when it made me love thee,
So much the stronger in its appeal to me
As it is now girt round with power and glory,
As everywhere it brings thee victory,
As I can better know the greatness of it,
And as it never hath belied my hopes.
But that same sense of duty which withstood thee
In Rome and gave me to a husband here,
Again so well resists thy dear attractions
That though my soul is torn, it is not shaken.
'Tis the same virtue, cruel to our desires,
Which thou didst praise of old, while railing at it.
Lament it still, but praise its resolution,
Which triumphs at once o'er thee and o'er my heart,
And realize that one whose sense of duty
Was not so steadfast or sincere could never
Have merited the love of great Severus.

SEVERUS.   Oh, dearest lady, pardon my blind grief
Which knows no longer aught but its own pain.
I called "inconstancy" and deemed a fault
The noblest workings of that sense of duty.
Reveal less clearly to my stricken spirit
The greatness of my loss and all thou art.
In pity, hide thy nature's rare perfection,
Which makes my love more ardent when it parts us,
And show me some defects which can instead
Lessen my grief together with my love.

PAULINE.   Alas, my rectitude, though still triumphant,
Does not hide well enough my bosom's weakness.
These tears attest it, and the unworthy sighs
Drawn from my breast by poignant memories—
Too cruel results of a beloved presence
'Gainst which my sense of duty ill defends me!
But if thou valuest that rectitude,
Preserve my fame therefor; see me no more.
Spare me the tears which to my shame must flow.

Spare me the feelings which reluctantly
I quell. In one word, spare me these sad meetings
Which but increase thy agony and mine.
SEVERUS.   Shall I renounce the only blessing left me!
PAULINE.   Save thyself from it; 'tis fatal to us both.
SEVERUS.   So this is love's reward! my labors' fruit!
PAULINE.   'Tis the sole remedy which can heal our sorrows.
SEVERUS.   I wish to die of mine. Hold dear their memory.
PAULINE.   I wish to cure mine. They would taint my honor.
SEVERUS.   Ah! since thine honor passeth sentence on me,
My grief must yield perforce to its best interests.
What would I not do for thine honor's sake?
Thou hast recalled me to the care of mine.
Farewell! I go to seek in the midst of battle
That immortality which a brave death brings
And fulfil worthily, by a noble end,
The promise given by my former deeds—
Provided, after this dire stroke of fate,
I still have life enough to search for death.
PAULINE.   And I, whose pangs the sight of thee increases—
I shall escape them by thy sacrifice,
And in my chamber, hiding my regrets,
I, all alone, shall pray for thee in secret.
SEVERUS.   May the just gods, content with my undoing,
Give all good gifts to Polyeucte and Pauline!
PAULINE.   And may Severus find, after such misery,
The happiness that he deserves!
SEVERUS.   In thee
He found it.
PAULINE.   I was subject to my father.
SEVERUS.   O duteousness, my ruin and despair!
Farewell, too virtuous and too lovely being!
PAULINE.   Farewell, my all-too-hapless, ideal lover!
(*Exeunt* SEVERUS *and* FABIAN.)
STRATONICE.   I pitied both of you; my tears still flow.
But now thy soul at least need fear no longer.
Thou seest clearly that thy dream was false.
Severus hath not come with vengeful hand.
PAULINE.   Let me draw breath if thou dost pity me!
At my grief's climax thou recallest my terror.

Allow some brief rest to my tortured spirit,
And do not crush me with redoubled woes.
STRATONICE. What! thou art still afraid?
PAULINE.   I shake with fear;
For though I have scant reason to be frightened,
My groundless dread continually brings back
The unhappy vision that I saw last night.
STRATONICE. Severus is magnanimous.
PAULINE.   Despite
His self-restraint, ever before mine eyes
Rises the bloody image of Polyeucte.
STRATONICE. Thou sawest his rival pray for his good fortune.
PAULINE. I even believe that he at need would aid him;
But whether my belief be false or true,
His sojourn here would keep my fears alive.
Howe'er his noble nature prompts him, power
Is his, he loves me, and he came to wed me.

Enter POLYEUCTE *and* NEARCHUS.

POLYEUCTE (*to* PAULINE). Thou hast shed too many tears; 'tis time to
dry them.
Let thy woe cease and all thy fear be over.
Despite the warning sent thee by thy gods,
I still live, madam; thou seest me again.
PAULINE. The day is yet young; and, what most affrights me,
Part of that warning hath proved true already:
I thought Severus dead, and he is here.
POLYEUCTE. I know it, but I feel regarding it
Little concern. I am in Melitene,
And be Severus e'er so great, thy father
Rules here and I am much esteemed by all;
Nor do I think that one can reasonably
Fear treachery from the heart of such a hero.
I was told that he was paying thee a call,
And I was coming to show him the respect
That he deserves.
PAULINE.   He has just gone from me,
Sad and with mind in turmoil; but I have
Obtained his promise ne'er again to see me.
POLYEUCTE. What! thinkest thou I am already jealous?

PAULINE. Nay, I would thus insult all three of us.
I seek mine own peace, which his sight disturbs.
Even the most steadfast virtue takes no risk.
To expose oneself to danger courts disaster;
And, to speak frankly to thee, since true worth
Can breed love, his continual presence here
Might well rouse mine. Not only must one blush
To find one's heart thus taken by surprise;
One suffers in resisting it, one suffers
In saving oneself from it, and though virtue
Can triumph over love, its victory is not
Easy, the struggle fills one's breast with shame.

POLYEUCTE. O utter purity! O soul of honor!
How greatly must Severus feel his loss!
Thou makest me happy at his heart's expense
And ever art considerate of my love.
The more I see mine own faults, and the more
I think of thee, the more I marvel . . .

Enter CLEON.

CLEON (*to* POLYEUCTE).   Sir,
Felix requires thy presence at the temple.
The victim hath been chosen, the people kneel,
And for thee only waits the sacrifice.

POLYEUCTE. Go; we shall follow thee.   (*Exit* CLEON.)
                              Wilt thither, madam?

PAULINE. Severus fears the sight of me. It stirs
His love. I mean to keep my word to him.
I do not wish to see him any more.
Farewell, then. Thou wilt see him there. Remember
His power and the favor he enjoys.

POLYEUCTE. Nay, all his influence does not alarm me;
And as I know his heart's nobility,
We shall be rivals in naught but courtesy.
                    (*Exeunt* PAULINE *and* STRATONICE.)

NEARCHUS. Where thinkest thou to go?

POLYEUCTE.   To the temple, where
I have been summoned.

NEARCHUS.   What! thou'lt join thy prayers
With those of unbelievers? Dost thou, then,

POLYEUCTE

Forget already that thou art a Christian?

POLYEUCTE. Dost thou, who madest me one, remember thou
    Art one?

NEARCHUS.   I hate false gods.

POLYEUCTE.   And I abhor them.

NEARCHUS. I think their worship wrong.

POLYEUCTE.   I think it fatal.

NEARCHUS. Then flee their altars.

POLYEUCTE.   I would fain o'erthrow them,
    Cast them to earth or in their temple die.
      Come, dear Nearchus, let us before all men
    Defy idolatry and show what we are.
    That is the will of heaven; we must obey it.
    I have resolved to do this, and I shall.
    I thank my God, whom thou hast made me know,
    For this occasion, which he so soon hath offered,
    Wherein his grace, ready e'en now to crown me,
    Deigns to make trial of my new-found faith.

NEARCHUS. Too ardent is thy zeal. Do thou restrain it.

POLYEUCTE. One cannot have too much zeal for one's God.

NEARCHUS. 'Twill mean thy death.

POLYEUCTE.   I seek death for his sake.

NEARCHUS. But if thy heart quails?

POLYEUCTE.   He will give me strength.

NEARCHUS. He hath not bidden us to embrace destruction.

POLYEUCTE. The more we do so of our own free will,
    The greater our desert.

NEARCHUS.   'Tis quite enough,
    Not seeking death, to abide and bear it bravely.

POLYEUCTE. He meets it with regret who dares not seek it.

NEARCHUS. But in this temple thou art sure to die.

POLYEUCTE. A crown e'en now awaits me in the sky.

NEARCHUS. A holy life is needful to deserve it.

POLYEUCTE. If I live on, my sins could make me lose it.
    Why put in hazard that which death assures?
    Can what will open heaven's gate seem hard?
    I am a Christian through and through, Nearchus.
    The faith now mine yearns to achieve fruition.
    He who flees hath a coward's faith, a dead faith.

NEARCHUS. Preserve thy life. It is of use to God.
   Live to protect the Christians in these regions.
POLYEUCTE. The example of my death will aid them more.
NEARCHUS. Thou wishest to die, then?
POLYEUCTE.   And dost *thou* love life?
NEARCHUS. I cannot hide the fact that it is hard
   For me to follow thee. I fear lest I
   Shall fail in fortitude 'neath ghastly tortures.
POLYEUCTE. One who goes boldly hath no dread of failing.
   God gives us of his boundless strength, at need.
   The man who is afraid he will deny Him,
   Denies Him in his heart; for he believes
   He could deny Him, doubting his own faith.
NEARCHUS. He who fears nothing, trusts in himself too much.
POLYEUCTE. I expect all from His grace, naught from my frailty.
   When thou shouldst urge me on, *I* must urge *thee* on!
   Whence comes thy slackness?
NEARCHUS.   God himself feared death.
POLYEUCTE. And yet he freely gave his life. Do like him.
   Let us rear altars to him on piled fragments
   Of idols. "We"—I well recall thy words—
   "Must in his service leave wife, wealth, and rank,
   And for his glory pour forth all our blood."
   Alas, where is that perfect love, which thou
   Didst wish in me—which I now wish in thee?
   If any remnant of it still is thine,
   Art thou not jealous when I, who am but now
   A Christian, display more of it than thou?
NEARCHUS. Thou comest fresh from baptism, and what fires thee
   Is God's grace, which no crime hath weakened in thee.
   It acts with full force, being still unimpaired,
   And all seems possible to its ardent flame.
   But this same grace, which is in me diminished,
   And which unnumbered sins make ever feebler,
   Acts in great matters so irresolutely
   That naught seems possible to its scant vigor.
   Such spinelessness, such cowardly pretenses
   Are mine in punishment for my offenses;
   But God, whom one should never fail to trust,
   Gives me, to fortify me, thy example.

Then come, dear Polyeucte, let us before all men
Defy idolatry and show what we are.
May I be an example unto thee
In suffering death, as thou hast been to me
In offering thy life freely.

POLYEUCTE.   In this fervor,
Which heaven implants in thee, I recognize
Again Nearchus, and I weep for joy.
    Let us lose no more time. The sacrifice
Impends. Let us go thither to uphold
The cause of the true God. Let us go trample
Beneath our feet that absurd thunderbolt
Wherewith a superstitious people arm
A rotting wooden statue. Let us go
And bring men light in this their fatal blindness.
Let us destroy these gods of stone and bronze,
Give ourselves wholly to this heaven-sent ardor,
And make God triumph—the rest be in his hands!

NEARCHUS.   Let us show forth his glory to all eyes,
And gladly do whatever will is his.

                                   (*Exeunt.*)

A C T   I I I

PAULINE *is discovered, alone.*

PAULINE.   What vague anxieties, what coils of gloom,
Raise up before me ever-changing pictures!
Sweet peace, to which I do not dare aspire,
How slow is thy divine ray to dispel them!
Countless emotions, bred of my distress,
By turns possess my shaken soul and die.
No hope comes thither in which I can persist.
No fear reigns there which I can think sufficient.
My mind, believing all that it imagines,
Sees now my happiness, now my life's ruin,
And follows each vain concept so unsurely
That I can wholly neither hope nor fear.
Severus without cease troubles my thoughts.
Now I have faith in his nobility,
And now I fear his jealousy; nor dare I

Suppose that Polyeucte will without displeasure
Look on his rival. As hate is natural
Between these two, their meeting easily
May terminate in a quarrel. This one will see
Her whom he thinks should rightly have been his
Another's wife, that one a desperate man
Who may attempt some wrong. However high
The minds that rule their hearts, the one will feel
Envy, the other anxiety. The shame
Of an affront that each believes he suffers,
Or has just suffered, or is about to suffer,
Destroys in the first instant all their patience,
Creates mistrust and anger, and, o'ercoming
At the same time the husband and the lover,
Makes them despite themselves their passions' slaves.
  But in what strange imaginings I indulge!
How badly I treat Polyeucte and Severus!
As if these noble-hearted rivals could not
Escape the faults of ordinary men!
They both alike are masters of their souls,
And of too lofty nature for such baseness.
They will behold each other in the temple
Like generous spirits—but alas! they will
Behold each other, and that may be too much!
What doth it serve my husband that he is
In Melitene, if Severus arms
The Roman eagle 'gainst him,—if my father
Rules here and fears this favorite of the Emperor
And even now repents the choice he made
Of a husband for me. The faint hope I have
Burns with a struggling flame. In the very instant
'Tis born, it dies and is replaced by dread.
What should confirm it, serves to dissipate it.
Gods, make my fears prove in the end mistaken!

(*Enter* STRATONICE.)

But let us learn the truth.

                    Well, Stratonice,
How was our solemn sacrifice concluded?
Did these two noble rivals meet each other
In the temple?

243

STRATONICE.   Oh, Pauline!

PAULINE.   Were my prayers futile?
    I see bad news imprinted on thy face.
    Was there a quarrel?

STRATONICE.   Polyeucte . . . Nearchus . . .
    The Christians . . .

PAULINE.   Speak! The Christians . . .

STRATONICE.   Nay, I cannot.

PAULINE. Thou seemest to prepare me for great sorrow.

STRATONICE. Thou couldst not have a better reason for it.

PAULINE. They have murdered him?

STRATONICE.   That would be little. All
    Thy dream hath come true. Polyeucte is no more . . .

PAULINE. He is dead!

STRATONICE.   No, no! He lives, but oh, vain tears!
    This heart so great, this nature so divine,
    No more is worthy of life, nor of Pauline.
    He is no more that husband thou didst love.
    He is alike the realm's foe and the gods' foe,
    A wicked, infamous, disloyal, faithless
    Scoundrel, a traitor, dastard, monstrous villain,
    A thing abominate to all good people,
    An impious blasphemer—in short, a Christian.

PAULINE. That word would have sufficed, without this torrent
    Of insults.

STRATONICE.   Are these words for Christians false?

PAULINE. He is all that thou sayest, if he hath
    Embraced their faith. But he is still my husband,
    And 'tis to me thou speakest.

STRATONICE.   Think no more
    Save of the God he worships.

PAULINE.   I in duty
    Have loved him, and that duty still is mine.

STRATONICE. He gives thee now good grounds for hating him.
    One who is unto all our gods a traitor
    Could well have been unfaithful unto thee.

PAULINE. I would have loved him still, though faithless to me,
    And if thou art astonished at such love,
    Know that *my* duty does not in the least
    Depend on him. Let him not do his duty

If so he pleases; I must yet do mine.
What! if he loved elsewhere, would it be lawful
For me to yield, like him, to some mad passion?
A Christian though he be, I shrink not from him.
I cherish him the while I hate his error.
    What feelings doth my father show towards him?
STRATONICE. An inward rage, an anger past all words,
    In spite of which a remnant of affection
    Still makes him have some pity for Polyeucte.
    He does not wish to visit justice on him
    Till he has seen the false Nearchus punished.
PAULINE. What! is Nearchus, then, involved?
STRATONICE.   Nearchus
    Corrupted him. Such is the shameful outcome
    Of their long friendship. That perfidious man,
    Tearing him from thine arms despite himself,
    Carried him off to be baptised. This project
    Was what the great, mysterious secret was
    Which all thine anxious love could not discover.
PAULINE. Thou blamedst me then for being importunate.
STRATONICE. I did not then foresee such dire misfortune.
PAULINE. Before abandoning my heart to grief,
    I must find out what power my tears can have.
    Being a wife and daughter, both, I hope
    They will o'ercome my husband or will sway
    My father. If they fail to influence either,
    I shall take counsel only with despair.
    But tell me what those two did in the temple.
STRATONICE. A sacrilege that hath no parallel.
    I cannot think of it without a shudder
    And fear I sin in telling thee about it.
    Hear briefly of their violence and daring.
      The priest had scarce secured a general silence
    And towards the east had turned his face, when they
    Exhibited their lack of all respect.
    At every moment of the ceremony
    They both alike displayed at will their folly
    And loudly mocked the sacred mysteries,
    Treating with scorn the gods who were invoked.
    The people murmured, and Felix was offended,

But both went on to worse impiety.
   "What!" Polyeucte cried to them, lifting his voice,
"Do ye adore vain gods of wood and stone?"
   Spare me from telling thee the blasphemies
Which they spewed forth 'gainst Jupiter himself.
Their mildest charge was incest and adultery.
   "Hear ye!" he then said. "Hear ye, all ye people!
The God of Polyeucte and of Nearchus
Is the almighty King of heaven and earth,
The one and only self-existent Being,
Sole master of our fate, the great First Cause
And sovereign end of all. It is this God,
The Christians' God, to whom our thanks are due
For all the triumphs of the Emperor Decius,
Since He alone holds victory in His hands.
He wills to exalt him; He can cast him down.
His goodness, power, and justice have no bounds:
He alone punisheth; He alone rewardeth:
Ye vainly worship monstrous, powerless gods."
   Seizing, at these words, on the wine and incense,
They flung the sacred vessels on the floor,
And without fear of Felix or Jove's thunder
They rushed with equal frenzy to the altar.
Ye heavens, have any like things e'er been witnessed!
The statue of the mightiest of the gods
We then saw overthrown by impious hands,
The mysteries interrupted, and the temple
Profaned, amid the uproar and the flight
Of the people, out of all control, who feared
Lest they should be o'erwhelmed by heaven's wrath.
Felix . . . But he is here, to tell the rest.

PAULINE.   How somber his face seems, and fraught with passions!
What sorrow he reveals, what indignation!

Enter FELIX.

FELIX.   To dare so foul an outrage! Publicly!
Before mine eyes! 'Twill cost his life—the traitor!
PAULINE.   Oh, let thy daughter clasp thy knees . . .
FELIX.   I spoke
Of Nearchus, not thy husband. Howe'er unworthy

  Of the fond name of son-in-law he is,
  My heart hath still a tender feeling towards him.
  The greatness of his crime and my displeasure,
  Hath not destroyed the love which made me choose him.

PAULINE. I looked for naught less from my father's goodness.

FELIX. I could have wreaked upon him my just anger.
  Thou art not ignorant of the horrid lengths
  To which his sacrilegious frenzy went.
  This, at least, thou couldst learn from Stratonice.

PAULINE. I know he is to see Nearchus punished.

FELIX. He will be better taught what course to take
  When he hath witnessed his corruptor's death.
   If one beholds the bloody spectacle
  Of a companion ere his own turn comes,
  The fear of dying and the love of life
  Will seize again so strongly on his soul
  That, viewing death, he ceases to desire it.
  Such sights can move one more than any threat.
  Polyeucte's rash zeal will soon be chilled, and we
  Shall see him beg of me with heart appalled
  A pardon for his great impiety.

PAULINE. Canst thou expect that he will thus lose courage?

FELIX. He should learn wisdom at Nearchus' cost.

PAULINE. He *should*; but oh, what prospect dost thou leave me,
  And what dread risk will not my husband run,
  If I from his inconstancy must hope
  The boon I did hope from my father's kindness!

FELIX. I show thee too much of it, in consenting
  To let him escape death by prompt repentance.
  I ought to give like crimes like punishment.
  In treating differently this guilty pair
  I betray justice, through paternal love,
  And make myself a criminal for his sake.
  I was expecting from thee in thy fear
  More thanks than there are plaints that now I hear.

PAULINE. Wherefore thank one who gives me naught? I know
  The temper and the spirit of these Christians.
  They remain obstinate to the very end.
  To insist that he repent, dooms him to die.

FELIX. His fate is in his own hands. Let him look to 't.

PAULINE. Give him, outright, his pardon.

FELIX.   He can win it.

PAULINE. Leave him not to the madness of his sect!

FELIX. I leave him to the laws I must respect.

PAULINE. Is this the aid thou givest thy daughter's husband?

FELIX. Let him do for himself as much as I
Do for him.

PAULINE.   But he is blind.

FELIX.   By his own will.
Who to his error clings would fain not know it
For what it is.

PAULINE.   Ah, father, in the name
Of all the gods . . .

FELIX.   Nay, do not call on them,
Our gods, whose sacred cause demands his death.

PAULINE. They hear our prayers.

FELIX.   Well, then, let *him* pray to them.

PAULINE. In the name of the Emperor, whence thou holdest office . . .

FELIX. I wield his power, but if he consigned it
To me, 'twas to employ it 'gainst his foes.

PAULINE. Is Polyeucte his foe?

FELIX.   All Christians are.

PAULINE. Do not apply to *him* that cruel maxim!
Wedding me, he became as of thy blood.

FELIX. I see his fault, not his relationship.
When crimes of State are joined with sacrilege,
Blood ties and friendship count with me no longer.

PAULINE. How great thy harshness!

FELIX.   Less great than his crime.

PAULINE. Too true fulfilment of my hideous dream!
Dost thou not see thou slayest thy daughter with him?

FELIX. My duty to the Emperor and the gods
Outweighs my duty to my family.

PAULINE. The loss of both of us, then, cannot stay thee?

FELIX. I have the gods and Decius, both, to fear.
But we have yet no grounds to expect aught ill.
Thinkest thou he will persist in madness still?
If he hath seemed to us to court destruction,
'Twas the first fervor of a recent convert.

PAULINE.   If thou still lovest him, give up the hope
That he will change his faith twice in one day.
Not only is it that Christians are more steadfast;
Thou dost expect too great inconstancy
In him. This is no error thoughtlessly
Imbibed in childhood with his mother's milk.
Polyeucte is by deliberate choice a Christian
And came with firm convictions to the temple.
Thou shouldst presume he is like all the others.
Death is to them not terrible nor shameful;
They glory in their hatred of our gods;
Blind to the things of earth, they covet heaven,
And, thinking its gates opened wide by death,
Care not if they are tortured, maimed, or slain.
They regard suffering as we do pleasure;
It leads them to the goal of their desires.
They call the vilest of deaths "martyrdom."

FELIX.   Very well, then! Polyeucte shall have his wish.
Speak we no more of it.

PAULINE.   Father . . .

(Enter ALBINUS.*)*

FELIX.   Is it over,
Albinus?

ALBINUS.   Yes, my lord. Nearchus hath
Paid for his crime.

FELIX.   And Polyeucte saw him die?

ALBINUS.   He saw him, but alas! with envious eye.
Instead of quailing, he longs to follow him.
His heart is not dismayed, but fortified.

PAULINE.   I told thee 'twould be thus. Once more, my father,
If my obedience hath ever pleased thee,—
If thou hast valued it,—if thou hast prized it . . .

FELIX.   Thou lovest too well an undeserving husband.

PAULINE.   Thou gavest him to me. My love is blameless.
He was thy choice, preferred above all others;
And I, to accept him, quenched the dearest love
E'er worthy of sanction in a gentle breast.
    Now, in the name of that prompt, blind obedience
Which I have always given thee as thy daughter,
If thou hast had complete sway over me,

Over my heart, now let me in my turn
Have some small sway o'er thee! By that just power
Of thine, at present so much to be feared,
By those dear feelings which I had to stifle,
Do not take from me what thou gavest me!
'Tis precious in my sight, and it hath cost me
Enough to be so.

FELIX.   Thou art too persistent.
Though I am kind of heart, I love not pity
Beyond the extent to which I wish to feel it.
Set for thy natural grief a task more fruitful.
To touch my heart despite me is a waste
Of time and tears. I mean to be the master
Of my emotions, and I would have it known
I disregard them when extorted from me.
Prepare thyself to see this wretched Christian,
And after I have done my best, do thine.
Go; vex no more a father who doth love thee.
Try to persuade thy husband to save for thee
His own life. I shall have him soon come hither.
But leave us now. I wish to talk with *him*. (*Indicating* ALBINUS.)

PAULINE. Ah pray, let . . .
FELIX.   Leave us, I say, here together.
Thy grief not only pains me; it annoys me.
Use all thy powers to win Polyeucte over.
Thou wilt gain more by pleading with me less.

                      (*Exeunt* PAULINE *and* STRATONICE.)
How met he death, Albinus?
ALBINUS.   Impiously,
With scorn of torments and contempt of life,
Without regret or murmur or dismay,
With obstinate and hardened heart—in short,
A Christian, blasphemy upon his lips.
FELIX. And the other?
ALBINUS.   As I told thee, nothing daunts him.
Far from aghast, his heart is higher now.
Force was required, to make him leave the scaffold.
He is in the prison, where I saw him led,
But thou art far from having tamed him yet.
FELIX. What misery is mine!

ALBINUS.　　　　　　　All pity thee.

FELIX.　None knoweth the woes which now assail my breast.
With grievous thought on thought 'tis sore distressed,
With care on care ever disquieted.
Hope and fear, love and hatred, joy and grief
Move it by turns. With feelings past belief
I am possessed—some fierce, some merciful,
Some generous, on which I dare not act,
Some even base, of which I am ashamed.
I love this wretch I chose for son-in-law;
I loathe the superstition which hath seized him;
I mourn his loss, but when I try to save him
I yet must guard the honor of the gods.
I dread their thunderbolts and those of Decius.
My office—nay, my own life—is at stake.
Hence now I court destruction for his sake,—
Now destroy *him* not to destroy myself.

ALBINUS.　Decius will pardon a father-in-law's affection.
Moreover, Polyeucte is of princely blood.

FELIX.　Strict are the orders not to spare a Christian.
The loftier their station, the more dangerous
Is their example. One can make no difference
Between them when they publicly offend;
And if one shields a crime done by a member
Of his own household, what authority,
What law, permits him to chastise in others
That which he sanctions in his family?

ALBINUS.　If thou dost not dare to have mercy on him,
Write unto Decius and leave all to *him*.

FELIX.　If I did that, Severus would destroy me.
His power and enmity cause my worst cares.
If I delayed to punish such a crime,
Though he be noble,—though he be magnanimous,—
He is a man, and not devoid of feelings,
And I disdained him. In his indignation
At having been so scorned, and with a heart
Reduced now to despair by Pauline's marriage,
He would use Decius' wrath to ruin me.
All seems permissible to avenge an insult,
And such an opportunity would tempt

Even the least vindictive. Possibly—
And there are reasons for my suspecting this—
Hope is rekindled in his breast already,
And, thinking he will soon see Polyeucte punished,
He cherishes anew a love which scarcely
Had he been able to renounce. Then judge
Whether his wrath, herein implacable,
Would hold me guiltless if I spared the guilty,
And whether he would spare *me* if he saw me
A second time frustrate his heart's desire.
    Shall I now tell thee an unworthy thought,
A base, vile thought? I stifle it; it comes
To life. It pleases and it vexes me.
Ambition always brings it to my mind
Afresh, and all that I can do is loathe it.
Here Polyeucte is the prop and stay of me
And mine; but if his death allowed Severus
To wed my daughter, I would thus acquire
A far more potent helper, who would set me
A hundred times as high as now I am.
My heart finds in that thought a perverse joy
In spite of me, but better heaven should blast me
Before thine eyes than e'er I should consent
To anything so infamous or I
To this extent mine honor should belie!

ALBINUS. Thy heart is much too good, thy soul too high . . .
Hast thou resolved to punish Polyeucte?

FELIX. I go now to the prison, to try my best
To cow his spirit with the threat of death;
And we shall, afterwards, see what Pauline
Can do.

ALBINUS.   But should he to the end remain
Obstinate, what wilt thou do finally?

FELIX. Nay, press me not. In this unhappy strait
I am unable to decide or choose.

ALBINUS. I ought to warn thee, as thy faithful servant,
That even now the city for his sake
Hath risen in revolt. It cannot see
Its last hope, the descendant of its kings,
Thus undergo the penalties of the law.

I deem his prison itself not sure to hold him:
I left all round it a great throng in tears;
I fear that they will force its doors.

FELIX. We must
Remove him from it, then, and bring him here
For safer custody.

ALBINUS. Thyself remove him
Thence; let the hope that thou wilt show him grace
Appease the frenzy of the populace.

FELIX. Come; if he will not cease to be a Christian,
Ere they know aught we shall dispose of him.

(*Exeunt.*)

A C T   I V

Enter POLYEUCTE, *led in by* CLEON *and three guards.*

POLYEUCTE. Guards, what is wished of me?

CLEON. Pauline would see thee.

POLYEUCTE. The encounter which I dread above all others!
Felix, I triumphed o'er thee in the prison,
Laughed at thy threats, saw thee unflinchingly.
To avenge thyself for thy defeat, thou takest
More potent weapons now. I fear much less
Thy executioners than her distress.
    O Lord, who seest the perils which I face,
Double thine aid in this my urgent need!
And thou who wentest lately hence victorious,
Look on my trials from thine abode of glory,
Nearchus! to o'ercome so strong a foe,
Stretch down a hand unto thy friend below!
    Guards, dare ye do me a kind favor? not
Save me from torture—it is not my thought
To escape a cruel death—but as three of you
Suffice to guard me, let the fourth oblige me
By going to fetch Severus. I believe
My wish can without risk be satisfied.
If I could tell him an important secret,
He would be happier, I would die contented.

CLEON. If thou so biddest me, I haste to obey.

POLYEUCTE.   Severus will reward thee, though I cannot.
  Go; lose no time; return immediately.
CLEON.   I shall be back here in a moment, sir.   (*Exit* CLEON.)
POLYEUCTE.

> Source of earth's joys and woes in equal store,
>   Deceptive pleasures, why trouble me anew?
> Shameful bonds of the flesh and the world, wherefore
>   Do ye not turn from me as I from you?
> Begone, delights and honors, my soul's foes! Alas,
>   Your entire felicity,
>   Being of the things that die,
>   Doth in a twinkling change and pass;
>   And though 'tis bright as clearest glass,
>   It hath the same fragility.

> Hope not that I shall sigh for you again.
>   To me your powerless charms ye vainly showed—
> Yea, showed throughout this empire vast in vain
>   The rich and prosperous enemies of God.
> He shows me in his turn their righteous overthrow:
>   How these great folk shall be undone,
>   And how the sword shall fall upon
>   Their guilty necks and fall but so
>   Much the surer as its blow
>   Shall have been foreseen by none.

> Tiger athirst for blood, Decius the cruel,
>   Long hath God left his children in thy power.
> See the dread sequel of thy haughty rule:
>   A little more, and thou shalt reach that hour
> When Scythians shall avenge the Persian and Christian dead.
>   Naught can save thee from that doom.
>   The thunderbolt that is to come,
>   Cleaving the sky, to cleave thy head
>   For thy sins, cannot be further stayed
>   By the hope that thou wilt turn therefrom.

> Let Felix sacrifice me to thy wrath.
>   Let a rival's power blind him. Let him have
> My rival for a son-in-law by my death,
>   And rule here still by making himself a slave.

I care no whit—nay, rather I to my fate aspire.
World, thou no more art aught to me;
My heart, now Christian utterly,
Burns only with a sacred fire;
And as an obstacle to higher
Things, and naught else, Pauline I see.

Delights of heaven, holy imaginings,
How full ye fill the heart that can receive
Such benisons. Those who possess these things,
And know their charm, henceforth cannot believe
That aught could daunt them. Ye promise much; ye give yet
more.
Your blessings are inconstant never,
And death, to crown my soul's endeavor,
Serves but as a kindly door
To bring us to that blessed shore
Where we shall find content forever.

'Tis thou, O fire divine, which naught can quench,
By whose aid I shall see Pauline, nor blench.

(*Enter* PAULINE.)

I see her, but my heart, which holy zeal
Enflames, no longer now doth feel her spell
As formerly, and mine eyes, that see the light
Of heaven, no more take pleasure in her sight.
Madam, what purpose makes thee have me brought here?
Wouldst thou contend with me or strengthen me?
Is this attempt, which showeth thy love complete,
Meant for mine aid or meant for my defeat?
Comest thou in enmity or in affection,
As my sworn foe or my soul's other half?

PAULINE.   Thou hast no foe at all here but thyself.
Thou hatest thyself, when everyone else loves thee.
Alone thou bringest to pass all that I dreamed.
Cease to desire thy doom, and thou art saved.
However great thy crime, thou wilt be reckoned
Guiltless if thou wilt on thyself have mercy.
Recall the stock from which thou art descended,
Thy glorious deeds, thy rare abilities.
Dear to the people, honored by thy sovereign,

    Son-in-law to the ruler of the province
    (I do not add thereto thou art my husband;
    'Tis my good fortune but no great thing for thee)
    Yet after thy brave exploits and high birth,
    After thy power, think of our just hopes
    And give not up to the executioner's hand
    All that a kind fate promised to our prayers!

POLYEUCTE.   I recall more. These my advantages
    I know, and know what hopes on such foundations
    Ambitious spirits build; yet they aspire,
    If truth be told, only to transient blessings
    Which cares will vex and dangers will attend.
    Death takes these from us; Fortune sports with them—
    Today a throne, a dunghill on the morrow—
    And their bright splendor rouseth so much envy,
    Few of your Caesars have enjoyed them long.
      I have ambition, but 'tis nobler, fairer.
    Those honors perish; I seek immortal honors,
    A bliss assured, eternal, infinite,
    Above the reach of envy and of fate.
    Is this too dearly bought with one poor life,
    Which soon and suddenly can be snatched from me,—
    Which gives me joy for but a fleeting moment
    And cannot promise safety after that?

PAULINE.   These are the foolish fancies of thy Christians.
    See with how strong a spell their lies have charmed thee:
    Such blessings are bought cheaply with thy lifeblood!
    But is that blood thine to dispose of thus?
    Thy life is thine only in sacred trust.
    The day which gave it to thee at the same time
    Bound thee with obligations: to thy sovereign
    Thou owest it, to the people, to the realm.

POLYEUCTE.   For them I would in battle lose it gladly.
    I know the joy and glory of so doing.
    The memory of Decius' ancestors
    Is reverenced, and the name he shares with them,
    Still precious to you Romans, placed the empire
    A full six centuries later in his hands.
    I ought to give my lifeblood for my country,
    My sovereign, and his crown; but how much more

I ought to give it for the God who gave me
My life! If dying for one's prince be glorious,
What must it be when for one's God one dies!

PAULINE. But such a God!

POLYEUCTE.   Soft, soft, Pauline! he hears thee;
For he is not a God like thy vain gods,
Deaf, mindless, powerless, broken, made of wood,
Of marble, or of gold as ye may choose.
This is the Christians' God, is mine, is thine;
And neither earth nor heaven knows any other.

PAULINE. Worship him in thy heart, and speak not of him.

POLYEUCTE. Be at once an idolater and a Christian?

PAULINE. Feign only for a moment. Let Severus
Depart, and give my father grounds for mercy.

POLYEUCTE. The mercy of my God is far more precious.
It saves me from the risks I might have run,
Leaves me no chance to turn back in my course
But crowns me ere I have begun the race,
Wafts me to harbor with the wind's first breath,
And straight from baptism sends me to my death.
If thou couldst know how small a thing life is
And by what ecstasy this death is followed!
But what availeth it to speak of these things
To one whom God hath not yet touched?

PAULINE.   Cruel man!
(For it is time my woe should find a vent
And crush a thankless soul with just reproaches)
Is this thy boasted love? are these thy vows?
Dost thou display the least affection for me?
I spoke not to thee of the cureless grief
In which thy death will leave thy hapless wife;
I deemed thy love would speak of it enough
To thee, and did not wish to force thy pity.
But can that steadfast, well-deservèd love
Which thou hadst promised me and I have given thee
Not draw from thee one tear, one single sigh,
When thou wouldst leave me, and when hence I die?
With joy, ungrateful wretch, thou goest from me.
Thou hidest it not; thou wishest me to see it.
Thy heart, unmoved by my sad charms, envisions

A happiness in which I have no part.
Is marriage, then, thus followed by aversion?
Thou loathest me after I have given thee all!
POLYEUCTE. Alas!
PAULINE.   Thou scarce couldst utter that "alas"!
Yet if it were the first step in repentance,
Though wrung from thee, how much it would delight me!
(*To herself*) But courage! he is moved; I see his tears.
POLYEUCTE. They flow; and would to God my shedding them
Could pierce at last this too hard heart of thine!
The lamentable state in which I leave thee
Deserves the tears my love accords to thee;
And if in heaven one can still feel sorrow,
I shall mourn even there thy woeful plight.
But if in that abode of bliss and glory,
This God who is entirely just and good
Can tolerate my prayer,—if he can deign
To hearken to thy husband's love for thee,—
Upon thy darkness he will shed his light.
   Lord, I must have this boon of thy great mercy.
She is too virtuous not to be a Christian.
It pleased thee to endow her far too richly
For her to know thee not and love thee not,—
To live a miserable slave of hell
And die as she was born, 'neath sin's sad yoke.
PAULINE. What sayest thou, wretched man? What darest thou hope?
POLYEUCTE. What I would gladly buy with all my blood.
PAULINE. Rather . . .
POLYEUCTE.   One strives in vain against this God.
He touches hearts when least they think on him.
For thee, that moment hath not yet arrived.
It *will* come, but I know not at what time.
PAULINE. Turn from these dreams, and love me.
POLYEUCTE.   I do love thee—
Far less than God, but far more than myself.
PAULINE. In the name of that love, oh, do not forsake me!
POLYEUCTE. In the name of that love, follow in my steps.
PAULINE. Is it not enough to leave me? Wouldst thou also
Lead me astray?

POLYEUCTE.   'Tis not enough to go
    Myself to heaven; I wish to guide thee thither.
PAULINE. Figments of fancy!
POLYEUCTE.   Nay, celestial truths!
PAULINE. Amazing blindness!
POLYEUCTE.   Nay, eternal light!
PAULINE. So thou preferrest death to Pauline's love!
POLYEUCTE. So thou preferrest the world to God's forgiveness!
PAULINE. Go, cruel man! Go, die! Thou ne'er hast loved me.
POLYEUCTE. Live happy in the world. Leave me in peace.
PAULINE. Yes, I shall leave thee there; no more be troubled.
    I shall go . . .

                         (*Enter* SEVERUS, FABIAN, *and* CLEON.)
                    But what brings thee here, Severus?
    Could it have been believed that one so noble
    Would come to mock the unfortunate?
POLYEUCTE.   Pauline,
    Thou treatest ill a nature such as his.
    Only at my request he visits me.
      I have not shown thee, sir, fit courtesies.
    This thou wilt pardon as due but to my chains.
    I have a treasure which I did not deserve.
    Let me, before I die, give it to thee
    And leave the rarest virtues that were ever
    Bestowed by heaven upon a mortal woman
    To the most honorable and valiant man,
    Adored by all, that Rome hath yet seen. Thou
    Art worthy of her, and she is worthy of thee.
    Do not refuse her from her husband's hand.
    He parted you; his death shall reunite you.
    May a love once so true, never grow less.
    Give her again thy heart; accept her vows;
    Live happily together, and each die
    Like me a Christian. That is the fair future
    That Polyeucte desires for both of you.
      Let me be led to death; I have naught more
    To say. Come, guards. 'Tis done.
                         (*Exeunt* POLYEUCTE, CLEON, *and guards.*)
SEVERUS.   I stand bewildered
    In my amazement at his mad resolve.

It is so nearly without parallel
That even yet I scarce can trust mine ears.
A man who loves thee—but what man so abject
That he could ever know thee and not love thee?—
A man loved by thee, just when thou wert his
Leaves thee without regret;—nay, he does more,
He yields thee to another; and as though
Thou and thy love were fatal gifts, he gives them,
Himself, unto his rival! Surely, either
Christians are in some wondrous way demented
Or their felicity must have no bounds,
Since to aspire to it they can renounce
That for which all the empire would not be
Too great a price. For *my* part, if my fortunes
Had prospered earlier and my devotion
Had been rewarded by thy hand in marriage,
I would have worshipped naught but thy bright eyes.
They would have been my kings, my deities.
Sooner had I been ground to dust or burned
To ashes . . .

PAULINE.   Stop! I fear that I might hear
Too much. Thy love's first ardor might impel thee
To utterance unworthy of us both.
Severus, know the whole heart of Pauline.
   My Polyeucte hath come to his last hour.
His life will end in but a moment more.
Thou art the cause of this, though innocently.
I know not if thy soul, swayed by its wishes,
Hath dared to found some hope on his destruction;
But understand, there is no death so cruel
I would not go to it with brow serene,
Nor hell hath horrors which I would not endure,
Ere I would stain my honor's purity
By wedding after *his* sad fate a man
Who in some fashion brought that fate upon him;
And if thou thoughtest I had a soul so vile,
The love I felt for thee would turn to hate.
   Generous art thou; be generous to the end.
My father will accord thee whatsoever
Thou wilt. He fears thee. And this one thing more

I tell thee: if he puts to death my husband,
'Twill be to thee that he will sacrifice him.
Oh, save this man! Bestir thyself for him.
Compel thyself to strive in his behalf.
I know how great a thing of thee I ask
But the more difficult it is to grant,
The greater glory thine in granting it.
To aid a rival whom thou enviest
Is a magnanimous act, meant for thee only,
And if that prospect of renown is not
Enough to urge thee on, 'tis no small matter
That thus a woman once so much beloved—
Who still, perhaps, can move thy heart—should owe
To thy nobility what is dearest to her.
Remember also that thou art Severus.
Farewell. Decide without my presence what
Thou dost prefer to do. If thou art not
Such a man as I dare to hope thou art,
To prize thee still, I do not wish to know it! (*Exit* PAULINE.)
SEVERUS.   What is this, Fabian? What new thunderbolt
Falls on my happiness and shatters it?
When I suppose it near, 'tis farthest off.
I find all lost when I believed all gained,
And Fortune, ever bent on injuring me,
Destroys my hopes as soon as they are born.
Before I urge my suit, I am refused—
Always sad, and embarrassed and ashamed
To see that hope could basely live again
In me, and still more basely show itself,
And, lastly, that a woman in distress
Should give me lessons in nobility.
    Thy fair soul is as lofty as unhappy,
But it is no less cruel than it is noble,
Pauline; and in thy grief thou dost too sorely
Mistreat a lover's heart entirely thine.
'Tis not enough, forsooth, that I must lose thee;
I needs myself must give thee to another;
I needs must serve a rival who forsakes thee,
And, that I may restore thee unto him,
Heedless of mine own pain, snatch him from death.

FABIAN.   Leave all that perverse family to its fate.
    Let that fate reconcile, if so it will,
    The father with the daughter, Polyeucte
    With Felix, and the husband with the wife.
    What reward hopest thou from such a task?
SEVERUS.   The glory of proving to this noble being
    That I am like her and am worthy of her,—
    That mine she should have been, and heaven's decree
    Wronged me when it denied her unto me.
FABIAN.   Accuse not Fate nor heaven of injustice.
    Rather, beware the perils thou wouldst incur.
    Thou riskest much; think better of it, sir.
    What! thou wilt undertake to save a Christian?
    Canst thou not know what is and always hath been
    The hate of Decius for that impious sect?
    What thou intendest is so great a crime
    In his sight, it may cost thee even his favor.
SEVERUS.   This warning would have weight with common souls.
    Though in his hand he holds my life and fortunes,
    I am Severus still, and all his power
    Can stay me not from honor or from duty.
    Honor constrains me now, and I will heed it.
    Henceforth let Fate be kindly or be adverse,
    As it by nature is inconstant ever,
    If I die nobly, I shall die content.
      More I shall tell thee, confidentially.
    Christians are not as they are thought to be.
    They are much hated—why, I do not know,
    And only in this matter Decius seems
    To me unjust. From curiosity
    I have desired to have some knowledge of them.
    'Tis thought that they are sorcerers, vile servants
    Of hell, and on account of this belief
    The celebration of their secret mysteries,
    Which we in no wise comprehend, is punished
    By death; and yet like them the Bona Dea
    And Eleusinian Ceres have their mysteries
    In Rome and Greece. Moreover, we permit
    Freely in every place all sorts of gods,
    Their God alone excepted. All the monsters

Of Egypt have their temples even at Rome.
Our ancestors made of a man a god,
And we inherit their errors with their blood
And in the skies set all our emperors;
But so much deification casts a doubt,
Frankly, upon such metamorphoses.
  The Christians have but one God, the supreme
Master of all things. By his will alone
He does whate'er he wills. Yet if I dare
Tell thee, between ourselves, my inmost thoughts,
Our gods are often little in accord
With one another, and—even though their anger
Blast me before thine eyes for saying this—
Are over-numerous to be true gods.
Besides, the life these Christians live is blameless.
Vice they abhor; virtue they cultivate.
They offer prayers for those that rack and slay them,
And in the whole time of their persecution
When have they struck back, when have they rebelled?
Have our commanders had more faithful soldiers?
Fierce in war, tame before our executioners,
They fight like lions and they die like lambs.
I pity them too much not to defend them.
Then let us go find Felix and begin
In the instance of his son-in-law to aid them,
And satisfy by one act in this fashion
Pauline, my honor, and my just compassion.

(Exeunt.)

ACT V

FELIX, ALBINUS, *and* CLEON *are discovered.*

FELIX. Seest thou not Severus' trickery,
        Albinus? Seest thou not in sooth his hate?
        And seest thou my misery?
ALBINUS.   I can see
        Nothing in him but a magnanimous lover,
        Nothing in thee but a relentless father.
FELIX. How ill thou readest from the face the mind!
        At heart he hates Felix and scorns Pauline;

And if he loved her formerly, he now deems
The leavings of his rival too unworthy
Of him. He speaks in Polyeucte's behalf,
Begs me, and threatens me; he will undo me,
He says, if I do not accord him mercy.
Pretending generosity, he thinks
To frighten me. The trick is much too clumsy
Not to betray his purpose. I know the wiles
Of people of the Court. Better than he
I know their cleverest shifts. It is in vain
He storms and feigns to be infuriated.
I see his real intentions with the Emperor.
If I should do that which he asks of me,
He would denounce it as a crime; and so,
Sparing his rival, I would be his victim.
   Now, if he had to deal with some dull blunderer,
His well-laid snare would doubtless ruin him.
But an old courtier is less credulous;
He can perceive when he is being played with,—
When someone is dissembling; and as for me,
So much of all devices have I seen
That I, if there were need, could give Severus
Lessons in them.

ALBINUS.   Gods! how thou torturest
Thyself by thy distrust of him!

FELIX.   The noble
Science of living in a Court is this:
When any man once hath good cause to hate us,
We must presume he seeks means to undo us,—
Must doubt whatever friendship he professes.
If Polyeucte, then, does not abjure his faith,
Whate'er Severus feels at heart towards him
I shall obey the imperial mandate strictly.

ALBINUS. Nay, mercy, my lord! Grant this to Pauline.

FELIX. The Emperor's mercy would not follow mine,
And far from saving Polyeucte from his plight,
My clemency would but destroy us both.

ALBINUS. Severus promises . . .

FELIX.   I do not trust him,
Albinus, and I know better than he

How great is Decius' hatred of the Christians.
If he offends the Emperor for their sake,
He will destroy himself along with us.
    But still I wish to try another tack.
    (*To* CLEON) Bring Polyeucte. If I send him hence again,—
If this last effort for him proves in vain,—
Let him, on leaving here, be put to death.

(Exit CLEON.)

ALBINUS. 'Tis a harsh order.

FELIX.   It must be obeyed
If I am to prevent a riot here.
I see the people roused in his behalf,
And thou thyself just now warned me against them.
With so much feeling shown for him already,
I know not if I could control them long.
Perhaps tomorrow, or tonight, or sooner,
Things would ensue that I would fain not see;
And then Severus would for his revenge
Fly with the news to Rome and slander me.
I must avert this blow, which would undo me.

ALBINUS. What a misfortune such keen foresight is!
Everything harms thee; everything undoes thee;
Everything causes thee anxiety.
Think of how Polyeucte's death will fill the people
With rage, and of how poor a way to quiet them
It is, to drive them to despair.

FELIX.   Their murmurs
Will be without avail when he is dead;
And if they dare proceed to violence,
'Tis but to bear a short while their presumption.
I shall have done my duty, come what may.
    But here is Polyeucte. Let us try to save him.

(Enter guards with POLYEUCTE.)

Soldiers, withdraw, and guard the portal well.

(Exeunt guards.)

    Dost thou, indeed, hate life so bitterly,
Unhappy Polyeucte, and do Christian precepts
Command thee to desert thy family?

POLYEUCTE. I hate not life; I love the living of it,
But am not bound to it with slavery's bonds.

2 6 5

       Always am I prepared to give it back
       Again unto the God from whom I hold it.
       Thus reason bids me feel, and Christian precepts,
       And thus I show you all how one should live
       If ye have hearts with courage to follow me.
FELIX. Follow thee to the abyss where thou wouldst plunge?
POLYEUCTE. Rather to glory, whither I shall mount.
FELIX. Give me at least the time to know of this.
       Serve as my guide, to make of me a Christian.
       Scorn not to instruct me in thy faith, or thou
       Thyself shalt answer to thy God for me.
POLYEUCTE. Nay, Felix, mock not; he will be thy judge.
       No refuge wilt thou find, when brought before him.
       Shepherds and kings are of the same rank there.
       He will avenge the blood of all his children
       Upon thee.
FELIX.   I will shed no more of it;
       And let come what come may, I will permit
       Christians to live in safety in their faith.
       I will protect them.
POLYEUCTE.   No, no; persecute them,
       And be the instrument of their happiness.
       True Christians find it only in their suffering.
       The cruelest torments are to them rewards.
       God, who repays good deeds a hundred fold,
       Sends persecutions as a crowning gift.
       But these are secrets which thou canst not fathom;
       To none but his elect does God reveal them.
FELIX. I tell thee truly: I wish to be a Christian.
POLYEUCTE. What, then, can stay thee from accomplishing
       Thy wish?
FELIX.   The ill-timed presence here . . .
POLYEUCTE.   Of whom?
       Severus?
FELIX.   On account of him alone
       Have I pretended so much wrath against thee.
       Feign for a moment, until he departs.
POLYEUCTE. Felix, is this, then, how thou speakest the truth?
       Bring to thy pagans, to thine idols bring,
       The poisoned sweetness of thy honeyed words.

A Christian feareth naught and feigneth naught.
In all men's sight he is a Christian always.
FELIX. The fervor of thy faith serves but to blind thee
If thou wouldst die now rather than instruct me.
POLYEUCTE. This is no time to tell thee of that faith.
It is a gift of heaven, not of reason,
And soon can I, seeing God face to face,
More easily obtain for thee his grace.
FELIX. But losing thee will fill me with despair.
POLYEUCTE. That loss 'tis in thy power to repair.
Losing one son-in-law, thou gainest another,
Whose fortunes accord better with thine own.
My loss is but a helpful change for thee.
FELIX. Talk not to me in this outrageous way.
I have been kinder unto thee than thou
Deservest. But in spite of my good will,
Which grew the more as thou didst flout me still,
Thine insolence must finally rouse mine anger.
I shall avenge our gods and myself, too.
POLYEUCTE. What! thou so soon changest thy mood and speech?
Zeal for thy gods re-entereth thy breast?
Gone is thy wish to be a Christian! I
By chance have made thee speak the truth indeed!
FELIX. Nay, do not think, whate'er I swore to thee,
That I believe the lies of thy new teachers.
I humored then thy madness, to prevent thee
From falling headlong to a shameful death.
I sought but to gain time to pardon thee
As soon as Decius' minion had gone hence;
But I have wronged too much our sovereign gods.
Choose: give to them the incense or thy blood.
POLYEUCTE. My choice is easy. But I see Pauline.
Ah heaven!
(*Enter* PAULINE.)
PAULINE. Which of you twain today will kill me?
Shall it be both at once or each in turn?
Can I make neither natural affection
Nor love yield to my prayers? Can I in no wise
Obtain aught from a husband or a father?
FELIX. Speak to thy husband.

POLYEUCTE (*to* PAULINE).   Wed Severus.
PAULINE.   Monster!
    Kill me at least without insulting me.
POLYEUCTE.   Because I love and pity thee, I seek
    To solace thee. I see what grief possesses
    Thy soul, and well I know another love
    Is the one remedy for this. Aforetime
    Severus by his true worth charmed thy heart,
    And hence, if near thee, he should still be able
    To charm it. Thou didst love him; he loves thee;
    And now his new-won glory . . .
PAULINE.   What have I
    Done to thee, cruel man, to be treated thus
    And be reproached—thou scorning my devotion—
    For the great love that I o'ercame for thee?
    Think of how sorely I have had to strive
    To vanquish for thy sake so strong a foe,
    What battles mine to give to thee a heart
    So justly won by its first conqueror;
    And if ingratitude does not rule *thy* heart,
    Use some compulsion on thyself in turn
    That thou mayest be restored unto Pauline.
    Learn thou from her to master thine own feelings.

    Let *her* course be thy guide in this thy blindness.
    Let her obtain thy life's gift from thy hands
    That she may always live beneath thy sway.
    If still thou canst refuse such lawful wishes,
    At least behold her tears and hear her sighs.
    Oh, drive not to despair one who adores thee!
POLYEUCTE.   I have already said, and say again,
    Live with Severus or else die with me.
    I do not scorn thy tears nor thy devotion,
    But howsoe'er our love pleads in my heart,
    Henceforth I know thee not unless thou art
    A Christian.
            Enough, Felix! Now resume
    Thy wrath and on a man so insolent
    Avenge thy gods together with thyself.
PAULINE.   Ah, father, though his crime be hard to pardon,
    If he is mad thou art not. Family ties

Are very strong, and natural affection
For those of one's own blood is never lost.
A father does not cease to be a father,
And so I still dare cling to some slight hope.
   Look on thy daughter with a father's eye.
My death will follow that of him I love.
The gods will deem his execution wrong
Because 'twill punish innocence as well
As guilt and by this double act become
No just requital but a dire injustice.
Our fates, which thou hast linked inseparably,
Must on us both confer like weal or woe;
And thou wouldst be cruel to the last extreme
Wert thou to sunder those thou hast united.
A heart once given to another heart
Cleaves to it and bleeds if they are torn apart.
But thou art moved, seeing my misery,
And viewest my tears with a fond parent's eye.

FELIX. Yes, child, a father is a father always:
   That is true. Naught can break that sacred tie.
   I have a tender heart; thy grief hath touched it.
   I join with thee in trying to save this madman.
     Wretched Polyeucte, art thou alone unfeeling?
   Alone wouldst keep thy crime from being pardoned?
   Canst thou behold such sorrow with indifference?
   Canst thou behold such love and not be moved?
   Seest thou thy father-in-law and wife no more
   With friendship for the one, love for the other?
   To make thee answer to the names again
   Of son-in-law and husband, is it needful
   That thou shouldst see us both cling to thy knees?

POLYEUCTE. What sorry grace have all these artifices!
   When twice thou hast attempted threats,—when thou
   Hast made me see Nearchus die,—when thou
   Hast tried love and love's prayers,—when thou hast shown me
   This eagerness for baptism, to oppose
   To God the interests of God himself,—
   Thou joinest in *her* plea. Ah, snares of hell!
   Must one so often conquer ere he triumphs?
   Too long a time thou needest for thy decisions.

Come! reach one now; mine has been reached already.
 I worship one sole God, master of all things,
Before whom tremble heaven and earth and hell—
One God, who, loving us with boundless love,
To save us chose to die a shameful death,
And who, as a result of this great love,
Desireth to be offered as a victim
Each day for us. But I do wrong to speak
Hereof to those who cannot understand me.
See the blind error that ye dare maintain!
To all your gods ye impute the blackest crimes.
Ye punish naught that hath not in the skies
Its patron. Lechery, adultery, incest,
Theft, murder—everything that men detest—
By their example is commended to you.
I have profaned their temple, broke their altars,
And I would do it again, were it still to do,
E'en before Felix, e'en before Severus,
Before the Senate, before the Emperor.

FELIX. My kindness now gives place to righteous wrath.
Worship the gods, or die.

POLYEUCTE.   I am a Christian.

FELIX. Blasphemer, worship them, I say, or live
No more.

POLYEUCTE. I am a Christian.

FELIX.   Art thou so?
O heart too obdurate!
 (*Raising his voice*) Soldiers, carry out
The orders that I gave.

          (*Enter guards.*)

PAULINE.   Where lead ye him?

FELIX. To death.

POLYEUCTE. To glory. Dear Pauline, farewell.
Do not forget me.

PAULINE.   I will follow thee
Where'er thou goest, and die if thou dost die.

POLYEUCTE. Follow me not, unless thou turnest from error.

FELIX. Away with him! Obey me! Since he wishes
To perish, I will grant him leave to perish.

POLYEUCTE

(The guards lead out POLYEUCTE. PAULINE *follows them.)*

    Albinus, I did violence to my feelings,
But I was forced to do it. The kindliness
Natural to me could easily have destroyed me.
    Now let the people manifest their rage,
Severus in his anger storm and thunder;
Having constrained myself thus, I am safe.
    But art thou not amazed at Polyeucte's
Callousness? Hast thou ever seen a heart
So hard, or impiousness in such degree?
At least I satisfied my troubled conscience.
I o'erlooked naught that might have softened him;
I even feigned—thou sawest me—utter baseness;
And truly, but for his last blasphemies,
Which filled me suddenly with wrath and terror,
I scarcely could have conquered my reluctance.

ALBINUS. The day may come when thou wilt curse that victory,
    Which in some aspects was a heinous crime
    Unworthy of Felix, or of any Roman,
    Shedding with thine own hand blood near to thee.

FELIX. Thus did, of old, Brutus and Manlius;
    But thence their honor, far from being impaired,
    Grew greater; also, had our ancient heroes
    Had any bad blood, to be rid of it,
    They gladly would have opened their own breasts.

ALBINUS. Thy zeal misleads thee, but whate'er it tells thee,
    When it hath once grown cool and thou reflectest,—
    When thou beholdest Pauline, and her despair
    Moves thee too sorely with her tears and cries . . .

FELIX. Thou causest me to remember that she followed
    This traitor, and the woe that she displayed
    Might make it hard to carry out my orders.
    Go, then; run where they are, and assume charge
    And see what she is doing. Override
    Whatever obstacles her grief may raise.
    Take her away from the sad sight, if thou canst.
    Try to console her. Go, I say. What stays thee?

ALBINUS. There is no need to go. She has come back.

Enter PAULINE.

PAULINE. Complete, complete thy work, barbarian father!
    Here is another victim for thy rage.
    Unite thy daughter with thy son-in-law
    Again. Nay, shrink not; why dost thou delay?
    Thou seest the selfsame crime, or selfsame virtue,
    In me that was in him. Thy cruelty
    Hath new occasion for its exercise.
    In death my husband left his light to me.
    His blood, in which thy executioners bathed me,
    Hath now unsealed mine eyes and opened them.
      I see, I know, and I believe; I am
    Released from error. With that blessed blood
    Thou seest me baptized. I am a Christian,
    In short. Have I not said enough? Preserve
    By slaying me thy station and prestige.
    Fear thou the Emperor; fear Severus, too.
    If thou wouldst live, my death is necessary.
    Polyeucte calls me to this happy fate.
    I see him and Nearchus stretching out
    Their arms to me. Lead, lead me to your gods,
    Whom I abhor. They broke but one of them;
    I will break all the rest. I shall be seen
    Defying there all that ye hold in dread—
    Those powerless thunderbolts wherewith ye arm them—
    In God's cause flouting the authority
    Which birth imposed on me, and for one time
    Failing in my obedience to thee!
      'Tis not my grief which I exhibit thus.
    'Tis Grace which speaks in me, and not despair.
    Must I repeat it, Felix? I am a Christian.
    Make certain, by my death, thy destiny
    And mine. The deed will be invaluable
    To both of us, because it will ensure
    Thy fortunes here and lift me up to heaven.

Enter SEVERUS *and* FABIAN.

SEVERUS. Unnatural father, miserable intriguer,
    Ambitious slave of unsubstantial fears!
    Polyeucte is dead, and by thy cruelty
    Thou thinkest to preserve thy wretched honors!

The favor that I offered thee for him,
Instead of saving him, hath sealed his doom!
I begged, I threatened, but I could not move thee.
Thou thoughtest me treacherous or of little power.
Well, thou wilt to thy cost learn that Severus
Makes no vain boast of that which he can do,
And in thy downfall thou shalt judge if he
Who can crush thee could have protected thee.
Continue faithfully to serve the gods.
Show them thy zeal by fresh atrocities.
Farewell; but when the storm breaks o'er thy head,
Doubt not from whose arm come its buffetings.

FELIX.   Stay, sir, and with a heart content allow me
To put an easy vengeance in thy hands.
    No more reproach me for my having tried
By cruelty to preserve my wretched honors.
I lay them, with their false charms, at thy feet.
The estate to which I dare aspire is nobler.
I find myself constrained mysteriously;
I yield to feelings quite outside my ken;
And by a change I cannot understand
From my late anger turn to Polyeucte's faith.
'Tis he, beyond a doubt, whose innocent blood
Begs the one God to save his persecutor.
His love, poured out on all the household, draws
Not his wife only, but her father also
To follow him. I made of him a martyr;
His death has made of me a Christian. I
Ushered him to his bliss; he now seeks mine.
That is the way a Christian becomes angry
And takes revenge. O blessed cruelty
Of which the consequences are so kind!
Give me thy hand, Pauline. Bring chains, Severus;
Immolate to the gods these two new Christians.
I am one; she is one: glut now thy wrath.

PAULINE.   How joyfully I find again my father!
This glad change makes my happiness complete.

FELIX.   To Him who caused it, child, be all the glory.

SEVERUS.   Who would behold unmoved a scene so touching?
A change like this must be miraculous.

Surely your Christians, whom we persecute
In vain, have something in them more than human.
They lead a life so pure that heaven owes them
Some recompense. To rise again with strength
The greater as they are the more downtrodden
Is no result of ordinary virtue.
Whate'er was said of them, I always loved them
And in my heart grieved when I saw them die.
Perhaps I yet, someday, shall know them better.
Meanwhile, I would that all should have their gods
And serve them in their own way, without fear
Of punishment. If ye are Christians, dread
My hate no longer, Felix; I love Christians
And will not, after being their protector,
Become at thy expense their persecutor.
    Keep thine authority; resume its tokens.
Serve well thy God; serve well our emperor.
I shall lose all my favor with his Highness
Or ye shall see his cruel commands revoked.
This unjust hate of his too sorely wrongs him.

FELIX.   May heaven deign to achieve its work through thee
And, to reward thee as thou well deservest,
Ere long breathe all its truth into thy soul!
    We others now should bless our happy lot.
Let us give burial to our martyrs, kiss
Their sacred bodies first, consign them straightway
To worthy sepulchers, and then acclaim
With glad cries everywhere God's holy name.

Rodogune

CHARACTERS IN THE PLAY

CLEOPATRE, *Queen of Syria; widow of Demetrius Nicanor.*

ANTIOCHUS ⎫
⎬ *sons of Demetrius Nicanor and Cleopatre.*
SELEUCUS ⎭

RODOGUNE, *sister of Phraates, King of Parthia.*

TIMAGENES, *tutor of Antiochus and Seleucus.*

ORONTES, *ambassador of Phraates.*

LAONICE, *sister of Timagenes; lady-in-waiting of Cleopatre.*

The scene represents a room in the royal palace in Seleucia, the capital of Syria.

The French form of the Queen's name, Cleopatre (a trisyllable, "Cle-o-patr'," accented on the last syllable), is retained in this translation because in the mind of everyone the name "Cleopatra" is inseparably associated with Antony's Cleopatra of Egypt. Himself conscious of the possibility of their confusion, Corneille uses the name of the Queen in stage directions only; in the spoken lines she is always called "the Queen."

"Rodogune" is similarly to be pronounced as a trisyllable, rhyming with "moon." "Laonice" is in English a word of four syllables, accented on the first and third syllables. The names of all the other dramatis personae are accented on the second syllable.

Rodogune

ACT I

LAONICE and TIMAGENES are discovered.

LAONICE. At last this great, this happy day has dawned
Which terminates the long, long night of strife—
This glorious day when marriage ends all vengeance,
Brings peace once more to us and Parthia,
Sets free its princess, and forever gives us
Instead of grounds for war a bond of concord!
This day has come, my brother, when our queen,
No longer keeping her uneasy crown,
Must break before all men her stubborn silence
And say which prince is older, of the twins.
The advantage of one moment's prior birth,
Whereof till now she hath concealed the truth,
Shall make of one a king, of one a subject,—
Shall give to fortune's favorite the scepter.
But art thou not amazed that this same queen
Gives him for wife the object of her hate
And names a king only to crown at last
Her whom she loved to torture when a captive?
Rodogune, treated as her slave till now,
Will see herself raised to the throne by her,
Since that one of the twins whom she declares
Our king is to be wedded to the Princess.
TIMAGENES. That I may marvel more, vouchsafe, I beg thee,
To let me learn from thee of Syria's troubles.
I saw the first of them and still remember
The hapless fate of the great king Nicanor,
Who, following fast the routed Parthians
In their adroit flight, fell into their hands
At the conclusion of his pursuit of them.
Neither have I forgot that this disaster
Caused the revolt of the perfidious Trypho.
Seeing the King in chains, the Queen forlorn,
He thought that he could seize the tottering throne

And bring the realm at once beneath his sway
If Fortune favored him in his wicked efforts.
The Queen, who feared the worst from this new danger,
Found shelter from it for those whom she held dearest.
Not to expose her sons of tender age,
She had me carry them away to Memphis
Unto her brother. There we have heard naught
Except from rumors, whose confused report,
Diversely borne, hath brought to even our ears
The story of those great reverses only
Obscurely in a hundred different forms.

LAONICE. Know, then, that Trypho, after four encounters,
Having reduced us to this single city,
Promptly besieged it; and, to crown our fears,
False tidings reached us that the King was dead.
The frightened populace, who were at heart
Already loath to obey a woman's orders,
Sought to compel the Queen to choose a husband.
What could she do, alone against them all?
Thinking the King dead, she espoused his brother.
The sequel showed this course was advantageous.
The prince Antiochus, the new sovereign, seemed
To bring success with him where'er he went.
The victories which accompanied his arms
Now gave our haughty foes our recent fear,
And in a final battle Trypho's death
Changed all our fortunes, won back all our land.
  Whatever promise King Antiochus
Had made the Queen to set her sons again
Upon their father's throne, he showed so little
Desire to do this that she never dared
To have them return home. When he had reigned
For seven years, his martial spirit made him
Revive that strife which caused his brother's downfall.
He attacked Parthia, thinking himself strong
Enough to avenge on it the imprisonment
And death of King Nicanor; for *his* sake
He carried the war thither, and became
On every side as feared as heaven's lightnings,
Joined battle there, and with unnumbered exploits . . .

But I shall tell the rest some other time.
One of the princes comes.

Enter ANTIOCHUS. *She starts to withdraw.*

ANTIOCHUS.   Stay, Laonice.
Thou canst, like him, do me a service. Sad
And full of care, in this my present plight,
If I have great hopes, I have fears as great.
One word tomorrow will decide my fate,
Will take from me or give to me the scepter
And Rodogune forever; and of all
Mortals the revelation of our secret
Will make me the most desolate or the happiest.
I see at stake all blessings that I long for,
And I cannot be fortunate without
My brother being unfortunate, a brother
So dear that our affection's sacred bond
Gives half of his unhappiness to me.
Then to risk less I fain would seek for less,
And to avoid the issue which my heart
Dares not abide, concede to him the one
Of the two prizes which is the more dazzling,
To assure myself of that one which is more
Precious to me—to me, who would be happy
If, without waiting for the tiresome question
Of our priority to be decided,
I might give up a doubtful throne and for it
Obtain the Princess, and by this division
Of blessings spare to both of us the sighs
Born of my pain or his dissatisfaction.
    Seek him for me, Timagenes, and tell him
That for this lovely maiden I resign
The kingdom unto him, but picture to him
The joys of reigning as so wonderful
That he will let the splendor of a throne
Prevail on him,—will let it blind him so
That he will not appreciate at what price
Do I consent to take him for my master.
    (*To* LAONICE) And thou, in my behalf, seek this dear being
And try to bring her glance down to a vassal

Who might perhaps ascend today the throne
If *his* eyes were not fixed on her alone
And he did not prefer her to that kingship
For which the noblest hearts shed all their blood.
TIMAGENES. Sir, the Prince cometh, and thou in thy love
    Canst offer him, thyself, the diadem.
ANTIOCHUS. Ah, how I tremble! The fear of a refusal,
    In which he would be wholly justified,
    Makes my tongue silent and my mind confused.

Enter SELEUCUS.

SELEUCUS (*to* ANTIOCHUS). Can I tell thee in strictest confidence
    My thoughts?
ANTIOCHUS.   Speak. Any doubt wrongs our affection.
SELEUCUS. Alas! Some wrong to it is what I dread.
    'Tis grounded, brother, in our equality;
    That is its basis, bond, and guarantee;
    And when on one of us every advantage
    Falls, I have reason to fear that the destruction
    Of our equality will destroy our tie
    And that this day will end our lives' good fortune
    By giving one of us but shame and envy.
ANTIOCHUS. As we have always shared the selfsame feelings,
    This fear assails me, brother, equally.
    But well I know its cure, if this thou wishest.
SELEUCUS. If this I wish? I bring it, and consign
    To thee all joys which in a crown inhere.
    Yes, sire, for I am speaking to my king,
    For the throne given thee, give me Rodogune,
    And I shall nowise envy thy good fortune.
    Thus in our fate there will be nothing shameful;
    Thus will our happiness be never doubtful;
    And we shall scorn this right of prior birth,
    Thou with the throne content, I with the Princess.
ANTIOCHUS. Ah me!
SELEUCUS.   Art thou displeased to hear my offer?
ANTIOCHUS. Canst thou call "offer" a desire to choose,
    Which, with the same hand that resigns a realm
    To me, wrests from me a yet greater thing
    And the sole blessing to which *I* aspire?

SELEUCUS.   Rodogune?
ANTIOCHUS.   Yes. These *(indicating* TIMAGENES *and* LAO-
     NICE) will bear witness for me.
SELEUCUS.   Thou settest such store by her?
ANTIOCHUS.   Dost thou set less?
SELEUCUS.   She is well worth a throne, I must confess.
ANTIOCHUS.   In *my* sight she is worth the whole of Asia.
SELEUCUS.   Thou lovest her, then, my brother?
ANTIOCHUS.   So dost thou.
     That is my whole misfortune, all my woe.
     I hoped the splendor which adorns a throne
     Would rouse thy longings more than this rare being,
     But even as I thou knowest the value of her
     And thou hast made, before me, the right choice.
     Ah, hapless prince!
SELEUCUS.   Ah, too contrarious fate!
ANTIOCHUS.   What would I do 'gainst any but a brother!
SELEUCUS.   O brother! Name too precious for a rival!
     What would I not do against all but thee!
ANTIOCHUS.   O brotherly affection, where wilt lead me?
SELEUCUS.   Love, which shall conquer here, thou or affection?
ANTIOCHUS.   Love, love shall conquer, and forlorn affection
     Shall be, between us, but a thing to pity.
     A great soul yields a throne, with honor yields it;
     This noble act makes memorable that soul;
     But when love's worthy object fires our hearts,
     He who yields that, is base and cannot love.
     Rodogune hath enchanted us alike.
     Let us no longer, through excess of yearning,
     Wrong her. She needs must wed, not thee, not me,
     But whichsoever of us shall be king.
     The crown still hangs uncertainly between us,
     But certain is it that she must be queen.
     Yet, blinded with our own vain purposes,
     We both would make of her a subject's wife!
     Let us seek to reign. The ambition well becomes us,
     Whether for her abandoned or resumed;
     And this throne, which we both would fain renounce,
     Let us alike desire—to place her on it.
     This in our circumstances is the only

Counsel to follow; we can sorrow o'er it,
But we must needs look forward to naught else.
SELEUCUS. Still more is necessary. Our affection
Must triumph on this great day, as well as love.
Those sieges world-renowned of Thebes and Troy,
Which deluged one with blood, swept one with flames,
Had as the basis of their untold evils
Only those ills which Fate combines for us.
It breeds between us all the jealousy
That once unpeopled Greece and ravaged Asia.
Two men, like us, had like hopes of the throne;
Two loved, like us, alike the same fair woman.
Thebes perished for the one cause, Troy for the other.
All must needs fall to thy lot or to mine.
Affection vainly made us try to share it;
And if I may be frank, 'tis a frail title—
Doubtful priority on a mother's word—
That will crown one with glory, one with woe.
With double stakes, the luckless one will have
What reasons for disputing a decision
Given upon such weak authority!
What grounds for wrath! Alas! judge the result.
Dread the fell outcome of all this, with me,
Or rather make with me a worthy effort
To fortify thy soul 'gainst such a fate.
Despite a throne's lure and a woman's love,
May our affection so well sway our hearts
That either of us in his loss will stifle
Any regret that counsels him amiss,
And in his brother's happiness find his own.
Thus what aforetime destroyed Thebes and Troy
In our accordant hearts will cause but joy.
Thus our affection, in its turn triumphant,
Will vanquish jealousy though we are in love,
Defy the cruel decrees of destiny,
And find some sweetness midst our coming woes.
ANTIOCHUS. Brother, canst thou do this?
SELEUCUS. Ah, do not press me!
At least I wish to, brother; that is enough;

And reason will maintain such sway o'er me
That if my heart sighs, I shall disavow it.
ANTIOCHUS.   Like thee, I cherish these noble sentiments;
But let us fortify them with an oath,
That, being witness to our sworn affection,
The gods will make it survive such a trial.
SELEUCUS.   Let us go bind ourselves before their altars
With holy bonds and everlasting pledges.

(*Exeunt* ANTIOCHUS *and* SELEUCUS.)

LAONICE.   Can one more thoroughly deserve the crown?
TIMAGENES.   I am no whit surprised by what astounds thee.
Assured of both, foreseeing their distress,
I have foreseen their constancy as well
And pitied their misfortunes. But I pray thee,
Finish the history which thou begannest.
LAONICE.   To take it up, then, where 'twas interrupted:
The Parthians, brought to battle by our forces,
Now almost conquerors, now almost conquered,
Beheld the uncertain victory hover long
Above both armies, equally successful;
But fortune turned against us finally,
So that Antiochus, pierced by countless wounds
And on the point of being made a prisoner
By a detachment of the enemy,
Chose to snatch from them his life's remnant, and,
Preferring honorable death to fetters,
Himself by his own hand achieved his end.
    Soon after the Queen learned of this sad news,
She received other tidings still more cruel:
That it had been a false report which she
Had heard and credited about the death
Of her first husband; that Nicanor lived;
That, bitterly resenting her remarriage,
He had resolved to do as she had done,
And, to escape the shackles of his foes,
Was soon to wed the King of Parthia's sister.
That was this princess Rodogune, in whom
Both the twin brothers find the same attractions
Their father found. Our queen to no avail
Sent messages to justify her conduct.

Fruitless was her defense, vain were her prayers,
Encountering an inexorable judge.
In his new love, he wished to think her guilty,
Her error was a crime, and that he might
Punish her better, it was his desire
To marry Rodogune before her face,
To tear the diadem from off her brow
And crown another in her very presence—
Whether because his vengeance thus would be
The more humiliating to her, or whether
Because the marriage in this way would have
Greater authoritativeness and he
Would by his cruel course better assure
To children born of it the throne of Syria.

    But when, impelled by wrath and love, he came
To disinherit her sons by his return,
And a great squadron of exultant Parthians,
Riding as to the chase, conducted hither
The betrothed couple, the Queen, in her despair
At having gained naught from him by her efforts,
Resolved to thwart this marriage or else die.
She recked not of a husband who was eager
To cease to be one and who wished to see her
No more save as her unforgiving master,
And with her love reluctantly transformed
To hate, gave o'er her heart to righteous anger.
She herself laid an ambush on their route,
Joined in the fight herself, was everywhere
In her mad rage, to which she set no bounds.
What shall I tell thee more? The Parthians fled;
Nicanor died—by her own hand, 'tis said;
Rodogune was her hated prisoner.

    The Princess would have suffered, but for me,
All evils that a slave endures in chains,
My brother. But the Queen, who found an endless
Delight in torturing her, entrusted only
To me the infliction of the woes decreed her;
And whatsoe'er that heart, aflame with hate,
Bade me, I promised much and did but little.

The King of Parthia, meanwhile, vowed revenge.
He fell upon us swiftly, sword in hand,
Took us quite by surprise, and so besieged
This city that in our extremity
We sued for peace. Made arrogant by success,
He would have turned a deaf ear, but well knowing
That Rodogune was a hostage in our hands,
Through fear for her he deigned to hearken to us,
Whence cometh that which must this day be done.
The Queen hath called our princes home from Egypt
To give the one first born her throne and realm.
Rodogune now appears, released from prison,
Like a bright sun new-risen in our skies.
The Parthian king has gone, to other wars
Against the Armenians, who lay waste his land.
Once a cruel foe, he has become our friend;
Peace ends his wrath; and for a fitting climax
(Ought I to say of good or evil fortune?)
Both of our princes worship Rodogune.

TIMAGENES. No sooner were they here at Court than they
Beheld her, and I have perceived they love her;
But though we pity them for being rivals,
Knowing their virtues, I see naught to fear.
For thee who servest her whom they both love . . .

LAONICE. I have not yet observed that she loves either.

TIMAGENES. Thou deemest me one with whom it is improper
To discuss such things. It is perhaps to do so
With thee that she comes hither now. Farewell.
I owe that station which will soon be hers
At least the chance to speak with thee in private.

(*Exit* TIMAGENES. *Enter* RODOGUNE.)

RODOGUNE. I know not what misfortune threatens me
Today and chills my joy with icy breath.
I tremble, Laonice, and I wish
To talk with thee, either to drive away
My fears or to console me for them.

LAONICE.   What!
On this day, madam, so full of glory for thee?

RODOGUNE. This day doth promise me so much that scarcely
Can I believe in all of it. Fortune treats me

With too great deference. Both the throne and marriage
Rouse my suspicions. Marriage seems to me
To hide some dreadful fate, the throne to open
A yawning gulf beneath my feet. I see
New fetters take the place of mine so lately
Broken, and all these blessings I regard
As evils in disguise. In brief, I fear
Everything from the dark heart of the Queen.

LAONICE. The peace which she hath sworn hath quenched her hate.

RODOGUNE. Hate rarely can be quenched among the great.
    Peace often serves them only as a respite,
And when I occupy the place I shall,
To speak to thee without dissimulation,
She will have reason to fear me, and I fear
This fear of hers. Not that I have not truly
Given up for the welfare of two kingdoms
The hate I rightly owed her for her deeds.
I made myself forget all that I suffered;
But by the very nature of great wrongs
Their doer doth ascribe unto the wronged one
A keen resentment, which he thinks is dangerous;
And though they seemingly be reconciled,
He fears him, hates him, and will never trust him,
But always anxious through such misconception,
Seizes the first chance offered to destroy him.
The Queen feels thus towards me.

LAONICE.   Ah, I swear, madam,
That thou dost wrong her with this false suspicion.
Thou shouldst forget the jealous desperation
To which her faithless husband drove her. If,
Stained with his blood and wholly frenzied, she
At that time treated thee as an odious rival,
The violence of her soul's first paroxysm
Constrained her vengeance to this cruelty.
A pretext was required to quell her anger,
Time was required, and, to hide naught from thee,
When I presumed to obey her orders badly,—
When I in thy behalf seemed false to her,—
Perchance with gentler and repentant heart
She was dissimulating in large part,

And shut her eyes on seeing herself deceived,
And was pleased better by a little pity.
At this time, when love takes the place of wrath,
She looks upon thee with a mother's fondness,
But should I find that she hath ceased to love thee,
I swear that I at once shall warn thee of it.
Thou knowest how utterly I am thine. Besides,
Would the King let her take thee unawares?

RODOGUNE. Whichever of the two is crowned today,
She, being his mother, will in all things sway him.

LAONICE. Whiche'er it be, I know that he adores thee.
Sure of their love for thee, canst thou still fear?

RODOGUNE. I fear their marriage, where I must be the bride.

LAONICE. How now! Are they unworthy of thy love?

RODOGUNE. As they are of one blood, of equal merit,
Reason solicits me alike for them;
But 'tis not easy, equals though they be,
For me, when thus beset, to incline towards neither.
There secretly are ties, are sympathies,
By whose sweet influence two kindred souls
Are linked to one another and are stirred
By feelings that are indescribable.
'Tis thus that one of them hath gained my preference.
I look upon the other with indifference,
But this indifference to him seems aversion
When I compare it with my heart's true passion.
Strange consequence of love! A thing incredible!
I fain were his, did I not love his brother;
Yet now the worst misfortune that I fear
Is that ill chance may destine me for him!

LAONICE. Could I not be of service to such love?

RODOGUNE. Think not to wrest its secret from my heart.
Whatever husband heaven decrees for me,
I wish to give myself to him completely.
If I should be the prize of him I dread,
With the same countenance shall I accept him.
Marriage will make me cherish him in turn;
Duty will do what love would else have done,
Without my fearing that I may be reproached,

When thus constrained, that any other man
Than mine own husband reigns within my thoughts.
LAONICE. Thou fearest that I would dare reproach thee so?
RODOGUNE. Would that I might conceal this from myself!
LAONICE. What thou concealest from me, I guess with ease;
    And, to declare to thee what I conceive,
    The prince . . .
RODOGUNE.   Nay, do not name him who hath won
    My heart. My blushes would betray its secrets,
    And I would take it ill if thy adroitness
    Should thus defeat the purpose of my silence.
    For fear that even one word, let slip by chance,
    Might show my heart to thee, and what shafts pierce it,
    I shall now end this talk, whose turn offends me.
    Farewell. Remember that 'tis through thy promise
    That I regain some measure of tranquillity.
LAONICE. Madam, have faith in my fidelity.

ACT II

CLEOPATRE *is discovered, alone.*

CLEOPATRE. False oaths and advantageous self-restraint,
    Which force imposed upon me, and of which
    I in my fear availed myself, O ye
    Blessed dissemblers of my deathless wrath,
    Ye empty phantoms of State policy,
    Begone! If terror bred by desperate peril
    Begot you, ye must vanish with that peril,
    Like to those vows made in a storm at sea,
    Which are forgotten once the waves are still.
      And thou by these concealed with so great skill,
    Recourse of helplessness, O Hidden Wrath,
    Thou virtue worthy of kings, thou noble secret
    Of Courts, burst forth; 'tis time; thy day hath come.
    Let us, both thee and me, be seen no more
    Like slaves, but as I am and as thou art.
    The King of Parthia is far away,
    And we can now dare all. We now have nothing
    To fear and nothing to disguise. I hate;
    I still reign. Let us leave illustrious memories

In quitting, if we must, this royal station
And make our going glorious and splendid,
And fatal unto her who doth await it.
Still, still is she the selfsame enemy
Who sought her honors in my ignominy,—
Who in her hate thinks she in turn will rule me
And reign by my command o'er me and thee.
   Thou deemest me base indeed, imprudent rival,
If thou believest that I will suffer this
And let a marriage vainly promised thee
Put in thy hand my scepter and thy vengeance.
Behold how far love of the crown hath borne me;
Behold what blood it cost me; and then tremble,
Tremble, I tell thee, for thyself, reflecting
That I too dearly bought it to bestow it
On thee, no matter what may be the treaty.

                            (*Enter* LAONICE.)

     Seest thou, Laonice, how the people
Prepare, in rich dress, for this great occasion?
LAONICE. The joy is general, and both the princes
Have won the favor of the enraptured Syrians.
Both have displayed such rare good qualities
That public preference hesitates between them;
And any leaning shown by some towards either
Has only the weak force of a first impulse.
They lean towards one, ready to swing to the other;
Their choice, to become fixed, still waits for thine;
And they so little care what will be done
That all will be content when told thy secret.
CLEOPATRE. Knowest thou that 'tis not what they suppose?
LAONICE. I, with them all, hope to learn which is older.
CLEOPATRE. For one brought up at Court, among great folk,
Thine eyes possess scant power to probe their hearts.
Learn, learn, my confidante, to know me better.
If I conceal the order of their birth,
See, see, that just as long as that is doubtful
Neither of them can reign, and I reign for them.
Though kingship is a blessing which both seek,
The fear of losing it will keep them silent.
Meanwhile, I rule, and their uncertain claims

Leave, like their fate, their scepter in my hands.
That, that, is my great secret. Knowest thou wherefore
I left those princes in my brother's care?
LAONICE. I thought Antiochus kept them away
That he might have the realm his sword regained.
CLEOPATRE. He sat upon their throne and feared their presence;
And this fear, rightly felt, made sure my power.
When I would threaten him with their return,
My orders were obeyed in every point.
Seeing this thunderbolt which I could hurl
At once if angered, he dared not displease me,
However much he might dare do for me;
And, forced to be content with the mere title
Of king, if in their place he reigned, he did so
But as my vassal. I will tell thee more.
I would without resort to violence
Have seen Nicanor espouse Rodogune
If he had with her love been satisfied
And, disregarding me, had lived with her
In Parthia, letting me still reign here.
His marriage irked me less than his return.
I could have loved her, would he not have crowned her!
Thou sawest how vainly he attempted that.
I did much then, and I would do yet more
If there were any means, lawful or wicked,
Which honor showed me or crime offered me
That could preserve for me a thing I prized
Enough to shed for it my husband's blood.
    In the predicament in which I am,
O my heart's joy, I needs must give thee up!
I must; I am forced to do so. But men soon
Will see the consequence to her who brought me
Unto this pass. The love I had for thee
Now turns to hate for her. As great as one
Hath been, the other will be cruel; and since
In losing thee I can on her take vengeance,
My loss is bearable and my grief is little.
LAONICE. What! thou still talkest of vengeance and of hate
For her of whom thou art to make a queen?

CLEOPATRE. And shall I make a king that he may be
Her husband, and that I may thus become
The target of her animosity?
Wilt thou ne'er learn, thou base and earthy soul,
To see but with the eyes of the vile herd?
Thou, who dost know this people, and dost know
How cravenly it followed to the fields
Of Mars the banners of a woman,—how
Trypho would have despoiled me, had it not
Possessed Antiochus,—how 'neath him its courage
Was suddenly reborn,—canst thou not guess
That if I name a king, it is that I
May rule him and that he may fight for me?
'Tis in my hands to choose him, as the first-born,
And since I needs must make of him an aid
To mine own weakness,—since without him war
Must not again be kindled,—I shall use
The power discreetly that I have to name him.
No one shall mount the throne whence I descend
Save by espousing my hate and not my rival.
'Tis only by avenging me that someone
Can take my place, and I shall let him reign
Who wishes to serve me.
LAONICE.   I knew thee ill.
CLEOPATRE. Know me thoroughly. When I consigned
Rodogune as a prisoner to thy charge,
It was not pity or deference for her rank
That stayed my hand and kept her blood unspilled.
Antiochus' death left me without an army,
And the great losses among those compelled
To follow me in my pursuit of vengeance
Stripped me of aid or strength to oppose her brother.
I saw that I was lost, without this hostage.
He came, and feared for her despite his rage.
He imposed terms on me, exacted oaths;
And I—to gain time I accorded all.
Time is a treasure great beyond conception.
I gained it, and I think the victory mine.
I thus contrived to catch my breath once more,
And under these misleading preparations . . .

But here are my two sons, whom I have summoned.
Listen, and thou shalt learn about the marriage
With which 'twas planned this festal day should end.

(Enter ANTIOCHUS *and* SELEUCUS.*)*

My children, come. This is at last the hour
So sweet to my desires, dear to my love,
When on the head of one of you I can see
What I have kept safe through so many storms,
And can to you restore, after so many
Misfortunes, a possession that hath cost me
Such anxious care and sorrow, for your sake.
It can recall to you what tears were mine
When Trypho caused me so great terror that,
Not to see you exposed to his attack,
I had to bring myself to part with you.
What pain, just gods, since then have I not suffered!
Each day made worse my woes and my disasters.
I saw your kingdom shrunken to these walls;
I thought your father dead, and at this rumor
The people rose and fain would have a king.
Vainly I called them dastards, recreants, traitors;
Their brutal wishes had to be fulfilled,
And lest they should take one, I chose them one.
To save your realm, what would I not have done?

'Twas with a mother's eyes I chose a husband—
Antiochus, your uncle; and I hoped
Your tottering throne would find a firm support
In him, but scarce his arm had stayed its fall
Ere through him Fate again afflicted me.
When master of the State, which he had saved,
He would not cease to occupy its throne.
To speak of you would cause him to make threats;
He routed Trypho but to take his place,
And, from the land's guardian and liberator,
Became a tyrant and a vile usurper.
His own hand punished him. Peace to his spirit!

There were, besides this trouble, many others.
Nicanor, my first husband and your father . . .
But wherefore give him still such tender names
Since, having been thought dead, he seemed to take

Renewed life only to deprive himself
Thereof in hounding us? No more of that!
I cannot, without trembling, call to mind
The deed by which I then prevented him
From ruining us. I know not if 'tis worthy
Of praise or horror,—if it pleased the gods
Or not,—if it were just or criminal;
But whether crime or justice, this, my sons,
Is certain: all that I have done, I did
Because of love for you. No love of greatness
Or love of life would in my heart have kindled
Such blind rage. I was weary of a throne
On which misfortunes without end would bring me
New griefs each day. My life was almost spent,
And the useless remnant of it would have found
With you a safe asylum with my brother.
But after twelve years filled with cares and woes,
To see your father rob you of the fruit
Of all my toil! To see your crown bequeathed
By him to children of a second marriage!
Upon this outrage, I forgot all else.
I deemed naught wrong to save your heritage.
  Receive, then, from a mother's hands, my sons,
A throne repurchased by a father's slaughter.
I thought that he was guilty of a crime
In taking it from you, and if I have
Committed one in my recovery of it,
May righteous heaven in its mercy deign
To punish me for this, and let you reign,—
To launch at me alone the thunder due me
And shower on you only prosperity!

ANTIOCHUS. Never hath anyone yet doubted, madam,
  The long, great toil thy love for us hath cost thee;
  And to thy loving care we deem we owe
  Our fond hopes of the throne, as well as life.
  Thy story makes us better know how much
  We ought to thank thee; it hath charmed our hearts.
  But that we may forever bless thy deeds,
  Spare us the memory of the last of them.
  There are dread things by which the troubled soul

Finds itself oft more swayed than fain 'twould be.
O'er a sad picture with such darkling hues
One needs must pass a sponge or draw a curtain.
A son is wicked if he looks upon it,
And whatsoe'er the gods ordain shall follow,
I will not think of it, but believe such things
Are best accorded silence and oblivion,
Not tears.

          We wait with like hopes of the scepter;
But though we wait, it is with no impatience.
We both can live contented without reigning.
The crown is thy toil's fruit; enjoy it long.
'Twill fall to us when thou art weary of it.
We shall receive it then with better grace,
And to accept it now would seem as if
We returned here only to snatch it from thee.

SELEUCUS. I shall add, madam, to what my brother says,
That though we both cherish fond hopes of it,
Ambition is not strongest in our hearts.
Reign; we shall both be glad to see thee do so,
And it is only right that we repay thee
With some obedience for the power thou givest us
And that the one of us whom heaven selects
Shall learn by thy example how to rule.

CLEOPATRE. Speak the whole truth, my sons: ye shun the crown—
Not that its splendor nor its weight dismays you;
The only source of your aversion to it
Lies in the shame incurred by its possession.
Your eyes find in it the same infamy
If ye must share it with our enemy,—
If an unworthy marriage makes it fall
Again to her who came to rob you of it.
O noble feelings of a lofty soul!
O sons indeed my sons! O happy mother!
  Your father's fate is shown in the true light
At last: no guilt was his; I, too, may have none.
He loved you always, and was a bad father
Only by spell of the sister or compulsion
Else of the brother. In that ambuscade
In which he strove so vainly, Rodogune

It was, my sons, that slew him by my hand.
Thus did the fatal power of their love
Cost you your father, me my innocence;
And if my hand had not dared all for you,
The fruit of that love would have cost you all.
  Ye will restore my innocence and fair fame
When ye have punished her who caused my crime.
This same hand, which saved all for you, could well
Have washed that from me with her hated blood;
But as she wronged you also, I reserved
For you a share in my revenge. And now,
To hold your spirits in suspense no longer,
That is the throne's price, if ye wish to reign.
Between two sons, whom I love equally,
To espouse my cause will give priority.
Rodogune's death will make one the first-born.
  What! ye both show a countenance dismayed?
Fear ye her brother? After the vile peace
Which, even while swearing it, I loathed at heart,
By secret orders I raised troops, now ready,
As ye will find, to follow you anywhere;
And while he copes with the Armenian princes,
We can with ease throw off his yoke. What, then,
Makes you turn pale at this just mandate? Is it
Pity for her? Or is it hate for me?
Do you indeed wish to wed her who braves me
And put me at the mercy of my slave? . . .
Ye do not answer! Go, ungrateful children,
For whom I vainly thought to save this realm!
I made your uncle king, and I can make
Another man king; and my name still hath
More power here than yours.

SELEUCUS.   But, madam, think:
  For our first exploit . . .

CLEOPATRE.   Nay! each of you
  Think what he owes to *me*. I of a truth
  Know that the blood which I demand of you
  Is not a fitting test of your high worth;
  But if ye have through me life and the scepter,
  This blood should be the token of your love

For me. Without that proof I ne'er could trust
What were your feelings toward my heart's hate. Only
By doing like me can ye vindicate me.
    It serves you naught to show surprise hereat.
Once more I tell you, that is the throne's price.
I can dispose of it because I won it.
No prior birth, no kingship can ye have
Except by bringing me her head, and since
My choice alone can crown you, to enjoy
My crime's fruit, ye must needs complete that crime.

                         (*Exeunt* CLEOPATRE *and* LAONICE.)

SELEUCUS.   Is there a heart so stout it can endure
    The thunderbolt of this inhuman mandate
    By which our hopes are shattered into dust?
ANTIOCHUS.   Is there a thunderbolt whose blow can rival
    The blow which this inhuman mandate deals us?
SELEUCUS.   O hate! O frenzy worthy of a Megaera!
    O woman, whom I dare not still call "Mother"!
    After thy crimes have reigned unchecked, canst thou
    Not bear for anyone to reign innocently?
    What charms, pray, thinkest thou the crown hath for us
    If given us for a deed as black as thine,
    And with what horror must it weigh upon us
    If we must be like thee to mount the throne?
ANTIOCHUS.   Let us have more respect for natural ties
    And but to Fate ascribe our hapless plight.
    We called Fate cruel, but it was kindly to us
    When giving us naught to strive with but each other.
    Being both mutually beloved and also
    Rivals, we thought no trouble was like ours,
    Yet when we found ourselves each other's rivals
    We did not know the half of our misfortunes.
SELEUCUS.   A sorrow so discreet and reverential
    Is either not great or too well restrained,
    And in such woes the heart is stout indeed
    That, knowing who causes them, blames Fate alone.
    For my part, I am weaker; for the more
    Their cause is dear to me, the worse my wound.
    Not that I dare to seek revenge. I still
    Would shed the last drop of my blood for her.

I well know what I owe her, but when thus
Constrained I stay my arm, I give free scope
To my repinings, and I deem that when
She injures us so greatly, he who only
Complains of her shows her enough respect.
Dost thou not see how infamous a task
She in her hatred dares exact of us?
Dost thou not see that in her eagerness
To perpetrate new crimes she seeks to make
Of her own sons—two princes—executioners?
If thou canst see that, how canst thou be silent?

ANTIOCHUS. I see yet more. I see she is my mother.
The more she is unworthy to be so,
The more the source of my own blood is foul.
I feel the violence of my grief increase;
But my confusion forces silence on me
When I behold her criminal lineaments
Engraven in our features, which she formed.
I towards that sight try to be blind or witless;
I venture to gloss o'er her monstrous deed;
I hide from mine own self a misery
In which our shame is equal to my sorrow;
And with mine eyes turned from so cruel a mother,
I blame all on the fate which made me born
Of her. Yet still I cling to one faint hope:
She is a mother, and ties of blood are strong;
And though she had been even more inhuman,
Tears from a son's eyes might allay her hatred.

SELEUCUS. Ah, truly, love cannot be very great
For children who have been brought up in exile,—
Whom she has let be reared almost as slaves
And now brings home only to serve her rage.
I see through her pretense of boasted tears.
In *her* heart thou and I have little place.
She loudly talks of her great mother-love,
But really loves and serves herself alone;
And whatsoe'er her sweet words tell us, she
Did all things for herself and naught for us.
The love is false that is controlled by hate.
Having embraced us, she now seeks our death

When, loathing the dear object of our love,
She asks her blood of us and offers to us
The throne at this price only. 'Tis no longer
From her hands that we can expect to have it;
It is ours, ours, if we but dare to take it.
    Such insurrection would be wholly blameless.
Thus one of us shall reign, if the other will
Consent, and thus her anger will be helpless.
That is the only way to save the Princess.
Let us go find her, and still act in unison;
That is the only way to end our troubles.
My love for her suggests so good a plan
To me, but thine accord must aid in this.
Our love, today well worthy of pity, cannot
Triumph save through our mutual devotion.

ANTIOCHUS.   This warning indicates a doubt of me
Which my affection for thee bears with patience.
Let us go; and be sure that death itself
Cannot break bonds between us that love cannot.

                                       (Exeunt.)

ACT III

RODOGUNE, ORONTES, *and* LAONICE *are discovered.*

RODOGUNE.   So that is how love takes the place of wrath,
How she looks on me with a mother's fondness,
How she loves peace, how she selects a king,
And how, in short, she treats her sons and me!
And only just now my suspicions wronged her?
She had done naught save in her own defense?
When thou deceivedst her, she shut her eyes?
Ah, how much better my distrust appraised her!
Thou seest, Laonice.

LAONICE.   And thou seest,
Madam, how faithfully my heart doth serve thee.
When I perceived her hatred and my error,
Aghast and shuddering, my breast swollen with sighs,
I broke the faith I owed to my queen's secrets
And told thee of my error and her hatred.

RODOGUNE. I think this information the one source
        I have for hope of any further life.
        But it is not enough that thou hast warned me:
        I must be shown how to escape these perils;
        I need thy counsel to help me to defeat . . .
LAONICE. Madam, in heaven's name, ask not this of me.
        It is enough that I should thus betray her
        For thy sake, without further undertaking
        To counsel thee against her. Thou hast with thee
        Orontes here, who as ambassador
        Was to do honor to this regal marriage.
        Since 'twas in *his* hands that the King thy brother
        Consigned the care of one so precious to him,
        I now shall leave thee to consult with him.
        Let me be ignorant of what ye decide.
        This only: doubt not the two princes' love.
        Rather than lose thee, they would lose the crown.
        But I cannot be sure that this cruel monster
        Will not avail herself of other hands
        When they refuse her theirs. I tremble all
        The while I talk with thee. If I were seen here,
        'Twould destroy me and make thy peril greater.
        Fly, noble princess. Let this be farewell.
RODOGUNE. Go. I shall yet repay thy service to me.

                                    (*Exit* LAONICE.)

        What shall we do, Orontes, in this strait
        In which a crown is offered for my blood?
        Flee to my brother? Tamely wait for death?
        Or make a worthy effort to prevent it?
ORONTES. Madam, our flight would be most difficult.
        I have seen troops posted throughout the city.
        Thou'rt watched, if thy destruction is intended;
        Or, if thou art allowed to save thyself,
        The counsel of Laonice is a ruse
        And, feigning to serve thee, she serves her mistress.
        The Queen, whose chief dread is to see thee reign,
        Rouses these fears in thee to make thee flee,
        Wishing, in order to break off a marriage
        Which she with difficulty can endure,
        To charge 'twas thou thyself who didst refuse

To proceed with it. She would gain through thee
The end which she desires, and would accuse thee
Of failing to observe the terms of peace;
And the King, seeing thee bring him a new war,
And therefore angrier with thee than her,
Would blame thy fears and our unstableness
For daring to doubt the good faith of the treaty,
And, being hard pressed by the Armenian princes,
Might leave thee laughed at and the Queen unpunished.
Adopt no such humiliating course.
'Tis here that thou must either reign or perish.
Heaven has not elsewhere offered thee a crown,
And none who will abandon one deserves one.

RODOGUNE.   How I would love the boldness of thy counsels,
Had we but might to match thy heroism!
But can we now defy this queen's fell hate
With the few followers whom my brother left me?

ORONTES.   I would have lost my wits had I dared boast
That with no more than these we could oppose her.
We at thy feet would die; 'tis the sole aid
That in our helplessness we now can give thee.
But shouldst thou quail when here thou hast, besides,
The master of all kings and gods to aid thee?
Love will do for thee everything thou needest.
    Make of the sons thy shield against the mother.
Use their love shrewdly; their whole hearts are thine,
And all adore these newly risen stars.
Whatever power a cruel queen hath here,
Thou, since thou swayest her sons, hast more than she has.
But let me try, in this dire strait, to assemble
Our widely scattered Parthians. They are few
But valiant, and their furious resistance
Might thwart a first surprise attempt against thee.
Be less afraid, and on this great day, madam,
If thou wouldst reign, vouchsafe that love shall reign.

(*Exit* ORONTES.)

RODOGUNE (*alone*).   What! I could stoop to the vile plan of begging
The aid of men who are in love with me,
And with appealing glances, falsely fond,
Attempt to find my safety in their hearts?
Those of high birth like mine recoil from baseness.

Their generous souls loathe such ignoble wiles.
Whate'er the help these princes can afford me,
I think I do enough when I accept it.
I shall behold their love and test its fervor
Without encouraging or luring them;
And if 'tis strong enough to serve my needs,
I then shall crown it but shall still control it.

Long stifled impulses of wrath and hate,
Rekindle now your torches by the Queen's
And end at last a forced forgetfulness
To render justice to a great king's ghost!
Call up before mine eyes his bloody image,
Still burning with the flames of love and anger,
Even as I saw him when, all pierced with wounds,
He cried to me: "Vengeance! Farewell! I die
For thee." Ah, dear shade, far from seeking vengeance,
I was to kiss the hand that took thy life
And be to her who shed thy blood a daughter!
Forgive the course to which my rank constrained me.
The nearer to the crown we are by birth,
The more our very eminence enslaves us;
Our hearts are not our own, to love or hate,
And all our passions end but in obedience.
When swords were drawn to avenge this heinous deed,
I was made surety for an ill-advised
Peace. To her crimes I shut mine eyes, accepting
The fate decreed me by State policy.
But when her blood-stained hand is found today
Still fiercely eager to assail whate'er
Is left of thee and pierce this hapless bosom
To seek the soul there which thou gavest me,
I seal no more a pact she violates;
I can with honor break my gilded yoke,
Can have again a breast that loves and hates,
And henceforth thee alone would fain obey.

Wilt *thou*, his living image, whom my heart
Adores, permit this violence to my love,
Dear prince, whose name midst all my fondest thoughts
I dare not yet trust to these palace walls?
I know what fear and anguish will be thine;

I see thy grief, I hear thy plaints, already;
But pardon me what I still owe to a king
Who gave thee life and for my sake lost his.
I have like sorrows, like anxieties.
'Twill cost me tears, if it will cost thee sighs . . .
    But, gods! with what dismay I see them both!
Love, which confoundest me, at least hide thy fires.
Be satisfied with mastery o'er my heart,
And do not in mine eyes reveal thyself.

Enter ANTIOCHUS *and* SELEUCUS.

ANTIOCHUS.   Be not offended, Princess, that we come
To tell thee of the power of thy glance.
'Tis not today that this enslaved our souls;
Both became thine at the first sight of thee;
But our respect for thee made love be silent,
And that respect compels us now to speak.
The happy hour now comes in which thy fate
Is thoroughly bound up, 'twould seem, with ours
Since a seniority still doubtful gives
To us a scepter and to thee a husband.
It is not fitting that our sovereign lady
Should owe the name of "queen" to one of her
Captives. For her to do so would offend
Our love, and, changing this arrangement, we
Leave it to her to choose a king for us.
No longer stoop to following the crown.
Give it; let not thyself be given with it.
Decide our fate, which heaven hath ruled but ill.
Our only law of primogeniture
Is to be pleasing in thy sight. The ardor
Enkindled in us by a love so pure
Makes us prefer thy choice to nature's choice
And come to sacrifice, as thou decidest,
Our every hope and every ambition.
Speak, then, madam, and create a king.
We shall submit, without shame, to thy mandate,
And whosoe'er shall lose thy heavenly person,
At least shall be the foremost of thy subjects.
His never-dying love will always tell him

That such a rank near thee is better than
An empire elsewhere; he will glory in it,
And amid such misfortune the great joy
Of being thy servant will assuage his grief.
RODOGUNE. Prince, I owe many thanks for being given
Disposal of your hopes and your ambitions.
I would accept the offer willingly
If those of *my* rank had the right to choose.
As monarchs use them without their consent
To strengthen thrones or put an end to quarrels,
Their fate is governed by the public good;
The terms of treaties wholly sway their hearts.
By these, not for the crown, shall mine be given.
I shall love one of you because they bid me;
From the disclosure of the truth about you
I shall derive the power so to do,
Nor will my love precede my obligation.
Hope for naught more, or ye shall hope in vain.
    The choice ye tender me is the Queen's right,
Which, doing as ye urge, I would usurp.
Have ye not heard how far her hate can go?
I ought to know this from experience
Sufficiently to shun reviving it.
What did I not endure, or she not dare!
I fain would think like you all wrath is ended,
But fear with me that if I made this choice
'Twould waken her dead hate to some new crime.
Forgive that word, which brings to memory what
The peace between us was to leave forgot.
Fire that seems out oft sleeps beneath its ashes;
Whoe'er rekindles it, may be its victim;
And I deserve to be consumed by it
If 'tis through me that it again is lighted.
SELEUCUS. Needest thou dread her resurrected hate
If thou hast means to make it powerless?
Select a king, madam, and reign beside him.
Her wrath will be disarmed, with none to aid it,
And all its fires, thus ineffectually
Rekindled, will send up but idle smoke.
Yet what concern to her is whom thou choosest,

That thou shouldst fear the harm thou dost conceive?
The crown is ours; and, without wronging her
Or failing in respect for ties of nature,
Each of us can yield *his* claims to the other
And leave the chance he hath to thy decision.
For our sake, put aside such trivial scruples.
Thy preference outweighs seniority,
Which would impose too harsh a yoke upon thee
If it were different from thy heart's desire.
Thou'dst be congratulated when thou shouldst
Be pitied; 'twould subject thee to constraint
To make thee reign; 'twould give the crown to thee
Only by tyrannizing over thee,
And poison all thy joy in this great gift.
   Then in the name of that fair flame of love,
Princess, by which we are alike consumed,
Divest our hopes of all such bitterness
And let the joys of him who is to wed thee
Be doubled by their being conferred by thee.

RODOGUNE.   This fervent love blinds you as well as burns you,
And, trying to further it, ye serve it ill.
Ye think this choice which ye both ask of me
Can make one of you happy without making
The other one dissatisfied; and I,
Howe'er ye steel your hearts, I fear to make you
Alike dissatisfied if I speak mine.
'Tis not that I disdain the suit of both;
I fain would be the wife of one of you.
But let me wed with him to whom Fate gives me.
Too high will be the price that I shall ask
If I must give myself to anyone.
Although I would obey most readily
The orders of my king, 'twould be indeed
Not easy to obtain me from myself.
Know ye what tasks, what toil, what services
I would exact in my capricious pride,—
What glory would be needed to deserve me,—
Into what fearful dangers ye would have
To rush? This heart is given you with the crown,
Princes. Beware of making *me* its mistress.

RODOGUNE

Ye may renounce all claim to it forever
When I have told you how much it will cost you.

SELEUCUS. What can the task, the toil, the service be
Which for love's sake we would not do for thee?
And, pray, what fearful dangers can we dread
If by defying them we may deserve thee?

ANTIOCHUS. Princess, lay bare thy heart and know ours better.
Know better love's fair flame that burns in us,
And tell us boldly at what price thy choice
Will make of one the happiest of kings.

RODOGUNE. Prince, ye desire this?

ANTIOCHUS.   It is our sole wish.

RODOGUNE. Your ardor will be followed by repentance.

SELEUCUS. Ere we repent, we both shall die.

RODOGUNE.   Ye really
Desire this?

SELEUCUS.   We implore this of thee.

RODOGUNE.   Then
So be it! The time has come for me to speak.
I shall obey my king, since one of you
Is to be such; but when I once have spoken,
If ye repine thereat, I call to witness
All of the gods that ye have made me do so,
And that it is despite myself that I
Am free again and hearken to a wrath
Which was forbidden me,—that a revived
Duty brings back to me a memory
No more prohibited by a treaty's terms.

    Tremble, Princes, tremble at the name,
Then, of your father. He is dead, because
Of me, and by your mother's hand. When bound
By other obligations, I forgot him;
But, free at last, I pay the debt I owe him.
It is for you to choose my love or hate.
I love the King's sons, and I hate the Queen's.
Act ye accordingly, and without further
Soliciting me choose which of your two parents
Ye wish now to renounce. Ye must perforce
Take sides, and your choice shall determine mine.
    I reverence one of them as much as I

Abhor the other, but if this great king's blood
Which I love in you is not worthy of him,
It is not worthy of me. That blood within you,
That throne which he has left you, well deserve
That in his quarrel your hearts should be enlisted.
Honor demands it, love requires it, of you.
What is there which can turn you against both?
If ye prefer to them a cruel mother,
Be ruthless, treacherous, and depraved like her.
Ye ought to punish her, if ye condemn her.
Ye should resemble her, if ye uphold her.
What! all your ardor gone? ye both heave sighs?
I had foreseen, I had predicted, this.

ANTIOCHUS. Princess . . .
RODOGUNE.   It is too late. I now have spoken.
When I would fain be silent, I could not be.
Call ye this duty "hatred," "harshness," "wrath,"
To win me ye must needs avenge your father.
That is the price at which I may be had.
Dare to deserve me. Let us see which one
Of you will deign to accept me. Farewell, Princes.

                                        (*Exit* RODOGUNE.)

ANTIOCHUS. Alas! 'tis thus, then, that the deference
Born of the truest love is treated!
SELEUCUS.   Brother,
She flees from us, after those cruel words!
ANTIOCHUS. She flees, but like a Parthian, launching shafts
That pierce our hearts.
SELEUCUS.   Oh, how unjust is heaven!
One with a soul so barbarous should have had
Our mother, and should have been born of her.
ANTIOCHUS. Let us lament without blaspheming.
SELEUCUS.   Ah,
How much thou frettest me by this self-restraint
In which thou art so persistent! Must we still
Seek to reign? Must we love her still?
ANTIOCHUS.   We must
Show greater reverence for our beloved.
SELEUCUS. 'Tis to desire o'ermuch the throne or her,
To wish to reign or love her at this price.

RODOGUNE

ANTIOCHUS. 'Tis to hold it and her of little value
To feel so quickly, utterly rebellious.
SELEUCUS. When to obey is such an impious thing,
To be rebellious becomes necessary.
ANTIOCHUS. This thy rebellion, brother, is too hasty
When that from which we shrink can be revoked,
And our desires are all too rash when we
Aspire to win such blessings easily.
By trials heaven would have us mount to glory.
To enjoy a triumph, one must gain a victory.
But how I vainly try to hide our plight!
Our woe is far too great to be glossed over.
It in its vastness seems a black abyss
To me, where hate awards a crown to crime,
Where good fame is not prized, virtue not honored,
Where happiness must be bought with matricide;
And seeing the dread picture of these ills,
I feel myself grow weak while I exhort thee;
I reel, I tremble, and my stricken heart
Gives heed now to its grief, now to its courage.
Brother, forgive these wild, disordered words,
Which show too well the turmoil in my soul.
SELEUCUS. I would do like thee if my shaken spirit
Did not cast off the yoke that crushes it.
Despite ambition, despite ardent love,
I know a throne's worth and a woman's worth,
And reckoning their possession 'gainst their cost,
I quench alike my love and my ambition.
I gladly would resign them both to thee
If, midst the peace which heaven restores to me,
The fear of giving thee a fatal gift
Did not afflict my heart with qualms too keen.
Let us, my brother, flee from these cruel women
That they may finish without us their feud.
ANTIOCHUS. Loving much, I still have a little hope;
For hope cannot be quenched where so great love
Burns, and some light its struggling flames allow me
To judge these haughty souls better than thou.
Believe me, they both dread our tears; their flight
Hath saved them from the sound of our lament.

307

But had they hearkened to it even briefly,
Their hate would have been vanquished by our grief.
SELEUCUS.   Then weep before them; sigh and groan; and I
Shall fear for thee that which thou hopest for.
Whatever boon thy sorrow wins from them,
Thou must ward off their mutual hate,—must save
One from the other,—and perchance their blows,
Finding thee 'twixt them, will pierce only thee.
'Tis this that calls for tears. Mother nor loved one
Can longer choose or prescribe aught for us.
Whate'er their wrath demands of thee or me,
I make thee king; hence Rodogune is thine.
Spare thy lament to both of them; since I
Have found my happiness, do thou grasp thine own.
I am not jealous of it; my affection
Will see it only with an eye of pity.

                                        (*Exit* SELEUCUS.)

ANTIOCHUS.   How great would be my bliss, did I not love
My brother! But when he declines to see
The injury which he fain would do himself,
In my devotion to him I shall oppose
His blindness.
                    I shall act in thy behalf,
Brother, no less than mine. I will not take
Advantage of the wrong thy indignation
Does to thy hopes.
                    A heavy blow oft stuns us.
We think ourselves unhurt when sorely smitten.
Whatever our instinctive pride at first
May tell us, he who knows not of his sickness
Is so much the more sick. 'Neath seeming health
May lurk unnumbered poisons, and death soon
May follow an apparent cure. Oh, deign,
Just gods, to render my forebodings vain!
But let me go and see if I can quell
The tempest, and if motherhood and love
Will speak for me against a wrath so fierce.

                                        (*Exit* ANTIOCHUS.)

ACT IV

Antiochus and Rodogune are discovered.

RODOGUNE. Prince, what have I just learned? Because I sigh,
Thou thinkest I love, although thou darest not say so!
Is it thy brother, is it thou, whose boldness
Imagines . . .

ANTIOCHUS.   Peace to thine offended heart,
Princess. Neither of us would be so rash
As to suppose that the good fortune might
Be his of being pleasing in thy sight.
I see thy virtues and my little worth,
And my beloved rival knows well his faults.
But if just now thy soul spoke by thy lips,
It wished us to believe that 'twas not loveless
And that 'twill hear my suit or his. Thou saidst
Thou fain wouldst be the wife of one of us.
If 'tis presumptuous to believe this marvel,
'Tis impious to doubt such an oracle;
And if we quench a hope thou biddest us have,
We shall deserve the woes to which thou doomest us.
Princess, in heaven's name—in our love's name . . .

RODOGUNE. One phrase doth not reveal one's inmost soul,
And your too hasty hope is too much flattered
By gracious words I spoke in courtesy.
I said them, true; but whatsoe'er they meant,
Deserve that love whereof thou seekest to know.
When I have uttered sighs, 'twas not for you;
I owed them to my plighted husband's ghost,
And they are the result of loyal memories
Which every hour his death recalls to me.
Be his sons, Princes, and espouse his cause.

ANTIOCHUS. Accept his heart, then, shared between us two,—
His heart, which a pure love brought 'neath thy sway,—
His heart, for which thou sighest at every moment,—
His heart, pierced undeservedly while loving
Thee; have thou back that blood, again to love thee,
Which once it shed. In us it hath this back;
It lives again; it loves thee, and it shows

In loving thee that it is still the same.
Ah, Princess, in the plight in which Fate placed us,
Can we prove better that we are his sons?
RODOGUNE. If 'tis indeed his heart which lives again
In you and loves me, let it do what he
Would do, were he alive in his own person.
Lend your avenging arms unto this heart
He leaves you. Can ye have it and not heed it?
If ill it tells you what it should expect
Of you, it borrows now my voice to make
Itself be better understood. Through me
A second time it speaks unto you. Prince,
It must have vengeance.
ANTIOCHUS.   I accept that mandate.
Name the murderers, and I shall make haste
To carry it out.
RODOGUNE.   What strange thing causes thee,
When thou acceptest it, not to recognize
Thy mother?
ANTIOCHUS.   Ah, unless 'tis thy desire
To see our thread of life cut short, name other
Avengers, or else other murderers!
RODOGUNE. Nay, I can see that in thy soul too much
Her cause doth reign. Prince, thou espousest it.
ANTIOCHUS. Yes, I espouse it, madam, and I bring
Unto thy feet blood which is truly hers,
Which nature locks up in this woeful breast.
Thou thyself satisfy that secret voice
Whereof thine deigns to be the interpreter
To us. Do its command, and forthwith punish
In me a queen and thus avenge a king.
But when my death has once acquitted thee
Of that stern duty, listen to a second
Duty, and bless thereby my brother. Take
Of these two princes who solicit thee
One for a victim, one to be thy husband.
Punish one of them for his mother's crime
But pay the other for his sire's devotion,
And leave an instance to posterity
Of complete rigorousness and perfect justice.

What! wilt thou hearken to neither love nor hate?
Can I not have reward nor punishment?
This heart which loves thee, and which thou disdainest . . .

RODOGUNE. Alas!

ANTIOCHUS.   Is it still the King for whom thou grievest?
Is that sigh uttered only for my father?

RODOGUNE.   Go, or at least bring back thy brother here.
The struggle was less dangerous to my soul
When I had both of you to fight against.
Thou art stronger than ye together were;
Then I defied you, and I tremble now.
I am in love. Do not misuse my secret,
Prince. To my great regret it hath escaped
My lips while hate so fills me; but it *hath*
Escaped them finally, and in modesty
I can no longer bear to meet thine eyes.
Yes, I love one of you despite my wrath,
And this last sigh says plainly it is thou.
Stern duty sets itself against this love.
Blame me not, for 'tis ye who are the cause
Of this. Ye who have broken the good terms
Of the compact have brought back to life that duty
When ye beset me to make choice between you.
See what your father's death for me entails:
If thus ye leave me free, I must avenge him,
And in my soul love's flames protest in vain;
I can bestow my hand at this price only.
   But not of thee can I expect it. *Thy*
Refusal is as just as my demand.
Filial respect will make thee false to love;
I fain would hate thee if thou hadst obeyed me,
Nor do I prize revenge so much that I
Could wish to be the guerdon of a crime.
Let us return to the conditions, then,
Imposed upon me by the treaty of peace,
Since to be freed from them is to lose thee
Forever. Prince, I can do nothing more
For thee. My heart still swells with pride of birth,
And whatsoe'er love's power over me,
Never shall I forget that I was promised

A king for husband. Yes, despite my love
I shall expect the throne with either thee
Or else thy brother, at thy mother's hands.
Till told her secret, thou wilt have my wishes;
And if it crowns him, thou wilt have my sighs.
My honor cannot grant more to my heart,
Nor can my heart dare promise more to thine.

ANTIOCHUS.   What more could I desire? His good is mine.
Give happiness to him, and I lose nothing.
Affection grants him this, if love shrinks from it.
I shall thank heaven for such great misfortune,
Give up the sweetness of my dubious hope,
And, though I die of sorrow, die contented.

RODOGUNE.   And I, if Fate gives me into his hands
And bids me live for someone else than thee,
My love . . . But fare thee well. My soul is shaken.
Prince, if thy heart's flame burns as mine doth burn,—
If thou art not cruel to this heart that loves thee,—
See me no more unless thou wearest the crown.

(*Exit* RODOGUNE.)

ANTIOCHUS.   My dearest wishes are at last fulfilled.
Love, thou hast conquered; but 'tis not enough.
If thou wouldst triumph in this present strait,
Having thus conquered, make a mother's instincts
Conquer no less. Inspire in her towards us
That tenderness which in true lovers' bosoms
Thine ardor wakens, that pity which reigns o'er them,
And those becoming weaknesses whose power
Destroys all vengeful wrath. . . . The Queen draws near.
Love, instinct, righteous gods, enable me
To touch her heart or die before her face.

Enter CLEOPATRE *and* LAONICE.

CLEOPATRE.   How now, Antiochus! canst thou claim the crown?
ANTIOCHUS.   Madam, thou knowest if heaven assigns it to me.
CLEOPATRE.   Thou knowest better than I if thou deservest it.
ANTIOCHUS.   I know that I shall die if thou wilt not
Hear me.
CLEOPATRE.   Too slow, 'twould seem, to serve my hate,
Thou hast allowed thy brother to act first.

312

He hath avenged me while thou tookest thought,
And unto him I owe what thou hast hoped for.
I pity thee, my son, for thy misfortune
Is great. To lose a throne is worse than death.
I know therefor only one remedy—
Grievous, dismaying, doubtful, sad for both
Of you. I would sooner die myself than name it;
But when a realm is lost, then all is lost.

ANTIOCHUS. The whole cure of our woe is in thy hands
And is not grievous, doubtful, or dismaying.
Thy wrath alone makes us unfortunate.
In losing Rodogune, we lose all, madam.
We both adore her; judge into what misery
The harshness of thy mandate plunges us.
The avowal of this love no doubt offends thee,
But with our silence our misfortune mounts;
And blinded by a little enmity,
Unless thou knowest our woes, thou canst not take
Pity upon them. As I see the matter,
There is no other remedy for them.

CLEOPATRE. What madness blind possesses thee thyself!
Hast thou forgotten that thou speakest to *me*?
Or darest thou think to be my king already?

ANTIOCHUS. I seek respectfully to show thee how
Strong is that love whereof thou wert the cause.

CLEOPATRE. *I*? *I* have kindled this presumptuous love?

ANTIOCHUS. What other pretext, pray, caused our return?
Didst thou for any reason summon us
Save that the rights of prior birth might give
To one of us the scepter and the Princess?
Thou hast done even more: thou hast made us see her,
And thus thy hand hath placed us in her power.
Which of us, madam, would have dared refuse her
When thou didst bid us both aspire to win her?
Had not her beauty lit love's flame within us,
Our obligation would have bound us to her.
The wish to reign would have caused like results.
According to the terms which the peace-treaty
Imposed, we were compelled to seek her hand
Alike by love, by duty, and by ambition.

Hence we have loved her, thinking thus to please thee.
Each of us feared only his brother's bliss,
And, now this fear hath yielded to affection,
I beg for each of us one moment's pity.
Could we have e'er divined thy hidden hatred,
Which even the treaty's terms have not uprooted?

CLEOPATRE.   No; but ye should have kept alive the memory
Of the humiliation that I spared you
And the base lot to which your Rodogune,
But for me—for my courage—would have consigned you.
I fancied that your hearts, conscious thereof,
Preserved a noble wrath because of this;
And I, by my feigned meekness, held in check
That wrath in order that when it had grown
Greater by reason of some slight restraint,
The torrent of resentment and of rage
Might be more headlong in its unleashed fury.
I now do more: I urge, beseech, command,
And threaten; yet naught rouses you. The scepter
With which my hand should have rewarded you
Holdeth no charms to make you for one instant
Waver; ye think not of it, nor my wrongs.
Love silenceth in you the voice of nature—
And could I cherish, forsooth, unnatural sons?

ANTIOCHUS.   Nature's tie and love have separate rights.
One does not rob the other of a heart
Which it possesses.

CLEOPATRE.   No, no; where love reigns,
The other hath no choice but to give way.

ANTIOCHUS.   Their spells have equal power o'er our hearts.
We both, if there is need, will die for thee;
But also . . .

CLEOPATRE.   Go on, thankless, recreant son.

ANTIOCHUS.   We both, if there is need, will die for her.

CLEOPATRE.   Die, die, then! Your rebelliousness deserves
More horror than compassion; and mine eyes
Could view your deaths and never shed a tear,
Beholding in you only her who charms you;
And I shall triumph, in seeing my sons die,
Over her votaries and my enemies.

ANTIOCHUS. Well, triumph o'er them, then; let naught restrain thee.
Does thy hand tremble? Wouldst thou borrow mine?
Madam, command; I shall at once obey thee.
Yes, I shall pierce this heart that dares betray thee,
Happy if I can satisfy thee so
And in my blood can wholly drown thine anger.
But if thou in the fierceness of thy hate
Still callest our love rebelliousness against thee,
At least do not forget that this hath taken
For arms only vain sighs and powerless tears.
CLEOPATRE. Ah, why hath it not taken sword and flame?
How much more easily I could cope with them!
My heart is too responsive to thy tears;
Almost have they destroyed my thirst for vengeance.
I cannot refuse sighs to them. I feel
I am a mother, when I see thy grief.
Thou hast thy will; I yield; my anger fades.
Rodogune—and the kingdom, too—is thine.
Give thanks to heaven, which made thee the first-born.
Possess her; reign.
ANTIOCHUS.   O fortune-favored moment!
O all too happy end of my great anguish!
I thank the gods who have dispelled thy hate.
Can this be, madam?
CLEOPATRE.   I in vain resisted.
Too strong is nature's bond; my heart surrenders.
I say no more to thee; thou lovest thy mother
And wilt conceal for me what needs concealment.
ANTIOCHUS. Ah! I then triumph when about to perish?
The hand which wounded me vouchsafes to heal me?
CLEOPATRE. Yes, I would fain reward a love so true.
Go, carry to the Princess this good news.
Her heart, like thine, will be o'erjoyed to hear it.
Thou dost not love her more than she loves thee.
ANTIOCHUS. Happy Antiochus! happy Rodogune!
Yes, madam, she and I share the same joy.
CLEOPATRE. Go, then. The moments which thou losest here
Are but so many stolen from your bliss.
This evening, destined for the ceremonies,
Will clearly show whether my hate is dead.

ANTIOCHUS. And we shall show thee that the goal of all
    Our wishes is to give thee two crowned subjects.

(Exit ANTIOCHUS.*)*

LAONICE *(to* CLEOPATRE*)*. So thy great heart hath overcome its anger?
CLEOPATRE. What power can sons lack in a mother's breast?
LAONICE. Thy tears again flow; and that heart, grown soft . . .
CLEOPATRE. Send unto me his brother, and leave us here.
    His woe will be extreme, I surely think,
    But I can soon allay its bitterness.
    Tell him naught; 'twill be less unpleasant for him
    To learn all from my lips rather than thine.

(Exit LAONICE.*)*

    (Alone) How ill thine eyes can read my inmost thoughts!
    If I shed tears, they are but tears of rage;
    And my fell hate, which thou supposest gone,
    Hath made them flow only to hoodwink thee.
    I do not wish to share with anyone
    The secret of what I intend; and thou,
    O credulous lover, by appearances
    Beguiled, whose petty soul clings eagerly
    To the deceptive charms of my pretenses,
    Go, triumph in fancy with thy Rodogune!
    Prefer thy lot to that of the immortals,
    Till I can plunge thee into new misfortunes
    And teach thee better how I take revenge.
    Not all at once doth pride like mine collapse.
    Snares should be feared from those who yield too soon,
    And 'tis not well to judge of hearts by faces
    And deem sincere a change that is so sudden.
    The result will make thee see if I have changed.

(Enter SELEUCUS.*)*

    Knowest thou, Seleucus, that I am avenged?
SELEUCUS. Alas, poor princess!
CLEOPATRE.   Thou lamentest her fate?
    Thou lovest her?
SELEUCUS.   Enough to regret her death.
CLEOPATRE. Thou still canst serve her as her faithful lover.
    If I have had revenge, 'tis not on her.
SELEUCUS. O gods! on whom, then, madam?

CLEOPATRE.   'Tis on thee,
    Ingrate, who seekest but to be her husband,
    And who adorest her, despite thy mother!
    On thee, who wilt not deign to serve my wrath!
    On thee, whose love, refractory to my will,
    Opposes my revenge, blights all my joy!
SELEUCUS. On me?
CLEOPATRE.   On thee, thou traitor! Know not of,
    Or else pretend to know not of, the ills
    That thou shouldst dread, or of the fire that burns thee;
    But if thou thinkest by ignorance to shun them,
    At least in learning of them begin to feel them.
    The throne was to be thine by right of birth.
    Rodogune, with it, fell into thy hands.
    Thou hadst the right to wed her, and be king.
    But since none knows this secret but myself,
    I can at will ascribe seniority
    And give thy crown and loved one to thy rival.
SELEUCUS. My brother?
CLEOPATRE.   Him have I declared the elder.
SELEUCUS. Thou causest me no grief by crowning him,
    And, for a reason quite unknown to thee,
    My own heart's wishes had outstripped thy deed.
    The blessings whereof thou deprivest me
    Did not have charms so sweet as to deter me
    From giving them, before thee, to my brother;
    And if to this thou limitest thy vengeance,
    Thy purposes and mine are in accord.
CLEOPATRE. 'Tis thus that one conceals great bitterness,—
    Thus that by shams one soothes it outwardly
    And thinks that he with seeming acquiescence
    Can deceive those whose natural distrust
    He fears at heart.
SELEUCUS.   How now! dost thou imagine
    That I might harbor still some secret wrath?
CLEOPATRE. What! dastard, canst thou lose without regret
    Her whom the gods gave thee to wed withal,—
    Her whose supposed death thou just now wert mourning?
SELEUCUS. To look upon her death with some compassion
    Is not to aspire to wed her.

CLEOPATRE.   Whether death
        Seizes her or a rival bears her off,
        A lover's grief is equally intense,
        And any man who seeks for consolation
        After that fatal blow cannot endure
        To see his treasure in his rival's arms.
        Cut to the quick, he tries to win her back;
        He feigns indifference, to achieve a better
        Surprise, so much the more incensed as she
        Whom he has lost was rightly his love's due
        By reason of his station or his merit.
SELEUCUS. Perhaps! but really with what mother-love
        Dost thou incite me so against my brother?
        Takest thou pains to make my spleen burst forth?
CLEOPATRE. I take them to know of it and to thwart it.
        I take them to preserve my work, despite thee,
        From foul deeds of thy hidden, jealous rage.
SELEUCUS. I fain would think so; but what other interest
        Makes each of us the elder when and as
        It pleases thee? Which of us twain should trust thee?
        And by what justice should it be that all
        The punishment on me alone must fall,
        And that when we are torn by the same love
        Thou shouldst reward him for it and punish me?
CLEOPATRE. As Queen, I can dispense justice or kindness
        According as I wish; and I am truly
        Nonplussed to learn where thou canst find such boldness,—
        Whence comes it that a son so traitorous towards me
        Dares to ask *me* the reason for my favors.
SELEUCUS. Then thou wilt pardon me if I speak out bluntly.
        I am not jealous of thy boons to him,
        And I can see what sort of love thou hast
        For both of us, better than thou believest
        And than I fain would see. Filial respect
        Forbids me to say more to thee of this.
        I have no lack of eyesight or of manhood,
        Madam; but hope not to find aught in me
        Save fondness for my brother, zeal for my king.
        Farewell.   (*Exit* SELEUCUS.)

CLEOPATRE *(to herself)*. What further woes can I endure?
    Their love offends me, their affection thwarts me;
    And to defeat my rage I find my offspring
    Two rebel sons and two devoted rivals.
    How now! lose placidly both throne and loved one?
    What spell is this thou workest, odious princess?
    And by what power, kindling such love, canst thou,
    Taking but one of them, rob me of both?
    Yet do not hope to triumph o'er my hate!
    Though reigning in two hearts, thou'rt not yet Queen.
    I know that since my sons are as they are,
    I needs must pierce them through to come at thee—
    But what of that? my hands, which slew their father,
    Will for an arm's refusal take their lives.
    Those lives are no less dangerous to me;
    With him did I begin, with them will I
    Conclude. Out of my heart, ye ties of nature,
    Or force my sons to obey me! Make them serve
    My hate, or else consent that they shall perish.
    But one of them already hath perceived
    That I desire to punish them. Quite often
    He who delays too long, permits himself
    To be forestalled. Let us go now and seek
    The time for me to sacrifice my victims
    And win my happiness by monstrous crimes.

A C T   V

CLEOPATRE *is discovered, alone.*

CLEOPATRE. At last, the gods be thanked, I have one foe
    The less. Seleucus' death has half avenged me.
    His ghost, awaiting Rodogune and his brother,
    E'en now can promise them to his father from me.
    They soon will follow him; all is prepared
    To reunite those whom I separated.
      Thou who delayest but till the ceremony
    To cast my rival, lifeless, at my feet,
    And by whose means two lovers at one stroke
    Of fate will gain marriage, the throne, and death,—
    O poison, canst thou give me back my crown?

Cold steel hath served me well; wilt thou do likewise?
Wilt thou not fail me?

            And *thou*—what wouldst thou with me,
Absurdly reawakening, stupid virtue,
Tenderness no less dangerous than ill-timed.
I want no son who weds with Rodogune.
I see no more aught of my blood in him
Who plucks me from the throne and sets her there.
  Ungrateful offspring of a faithless husband,
Heir of a love that did me deadly wrong,
Dote on my enemy and perish like her!
To achieve her fall, I strike down her support.
As well dig an abyss beneath my feet
As stop now with my crimes but half complete;
And to make thee my king would be too rash,
Leaving thee to avenge on me a father
And brother. He who takes but half his vengeance
Rushes, himself, to his own punishment.
He must forswear or satisfy his hate.
Even though the populace, in rage of grief
For its new masters, should bedew their graves
With my loathed blood,—though the avenging king
Of Parthia should find me quite defenseless,—
Though heaven should make my punishment as great
As my misdeeds,—throne, I cannot consent
To give thee up. 'Tis better far to perish
Beneath the thunderbolt. 'Tis better far
To earn the direst fate. Fall on me, skies,
Provided that I may avenge myself!
I shall receive the blow with face serene.
'Tis sweet to die after one's enemies;
And with whatever sternness Fate may treat me,
My loss is less to die than live their subject.
  But here is Laonice. I must hide
What shall be soon apparent from my deeds.

                          (*Enter* LAONICE.)
Come they, these lovers of ours?

LAONICE.   They draw near, madam.
  Their spirits' joy is pictured in their faces.
  Love there is seen with majesty commingled,

And, following the old usage of the Syrians,
They both come, full of an august and royal
Charm, to partake here of the bridal cup
And then go from the palace to the temple
To be made one forever by the hands
Of the high priest. 'Tis there that he awaits them,
To bless their union. All the populace,
Delighted by their nuptials, precede them
And with loud cries ask of the gods for them
Whate'er is sought by prayers at any altar,
Eager for their sakes that the ceremonies
Soon should begin and soon should be completed.
Parthians and Syrians jostle in the crowd;
All banish from their souls our former quarrels
And swell the gathering; they vie in blessing
As with one voice the Prince and Rodogune.
    But I e'en now espy them. 'Tis for thee,
Madam, to begin here the scenes of joyance.
    (*Enter* ANTIOCHUS, RODOGUNE, ORONTES, *and a throng of*
      Parthians and Syrians.)

CLEOPATRE.   Hither, my children—for maternal love,
    Madam, within my heart accounts thee one
    Of them already, and I think this name
    Will not displease thee.

RODOGUNE.   I shall cherish it,
    Even unto death. It is most dear to me,
    Madam; and the sole joy I hope for is
    To obey thee and respect thee as my mother.

CLEOPATRE.   Do naught but love me; ye shall be the sovereigns,
    And, if respect is to be shown, 'tis I
    Who owe it to you.

ANTIOCHUS.   Ah, if we shall acquire
    The supreme power, it is not to depart
    From our obedience to thee. Thou shalt reign
    O'er us while we are reigning o'er this land,
    And it shall be thy laws that we dispense.

CLEOPATRE.   I dare to think 'tis so. But take your places;
    'Tis time to set about what I must do.
    (ANTIOCHUS *seats himself in a chair, with* RODOGUNE *on his*
      left beside him, and CLEOPATRE *on his right but on a lower*

level indicating some inferiority in rank. ORONTES *sits
similarly on the left of* RODOGUNE *on a similar lower level.*
CLEOPATRE, *while they are taking their places, whispers to*
LAONICE, *who goes to fetch a cup that is filled with poisoned wine. After she has gone out,* CLEOPATRE *continues.*)

All ye who hear me, Parthians and Syrians,
Whether the subjects of the King her brother
Or mine till now, this is of my two sons
He whom the right of primogeniture
Sets on the throne and gives unto the Princess.
To him I now yield up the realm which I
Have saved for him; this day I cease to reign
And he begins. Let no one longer treat me
As ruler here. People, behold your king,
Behold your queen. Serve them, revere them both,
Love them, and die, if necessary, for them.
   Orontes, thou observest how willingly
I give to them the power which I resign.
Observe the rest, and note how the results
Follow in every point the treaty's terms.
               (LAONICE *re-enters with a cup in her hands.*)

ORONTES. Thou makest thy sincerity evident,
   Madam. I so shall tell the King my master.
CLEOPATRE. The wedding now is our chief business. Custom
   Requires, my son, that here it should begin.
   Take from my hands the nuptial cup, and be
   Later united by the bonds of marriage.
   May it be a token, in thy partner's eyes,
   Of both your love and my affection.
ANTIOCHUS *(taking the cup).*   Ah,
   What do I not owe to my mother's kindness!
CLEOPATRE. Time flies, and thus thy happiness is postponed.
ANTIOCHUS *(to* RODOGUNE*).* Then, madam, let us speed these blessed
   moments.
   They are the glad beginning of our joy.
   But if my brother were thereof the witness . . .
CLEOPATRE. 'Twould be too cruel to wish for him to see it.
   A sight is this which he does well to spare
   Himself and shun, feeling such griefs at heart.
ANTIOCHUS. He had assured me that he would look on it

Without pain. But no matter. Let us proceed.

TIMAGENES *rushes in.*

TIMAGENES. Ah, sir!

CLEOPATRE.   Timagenes, what dost thou mean
  By this presumption?

TIMAGENES.   Alas, madam!

ANTIOCHUS (*giving the cup back to* LAONICE). Speak.

TIMAGENES. Grant me a moment to regain my senses.

ANTIOCHUS. What thing, then, hath occurred?

TIMAGENES.   The Prince thy brother . . .

ANTIOCHUS. How now? Would he oppose my happiness?

TIMAGENES. When I had long sought for him to dispel
  The misery he might feel in his misfortune,
  I found him at the end, sir, of a lane
  In which the light of heaven is always dimmed.
  Outstretched upon the grass because of weakness,
  He seemed to mourn for that which he had lost,
  With soul abandoned wholly to such thoughts,
  His head upon a shoulder limply drooping,
  Dreamy and motionless like a hapless lover . . .

ANTIOCHUS. What was he doing, then? Come to the point.

TIMAGENES. From a deep wound wherewith his side was pierced,
  His blood in great spurts on this grassy couch . . .

CLEOPATRE. He is dead?

TIMAGENES.   Yes, madam.

CLEOPATRE.   Ah, contrarious Fortune,
  Which enviest me the blessings I expected!
  This is the thing that in my heart I feared,
  This the despair to which his love reduced him.
  (*To* RODOGUNE) He loved thee over-much to live without thee,
  Madam, and his own hand robbed him of life.

TIMAGENES (*to* CLEOPATRE). Madam, he spoke. His hand herein is
    guiltless.

CLEOPATRE (*to* TIMAGENES). Then thine is guilty, and with villainy
  Unequalled, thou in thy mad insolence,
  When thou hast murdered him, still makest him speak.

ANTIOCHUS. Timagenes, bear with a mother's grief
  And the suspicions prompted by blind wrath.
  As this fell deed hath had no other witness,

I would think like her if I knew thee less.
But what was it he said? Go on, I pray thee.
TIMAGENES.   O'erwhelmed by such a sight, I cried aloud;
And at my cry this prince, amid his gasps,
Half opened, though 'twas hard, his dying eyes;
And this last wandering, beclouded gaze
Showing him his dear brother in my stead,
He spoke to me, thinking he spoke to thee,
These words in which affection outweighed anger:
   "A hand that was beloved of us
Avenges a cruel deed's refusal thus.
   Reign; and above all, brother dear,
   Of that same hand beware, beware.
It is . . . " Fate at this word cut short his utterance;
His life was ended, and his soul took flight;
And I, affrighted by a death so tragic,
I rushed to thee to tell thee the sad news.
ANTIOCHUS.   News sad indeed, and death indeed most tragic,
Which soon will change the people's joy to tears!
O brother dearer than the light of day!
O rival precious to me as my love!
I lose thee, and I find midst all my grief
Over thy death a torture worse than that.
How fatally obscure thy last words were!
Into what depths of horror do they plunge me!
When I would seek the hand that murdered thee,
I feel that my suspicions all are monstrous;
But with the evidence which thou hast supplied me—
Fatal obscurity!—what must I think?
   "A hand that was beloved of us"?
   (*To* RODOGUNE) Is it thine, madam, or is it my mother's?
Ye both besought of us too cruel a deed.
Both of us have refused to do it for you.
Which of you took revenge? Was it this or that one
Whose hand did thus when we refused her ours?
   (*To* RODOGUNE) Is it thou whom I must needs believe was
      guilty?
   (*To* CLEOPATRE) Is it thou of whom I henceforth must
      beware?
CLEOPATRE.   What! thou suspectest *me*?

RODOGUNE.   *I* am suspected
    By *thee?*
ANTIOCHUS.   I am both son and lover. I
    Revere and love you. But however great
    The power of names so sweet over my heart,
    I know of none to whom these indications
    Apply save you.
                        But didst thou hear aright,
    Timagenes? Gavest thou a true report?
TIMAGENES.   Before I would suspect of such a crime
    The Princess or the Queen, I fain would die
    A thousand deaths; but truly my report
    Told all that the Prince said, and nothing more.
ANTIOCHUS.   The crime, by either of them, was so heinous
    That though I cannot doubt it, I still dare not
    Believe it. Oh, whichever of you twain
    Hath shed his blood, trouble thyself no longer
    With planning in what way to pierce my bosom.
    We ill have served your mutual hate when ye,
    Equally cruel, each sought the other's life;
    But if I have refused this task abhorred,
    I willingly serve you both against myself.
    Whichever, then, it be, accept a life
    Whereof your rage e'en now has half deprived me.
                    (*He raises his dagger to stab himself.*)
RODOGUNE.   Oh, stop, sir!
TIMAGENES.   Sir, what doest thou?
ANTIOCHUS.   I am serving
    One or the other of them, and I only
    Make *their* blows needless.
CLEOPATRE.   Live. Reign happily.
ANTIOCHUS.   Then rid me of all doubt. Show me the hand
    Which I must dread and which dares succor me
    Only in order to assassinate me
    And saves me from myself to achieve my death.
    How can I live racked by this endless torment
    Of knowing not the innocent from the guilty,—
    Live and no more without anxiety
    Behold you,—fear you both yet love you both?
    To live thus tortured is to die each moment.

Remove me from this plight or let me die;
Yes, let my anguished soul by a brave blow
Save one of you from doing a foul deed.

CLEOPATRE.   Since on the day I crown thee I have lost
One of my sons and the other one suspects me,
And since amid my tears, which I must dry,
His scant love forces me to defend myself,
If thou no better canst console thy mother
Than by thus setting her in the same scale
As that in which thou settest a foreigner,
Sire, I shall tell thee (for I can no longer
Call by a different name my judge and king)
Thou seest the results of that old hatred
Which this fell tigress hath preserved for me
Despite the peace, and which within her bosom
The memory of past things keeps alive,
And which I naturally desired to frustrate.
She thirsteth for my blood, she sought to shed it;
I well foresaw what hath just now been shown me,
But I allowed thee to disarm my anger.

   (*To* RODOGUNE) Persuaded by his tears, I ceased to fear thee,
Madam, but, O great gods, what hate is thine!
I give thee one son, and thou slayest the other,
Robbing me suddenly of the sole weak aid
That, when assailed, I could have found in him!
When thou wouldst crush me, what can be my refuge?
If to the King I turn, thou hast his heart;
And if he dares to hearken to me, he may,
Alas, try vainly to protect himself
From that same hand. In brief, I am their mother,
Thou art their foe; my aim hath been their glory,
Thine their abasement; and, had I not loved
Those sons thou takest from me, thy first coming
To this place would have disinherited them.
The King ought now, when thus we stand opposed,
To let this difference govern his suspicions
As to which one of us he should distrust—
Unless thy spell can make him favor thee.

RODOGUNE.   Ill shall I plead my cause; for innocence
Cannot conceive, when taken so by surprise,

That it can be suspected, and since nowise
Hath it foreseen so great a crime, whoever
Cares to accuse it, can indeed surprise it.
I do not think 'tis strange to see thy hatred
Turn from Timagenes to declare me guilty.
At the least chance to lay all blame on me,
His story is found worthy of thy credence,
Although thou didst accuse *him* when thy heart
Feared that thy son in dying had named *thee*;
But seeing the doubtful sense of his last words,
To one of us two thou ascribest the crime.

    Truly, if thou wouldst have it believed certain
That one of us was guilty of his death,
I would not, from respect, charge thee with aught;
But thy hand is more stained with crime than mine,
And she who on a husband first does murder
May well complete her work by slaying a son.
I do not, for thou knowest them, deny
The feelings naturally bred in my soul.
Thou askedst for my blood, I asked for thine;
The King knows well the motives which impelled us.
As his discretion hath appeased us both,
Perhaps he knows thy heart, and also mine.

    (*To* Antiochus) 'Tis claimed, sir, that I best can win thy love
By slaying thy brother as a nuptial gift.
Nay, more: 'tis charged I did this monstrous deed
To give my dagger passage to thy bosom.

    (*To* Cleopatre) Where, after such mad crimes, could I
      escape thee,
Madam? and what would all thy Syria do?
Where, lone and helpless when assailed by thee,
Could I find . . . But thou dost not hear me, sir!

Antiochus. No, I hear naught. As to my brother's murder
I will not judge betwixt thee and my mother.
Assassinate a son, slaughter a husband,
I will not guard my life from her or thee.
I blindly follow my sad destiny.
To bare my breast to all, on with the marriage!
Dear brother, 'tis for me the road to death.
The hand that stabbed thee dead will not spare me.

I seek but to rejoin thee, not defend
Myself. I wish, indeed, to give that hand
Every chance to take me unawares,
And shall be happy if its rage, which hath
Deprived me of thee, will soon reveal itself
By finishing its task with me, and if
Its double crime can snatch from heaven's grasp
The thunderbolt too slow in smiting it.
Give me . . .   (*He reaches for the cup.*)

RODOGUNE (*staying him*). What, sir!

ANTIOCHUS.   Thou vainly stayest me.
Give it.

RODOGUNE.   Ah, nay! Protect thyself from both
Of us. This cup is subject to suspicion.
'Twas given thee by the Queen. Fear from us both
A secret hate.

CLEOPATRE.   Doth she who only now
Would spare me dare at last to accuse me?

RODOGUNE.   Madam,
He must refuse all things from either of us.
I accuse no one, and assume thee guiltless.
But a sure, instant proof hereof is needed.
I wish the same rule to apply to me.
One cannot be too careful of kings' safety.
Submit, then, to this test: for thy sole answer
Make trial of the cup upon some servant.

CLEOPATRE.   I shall make trial of it on myself.

                       (*She drinks from the cup.*)
Well, dost thou fear some dread thing from my hatred
Still? I have borne this insult patiently.

ANTIOCHUS (*taking the cup from her hands*). Forgive her, madam, for
     a little doubt
Of thee. Thou didst accuse her, she attempted
To hurl back in thy face the horrible charge;
And be it love for me or be it shrewdness
In her own interest, her solicitude
Makes her appear somewhat less like a criminal.
As for me, who with mind all turmoiled now
See naught but an abyss of misery,
Naught but a well of sorrows, while I wait
Until the truth shall fully come to light,

I leave all vengeance to the gods who know it,
And without more delay shall . . .

RODOGUNE (*pointing to* CLEOPATRE).　　　See her glance
Already wandering, sir, confused and wild!
That ghastly sweat running down o'er her face!
That swollen throat! O righteous gods! what frenzy!
To kill thee after her, she chose to die.

ANTIOCHUS (*giving the cup to an attendant*). No matter! 'tis my
mother; I must aid her.

CLEOPATRE. Back! thou in vain desirest to save my life.
My hate's device too well and surely serves me.
'Tis shown too quickly to destroy thee with me.
That is the one regret I feel in dying,
But in this failure I still find a comfort:
I shall not see my rival on my throne.
Reign! Crime hath followed crime, and thou art King!
I rid thee of thy father, of thy brother,
And of myself. May heaven let its vengeance
Fall on your heads, making you both its victims
In payment for my deeds. May ye in marriage
Find naught but horror, jealousy, and strife;
And, to wish for you all bad things at once,
May there be born to you a son like me!

ANTIOCHUS. Ah, live to change this hate to love!

CLEOPATRE.　　　　　　　　　　　　　I would
Curse the gods, if they gave me back my life.
Help me hence; I am dying, Laonice.
If thou dost wish to oblige me by a last
Service, after my enmity hath wrought
So vainly, save me from the humiliation
Of falling at their feet.

　　　　　　　(*She goes out,* LAONICE *helping her.*)

ORONTES.　　　　　　　　　In the stern justice
Of such a fate, sir, righteous heaven indeed
Is kind to thee: it hath preserved thy life,
When almost lost, from the most deadly danger
Which thou couldst undergo; and by a noble
Manifestation of its gracious power
Hath punished guilt and left thy hands unstained.

ANTIOCHUS.   Orontes, in her fell career I know not
       Which grieves my soul the more, her life or death.
       Both hold for me incomparable woe.
       Pity my plight.
          (*To the others*) And ye, go to the temple,
       To change the joy there into deepest mourning,
       The wedding pomp into funereal show;
       And later we shall see whether, when next
       We come with offerings as worshippers,
       The gods will be more heedful of our prayers.

Nicomède

(NICOMEDES)

CHARACTERS IN THE PLAY

PRUSIAS, *King of Bithynia.*
FLAMINIUS, *ambassador of Rome.*
ARSINOË, *Prusias' second wife.*
LAODICE, *Queen of Armenia.*
NICOMEDES, *Prusias' eldest son, born of his first marriage.*
ATTALUS, *son of Prusias and Arsinoë.*
ARASPES, *captain of Prusias' guards.*
CLEONE, *lady-in-waiting and confidante of Arsinoë.*
Guards.

The scene represents a room in the palace of Prusias, in Nico-
    media, the capital of Bithynia.

The names "Prusias" and "Attalus" are accented on the first
syllable; "Flaminius," "Arsinoë," "Laodice," "Araspes," and
"Cleone" on the second syllable. "Nicomedes" is accented on
the first and third syllables. The final "e" in the names of the
three women is in each case a separate syllable.

Nicomedes

ACT I

NICOMEDES *and* LAODICE *are discovered.*

LAODICE.   After such mighty deeds, sir, it is sweet
To see that I still reign within thy bosom,—
To see that though his brow is crowned with laurels,
I still hold captive this great conqueror's heart,
And that, with all the glory of his exploits,
He now does homage to unworthy me.
Yet whatsoever blessings heaven sends me,
My anxious heart can find no joy in them.
I see thee with regret, my love so clearly
Perceives the Court a dangerous place for thee.
Here reigns thy stepmother, and the King thy father
Views naught save through her eyes, makes her desires
His sovereign law, and thinks of her alone.
Judge of thy safety in the light of this.
The hate that naturally she has for thee
Is now renewed because of me. Thy brother,
Her son, returned a short while since . . .

NICOMEDES.   I know it,
My princess, and that he pays court to thee.
I know that he, who was the Romans' hostage,
Has finally been sent back for something worthier;
That this gift to his mother was the price
Which their Flaminius paid for Hannibal;
And that the King would have pronounced the order
To give up that great man if he himself
Had not by poison shunned the grasp of Rome,
Frustrating thus the stately shows to which
The terror of his name destined him there.
By my last battle I saw reunited
The whole of Cappadocia with Bithynia,
When on these tidings, filled with wrath at losing
My master and with fears for thee, I left
My army in Theagenes' command

333

To fly here to the succor of my queen.
This, madam, thou dost need, as I perceive
Well, for Flaminius still besets the King.
If Hannibal was the reason for his coming,
Him dead, this long stay hath some other object;
And I can see but one which could detain him:
To aid my brother in his pursuit of thee.

LAODICE.   I would not doubt that he, as a good Roman,
Takes ardently the Queen's side. Hannibal,
Whom she has just now sacrificed to him,
Enlists him in her cause; hence I distrust him.
But, sir, thus far I cannot complain justly;
And whatsoever he attempts, hast thou
Grounds for alarm? My honor and my love
Have very little influence on me
If to keep faith with thee I need thy presence;
And can I be so mad as to prefer
Attalus to the conqueror of Asia—
Attalus, whom the Romans reared, a hostage
Or a slave, rather, whom their hands have fashioned,
Teaching but servile fear to him, who trembles
To see an eagle and respects an edile!

NICOMEDES.   Nay! better, better death than that my thoughts
Conceive ideas so little worthy of thee!
'Tis violence I dread, and not thy weakness;
And if Rome once concerns herself against us . . .

LAODICE.   I am a queen, sir; Rome in vain will thunder.
She cannot bid me aught, nor can thy king.
If he is guardian of my youthful years,
'Tis but to carry out my father's orders.
He gave me unto *thee*, and no one else
Hath any right to change this and to choose
A king for me. By his command and mine
Armenia's queen belongeth to the heir
Unto Bithynia's throne, and she will never
Have a soul base enough to let herself
Marry a subject. Put thy mind at rest.

NICOMEDES.   But can I do so, madam, seeing thee
Endangered by the passions of a woman
Who is all-powerful here and thinks all things

Legitimate to enable her to see
Her son reign? There is naught that is too sacred
For her to violate. One who would surrender
A Hannibal might well use force with thee
And treat thee no more honorably than she
Treated the claims of hospitality.

LAODICE. But have the claims of natural ties a power
Of which thou canst be sure, after this outrage?
Sir, thy return, far from undoing her schemes,
Exposes thee thyself to them, then me.
Being unbidden, 'twill be deemed a crime;
And thou wilt soon be the first victim whom
This mother and son, because they cannot cow me,
Will seek to slay, to rob me of support.
If thee I need, that no one may constrain me,
My need is that the King and she shall fear thee.
Return to the army. To protect me, show them
A hundred thousand swords that would avenge me.
Speak armed with power and beyond their reach;
If here they hold thee, they have naught to dread.
Put no vain trust in thy heroic heart
Nor the distinction of thy conquering name;
However great thy valor, in this palace
Thou hast but two hands, like all other men;
And though thou wert the world's delight and terror,
He who comes hither brings his head to the King.
I say to thee again: go back to the army;
Show to the Court nothing but thy renown;
Safeguard thy fortunes, and thus safeguard mine;
So act that thou art feared, and I shall fear not.

NICOMEDES. Go back to the army? Ah! know this: the Queen
Fills it with murderers, whom her hate hath purchased.
Two have been found there; I have brought them with me
To prove her guilt and undeceive the King.
Although her husband, he is still my father;
And even though he should silence nature's tie,
Three scepters added to his own by me
Will speak instead of it and will not be silent.
Then if our destiny, bent on my death,
Prepares it here no less than in the army,

When the same peril everywhere is mine
Dost thou forbid that I should die beside thee?
LAODICE.   Nay, I no more shall tell thee that I tremble,
But that, if death comes, we shall die together.
    Let us be armed with courage, and we shall make
The dastards quail who now expect to crush us.
The populace love thee and hate these wretches,
And one is strong who reigns in hearts so numerous.
But mark, thy brother Attalus approaches.
NICOMEDES.   He has never seen me. Do not make me known.

Enter ATTALUS.

ATTALUS.   What, madam! ever an unrelenting mien?
May I not see one kindly glance escape thee,
One glance not armed with such severity
But as it is when it wins hearts for thee?
LAODICE.   If this mien is ill suited to win *thy* heart,
When I so purpose, I shall assume another.
ATTALUS.   Thou wilt not win it, for 'tis thine already.
LAODICE.   I have no need, then, of a more gracious face.
ATTALUS.   Keep my heart, prithee, having taken it from me.
LAODICE.   'Tis an ill-gotten prize, which I had rather
Give back to thee.
ATTALUS.   Too little thou esteemest it
To wish to keep it.
LAODICE.   Thee I esteem too highly
To wish to gloss o'er anything. Thy station
And mine would not permit that I should do so.
To keep thy heart, I have not where to put it.
The place is occupied, as I have told thee.
I must forbid thee, Prince, to speak like this.
At first one suffers it; but persisted in,
'Tis wearisome.
ATTALUS.   How fortunate is the man
Who occupies that place! How happy he
Would be who could dispute it and prevail
O'er him!
NICOMEDES (*interposing*).   'Twould cost some lives to take that place,
    sir,
From him. This conqueror guards his conquests well,

And none among his enemies yet hath learned
How to retake a fortress which he once
Hath taken.
ATTALUS.   Yet this fortress can be so
Assailed that, valiant though he is, he may
Have to abandon it.
LAODICE.   Thou couldst be mistaken.
ATTALUS. And if the King so wills?
LAODICE.   Being just and prudent,
The King wills only what is in his power.
ATTALUS. And what can sovereign power not do here?
LAODICE. Speak not so loudly. If he is a king,
I am a queen; and towards me all the force
Of his authority cannot be exerted
Save by requests and courtesies.
ATTALUS.   'Tis true;
But when exerted thus, it oft speaks volumes
To queens like thee, who dwell within his realm;
And if a king's requests are not enough,
Rome, which reared me, will speak to thee for me.
NICOMEDES. Rome, sir?
ATTALUS.   Yes; Rome. Hast thou a doubt of it?
NICOMEDES. Sir, I fear for thee, lest some Roman hear thee;
And if Rome knew with what love thou dost burn,
Far from aiding thee as thou sayest, she
Would be indignant to behold her creature
Doing such outrage to her honored name,
And would perhaps take from thee on the morrow
The glorious rank of Roman citizen.
Hast thou received it from her but to earn
Her hatred for degrading it by loving
A queen? Dost thou not know that there is neither
Prince nor king whom she would deign to set
Beside her lowliest commoner? To have lived
So long among these lofty beings, thou
Forgettest their maxims quickly. Reassume
A pride more worthy of her and thee. Uphold
Better a name before which we all tremble,
And without further humbling it to the dust
By vainly worshipping Armenia's queen,

Reflect that thou shouldst need, to thrill thy heart,
At least a tribune's daughter, or a praetor's,—
That Rome permits thee such a noble union,
Which thy defect of birth would have forbidden
If the unrivaled honor of adoption
By her had not allowed thee this ambition.
Wrench open, shatter, burst love's shameful bonds;
To kings, whom she despises, leave all queens;
And cherish loftier desires, to merit
The blessings which have been reserved for thee.

ATTALUS *(turning to* LAODICE). If this is one of *thy* men, impose silence
Upon him, madam, and put an end to such
Insolence. To see how far 'twould go,
I have compelled my wrath to let him speak.
I fear it will break out; if he continues,
I shall persist no more in such restraint.

NICOMEDES.   If I speak truth, what matter who I be, sir?
Does borrowing my voice destroy truth's value?
Thyself, thy love aside, be judge hereof.
   The name of "Roman" is a precious thing.
The King and Queen have purchased it too dearly
To be content to see it cast away,
Since they deprived themselves, for its great sake,
Of the sweet joys of rearing thee from childhood.
When thou wert four years old, they sent thee from them.
Say thou if 'twas to see that name disdained—
See thee renounce, by marriage with a queen,
The portion which they had in Roman greatness.
Both alike jealous of so rare a prize . . .

ATTALUS.   Madam, once more, is this man one of thine?
And is he so essential to thy pleasure
That thou canst not command him to be silent?

LAODICE.   Since he displeased thee, treating thee as a Roman,
I wish to treat thee as a monarch's son.
   As such, thou oughtest to recognize that a prince
Who is thy senior is by rights thy master,
Fear to offend him, and know well that kinship
Does not prevent your differing in rank.
Keep for him the respect owed to his birth,
And, far from stealing his treasure in his absence . . .

ATTALUS. If the honor of being thine is now his treasure,
Say one word, madam, and it will be mine;
And if my age makes somewhat less my rank,
Thou canst amend the inequity of that.
But if I owe him much as the King's son,
Allow me once to address thee as a Roman.
Know that there is not one whom heaven did not
Create to rule o'er kings and have no master.
Know that in loving thee I nobly seek
To avoid the shame of seeing myself a subject.
Know . . .

LAODICE.   I suspected, sir, that indeed my crown
Charmed thee at least as much as did my person;
But all I am, my crown and I, belong
To that first-born who is to be thy king;
And were he here, thou mightest in his presence
Think twice before offending him.

ATTALUS.   Why can I
Not see him here! My heart, aflame with love . . .

NICOMEDES. Conceive desires which are less dangerous,
Sir; if he knew them, he might well himself
Come to avenge his loved one for such love.

ATTALUS. Insolent man! is this the respect thou owest me?

NICOMEDES. I know not, of us two, sir, which has lost it.

ATTALUS. Canst thou indeed know me and speak these words?

NICOMEDES. I know to whom I speak, and it is *my*
Advantage, Prince, that as I am not known
To thee, thou knowest not if I owe respect
To thee, or if thou owest it to me.

ATTALUS. Ah! Madam, let my just wrath . . .

LAODICE.   As to that, sir,
Consult the Queen thy mother. She is here.

                    (*Enter* ARSINOË *and* CLEONE.)

NICOMEDES (*to* ARSINOË). Madam, instruct better the Prince, thy son.
Tell him, pray, who I am. Not knowing me,
He rageth—is beside himself. This frenzy
Is most unfortunate in a soul so rare.
I grieve to see it.

ARSINOË.   Sir, art thou, then, here?

NICOMEDES. Madam, I am, and Metrobates also.

ARSINOË. Metrobates! Ah, the traitor!

NICOMEDES.   He
    Has said naught, madam, which should at all disturb thee.

ARSINOË. But why, sir, this return so unexpected?
    What of thine army?

NICOMEDES.   'Tis under a good lieutenant.
    When I rejoin it, matters very little.
    I had left here my master Hannibal
    And her who is the mistress of my heart.
    Thou'st robbed me of one—thou, I say, or the Romans;
    I come to save the other from them and thee.

ARSINOË. This brings thee here?

NICOMEDES.   Yes, madam, and I expect
    Thy kindly services with the King my father
    In this.

ARSINOË.   I will serve thee there as thou expectest.

NICOMEDES. Of thy good will we are assured.

ARSINOË.   It shall
    Extend to deeds, unless the King forbids.

NICOMEDES. Thou wishest to do both of us this kindness?

ARSINOË. Be very sure that I shall forget nothing.

NICOMEDES. I know thy heart. Have thou no doubt of mine.

ATTALUS (*to* ARSINOË). Madam, is this man, then, Prince Nicomedes?

NICOMEDES. Yes—here to see if I must yield to thee.

ATTALUS. Ah, sir! pray, pardon me if, not knowing thee . . .

NICOMEDES. Prince, let me find in thee a worthier rival.
    If 'twas thy purpose to besiege this fortress,
    Do not give up so brave and bold a project;
    But as I am its only garrison,
    No longer threaten it with the King or Rome.
    I shall alone defend it; thus do thou
    Attack it—with the respect which is a crown's
    Just due. I choose indeed to put aside,
    Together with the title of first-born,
    My destined rank of lordship over thee;
    And we shall see which better makes a man
    Of honor and of spirit, the lessons taught
    By Hannibal or those taught by Rome.
                      Adieu.

Reflect on this. I leave thee to thy thoughts.

(Exeunt NICOMEDES *and* LAODICE.)

ARSINOË *(to* ATTALUS). What! make excuses to a man who dared
    Defy me!
ATTALUS.   But I was so much surprised!
    His swift return undoes me and defeats
    Thy plans.
ARSINOË.   Ill dost thou know them, Attalus.
    It puts their consummation in my grasp.
    Go find the ambassador of Rome for me.
    Bring him alone into my private rooms
    And leave to me the care of thy good fortune.
ATTALUS. But, madam, if 'tis needful . . .
ARSINOË.   Go; fear nothing,
    And to help matters, speed this interview.

(Exit ATTALUS.)

CLEONE. Thou hidest from him a purpose which concerns him,
    Madam?
ARSINOË.   I fear that if he learns of it,
    His heart will be dismayed. I fear that he,
    Because of his instruction by the Romans
    In virtue, will deprive me of the fruit
    Of all my toil and will not understand
    That there is neither trickery nor crime
    Which a throne won thereby does not absolve.
CLEONE. I would have deemed the Romans somewhat less
    Scrupulous, for the death of Hannibal
    Would make me think unfavorably of them.
ARSINOË. Do not impute to them so great a wrong.
    One Roman wrought that, and by my contrivance.
    Rome would have let him live; her mandate would not
    Have violated the laws of hospitality.
    Well knowing at her cost what he could do,
    She would not with a foe have let him dwell;
    But though, from prudence by sad memory taught,
    She forced Antiochus to banish him,
    Without ill will or fear she would have seen
    The last days of his life passed with a prince
    Allied to her. Flaminius alone,
    Stung by the shame with which his sire's defeat

Reddened his brow—for, I believe, thou knowest
That when the Roman eagle saw his legions
Slaughtered beside Lake Trasimenus' shores,
Flaminius his father was their general
And that he perished there by Hannibal's hand—
This son, I say, spurred by his thirst for vengeance,
Easily reached an understanding with me.
The hope of seeing his prey delivered to him
Has led him to procure my son's return;
Through him I have enflamed Rome's jealousy
At sight of Nicomedes' Asian conquests
And at Laodice's marriage with this prince,
Uniting her domains and those of Prusias,
So that the Senate feels a natural dread
Of such a great realm's being ruled by one
So great of heart; and he has had himself
Made their ambassador, to break off this marriage
And set a bound to Nicomedes' power.
That is the whole extent of Rome's concern.

CLEONE.   So Attalus to this end woos his lady!
But why did Rome not act ere the return
Of her dear lover fortified her love?

ARSINOË.   To offend a conqueror who commands an army
Ready to follow his wrath anywhere,
Would risk too much; and I have thought it best
That he should from his covert be lured hither.
So Metrobates hath contrived, pretending
Through panic to betray to him my orders,
And, saying he was suborned to murder him,
Easily brought him here, the gods be thanked!
He comes to complain of it to the King
And ask for justice from him, and his plaint
Will bring him to the brink of an abyss.
Without an effort to defend myself,
I can use this to strengthen my position.
As soon as I beheld him, I exhibited
Dismay, changed color, and cried out. He thought
That he surprised me, and he wrongly thought so,
For his return was mine own handiwork.

CLEONE. But whatsoe'er Rome does and Attalus
    Attempts, how win Laodice for him?
ARSINOË. I interest my son in wooing her
    Only to blind the King, the Court, and Rome.
    I have no wish, Cleone, for Armenia's
    Crown; I but seek to make sure of Bithynia's,
    And if its diadem is once our own,
    Then let this queen choose for herself a husband.
    I shall constrain her only to provoke
    Resistance in her—only to incense
    Her lover's heart and hers. The King, urged on
    Vigorously by Flaminius, will through fear
    Of giving offense to Rome act in hot haste;
    And this prince, justly angered, will no doubt
    Quite lose his head, then, and defy his father.
    He is quick-tempered, and the King no less so;
    And as I shall take pains to exasperate him,
    If such things in the least can move this lover,
    My triumph is assured, his ruin certain.
    There is my heart laid bare, and all its purpose.
    But in my rooms Flaminius awaits me.
    Come, and guard well the secrets of thy queen.
CLEONE. Thou knowest me too thoroughly to feel anxious.

                                           (Exeunt.)

A C T   I I

PRUSIAS *and* ARASPES *are discovered.*

PRUSIAS. Returns without my orders, and comes here?
ARASPES. Sire, thou wouldst wrongly be disturbed by this,
    And the high virtues of Prince Nicomedes
    Are potent medicine against every fear.
    Yet anyone but him should be suspect;
    So sudden a return fails in respect
    And offers grounds for having some misgivings
    About his secret reasons for such impatience.
PRUSIAS. Only too well I see them, and his boldness
    Directly challenges my authority.
    He would no longer be dependent on it,
    And thinks that there is left, after his conquests,

No more a sovereign head to rule his arm,
That he is his own law, and that such heroes
Are false to their own selves if they obey.

ARASPES. 'Tis thus that those like him most often act:
Their mighty deeds make them unapt for duty,
And these proud spirits, puffed up by their renown,
Supreme in the army and among their soldiers,
Are prone to acquire a habit of commanding,
Because of which they find obedience irksome.

PRUSIAS. Say all, Araspes: say that the name of "subject"
Sets all their glory in too low a station;
That though their birth destines them for the throne,
If they are slow to reach it, their great souls
Are mutinous; that a father keeps o'erlong
A prize which is their due and loses value
With being too long awaited; and that thence
Are seen to rise a thousand secret doings
Among his people and his retinue;
And that if no one actually cuts short
Alike his tedious reign and his sad days,
At least an insolently feigned obedience
Usurps his power and leaves him but his title.

ARASPES. 'Tis this which should be feared in any other,
Sir, and in any other should be balked.
But not for thee is such advice required.
The Prince is virtuous, and thou art a good father.

PRUSIAS. If I were not one, he would be a criminal.
He owes his innocence to paternal love.
'Tis this alone which finds excuses for him
And justifies him—or this alone, mayhap,
Which hoodwinks me and makes a victim of me;
For truly I should fear that his great virtues
Have struggled vainly 'gainst ambition in him,
Which makes the filial instincts in his breast
Be silent. He who wearies of his king
May weary of his father. This is taught us
By many dire examples. There is nothing
So powerful as the desire to reign,
And when it once hath seized us, nature's tie

Is blind, and virtue mute.
                              Shall I confess it
To thee, Araspes? he too well hath served me.
In adding to my power, he has snatched
All of it from me. He is now my subject
Only so much as he may wish to be;
And he by whom I reign is in reality
My master. Thus to have appeared before me,
His merit is too great. One does not love
To look on those to whom one owes too much.
All that he did finds voice when he approaches me,
And his mere presence secretly reproaches me.
Ever it tells me that he has thrice over
Made me a king; that I hold more through him
Than he will hold through me; and that if I
Shall someday leave a crown to him, my head
Wears three crowns which his valor gave to me.
At heart I blush at this, and my confusion—
Which is renewed, and mounts, on each occasion—
Constantly brings this troubling thought to me:
That he can take my crown who gave me three.
He only needs to try, and he can do
All that he wills to do. Consider, then,
Araspes, in what plight I am, if he
Wills to do all he can!
ARASPES.   Regarding any
Other than he, I know how to expound
The principles of sound, wise policy.
    As soon as any subject grows too great,
Though guiltless still, he is not innocent.
One does not wait till he dares use all license.
'Tis treason to be able to commit
Treason, and he who knows the art of reigning
Prevents with prudence anyone's deserving
A just and greater punishment, and forestalls
By a command, wholesome for both alike,
The ill deeds which he plans or could perform.
But, sire, as for the Prince, he is too virtuous.
I have already said so.

PRUSIAS. And wilt thou
    Answer to me for that? wilt guarantee me
    Against what he can do, to have revenge
    For Hannibal or to destroy his brother?
    And dost thou take him for a man to see
    Unmoved his brother's wooing and the death
    Of Hannibal? Nay, let us not beguile
    Ourselves. He seeks revenge. He has the pretext
    For it; he has the might. The rising star
    Is he which all my realm adores—the god
    Of both the army and the populace.
    Sure of the one, he no doubt comes to rouse
    The other, to swoop down with all his power
    On what is left of ours. But this small portion
    Of it which yet is mine, although 'tis weak,
    Is still perhaps not altogether helpless.
    However, I would fain act with adroitness
    And join with much laudation some slight harshness,
    Drive him away with honors, and mix sweetly
    Acclaim of his high worth with my resentment.
    But if he disobeys me, or if he dares
    Complain of this, whatever he hath done
    For me, whatever I perceive to fear
    In him, if I should see the whole realm thus
    Endangered . . .

ARASPES. He approaches.

(Enter NICOMEDES.*)*

PRUSIAS. 'Tis thou, Prince!
    Who bade thee come here?

NICOMEDES. Only the ambition
    That I might lay in person at thy feet
    Another crown, sir, and enjoy the honor
    Of thy embrace, and see thy satisfaction.
    With Cappadocia happily united
    Now to the realms of Pontus and Bithynia,
    I come to thank my father and my king
    For having graciously made use of me
    And having chosen my arm for such distinction
    And given me the glory of his victory.

PRUSIAS.   Thou mightest have dispensed with my embrace
   And have expressed thy thanks to me by writing.
   Thou shouldst not have enshrouded in a crime
   Thy victory's augmentation of thy fame.
   It is a capital offense to leave
   My camp, in all men inexcusable,
   Still more so in the General; and if any
   Other than thou had come without my orders,
   Despite this conquest, 'twould have cost his head.
NICOMEDES.   I erred, I must confess, and my rash heart
   Listened o'ermuch to its too ardent wishes.
   My love for thee committed this offense.
   That love alone hath made me fail in duty.
   If seeing thee were not so precious to me,
   I would be innocent but so far from thee
   That I would rather, sir, forfeit a little
   Of thy esteem, and that so great a pleasure
   Should cost me a small crime, for which I never
   Shall fear too stern a sentence, if in thee
   Love is the judge of love's result in me.
PRUSIAS.   The worst excuse suffices with a father,
   And every fault is trifling in a son.
   I would fain see only my sole support
   In thee.
      Receive today the honors due thee.
   The ambassador of Rome asks for an audience
   With me. He shall be shown how much I trust thee.
   Thou, Prince, shalt hear him and reply for me.
   Thou, after all, art the real king; no longer
   Am I aught but his shadow, and age leaves me
   Only an empty title, with which honor
   Is paid to my last years. I have, perhaps,
   No more than a few days yet left to keep it.
   To thee alone the interests of the realm
   Must look. Show now the strongest evidence
   'Tis so. But still forget not thine offense;
   And as it wronged sovereign authority,
   To make atonement for it, go hence tomorrow.
   Restore to royal power its distinction.
   Await it from me as I once received it,

Inviolablè, entire; and do not teach
Men worse than thou to treat it with dishonor.
The people and the Court, seeing thy conduct,
Would disobey thee by thine own example.
Set them another, and demonstrate to them
That our first subjects are the most obedient.

NICOMEDES. I shall obey, sir—sooner than expected.
But a reward I ask for my obedience.
Armenia's queen belongs in her own realm,
And by our wars the road to it lies open.
'Tis time this star should light its skies again.
Grant me the honor, pray, to escort her thither.

PRUSIAS. It is thy due, alone. This noble task
Requires a king himself or a king's heir;
But to restore her to Armenia
Thou knowest that pomp and circumstance are needful.
While I prepare for her departure, thou
Wilt go and in my camp await her from me.

NICOMEDES. She is ready to go now, without more train.

PRUSIAS. I will not thus offend against her rank.
But here the envoy is. He must be heard;
Then we shall see what needeth to be arranged.

Enter FLAMINIUS.

FLAMINIUS. When I was on the point of going, Rome
Hath bidden me, sir, to make one more request
Of thee for her.
                              She hath for twenty years
Nurtured a prince, thy son, and thou canst judge
The pains which she hath taken for his sake
By the great virtues and the striking signs
Which he displayeth of his royal blood.
He hath been taught, above all, how to reign.
So oughtest thou to believe and demonstrate.
If thou dost value rightly his upbringing,
Provide that he shall reign; this doth she ask;
And thou wouldst flout the esteem in which she holds him
If thou shouldst let him live and die a subject.
Then make me able to send her word today
Where thou designest for him a sovereign sway.

PRUSIAS. · Her people and her Senate ne'er will find me
A father little grateful for the pains
Taken with him. I think that he possesses
The qualities for reigning, and I would
Be loath to doubt it after what thou sayest.
But here, sir, is the Prince his elder brother,
Whose gallant arm hath won me, thrice, a crown.
He hath just gone forth to one victory more,
And I some guerdon owe him for his exploits.
Let his the honor be of answering for me.
NICOMEDES (*to* PRUSIAS). Sir, 'tis for thee alone to make a king
Of Attalus.
PRUSIAS. 'Tis alone thine interests
That his request affects.
NICOMEDES. Of thine alone,
However, I shall speak. Wherefore does Rome
Now interfere? and whence assumes the Senate,
Thou living still, thou reigning still, such rights
Over thy realm? Live, reign, sir, till thou diest,
And then let Rome act, or thy natural heir.
PRUSIAS. For such friends one must needs go to some trouble.
NICOMEDES. Those who partition what is thine desire
Thy death, and with such friends the wisest course . . .
PRUSIAS. Nay, nay, embroil me not with the Republic!
Have more respect for such allies.
NICOMEDES. I cannot
Bear to see kings humiliated by them;
And be whate'er he may this son whom Rome
Sends back to thee, I would return her gift
Gladly to her. If he hath been so well
Instructed in the art of governing,
'Tis a rare treasure which she ought to guard,
Keeping her cherished foster child with her
To serve as either consul or dictator.
FLAMINIUS (*to* PRUSIAS). Sir, in these words so little friendly to us
Thou seest the lessons taught by Hannibal.
This faithless enemy of Rome's greatness hath
Put in his heart only disdain and hatred
Of her.

NICOMEDES.   Not so, but he has above all things
　　　　　　Left me confirmed in this: to estimate
　　　　　　Rome highly, and to fear her not at all.
　　　　　　I am called his pupil, and I glory in it;
　　　　　　And when Flaminius assails his memory
　　　　　　He ought to know that someday he must give me
　　　　　　Full satisfaction for his having driven
　　　　　　My master to take poison, and remember
　　　　　　That 'twas against *his* father that this great man
　　　　　　Began of old his victories over Rome.
FLAMINIUS.   Oh! thou too much insultest me!
NICOMEDES.　　　　　　　　　　　　Do thou
　　　　　　Insult no more the dead.
PRUSIAS *(to* NICOMEDES*)*.　　　And thou, seek not
　　　　　　To foment discord. Speak, and speak in plain words,
　　　　　　Concerning that which he proposes to me.
NICOMEDES.   Well, then! if there is need of further answer,
　　　　　　Attalus needs must reign: Rome has decreed it;
　　　　　　And since her power is everywhere supreme,
　　　　　　Kings must obey whenever she commands.
　　　　　　　Attalus hath a great heart, a great mind,
　　　　　　And a great soul—all the great qualities
　　　　　　Which go to make a great king. But 'tis not well
　　　　　　That we should trust a Roman's word for this.
　　　　　　Let us discover by some noble deed
　　　　　　If he is worthy to be crowned a king,—
　　　　　　If he such valor hath, such eminent virtues.
　　　　　　Give him thine army, and let us note his exploits.
　　　　　　Let him do for himself what I have done
　　　　　　For thee; let him reign proudly o'er his own
　　　　　　Conquests and by his victories crown his brow.
　　　　　　I offer him my aid and now will gladly
　　　　　　Be his lieutenant if he will accept it.
　　　　　　The example of the Romans authorizes
　　　　　　This course for me. The famous Scipio
　　　　　　Acted thus for his brother; and when by them
　　　　　　Antiochus was dethroned, the elder marched
　　　　　　Beneath the younger's leadership. The shores
　　　　　　Of the Hellespont and of the Aegean Sea,

And what of Asia lies along our borders,
Offer material for his ambition . . .
FLAMINIUS. All this hath Rome placed under her protection,
And ye cannot make further conquests there
And not draw fearful tempests on your heads.
NICOMEDES. I do not know the wishes of the King
On this point; but perhaps I shall someday
Be mine own master, and we then shall see
The consequences of such threats.
Ye can
In the meantime have these places fortified,
Prepare an obstacle to my new designs,
Arrange betimes for sending help from Rome—
And if Flaminius leads it, we may find
A new Lake Trasimenus for him.
PRUSIAS. Prince,
Thou dost abuse too soon my favor shown thee.
Every ambassador must be respected,
And the honor which I have bestowed on thee . . .
NICOMEDES. Sire, either let me speak or silence me.
I know not how to answer otherwise
In a king's stead to whom upon his throne
Anyone seeks to dictate.
PRUSIAS. Thou dost give
Offense to me myself in speaking thus,
And thou shouldst curb the impetuosity
Which carries thee away.
NICOMEDES. What! shall I see
Someone set limits, sire, to thy domains,
Arrest my conquering arm in mid-career,
Have e'en the audacity to threaten thee,
And I must not reply with threat for threat!
And I must thank one who says arrogantly
That I no more may conquer and not be punished!
PRUSIAS (to FLAMINIUS). Sir, thou wilt pardon youth's hotheadedness.
Time and good sense can make him wise.
NICOMEDES. Good sense
And time have opened mine eyes wide enough,
And age will only open them the wider.
If I had lived till now like this my brother,

With virtues which were but supposititious
(For thus I call those which have borne no fruits,
And the admiration of heroic men,
Whose high worth he has seen displayed in Rome,
Is no great virtue unless one imitates them)—
If I had, then, lived in such quiet ease
As he hath lived in Rome beside these heroes,
She would let *me* have all Bithynia
Just as the eldest son hath from his father
Always received it, and would be less eager
To make him reign if under me thine armies
Had been unable to win aught. But because
She seeth, by the conquest of three crowns,
Such formidable power given Bithynia,
It must be split up; and with this fine project
In view, she deems the Prince of too high birth
To be my subject! Because he can serve her
By making me step down, he has more valor
Than Alexander had, and I must forfeit,
To put him in the station rightly mine,
My heritage or what my blood hath purchased.
I thank the gods, the brave deeds I have done
And my expected greatness have made Rome
Take umbrage. Thou, sir, canst allay it quickly;
But do not ask thy son to assent thereto.
The master who so carefully instructed
My youth, ne'er taught me to do aught unworthy.
FLAMINIUS. So far as I can see, Prince, thy objections
Rise from self-interest rather than from virtue.
The greatest exploits which thou hast achieved
Have only loaned thy father crowns, not given them.
He is a mere custodian of thy prizes,
And 'tis but for thyself that thou hast conquered.
Since, then, his glory and therewith his throne
Must go inseparably to thee alone,
I thought thou surely wouldst be somewhat more
Magnanimous. When Romans are magnanimous,
They for themselves do nothing. Scipio,
Whose spirit thou so greatly hast extolled,
Ne'er sought to reign over the walls of Carthage;

And in reward for all he did to make
Rome great, he won but glory and the name
Of Africanus. Yet in Rome alone
Does one see virtue so disinterested.
Everywhere else on earth is different.
  As for the reasons of State which thou imaginest
Make us fear so much power combined in thee,
If thou'lt consult with wiser heads than thine,
They will divest thee of these subtle thoughts.
In deference to the King, I say no more.
Employ thy leisure to reflect hereon.
Let not thy camp-fires smoke so martially,
And thou wilt have more penetrating vision.

NICOMEDES. Time will decide whether my thoughts are subtle
Or visionary. Yet . . .

FLAMINIUS.   Yet if it charms
Thy heart to extend the glory of thy arms,
We stint not that; but as one is permitted
To serve his friends against a foe, whoever
It be, if thou dost not know this, I wish
To teach it to thee and to give thee counsel
About it, that thou mayest not be surprised.
  As for the rest, be sure that thou shalt have
All that thou in thy heart devourest already.
Pontus shall be thine with Galatia,
With Cappadocia, with Bithynia.
Thy heritage, these lands thy blood hath purchased,
Shall not give Attalus thy lofty station;
And since it paineth thee to share them with him,
Rome does not wish to act unjustly towards thee.
This prince shall reign and yet take naught of thine.
  (*To* PRUSIAS) Armenia's queen needeth a husband, sir.
No opportunity could be better. She
Lives 'neath thy sway; thou hast disposal of her.

NICOMEDES. That is the real way to make Attalus king,
As thou hast said, and yet take naught of mine.
The stratagem is neat, and its devisers
Have by wide circuits reached a worthy end.
I shall say only this, not being concerned:

Treat this princess like the queen she is.
Touch not in her her royal rights, or I
Myself in their defense at need will die.
I give thee this advice; for ne'er do sovereigns,
By living in our realm, live 'neath our sway.
They, they alone, dispose here of themselves.

PRUSIAS. Hast thou naught else to say to him, Nicomedes?

NICOMEDES. Naught, sir, unless thy Queen should finally,
Though knowing what I can do, too far provoke me.

PRUSIAS. Insolent youth, in *my* Court what canst *thou* do
Against her?

NICOMEDES. Naught but keep or not keep silent.
Once more, I say, may it please thee, be advised
To treat Laodice like the queen she is.
'Tis I who beg this of thee. (*Exit* NICOMEDES.)

FLAMINIUS. What! always
Some obstacle?

PRUSIAS. 'Tis not strange, in a lover.
This haughty spirit, made drunk by his success,
Thinks to prevent our access to her heart;
But everyone must follow his own fate.
Love does not make the marriages of sovereigns;
And reasons of State, whose bonds are stronger far
Than love's, can find the means to quench its fires.

FLAMINIUS. Being in love, she will be obstinate.

PRUSIAS. No, no; I will be answerable to thee,
Sir, for Laodice. But 'tis true she is
A queen, and this her rank seems to require
Of us some courtesy. I, after all,
Have complete power over her; but I like
To cloak it with the semblance of entreaty.
Let us, then, visit her; and as ambassador
Thyself propose this marriage to her ambition.
I will support Rome, and will bring thee to her.
Since she is in our hands, love cannot balk thee.
Come, then; if she refuses thy request,
Take the chance offered to speak roundly to her.

(*Exeunt.*)

NICOMEDE

ACT III

PRUSIAS, FLAMINIUS, *and* LAODICE *are discovered.*

PRUSIAS.   Queen, since this title hath such charms for thee,
Thou oughtest to fear the loss of it. Whoever
O'er-acts the part of king does not reign long.
LAODICE.   I shall remember, sir, this weighty counsel;
And if I ever reign, I shall exhibit
Its salutary and noble policy.
PRUSIAS.   Thou followest ill the path of sovereignty.
LAODICE.   Sir, if I go astray, it can be taught me.
PRUSIAS.   Thou holdest Rome too lightly, and owest more
Respect to a king who is a father to thee.
LAODICE.   Nay, thou wouldst see that to them both I render
That which I owe, if thou didst more desire
To understand what being a king means.
   If I received ambassadors as a queen,
I would be playing the sovereign in thy presence,
Encroaching on thy rights, and in thy realm
Committing an offense to thy authority.
I hence decline, sir, and deny myself
The honor due me only in my Armenia.
'Tis there that on my throne with greater splendor
I can pay Rome fit honor in her envoy,
Can answer as a queen, and as deserve
Both whence I am addressed and he who speaketh.
Here such a part I know not how to play,
For I, save in Armenia, am nothing;
And elsewhere this great name of "queen" doth only
Empower me to recognize no throne
To which I must be subject, to live free,
And in all lands to have for master no one
Except myself, right reason, and the gods.
PRUSIAS.   These gods thy masters and the king thy father
Have given me their authority over thee;
And thou mayest learn, perchance, another day
What in all lands right reason is for monarchs.
To prove it, let us go now to Armenia.
With goodly numbers I shall bring thee there.

355

Come; and tomorrow, since thou so wilt have it,
Prepare thyself to see thy land laid waste;
Prepare thyself to see throughout thy country
All the most dreadful ravages of war,
The dead piled mountain high, rivers of blood.

LAODICE. Then I shall lose my realm and keep my rank,
And these huge evils which my pride brings on me
Will make of me thy slave, but not thy vassal.
My life is in thy hands, my honor is not.

PRUSIAS. We shall ere long change this unbending courage;
And when thine eyes, assailed by all these woes,
See Attalus upon thy fathers' throne,
Then perhaps—then—thou wilt beseech in vain
His hand of him, to raise thee there again.

LAODICE. If ever unto this thy war should bring me,
My soul and courage will indeed be changed.
But thou, mayhap, sir, wilt not go so far.
The gods will have some small care of my fortunes.
They will influence thee, or find a man
To oppose the many heroes Rome will lend thee.

PRUSIAS. Thy hopes depend on one presumptuous youth.
He rushes to his ruin, and drags thee with him.
Bethink thee, madam; do not wrong thyself.
Choose: be a queen or mere Laodice.
And for the last advice that I shall give thee:
If thou wouldst reign, make Attalus a king.
Farewell.   (*Exit* PRUSIAS.)

FLAMINIUS.   Madam, indeed the highest motives . . .

LAODICE. Follow the King, sir; thou hast done thy errand,
And I shall further say, not to mislead thee,
That here I neither ought nor wish to hear thee.

FLAMINIUS. And I speak thus to thee, in thy predicament,
Less as ambassador than as a friend
Who, touched with pity at the fate thou courtest,
Is trying to stay thy mad course to disaster.
I shall presume, then, as a friend to tell thee
Candidly that true virtue includes prudence,
And that we, for our own sake, should consider
The times in which we live and where we are.
The grandest courage in a royal soul

Without such prudence is but brutish virtue
Which its own fervor blinds and which false notions
Of honor so divert from real good
That it consigns us to the things we ought
To fear, arousing admiration only
To arouse pity—only to make us able
To tell ourselves, with a great sigh, "We had
Erewhile the right to reign and could not use it."
 Thou angerest a king whose troops thou seest,
Numerous, loyal, knowing naught but victory.
Thou'rt in his hands; thou livest in his Court.
LAODICE. I do not know if there was e'er a false
Notion of honor, sir; but I am willing
To answer thee as a friend.
      My prudence is not
Wholly asleep, and without trying to learn
By what unkindly fate it is that greatness
Of soul appears so wrong to thee, I wish
To make thee see that when I manifest it,
It is not, as thou deemest, a mere brute courage,—
That if I have the right to mount the throne,
I wish to avail myself thereof, and can
Defeat whoever fain would snatch it from me.
 I see on the frontier, as thou hast told me,
A mighty army, knowing naught but victory—
But led by whom? under what general?
The King, if he relied on it, might find
That he was wrong in doing so, and if he
Should wish to pass from his land into mine,
I would advise him to use other soldiers.
But I am in his Court—in his domains—
And I have little right, then, not to fear him?
Outside Armenia—even, sir, in his Court—
'Gainst tyranny virtue can find support.
His people all have eyes to see what mischief
His policies have done the common weal.
They know Nicomedes, know his stepmother;
They know, they see, her stubborn hatred of him;
They see the servitude their king accepts
And know so much the better their false friends.

As for me—on a chasm's brink, thou thinkest—
Far from disdaining Attalus perversely,
I wish to save him from the scorn that I
Would needs feel for him if he owed to me
The rank of king. I would regard him then
As an ignoble soul, as a man born
More fit for other fortunes, as my subject
More than my husband, and our marriage bond
Could not suffice to make him equal to me.
My people would, like me, esteem him little.
'Twould be too much, sir, for a noble heart
To suffer. By refusing him I really
Am gracious to him, and despite his wishes
I save him from lifelong unhappiness.

FLAMINIUS. If what thou sayest is true, *thou* art queen here.
I see thou swayest the army and the Court.
The King is but a name and has no power
Save that which thou accordest him through pity.
What! thou e'en goest so far as to be gracious!
After that, madam, pardon my bold words.
Let Rome, in short, speak to thee through my voice.
To grant an ambassador an audience
Is now within thy rights; or if this term
Offends thee anywhere but in Armenia,
Then let me simply as a Roman tell thee
That being Rome's ally, supported by her,
Is the sole means by which one rules today;
That thus are neighboring nations kept in check,
One's people quiet and enemies afraid;
That any ruler is established firmly
Forever on his throne when he is honored
By being called Rome's friend; that Attalus
Is, with this title, more a king, a sovereign,
Than any who wear crowns upon their brows;
And that . . .

LAODICE.   Enough! I well know what thou meanest.
All kings are kings only as ye permit;
But if Rome at her pleasure doth dispose
Of their domains, she certainly does little
For her dear Attalus, and since she hath

The power to bestow so much on him,
She ought not to persist in begging for him.
Her chariness towards so beloved a prince
Astounds me. Why does she not offer me
Him and a crown together? It offends me
To be so urged for a mere subject—me,
Who would not deem a king was worthy of me
If 'twas by thy command he came and *thy*
Alliance shamed his regal power. These
Are sentiments to which I must be true.
I will not wed a king who can obey;
And since thou hast been shown my inmost heart,
Sir, waste no more thy threats or prayers on me.

FLAMINIUS. May I not pity thee in this thy blindness?
Madam, again I beg of thee, bethink thee.
Remember what Rome is, what power is hers,
And if thou lovest thine own good, beware
Of her displeasure. Carthage overthrown,
Antiochus defeated, nothing now
Can hamper the achievement of our wishes;
All bow on land, all tremble on the waves,
And Rome today is master of the world.

LAODICE. Rome master of the world! Thou'dst frighten me
Were not Armenia and my heart still free,
Had the great Hannibal had no successor,
Did he not live again in Nicomedes,
And had he not left in such worthy hands
The secret of sure victory o'er the Romans.
So brave a pupil will not lack the courage
To put in practice all that he hath learned.
Asia hath proved it, where three conquered crowns
Show in what school he hath been taught so much.
These are his 'prentice work, but such that haply
The Capitol should fear his masterpiece,—
Should fear he may someday . . .

FLAMINIUS. That day is still
Far distant, madam, and some, if it be needful,
Will tell thee who those gods are that hurl down
From high to low estate the rash, and how
E'en on the Trebia's and Cannae's morrow

The Capitol's shadow awed thy mighty Hannibal.
But here he is, this arm so dire for Rome.

Enter NICOMEDES.

NICOMEDES. Either Rome gives wide powers to her agents
Or thou art long in carrying out thy mission.
FLAMINIUS. I know what is commanded me, and whether
Or not I go beyond it. 'Tis to others
Than thee that I shall render an account.
NICOMEDES. Then prithee go to them, and leave to me
In turn the pleasure of talking with the Princess.
Such an impression hast thou made on her,
And what thou sayest hath such attractions for her,
That I cannot refute without great effort
That which thou soughtest to put into her heart.
FLAMINIUS. The woes which an unworthy love will bring her
Have made me give her some advice, through pity.
NICOMEDES. To give her therefore kind advice is gentle
And merciful in an ambassador.
    Did he advise thee to be very base,
Madam?
FLAMINIUS.   Ah, this is too much. Thou art mad.
NICOMEDES. I mad?
FLAMINIUS.   Know thou that there is no land where
The sacred dignity of an ambassador . . .
NICOMEDES. Cease thou to boast to us of that distinction.
He who doth play the counselor is no longer
Ambassador. He oversteps that office
And he himself repudiates it thus.
    But tell me, madam, hath he had his answer?
LAODICE. He hath.
NICOMEDES (*to* FLAMINIUS). Know, then, that I shall henceforth treat
    thee
Only as Attalus' agent, as Flaminius,
And if thou irkest me, I perhaps shall add
As him who poisoned Hannibal, my master.
Those are the only names that I shall call thee.
If they displease thee, go and tell the King.
FLAMINIUS. Though a good father, he will give me justice;
Or Rome, should he refuse, will give it to me.

NICOMEDES.   Go and in suppliance clasp the knees of both.
FLAMINIUS.   Results will follow. Prince, look to thyself.
                                        (*Exit* FLAMINIUS.)
NICOMEDES.   This warning should be rather given the Queen.
 Her hate o'ercomes my magnanimity.
 I have spared her long enough by not disclosing
 Her infamous attempts to murder me,
 But I at last am driven to blazon forth
 Her entire crime. I have contrived to bring
 Zeno and Metrobates to the King,
 And as their story must astonish him,
 He will himself question them carefully.
LAODICE.   I do not know, sir, what will come thereof;
 But I quite fail to understand the whole
 Of this affair or why the Queen compels thee
 To such a step. The more she ought to fear thee,
 The less she fears thee, and the more thou'rt able
 To cover her with infamy, the more
 Doth she with deadly enmity assail thee.
NICOMEDES.   She anticipates my charges, and adroitly
 Attempts to make them seem inspired by hatred;
 But this deceitful mask of fictive boldness
 Disguiseth fear and hideth weakness in her.
LAODICE.   The mysteries of the Court are so obscure
 That oft the most discerning are bewildered.
  When thou wert nowhere near for my defense,
 I did not need to fight off Attalus;
 Rome never dreamed of troubling our love thus.
 Now hast thou been here but a single day,
 And in that very day, Rome in thy presence
 Besets me urgently to marry him.
 For my part, I can grasp no whit the logic
 Of this course, which awaits not thy departure.
 Ever have I as 'twere a cloud before me,
 Which dims my sight and casts its shadow o'er me.
 The King adores his wife and he fears Rome,
 And as for thee, if he does not behold
 Thy great deeds with a somewhat jealous eye,
 At least I must, in candor, not refrain

From saying to thee that he is much too good
A husband to be also a good father.   (*Enter* ATTALUS.)
    Mark how unseasonably Attalus comes!
What brings him to us? what intent? what scheme?
I hardly know, sir, what to think it is;
But I shall foil him if it needs my presence.
I leave thee.   (*Going.*)

ATTALUS.   Madam, such delightful converse
Charms thee no more if I take part in it.

LAODICE.   I shall be frank: thou greatly didst intrude.
Thou canst talk with me in my second self.
He knows my whole heart and will answer for me,
As he hath for the King answered Flaminius. (*Exit* LAODICE.)

ATTALUS.   Since I have driven her hence, I shall withdraw, sir.

NICOMEDES.   No, no; I have some things to say to thee
Prince. I have put aside the name of first-born
And the advantage of my destined throne,
And wishing to defend here my heart's prize
Unaided, I have asked thee to attempt
To win it from me in the selfsame way,
And above all not to avail thyself
Of the King's help or of the Romans' help.
Either thy memory is not very good
Or else thou wilt not do as thou art bidden.

ATTALUS.   Sir, thou compellest me to remember badly,
When thou dost not proceed to make all equal
Between us. Yes, thou dost divest thyself
Of certain rights of primogeniture,
But dost thou of the heart, too, of the Princess,
Or of the virtues which have made her love thee—
Those qualities that could well charm any heart—
Or of thy conquest of three realms, thy triumph
In six great battles, thy heroic storming
Of countless walls? With such aids thou canst have
No doubt of thy success. Then make the Princess
View us impartially. Let her no more
See this accumulation of renown
That victory has heaped up so lavishly
And long for thee; let her awhile forget
Thy lofty merits and thy famous deeds;

Or suffer me to have against her love,
Against thy valor, in the other scale
Rome and the King. The scantness of the help
That they have given me should cause thee to see
Clearly how light a counterweight they are.
NICOMEDES. That thou canst make so courtly a defense
Proves that thy time in Rome was not all lost.
Thou hast no lack of wit, if not of courage.

Enter ARSINOË *and* ARASPES.

ARASPES (*to* NICOMEDES). Sir, the King summons thee.
NICOMEDES. Summons me?
ARASPES. Yes, sir.
ARSINOË. Prince, calumny is easy to demolish.
NICOMEDES. I know not in regard to what thou comest
To tell me this fact—me, who nowise doubt it,
Madam.
ARSINOË. If thou hadst never doubted it,
Thou wouldst not, flattered by false hopes, have brought
From so far off Zeno and Metrobates.
NICOMEDES. I tried persistently to hide all, madam,
But thou hast forced me now to make them speak.
ARSINOË. Truth forces them, much better than thy bribes.
Such commoners keep ill their promises.
They both have said more than they meant to say.
NICOMEDES. I am sorry for thee, but thou wouldst have it so.
ARSINOË. I still would have it so, nor am I sorry
That I have seen thine honor thus attainted
And that the name of infamous suborner
Was almost added to thy noble titles.
NICOMEDES. *I* suborned these men against *thee* herein?
ARSINOË. *I* am outraged, *thou* art shamed thereby.
NICOMEDES. And thinkest thou to destroy all credence of them?
ARSINOË. Nay, sir. I hold by what they said.
NICOMEDES. What said they
Which pleases thee and which thou wishest believed?
ARSINOË. Some true words, which have crowned thee with fair fame.
NICOMEDES. May I not know these words of such importance?
ARASPES (*interposing*). The King grows tired, sir. Thou delayest too
much.

ARSINOË (*to* NICOMEDES). From him thou'lt learn them. He too long
  awaits thee.
NICOMEDES. I finally begin to understand thee.
  A husband's love drives out a father's love
  In him. 'Twill make thee innocent, me guilty.
  But . . .
ARSINOË.   Go on, sir. This "but"—what wouldst thou say?
NICOMEDES. Some true words, which permit life's breath to me.
ARSINOË. May I not know these words of such importance?
NICOMEDES. Thou'lt learn them from the King. I stay too long.
         (*Exeunt* NICOMEDES *and* ARASPES.)
ARSINOË. We triumph, Attalus. This great Nicomedes
  Shall see his villainy end as it should.
  The two accusers whom he hath himself
  Suborned to slander me, saying that I
  Hired them to murder him, forsooth, have ill
  Contrived to carry out this vile pretense.
  Both have accused me; both have then confessed
  To the foul trick this prince hath played on me.
  How strong is truth before a king! How many
  Gates doth it find to issue from the heart!
  How easily is falsehood there confounded!
  Both sought to ruin me; they have ruined him.
ATTALUS. I am delighted that such foul imposture
  Hath left thy fair fame greater, purer still;
  But if thou wouldst a little put aside
  Thy prejudice, to probe this matter well
  And learn the truth of it, thou ne'er couldst have
  A mind so credulous as to believe
  Without the least misgivings two such knaves.
  These faithless men both have declared themselves
  Alike suborned by thee, suborned by him.
  Against so many victories and virtues
  What credence can be owed to souls so black?
  He who confesses that he is a traitor
  Should not be trusted.
ARSINOË.   Thou art generous-minded,
  Attalus, and I see thou holdest dear
  The honor even of thy rivals.

ATTALUS.   Though
    I am his rival, I am his brother, too.
    We are of one blood, and my heart, which holds it,
    Can scarcely think him a calumniator.
ARSINOË.   And canst thou easier believe *me* a murderer—
    Me, who am doomed unless he be destroyed?
ATTALUS.   If I can scarce believe these witnesses
    Against him, when they were accusing thee
    I could believe them even less. Thy virtue,
    Madam, can never stoop to crime. Permit me,
    Then, to have some esteem for him. His glory
    Hath made a thousand people in the Court
    Jealous of him, some one of whom hath wished
    To ruin him along with thee; and this
    Base charge is nothing but a shaft of envy
    Which seeks to blacken his fair life.
                              For my part,
    To judge another from oneself, what I
    Feel in my heart, I shall presume in him.
    I use force openly against so mighty
    A rival, without trying to besmirch
    His good name or procure his overthrow.
    I accept aid, but this I do quite frankly.
    I think that he acts not less generously,
    That he hath only purposes whereto
    Honor impels him, and that he opposes
    Unto my courtship naught but his own merit.
ARSINOË.   Little thou knowest the world—or the Court, either.
ATTALUS.   Should one love otherwise than as a prince?
ARSINOË.   Thou lovest, my son, and speakest as a young man.
ATTALUS.   Madam, at Rome I have seen only virtues.
ARSINOË.   Time now, by setting thee new tasks, will teach thee
    What virtues one must have at a king's Court;
    But meanwhile, if the Prince is still thy brother,
    Remember also that I am thy mother.
    Come, then, despite the doubts thy mind conceives,
    And as to this learn what the King believes.

                                        (*Exeunt.*)

NICOMEDE

ACT IV

PRUSIAS, ARSINOË, *and* ARASPES *are discovered.*

PRUSIAS. Bring the Prince in, Araspes.   (*Exit* ARASPES.)
                                        And thou, madam,
      Restrain the sighs with which thou piercest my soul.
      Why burden my heart with thy distress when thou
      Canst wholly sway it without the help of tears?
      Why should those tears enlist in thy defense?
      Do I doubt *his* crime or *thy* innocence?
      Seest thou some sign that aught he said to me
      Hath so impressed me as to change my mind?

ARSINOË.   Ah, sir, can anything repair the harm
      Which one imposture doeth to innocence?
      And can a lie miscarry soon enough
      For virtue to recover all its purity?
      Ever some ugly memory of it lingers
      Which leaves a blot upon the fairest honor.
      How many slanderous tongues are in thy Court?
      How many blind adherents hath the Prince
      Who, knowing once that I have been impugned,
      Will deem thy love alone acquitted me?
      And if the least stain clings to me, if the least
      Part of the people cease not to suspect me,
      Am I then worthy of thee? Doth such a danger
      Touch me too little to deserve my tears?

PRUSIAS.   Ah, thou'rt too scrupulous and presumest too much
      Wrong from a husband who loves thee and should love thee!
      Honor is more unshakable after slander
      And shines the more for having once been tarnished.
      But here is Nicomedes. I would now . . .

                              (*Enter* NICOMEDES, ARASPES, *and guards.*)

ARSINOË (*pretending to supplicate the King, as soon as she sees* NICO-
      MEDES).   Have mercy, mercy on our sole support,
      Sire! on an arm that wins so many laurels!
      Have mercy on this conqueror, on this taker
      Of cities! mercy . . .

NICOMEDES.   Why? Because I conquered
      Three crowns, which my destruction will deliver

Unto thy son, madam? Because I carried
Your arms so far into the heart of Asia
That even thy Rome was seized with jealousy?
Because I have upheld the majesty
Of kings too well, have filled this Court too full
Of the renown of my great deeds, have practiced
Too much the precepts of great Hannibal?
If I need mercy, choose one among my crimes.
These are all of them, madam; and if thou addest
To them that I have trusted certain miscreants,
The tools of someone else, and that I have
A frank and guileless heart, which was not able
To fathom their devices, 'tis a noble
Distinction, not a crime, in one who sees
The light of day only amid an army
Far from thy Court, who is acquainted only
With manly virtues, and who, because he liveth
Untroubled by remorse, goeth his way
Untroubled by suspicions.
ARSINOË (*to* PRUSIAS).   I was wrong, sir;
He is no criminal. If he sought to blacken
My fair fame with eternal infamy,
He hath but done the dictates of that hatred
Usual in men like him towards a stepmother.
Biased by this aversion, he ascribes
To me each shaft that wounds him. When his mentor,
Hannibal, despite the law of nations,
Gave way to a mad rage of panic fear,—
When this old man sought to preserve his honor
And freedom rather through his own despair
Than through our hospitality,—his fear,
His madness, were my doing. Whatever charms
He himself findeth in Laodice,
'Tis I who give like eyes to Attalus;
'Tis I who make Rome act to aid my son;
From me proceeds all that displeases him;
And if, to avenge his mentor and to save
The mistress of his heart, he hath endeavored
To alienate thee from me, sir, all this
Can be forgiven in a jealous lover.

His feeble, vain attempt doth move me not.
   I know that my whole crime is being thy wife;
This name alone impels him to attack me.
For, really, with what else can I be charged?
In the ten years that he hath led an army
Did my voice ever fail to swell his fame?
And when he was in desperate need of help
And even the least delay would have allowed him
To perish, who hath been more prompt to aid him?
Who better hath repaired his broken fortunes?
Has he had near thee one more diligent
In keeping him supplied with men and money?
Thou knowest he hath not, sir, and to requite me,
When I have served him all I could, I see
That he would fain destroy thy love for me.
But all can be forgiven in a jealous
Lover. I have already told thee that.

PRUSIAS (*to* NICOMEDES).   Ingrate! what canst thou answer?
NICOMEDES.   That the Queen
Hath done me kindnesses at which I marvel.
I shall not say to thee that all this aid
With which she hath preserved my life and glory,
And which she so pretentiously parades
Before thine eyes, was working for the greatness
Of Attalus through me, that she was garnering
For him with *my* hands, and was thus preparing
For just the state of things one sees today.
Whatever motives have impelled her, I
Shall let heaven judge thereof; it knows her thoughts.
It knows in what way she hath sought my safety.
It will be just to her—to both of us.
   Yet, since indeed all hath so fair a semblance,
As she hath spoken for me, I ought to speak
For her and call for her sake to thy mind
That thou art slow in punishing two scoundrels.
Send to the rack Zeno and Metrobates.
Thou owest this sacrifice to her fair fame.
Both have accused her, and if they gainsay
Their own words to declare her innocent
And to accuse thy son, they have not cleared
Themselves thus, and their death is naught but just

For daring to make a mock of a great queen.
Such an offense against those of our station
Can nowise be atoned except by blood.
To unsay what one hath said, doth not suffice;
Falsehood must perish 'neath the torturer's hands;
Or thou wilt all thy royal house expose
To the frivolity of disloyal souls.
The example of these slanderers left unpunished
Is dangerous; it well might cost our lives.

ARSINOË (*to* PRUSIAS).   What, sire! punish them for the honesty
Which suddenly has in their mouths put truth,
Has bared to thee his knavery against me,
Has given thee back thy wife, saved me from death,
Withheld thee from decreeing it to me,
And say such punishment is for *my* sake only!
    Thou art too clever, Prince, and too sagacious.

PRUSIAS (*to* NICOMEDES).   No more of Metrobates! make thine own
Defense. Clear thyself of so vile a crime.

NICOMEDES.   Clear myself? *I*, sir? Nay, thou dost not mean it!
Too well thou knowest that a man like me
Would not be guilty at so cheap a price,—
That he requires, to tempt him, a reward
So dazzling that his crime leaves bright his glory.
    To make thy people rise; to hurl thine army
Into the cause of a mistreated princess;
To come, sword drawn, to pluck her from thy hands
In spite of Attalus and of the Romans,
And here unite against their tyranny
All thine armed host and all Armenia—
That is the thing a man like me might do
If he decided to be disloyal to thee.
Low trickery is the work of petty souls,
And it especially belongs to women.
    Then punish, sir, Zeno and Metrobates.
Do justice on them for the Queen or me.
Conscience is clamorous in life's last moments;
To appease the gods, one recks no more of mortals;
And these inconstant spirits, brought to bay,
Might well disown their words a second time.

ARSINOË.   Sire . . .

NICOMEDES.　　Madam, speak, and say why thou opposest
So obstinately their just punishment;
Or let us think that they would at death's door
Be subject to remorse which would not please thee.
ARSINOË (*to* PRUSIAS).　Thou seest how cruel his hatred of me is:
When I excuse him, he declares me guilty.
But, no doubt, sire, my presence irritates him,
And my withdrawal hence will mend his temper.
'Twill restore calm unto his noble breast
And doubtless spare him more than one misdeed.
　　I shall not ask that thou in pity shouldst
Make certain that a scepter will protect me,
Nor that, to assure safety for Attalus,
Thou shouldst divide the royal power between them;
And if thy friends in Rome have taken some pains
Unto this end, 'twas without my consent;
I felt no need for it. I do not love thee
So little that I shall not follow thee
As soon as in my arms thou liest dead,
And on thy tomb my new-born grief will shed
At the same time my tears and blood alike.
PRUSIAS.　Ah, madam!
ARSINOË.　　　　Yes, sire, that unhappy hour
Shall end, with thy last sigh, my destined span;
And thus, as he will never be my king,
How can I fear him? how can *he* harm *me?*
All that I ask for this dear bond between us,
This son who gives him such offense already,
Is that he may return to Rome to finish
His life, which there thou madest him begin.
Let him return and carry with him there,
Alike removed from danger and from glory,
The futile memory of thy love for me.
This great prince serves thee, and he will serve thee better
When he no more hath aught to offend his eyes.
And fear not thou Rome nor her vengeance: he
Hath too much valor, despite all her might;
He knoweth all the secrets of the famous
Hannibal, of that hero everywhere
So terrible to Rome that Africa

And Asia marvel at the great assistance
He gave to Carthage and Antiochus.
    I shall withdraw, then, that without constraint
Thy natural love shall make thee kind to him;
And I no longer wish to see a prince
Whom I esteem insult me shamefully
Before thy face, nor be myself compelled
To rouse thy wrath against a son so valiant
And worthy of thee.

(Exeunt ARSINOË *and guards.)*

PRUSIAS.   Nicomedes, this
Trouble, to put it briefly, gives me pain.
Whatever anyone dares impute to thee,
I nowise think thee base, but something let us
Concede to Rome, which makes complaint, and also
Attempt to reassure the Queen, who fears thee.
I love her dearly, love her passionately.
I do not wish to see this endless strife
Nor let those feelings which I fain would cherish
Always, reign in my heart only to rend it.
I wish to heed both love and natural ties
And be a father and a husband now . . .

NICOMEDES. Sir, wouldst thou trust me as to this? Be neither
One nor the other.

PRUSIAS.   And what should I be?

NICOMEDES. A king. Resume proudly this noble role.
A true king neither husband is nor father;
He looketh to his throne, and naught else. Reign.
Rome then will fear thee more than thou fearest her.
Despite her power so vast and so imposing,
Thou canst already see how she dreads *me*,
How much she hopes to gain by my undoing
Because she sees that I could really reign.

PRUSIAS. I shall reign, then, ungrateful youth! since thou
So biddest me: choose either Laodice
Or my four crowns. Thy king makes this division
Between thy brother and thee. I am no longer
Thy father. Obey thou thy king.

NICOMEDES.   If thou
Wert the king also of Laodice

To offer her to my choice with any justice,
I would ask time of thee to think of this;
But still to please thee, and offend thee not,
I shall obey, sire, without frivolous
Replies, thy meaning—not thy words.

                              Transfer
To this loved brother all my rights, and leave
Laodice her liberty of choice.
That is *my* choice.

PRUSIAS.   What abjectness of soul,
What madness blinds thee for a woman's sake?
Wretch, thou preferrest her to those glorious prizes
Thy valor added to thy patrimony!
Dost thou deserve to live after such baseness?

NICOMEDES.   I find a pride in following thy example.
Preferrest thou not a woman to that son
By whom these lands were added to thine own?

PRUSIAS.   Dost *thou* see *me* renounce the crown for her?

NICOMEDES.   Dost *thou* see *me* renounce it for the Princess?
What do I really give up to my brother
In giving up thy domains? Have I a right
To claim them ere thy death? Forgive my using
That word; the utterance of it is unpleasant;
But a king dies at last like other men,
And then thy people, when they need a sovereign,
May wish to choose between this prince and me.
    Sire, he and I are not so much alike
That one must have good eyes to see a difference,
And this old law of primogeniture
Hath so great power that one far away
Is oft recalled to fill his rightful throne.
But if this people's sentiments are like thine,
I have brought others 'neath thy sway, and were
The Romans jealous of me still, I might
Do for myself what I have done for thee.

PRUSIAS.   I shall provide 'gainst that.

NICOMEDES.   Yes, if their schemes
Force thee to sacrifice thy son to them;
Or thy domains, committed to this prince,
Will only while thou livest be in his hands.

Not as a secret do I tell thee this;
To him I say it, too, that he may be
Prepared for it. There he is now, and hears me.

PRUSIAS. Go; without shedding mine own blood I still
Can make him sure, thou ingrate, to succeed me.
Tomorrow . . .

Enter FLAMINIUS, ATTALUS, *and guards.*

FLAMINIUS. If for *my* sake thou art angry,
Sir, I have suffered only a small wrong.
The Senate might indeed be outraged at it,
But I have friends who can prevail with them.

PRUSIAS. I shall right all. Tomorrow Attalus
Shall from my hands receive the royal power
And become King of Pontus, my sole heir.
As for this rebel, for this haughty heart,
Rome shall adjudge the wrong 'twixt him and thee.
He shall in place of Attalus be her hostage,
And will be given thee to be taken thither
As soon as he hath seen his brother crowned.

NICOMEDES. Thou sendest me to Rome?

PRUSIAS. Rome is most just.
Go, ask of her thy dear Laodice.

NICOMEDES. I shall go, sir,—shall go, as thou so wishest,
And there be more a king than thou art here.

FLAMINIUS. Rome knows thy great deeds, and already loves thee.

NICOMEDES. Soft, soft, Flaminius! I am not there yet.
Unsure, all things considered, is the way,
And he who brings me there may go astray.

PRUSIAS. Lead him hence. Double his guard, Araspes.
(NICOMEDES *is led out by some of the guards.*)
(*To* ATTALUS) Do thou give thanks to Rome, and ever know
That, as her power is the source of thine,
By losing her support thou wilt lose all.
(*To* FLAMINIUS) Pardon me, sir, if being in distress
Because the Queen hath made me see her grief,
I go to comfort her, and leave thee with him.
Remember, Attalus, thank thy great helper.
(*Exeunt all but* FLAMINIUS *and* ATTALUS.)

ATTALUS. What shall I say, sir, having received boons

Beyond the ambition of the noblest minds?
Thy favors have no bounds, and thy affection
Grants more than thou didst promise or than I sought.
I shall confess, though, that my father's throne
Holds not the happiness which I most desire;
What thrills my soul, what charms my fancy, is
To win Laodice, whom I love so truly.
The royal rank which makes me worthy of her . . .
FLAMINIUS. Will make her no less hostile to thy wooing.
ATTALUS. Nay, circumstances cause a heart to change.
Besides, her dying father gave express
Commands; she says, herself, Armenia's queen
Belongeth to Bithynia's monarch's heir.
FLAMINIUS. This is no binding law; and, being a queen,
She really can make of it what she pleases.
Is she to love thee for a crown of which
Thou hast dispossessed a great prince whom she loves?—
Thee, who deprivest her of her dear protector?
Thee, who art sole author of his ruin?
ATTALUS. This prince gone elsewhere, sir, what will she do?
Who will sustain her cause 'gainst Rome and us?
For I dare still promise myself thy aid.
FLAMINIUS. Matters sometimes take a new course. Frankly,
I am not willing to assure thee of it.
ATTALUS. This, sir, indeed is wholly to confound me,
And I would be less king than something piteous
If any crown could rob me of thy friendship.
But I alarm myself too much, and Rome
Is not so changeable. Are not these thy orders?
FLAMINIUS. Yes, for Prince Attalus, for a man from birth
Nursed in Rome's bosom. But for the King of Pontus
There needs must be new orders.
ATTALUS.   Needs must be
New orders! What! Could it, then, be that Rome
Should become adverse to her own hands' work?
That my new greatness should rouse jealousy?
FLAMINIUS. What dreamest thou, Prince? What sayest thou to me?
ATTALUS. Thyself to me say how I must explain
This inconsistency of thy republic.

FLAMINIUS.   I shall explain it to thee. I wish to save thee
From making, it would seem, a fatal error.
    Rome, serving thee as to Laodice,
Was willing to commit a wrong to give
Her crown to thee; thus friendship did prescribe.
But Rome by other means hath made thee king;
Regard for her own honor now exempts her
From using, for thy sake, such violence.
Leave, then, this queen completely free, and turn
Thy wishes in some new direction. Rome
Herself will make thy marriage be her care.

ATTALUS.   But if Laodice should come to love me?

FLAMINIUS.   That would be still to risk Rome's being thought
To have used artifice or force herein.
This marriage would becloud her fair fame. Think
No more of it, Prince, if thou canst credit me;
Or if thou reckest little of my counsels,
Think no more of it without the Senate's sanction.

ATTALUS.   To judge by this quick change from love to coldness,
Rome does not love me; she hates Nicomedes;
And when she feigned to favor my desires,
She wished to destroy him, not make me great.

FLAMINIUS.   To give thee no reply too sharp to this
Fine trial flight of thy ingratitude,
Follow thine own caprice; offend thy friends.
Thou art a king; all is permitted thee;
But since this day must surely make thee see
That thou dost owe to Rome all thou shalt be,
And losing her support, thou shalt be naught,
Of what the King told thee, forget not aught.

(Exit FLAMINIUS.*)*

ATTALUS.   Was it thus, Attalus, that thy fathers reigned?
To be called "king," wouldst have so many masters?
Ah, at this price e'en now that title irks me!
If we must have a master, be it one only.
Heaven hath given us one too great, too noble
To be allowed to be the Romans' victim.
Let us prove proudly that we are not blind,
And let us free this land from their harsh yoke.
Since all they do is done to serve their interests,—

Since their false friendship yields to policy,—
Let us in turn be jealous of their greatness,
And as they act for their ends, act for ours.

A C T   V

ARSINOË *and* ATTALUS *are discovered.*

ARSINOË. I had foreseen this riot, and see nothing
    To fear from it. A moment kindled it
    To flame, a moment can extinguish it,
    And if the darkness lets its uproar grow,
    Day will dispel the shadows of the night.
    I grieve less that the populace revolts
    Than that thy heart clings stubbornly to its passion
    And, filled with abject and unworthy love,
    Does not feel scorn for her who scorneth thee.
    Avenge thyself on that ungrateful woman;
    Have done with that cruel woman, now when Fate
    Hath made thy lot the higher. It should have been
    Her throne, and not her face, that charmed thee. Thou
    Shalt reign without her; wherefore love her, then?
    Seek, seek a kindlier lady for thy heart.
    Now thou art king, Asia has other queens,
    Who, far from making thee endure their frown,
    Will spare thee soon the task of wooing them.
ATTALUS. But, madam . . .
ARSINOË.   Well, so be it; may she yield!
    Dost thou foresee the ills which then I fear?
    When she hath once made thee Armenia's king,
    She will involve thee in her hate of me.
    But can she end, O gods! her vengeance there?
    Canst thou sleep with assurance in her bed?
    Will she refuse to employ, in her resentment,
    Dagger or poison to avenge her lover?
    What will a woman's fury not essay?
ATTALUS. False reasons, to conceal from me the true!
    Rome does not like to see a powerful king;
    She feared in Nicomedes such a one,
    And would fear such a one in me. I must
    Aspire no more to marriage with a queen

If I would not displease our sovereign mistress;
And since to offend her would be my undoing,
That she may suffer me, I had best obey.
I well know by what means her wisdom led her
So swiftly to dominion o'er the world.
When any land becomes in the least too mighty,
Its fall must needs end the distrust she feels.
To make a conquest is to wrong the Romans;
It gives too many subjects to one ruler;
And rightly they wage war after this crime,
A capital offense against their greatness.
They, who in governing are the first of men,
Would have all docile to their will, like us,—
Would have so great a power o'er all kings
That they themselves alone would remain free.
    I know them, madam, and I have seen their fears
Destroy Antiochus and ruin Carthage.
Lest I should fall like these, I fain would kneel
And act through policy as I cannot feel.
I the more rightly do this in my weakness
When I see Nicomedes in their hands.
So great a foe assures them of my faith;
He is a lion that they can loose against me.

ARSINOË. It was of this I meant to speak with thee;
But thou delightest me by showing such prudence.
Times change; meanwhile take care to reassure
These jealous masters, whose good will thou needest.
                            (*Enter* FLAMINIUS.)
    (*To* FLAMINIUS) 'Tis to achieve, sir, a great victory
To make a lover be advised by me.
I have recalled him to the path of duty,
And reason hath resumed her sway o'er him.

FLAMINIUS. Then, madam, see if thou art able to make
This rabble, too, accessible to reason.
The trouble grows. 'Tis time for thee to act,
Or, when thou wouldst act, it will be too late.
Do not suppose that if thou givest free scope
To them and heedest them not, it will confound them.
Rome hath of old seen passions loosed like these,

But never did she take the course thou takest.
When there was need to quiet the populace,
The Senate spared not promises nor threats
And thus recalled the hosts of her insurgents
From both the Quirinal and the Aventine,
Whence they would have swept down with fearsome havoc
Had they been treated long as if their rage
Were powerless, and been left to their devices,
As thou appearest now to treat thy people.

ARSINOË. With this example, more talk would be useless.
The Senate's course shows me what mine must be.
The King . . . But here he is.

Enter PRUSIAS.

PRUSIAS (*to* FLAMINIUS).   I can no longer
Doubt, sir, whence comes the mischief which I see.
This mob is led by minions of Laodice.

FLAMINIUS. I had already guessed her handiwork.

ATTALUS (*to* PRUSIAS). Thus is thy tender care of her repaid!

FLAMINIUS. Sir, we must act; and if thou wilt be counseled . . .

Enter Cleone.

CLEONE. All is lost, madam, unless aid be prompt.
The people loudly demand Nicomedes.
They take the law into their own hands. They
Have torn to pieces Zeno and Metrobates.

ARSINOË. No more, then, need be feared; they have found victims.
Their criminal frenzy will in these men's blood
Be quenched. They will congratulate themselves
And think that Nicomedes is avenged.

FLAMINIUS. If this uprising had no leadership,
I would, like thee, fear less its consequences.
These men's deaths would appease the populace.
Sedition with fixed aims, not ceasing thus,
Pursues its objects till it hath attained them.
The first blood spilled gives it the taste thereof,
Inflames it more, destroys its sense of horror,
And leaves it thenceforth neither fear nor pity.

Enter ARASPES.

ARASPES. Sire, from all sides the people come in throngs;
Thy guards at every moment are deserting;
And if we judge by what is heard e'en here,
The Prince will not be in my hands much longer.
I can no more be answerable for him.

PRUSIAS. We shall, we shall restore to them this precious
Object of so affectionate a love.
Madam, let us obey our faithless people,
Who weary of obeying me and wish
To choose their king themselves; and from the height
Here of a balcony, to calm this tempest,
Let us throw down his head to his new subjects.

ATTALUS. Oh, sire!

PRUSIAS.   'Tis thus that I shall give him to them.
Those who thus seek him, ought to have him thus.

ATTALUS. Ah, sire! that will lose all, and to their rage
Deliver those that to thy heart are dearest;
And I dare say now that thy Majesty
Will have, himself, trouble in finding safety.

PRUSIAS. Then I must needs do whatsoe'er they bid me
And give them Nicomedes with my crown.
I have no other choice; and if they are
The stronger, I unto their idol owe
Either my scepter or my death.

FLAMINIUS.   Although
Thy purpose, sire, is not devoid of justice,
Is it for thee to say this prince shall perish?
What power is left thee, now, over his life?
This is thy son no more; this is Rome's hostage.
I must remember it when thou forgettest it.
To give commands concerning him wrongs us.
I am responsible to the Senate for him
And hence cannot consent to it. My galley
Lies in the harbor, ready to set sail.
A secret door leads thither from the palace.
If thou dost mean to kill him, let me go;
Let my departure make it clear to all
That Rome's intents are kindlier and more just.
Do not expose her to the shameful outrage
Of seeing her hostage slain before mine eyes.

ARSINOË. Sire, wilt thou heed my thought? May I explain it?
PRUSIAS. Nothing from thee could be unwelcome to me.
      Speak.
ARSINOË.   Heaven inspires me with a plan which will,
    I hope, satisfy Rome and not displease thee.
      If he *(indicating* FLAMINIUS*)* is ready to depart, he now
    Can carry his hostage with him easily.
    This secret door here is convenient for us;
    But to facilitate this course so much
    The better, show thyself unto the people
    And, bowing to their wrath, at least beguile them
    By arguing with them. Thus consume the time
    Till it is sure the galley is at sea
    Bearing their hero on it. If they force
    Their way into the palace and do not find him
    There, thou wilt seem like them surprised, bewildered;
    Thou wilt accuse Rome, and wilt promise them
    Vengeance on whosoe'er is her accomplice,
    Saying thou wilt launch pursuit when morning comes,
    And rousing hopes in them of speedy rescue,
    Wherewith the countless obstacles which thou
    Thyself wilt raise at every point can aid
    Our ruse. Whatever blind rage they exhibit
    Today, they will do nothing while they fear
    For him and while they deem their efforts useless.
    Here his release appears too easy, sire;
    And if they gain it, thou and I must flee.
    With him to lead them, they will make him king.
    Thou thyself judge.
PRUSIAS.   Ah, madam, I confess
    That heaven hath put this counsel in thy heart!
      Sir, could there be a better plan?
FLAMINIUS.   It makes thee
    Certain of life and liberty and honor.
    Thou hast, besides, Laodice as a hostage.
    But he who loses time, now, may lose all.
PRUSIAS. Then we no more must lose it: let us hasten.
ARSINOË *(to* FLAMINIUS*)*. Take but Araspes and three soldiers with thee.
    A larger number might include some traitor.

I shall go find Laodice and make sure
Of her.
        But, Attalus, where hurriest thou?
ATTALUS. I go, in my turn, to beguile the pride
Of this insurgent people, and to add
Another, different stratagem to thine.
ARSINOË. Remember that thy fate and mine are one.
Only thy interests lead me into danger.
ATTALUS. I shall remove thee from it, or die, madam.
ARSINOË. Go, then. I see Armenia's queen approaching.
    (*Exeunt* PRUSIAS, ATTALUS, FLAMINIUS, *and* ARASPES.
      Enter LAODICE.)
    (*To* LAODICE) Must she who caused these ills remain un-
    punished?
LAODICE. No, madam; and if she has the least ambition,
I can already promise thee she will not.
ARSINOË. Thou knowest her crime. Prescribe the penalty.
LAODICE. To suffer even a slight humiliation
Sufficeth for a queen. It is already
Enough that she hath seen her purpose foiled.
ARSINOË. Say that to punish her temerity
The crown should, rather, from her brow be torn.
LAODICE. Not thus do generous spirits think. When they
Once have the upper hand, they can forget.
They only wish to see their foes confounded.
ARSINOË. Whoe'er can deem thee such a one, is surely
Credulous.
LAODICE.   Heaven did not make my soul
More fierce.
ARSINOË.   To rouse subjects against their ruler,
To put a sword or torch in every hand,
So that they come and threaten even the palace—
Dost thou call this to have but little fierceness?
LAODICE. Madam, we understand each other ill.
I see that thou appliest to me whatever
I say to thee.
        About myself I have not
The least anxiety. I came to seek thee
That I might take thee under my protection
And not expose thee to the disrespect

Of a great people stirred to anger. Make
The King come, call thy Attalus, that I
May save for them their royal dignity.
This mob might in its fury treat them badly.

ARSINOË. Can any pride equal to thine be found?
Thou, who alone didst cause this whole disturbance,
Who seest thyself my prisoner in this palace,
Who with thy blood wilt give me satisfaction
For any outrage done to me as queen—
Thou speakest to me still with the same boldness
As if I needed to ask *thee* for mercy.

LAODICE. Madam, thou dost persist in talking thus.
'Tis simply to refuse to see that I
Command here, and that thou wilt be my victim
Whene'er it pleases me. Do not impute
This great uprising to me as a crime.
Thy people are to blame, for in all subjects
Seditious cries are heinous; but as for me,
Who am a queen and who have in our strife,
To triumph o'er thee, made this folk rebel,
'Tis by the laws of war permitted always
To kindle revolt among one's foes. To snatch
My husband from me is to be one of them.

ARSINOË. I then am thine, madam; and come what may,
If once the people break into this palace,
Thy life is ended. That I promise thee.

LAODICE. Ill thou wilt keep thy word, or on my grave
This royal family will soon be slaughtered.
But hast thou still another Metrobates
Among thy household, or another Zeno?
Fearest thou not that all who serve thee here
Have been corrupted by my secret dealings?
Knowest thou e'en one so ready to betray
Himself, so tired of life, as to obey thee?
I have no wish to reign o'er thy Bithynia.
Open to me the road unto Armenia;
And, to see all thy woes end in a twinkling,
Give me my husband, whom in vain thou holdest.

ARSINOË. Thou must go seek him on the road to Rome.
Flaminius leads him there, and can restore him

To thee. But hasten, prithee, and row hard:
His galley now hath reached the open sea.
LAODICE. If I believed thee!
ARSINOË.   Do not doubt it, madam.
LAODICE. Then flee the wrath that seizes on my soul.
   After this fatal and outrageous deed,
   No more respect nor generosity!
     But rather stay to serve me as a hostage
   Until my hand can free him from his chains.
   I shall go even to Rome to break those fetters,
   With all thy subjects and with all of mine.
   Hannibal truly called it mad to try
   To conquer Rome except in Italy.
   May she behold me deep in her domains
   Assert my fury with a million swords
   And curb her tyranny with my despair . . .
ARSINOË. Thou *dost* wish, then, to reign here in Bithynia?
   And will the King permit thee, in this frenzy
   Which now possesses thee, to rule for him?
LAODICE. Madam, I shall rule here and yet not wrong him,
   Since he would fain be king only in semblance.
   What matters it to him who makes the laws
   And who reigns for him here, I or the Romans?
     But a second hostage falls into my hands.

                    (*Enter* ATTALUS.)

ARSINOË. Attalus, dost thou know how those who left us
   Have fared?
ATTALUS.   Ah, madam!
ARSINOË.   Speak.
ATTALUS.   The angry gods
   Have brought upon us the most dire misfortune.
   The Prince escaped.
LAODICE.   Fear nothing further, madam.
   My heart forthwith is generous again.
ARSINOË. Attalus, dost thou enjoy frightening me?
ATTALUS. Nay, flatter not thy soul with such a thought.
   Luckless Araspes with his meager escort
   Had brought him to the secret door; the Roman
   Ambassador had passed through this already,
   When, at the feet of the Prince, Araspes fell,

NICOMEDE

A dagger in his breast. He gave one cry,
And, fearing a like fate, his followers
Immediately· took flight.

ARSINOË.   And who, who was it
Who stabbed him in that doorway?

ATTALUS.   Ten or twelve
Soldiers who seemed to guard it; and the Prince . . .

ARSINOË.   Ah, my son! traitors are on every side!
Few are the subjects faithful to their master!
But who hath told thee of this great disaster?

ATTALUS.   Araspes' comrades and the dying Araspes.
But hear yet more what fills me with despair.
I ran to make a stand beside the King
My father, but it was too late. Dismayed,
He had already yielded to his fears
And taken a skiff in order to rejoin
The Roman, who perhaps is not less frightened.

Enter PRUSIAS *and* FLAMINIUS.

PRUSIAS (*to* ARSINOË).   Nay, nay! we both have come back to defend
Thy honor here, or die before thine eyes.

ARSINOË.   Then let us die, sir—die, and free ourselves
From the utter power of our raging foes.
Let us not wait their bidding; let us show
That we are jealous of the glory they
Would have in making disposition of us.

LAODICE.   Such despair, madam, wrongs so great a man
More than thou wrongedst him in sending him
To Rome. Thou shouldst have understood him better,
And, since he has my troth, thou shouldst presume
That he is worthy of me. I would renounce him
If he were not magnanimous, if he failed
To measure up to my esteem, if he
Did not display a heart always the same.
But here he is. See if I know him ill.

Enter NICOMEDES.

NICOMEDES.   All is calm, sire. The people instantly
Have been appeased by the mere sight of me.

NICOMEDE

PRUSIAS. What! comest thou to defy me in my palace,
Rebel?
NICOMEDES. That is a name I ne'er shall have.
    I come not here to show the hated face
To thee of one made insolent by having
Broken the chains of his captivity.
I come as a good subject, to restore
That peace to thee which others, for their own ends,
Disturbed unseasonably. Not that I
Wish to charge Rome with any crime. She follows
The precepts of the noble art of ruling,
And her ambassador only does his duty
When he would fain divide the power between us.
But do not suffer her to constrain thee thus.
Give me thy love again, that she may fear thee.
Pardon thy subjects' somewhat too great fervor,
Which sympathy for me aroused in them.
Pardon misdeeds which they thought necessary
And which will bring nothing but good results.
    (*To* ARSINOË) Thou, too, forgive them, madam, and permit me
To adore thy kindness to my dying day.
I know the reason thou wert so hostile to me:
Maternal love made thee desire to see
My brother reign; and I myself will lend
My aid to let thee do so, if thou canst
Allow him to become a king through me.
Asia still offers conquests to my arm;
My sword is ready to enthrone him in them.
Only command, choose whatso land thou wilt,
And I will bring the crown thereof to thee.
ARSINOË. Sir, must thou push thy victory so far;
And having in thy hands my life and honor,
Is such a mighty conqueror ambitious
To conquer also even in my heart?
Against thy goodness I cannot defend it;
It is itself impatient to surrender.
Unite this conquest to three conquered scepters,
And I shall think that I have gained in thee
A second son.

PRUSIAS.   Then I surrender also,
Madam; and I would fain think that to have
A son so noble is my greatest glory.
But midst the joys that finally are ours,
Let us know, Prince, to whom we owe thy presence.

NICOMEDES. The striker of the blow concealed his face
But asked my diamond of me as a pledge
And is to bring it to me here tomorrow.

ATTALUS (*to* NICOMEDES, *holding it out*). Sir, dost thou wish to have it
from my hand?

NICOMEDES. Ah, let me always by this worthy proof
Know that true kingly blood flows in thy veins!
This is no more the ambitious slave of Rome;
This is the liberator of his kindred.
Brother, thou breakest other chains than mine:
The King's, the Queen's, Laodice's, and thine.
But why keep hidden in saving all the realm?

ATTALUS. To see thy noble nature at its best,
See it alone displayed 'gainst our injustice
Without being influenced by my slight service—
Or on myself or thee to avenge myself
If I had judged amiss all I had seen.
But, madam . . .

ARSINOË.   Enough! That was the stratagem
Which thou hadst promised me. 'Twas against me.
(*To* NICOMEDES) My heart, sir, is the better satisfied
Because my son thwarted the wrong I did.

NICOMEDES (*to* FLAMINIUS). Sir, to speak frankly, every noble soul
Must feel itself twice blest to have Rome's friendship;
But we no longer wish it when accompanied
By the harsh yoke 'neath which it bows all kings.
We ask Rome for it without servitude,
Or to be called her foe is preferable.

FLAMINIUS. The Senate must take counsel as to that;
But meanwhile I will venture to assure thee,
Prince, that if not her friendship, thou shalt have
Her true esteem, such as a heart so noble
As thine can hope for, and that she will feel
That she hath made a worthy foe if she

NICOMEDE

Does not accept thee as a gallant friend.

PRUSIAS.　The rest of us, happily reunited,
Tomorrow will prepare fit sacrifices,
And of the gods, our own great sovereigns, ask,
To crown our blessings, for the good will of Rome.